NORMAN ST. JOHN-STEVAS

The Agonising Choice

BIRTH CONTROL, RELIGION AND THE LAW

INDIANA UNIVERSITY PRESS

Bloomington/London

Library of Congress catalog card number: 77–163516
ISBN: 0–253–10060–7

by the same author

LIFE, DEATH AND THE LAW
LAW AND MORALS
THE RIGHT TO LIFE
WALTER BAGEHOT

The Agonising Choice

'I want the intellectual layman to be religious and the devout ecclesiastic to be intellectual.'

Cardinal Newman

'I think, dearest Uncle, you cannot really wish me to be the "maman d'une nombreuse famille", for I think you will see with me the great inconvenience a large family would be to us all, and particularly to myself; men never think, at least seldom think, what a hard task it is for us women to go through this very often.'

Queen Victoria in a letter to her uncle
King Leopold of the Belgians in 1841

'Recollect, to write theology is like dancing on a tightrope some hundred feet above the ground. It is hard to keep from falling and the fall is great.'

Cardinal Newman in a letter to
Miss Emily Bowles in 1866

'What you say of the pride of giving life to an immortal soul is very fine, dear, but I own I cannot enter into that; I think much more of our being like a cow or dog at such moments; when our poor nature becomes so very animal and unecstatic, but for you dear if you are sensible and reasonable, not in ecstasy nor spending your day with nurses and wet nurses, which is the ruin of many a refined and intellectual young lady, without adding to her real maternal duties, a child will be a great resource.'

Queen Victoria in a letter to her
daughter the Princess Royal later
Empress of Germany in 1858

1975

.y e kept

DA S

To Hans Küng with admiration for his
courageous Christian witness and fidelity to
the Catholic and Roman Church

Contents

Contents

Acknowledgements

I would like to express my gratitude to all those who have given me permission to quote from their books and articles. I am especially indebted to Bishop Christopher Butler of Westminster, who kindly read before publication my chapter 'Theological Perspectives'. Needless to say the opinions expressed in that chapter are my responsibility alone as are any errors in it. I am also grateful to my secretary Mrs J. E. Ross and to my former secretary Miss Sally Coles for their heroic efforts in typing a large part of the book. I am indebted to Mr Graham Zellick for his assistance in legal research.

Norman St. John-Stevas

Hampstead,
April 1971

The Agonising Choice

Introduction

Birth control today is a matter of interest to almost everybody. Family planning is accepted as a normal part of married life in all advanced societies and is commended by all the major religions. Technological advances have created new and more effective forms of birth control and further discoveries are continually taking place. Yet at the same time no method of birth control has been developed which is wholly satisfactory. Personal and aesthetic objections to various methods of birth control still remain. The medical difficulties have not been wholly disposed of – the pill, for example, has undesirable side effects, and its long-term effects will not be known for several decades. There are still strong religious objections to the employment of contraceptives, which are not confined to members of the Roman Catholic Church, and are felt by those of all religions and of none.

Birth control has created social and legal as well as religious problems and these have not been solved. In the past, the law in Western countries, and especially in England and the United States, treated birth control as an aspect of obscenity: today the law has largely withdrawn from this field but certain difficulties remain. What limitations should be imposed on the dissemination of contraceptive information and the sale and distribution of contraceptives? Should there be a ban on sales to minors? Should instruction be confined to the married or those about to enter the matrimonial state? What restrictions should be laid down for advertising?

There is a general awareness that a society in which knowledge of birth control is widely diffused faces grave new problems. The old restraints of fear of the consequences no longer deter citizens from extra-marital intercourse. Is it the business of the state to impose new ones? Or should they be provided by theologians and moralists and if so how are people to be persuaded to follow them? Contraception is having a profound effect on society's concept of the institution of marriage. If it becomes wholly effective and available to all, many of the arguments which have been advanced in the past for the permanence of marriage will lose their force and are already doing so at the present time. If permanent marriage is to survive as an institution it will have to be on personalist rather than on procreative grounds, on the conviction that for the majority of human beings a permanent, life-long association and commitment is the best means to achieve the greatest personal fulfilment and the highest form of human relationship.

Should the state provide a full family planning service available to all, free of charge or at subsidised rates, as part of the normal health service? As I write, Britain is half-way towards this position. Local authorities are empowered to supply such a service but they are not under any obligation to do so. The same problem has arisen in the international field where the growth of world population is causing acute problems, especially in the underdeveloped countries where the fastest population growth is concentrated. What is the part of family planning in aid to the poorer countries of the world and what priority should it be given? What are the moral principles which should regulate international family planning programmes? This book is an attempt to answer some of these questions and they cannot be answered satisfactorily without first considering the attitude of the great world religions to birth control and especially that of the Roman Catholic Church.

Much of this book is taken up with tracing the development of Christian attitudes in general to birth control and those of the Catholic Church in particular. The theological problems causing controversy today within the Catholic Church are fully discussed. The insights of Catholicism and the outcome of the disputes are of great interest to Roman Catholics but also to all men who are concerned with the ethics of the issue and the effect of its resolution on the future of mankind. The publication of the encyclical *Humanae Vitae* on birth control was a traumatic event for Roman Catholics but its attitudes aroused intense discussion among non-Catholics. It caused many people to ask questions about their own views on birth control. It raised in a particular form one of the most searching questions of our time, the limits which morality should seek to impose on an ever-advancing technology, which offers both a promise and a threat to the humanity of man. Mankind now finds itself in the position where it can do all manner of things but has not answered the question whether it should. This question cannot be answered by technologists, using the language of a value-free discourse but only by those who have some kind of vision of man and his ultimate destiny and commitments. In the widest sense, then, a theological answer is required.

In the course of this book, which sets out to be an objective account of events as they have taken place and opinions as they have developed, my own views on the issue are made plain, especially in the two final chapters. I did not always hold them and they have changed over the years. Others have gone through a similar experience but here I am writing only of myself. My point of departure was a complete acceptance of the traditional Catholic condemnation of birth control as being contrary to both revealed religion and the natural law. This was the tradition I was brought up in and along with many other Catholics it never occurred to me to question it.

In January 1950, as an undergraduate, I took part in a debate which I had arranged at the Cambridge Union on birth control. The motion read: 'This House would welcome the wider application of Birth Control as being in the best interests of Morality and Social Welfare.' It was supported by Mr Norman Haire, a well-known 'sexologist', and opposed by Dr George Andrew Beck, then co-adjutor bishop of Brentwood, and later Archbishop of Liverpool. I vigorously opposed the motion.[1] My peroration was unqualified and caused me some wry amusement when I re-read it recently: 'Let us, sir, tonight reject this motion. Let us read the lessons of history aright. The mighty empire of Greece was conquered because of the practice of birth control and the consequent

[1] The motion was carried; 342 votes for to 260 against.

declining population. The Emperor Augustus was faced with the same problem and the penalty for his failure to solve it was the fall of the far-flung Roman Empire. The information available to us all in the reports of the Royal Commission convey as clearly as did any writing on ancient palace wall, a solemn warning. And it says "populate or perish", "increase and multiply or vanish for ever into the dust of the civilisations of the past." [1]

I had no difficulty in accepting the Roman Catholic position nor the arguments put forward to support it until some doubts began to assail me in 1958, when I was working on my doctoral thesis at Yale on the subject of 'Law and Morals'. In the course of my researches on birth control and its treatment by the law I studied various contributions which had been made on the religious aspects of birth control by Roman Catholic writers in theological journals. I was struck by the fact that no one seemed prepared to make any original contribution to the discussion but invariably referred back to some previous authority. It all seemed to me to be being done by mirrors (rather as in some law journals) and if one had read a single article one had read them all. I contrasted this slavish following of authority with the treatment of the issue by Anglican theologians and Protestant thinkers such as Reinhold Niebuhr. I was particularly struck by an Anglican publication, *The Family in Contemporary Society*,[2] in which the issues were honestly faced and the contributors expressed varying degrees of approval for the employment of contraception by Christians. I found their line of argument persuasive and attractive but was not entirely convinced by it. Perhaps I did not allow myself to be and contented myself with presenting their arguments with the minimum of comment. I did however conclude that in view of the general acceptance of contraception in England and the United States legal sanctions against the distribution of contraceptives and the dissemination of birth control information were no longer appropriate. This view was put forward in my pamphlet *Birth Control*

[1] A year or so later I debated the subject again at the London University Union with Dr Marie Stopes, the birth control pioneer, using much the same arguments. At the end of my speech Dr Stopes leaned over the table and hissed at me: 'Very clever but very meretricious, like all Roman Catholics.'
[2] S.P.C.K. (London, 1958).

and Public Policy, published in the United States in 1960, and which attracted widespread attention.[1]

My intellectual position in the early 1960s was, then, that I was attracted to the Anglican position on birth control: I found their theological reasoning more convincing than that of the traditional Catholic natural law approach but I was not prepared to make a change. It must be remembered that at that time freedom of discussion and, indeed, of thought were severely circumscribed within the Roman Catholic Church and the emotional feeling against contraception was strong. I shared this revulsion from the idea of contraception and indeed still feel it to a certain extent. I have always felt uneasy about the simplistic viewpoint of the anti-fertility crusaders.

In the early 1960s tremors began to be felt in the Roman Catholic theological world about birth control which are described later in this book. In 1963 Father Janssens of the University of Louvain published his revolutionary article in which he suggested that the birth control pill was not a true contraceptive and that its use might therefore be legitimate for Catholics. I read this article eagerly and myself published an article in the *Observer*, setting out his arguments but without committing myself to them. In 1964 came the statement of Archbishop Roberts that he was no longer convinced by the natural law arguments against contraception although he was prepared to accept the ban on contraception on the authority of the Catholic Church. This was more or less my own position and from that time I found myself unable to put forward the natural law arguments. In May 1964 I took part in a television discussion on the English hierarchy's restatement of the traditional Catholic position and while I was unable to defend it I was restrained by feelings of loyalty from attacking it.[2]

By this time, thanks to the calling of the Second Vatican Council, discussion on this and other matters was much freer within the Catholic Church, and the traditional position was under open attack. In February 1965 I became involved in a public controversy with Miss Dee Wells when we both appeared on a television

[1] President Kennedy used this report to counter objections that a Catholic was 'unfit' to be President of the United States.
[2] See *Daily Telegraph*, 11 May 1964. Father Joseph Christie, S.J. championed the ban on contraception.

B

programme in the series 'Not so much a Programme more a Way of Life'. The item we were discussing was a highly offensive sketch about birth control which presented a Catholic priest in Liverpool as extorting money from a poor family, while enforcing the Catholic ban on contraception. I strongly condemned the sketch but on the actual issue of contraception confined myself to saying that the whole issue was under discussion within the Catholic Church, and that in relation to underdeveloped countries the most pressing need was for the necessary capital to advance industrial development. The programme gave rise to a dispute which raged in the Press and Parliament and the sketch was denounced by a number of Liverpool and other Members.[1]

By this time I had become convinced that a revision of the traditional Catholic teaching was inevitable and that it was only a matter of time before this came about. In July 1967 I expressed these views publicly for the first time at a conference on population policies at the Catholic University of Georgetown in Washington and suggested that the normative Catholic position in the future would be to leave the matter principally to the individual consciences of Catholics. I could not know what form the revision would take but felt that it would either be a new position altogether, legitimating the use of contraceptives in certain circumstances, or else the presentation of new arguments to justify the ban. What I did not anticipate was a flat restatement of the old position with virtually no modification in either practice or theory. Yet this is precisely what came about with the issue of the encyclical *Humanae Vitae*.

The Encyclical was published on 29 July 1969. Rumours had been circulating for some days that a Vatican statement was imminent, but these had proved false on so many previous occasions that not everyone took them seriously. On this occasion they proved well founded. On the morning of publication, before accounts of the contents had appeared in the newspapers, I had spoken to the Apostolic Delegate, Archbishop Cardinale, and he sent me round by car a copy of the Encyclical. I read it with

---

[1] The programme went out on 27 February 1965. The controversy was reported in the Press during the ensuing week. Miss Wells became very emotional and annoyed during the programme crying, 'You silly man.' her last words.

incredulity and dismay.[1] I was requested to appear on 'Panorama' that evening with the Bishop of Leeds, Lady Antonia Fraser and various other Catholics and passed the day resolving what I should say. As the day went on I became convinced that the time had come to speak out quite openly on the whole issue. For me this was especially difficult as for over twenty years I had been defending Catholic attitudes, putting the most favourable arguments for papal positions, and had never uttered a word of criticism of the Pope in public. Nevertheless I felt that I had come to a turning-point and that I would be failing in my duty both as a Churchman and a legislator if I failed to speak out.[2] The situation was the more agonising because of the personal friendship I enjoyed with the Pope and of the high esteem in which I held him. While the broadcast was a traumatic experience for me, I found that my religious faith far from being destroyed was strengthened, my belief in the Catholic Church never wavered, and I remain convinced of the validity and importance of the Roman Primacy. Others, as I know, have been less fortunate, and for them *Humanae Vitae* marked a parting of the ways, leading them to the abandonment of the Roman Church.

Humanae Vitae has precipitated for the Church as grave a crisis as any she has faced since the Reformation. Birth control is in itself a highly important and emotive issue. Paul VI, by forthrightly rejecting any artificial means of birth control as contrary to the law of God and using his ecclesiastical prerogatives to do so, linked it up with another equally explosive issue, which had already been half-detonated by the Vatican Council, the place of papal authority in the contemporary Church. *Humanae Vitae* highlighted what was already an issue within the Church and concentrated Catholic and world attention on it. What might previously have been thought of as a rather academic dispute among theologians was suddenly transformed into a dispute of immense practical importance affecting millions of people in their daily lives. And this was not surprising. The Encyclical was an attempt both to find a solution to a moral dilemma and to stem the undermining

[1] One of its tragic aspects was that it was on the wrong subject – birth control – when what was needed was a statement on abortion. The Papacy's moral influence was squandered on the subsidiary issue instead of being mobilised on the major one.
[2] The text of this and other statements is given on pp. 136–7.

of papal authority and to reassert it in the old style. It failed on both counts. Since its issue the debate on birth control has continued and the meaning, extent and limits of papal authority have been scrutinised by Catholics as never before. A document intended to restore a position fomented a revolution.

This book is not intended to stir things up further: rather it is an attempt to assess what has actually happened in the last two and a half years, to set it in historical perspective, and to make a contribution to what is a continuing dialogue. My hope is that it may prove helpful to the many Catholics who, like myself, find themselves in a position in which they accept the Roman Primacy but cannot accept this particular manifestation, an encyclical which is based on an outmoded legalism and scholasticism rather than on contemporary theological thought. I hope, too, that it will help all those who are concerned about religion as a part of human culture to understand better just what is happening inside the Catholic Church at the present time.

Some Catholics have dismissed the Encyclical as a sport, a mere aberration or *jeu d'esprit* of no present or ultimate importance. This is not an attitude which can reasonably be taken by anyone who accepts the claims of Rome in anything more than a nominalist way. A Catholic cannot honestly dismiss a solemn papal statement of this character *a priori*. Others have by-passed the intellectual issue altogether and have simply gone on practising their religion and contraception, at the same time ceasing to mention it in the confessional. This leaves the theological issue shelved. From the papal as well as from the individual's point of view this is highly dangerous because it could lead to a discrediting of all papal authority on other issues as well as the one under immediate discussion. What needs to be done has been admirably summarised by Bishop Butler when he wrote: 'What we have got to teach the faithful is that papal inerrancy – the incapacity of Popes to be wrong – has its limits. Plainly this is a most unpopular doctrine in some circles in the Church. But it is theologically true and with the spread of education it becomes more and more necessary to make it clear.'[1]

Development in moral and theological attitudes has taken

[1] 'The Dictates of Rome', *Sunday Times*, 6 October 1968.

place throughout the history of the Church: the idea of a Church which has never changed is more a myth than an historical reality, but in the past these changes have taken place slowly over many decades and sometimes centuries. What is new in the present situation is the speed with which, thanks to modern communications, change now takes place. Within a period of months, great bodies of clergy and laity, whole national hierarchies, have had to make adaptations which would formerly have been made over periods of years. The speed and the scale of the dissent from *Humanae Vitae* have been literally unprecedented and together constitute a new theological factor which has to be taken into account.

Catholics have also to grow accustomed to the idea of living with dissent, and peacefully co-existing with brethren who take different views on matters of major moral importance. This no doubt entails a higher degree of uncertainty on a number of matters than has been common in the recent past but this is a price which has to be paid if conscience and reason are not to be entirely subjugated by law. There is nothing new about this either: it has been the common experience of other Christian Churches for a considerable time but the Catholic Church has not yet grown accustomed to it. The Catholic Church has not for centuries, since the shock of the Reformation, been an 'open' institution, and the Vatican has been the most closed part of it, yet painfully and swiftly it has had to become one today. A uniformity which was thought of as a dispensation of the Holy Spirit now seems to have been little more than a cultural time-lag.

The view on birth control which informs this book, sometimes explicitly but more often implicitly, is that Catholics should be free to decide according to their own consciences what methods of birth control to employ. I make no claim that this is the only Catholic view but it is *a* Catholic view compatible with acceptance of the idea of the Roman Primacy, although not with some of its recent exercises. The conscience of any Catholic always operates within the framework of Catholic truth – it is not something wholly autonomous – but it is a true conscience none the less and is entitled to freedom. A genuinely conscientious decision must be made by the individual for himself: it cannot be made for him by others. As Father Enda McDonagh has put it: 'The moral guidance which is available to him in the community, Christian or general, may outline authentically and authoritatively (in the case of the Church) the basic structure of the demand, but his judgement, while incorporating this, must be his own personal assessment of the demands of truth and love in each particular case. To remove from the individual this personal assessment would be to rob his response of its dynamic, creative and genuine love quality, as if a man could only make love responses in accordance with a detailed recipe. The intrinsic structure of his situation and its demands can only be generally described in the moral teaching of the community. To force it into detail is to falsify it as well as to deprive the individual of his right and obligation to make his own assessment.'[1]

The debate sparked off by *Humanae Vitae* started with birth control but has gone on to raise wider questions of the nature of conscience, authority, and the future structure of the Church. The Church has been confronted by a situation which has compelled her to understand herself. As Cardinal Suenens has stressed on a number of occasions but notably in a famous interview given to the world religious press in May 1969, at the root of the conflicts going on within the Roman Catholic Communion today is a clash of views as to the nature of the Church.[2] On the one hand there are those, centred principally but not exclusively in the Roman Curia, whose concept of the Church is juridical and formal. They see the local 'Churches' as part of a whole 'which must be unified as closely as possible in relation to the centre, through a rigid network of detailed rules and regulations.' Cardinal Suenens characterises this view as being essentially 'bureaucratic', typical of men more aware of the established order and the past than of the demands of the future, looking backwards to the days of the first Vatican Council rather than forward to the needs of the world in the year 2000.[3] This is a view of the Church which

[1] 'Conscience: The Guidance of the Spirit' in *Truth and Life* (Dublin, 1968), p. 133.
[2] For the full English text of the interview see the *Tablet*, 16 May 1969.
[3] Cardinal Newman foresaw this development at the time of the dispute over the definition of papal infallibility which he thought 'inopportune': 'It is the increased executive force which the Definition will place in the hands of the Holy See that, in the human point of view, is the real secret of the Opposition.' See Meriol Trevor, *Newman – Light in Winter* (London, 1962), p. 474.

puts the Pope almost above the Church, laying down through the medium of the Curia detailed rules and guidance, to be enforced by bishops thought of primarily as papal agents. Priests in their turn carry out the bishops' rulings and enforce them on the laity. Women come at the very bottom of the heap. The reign of Pius XII marked the high point of this development of papal authoritarianism and prestige, with the Pope making his wishes known in a never-ending stream of addresses, discourses and radio messages.

With the election of Pope John XXIII a new era opened, advanced by the Second Vatican Council, in which the Church has been seen as a sacramental and mystical reality first, rather than a juridical society, which it is but only secondarily. 'From this viewpoint,' writes Cardinal Suenens, 'at once evangelical and historical, the first thing one sees is the local Churches, the Church of God in Paris, the Church of God in London, or New York, and one goes on from there to see the structure of the Church as a communion of individual Churches linked to the Church of Rome, and its head as their centre of unity.' The Church, from this point of view, is primarily the whole people of God, wending its way through history to salvation, a society hierarchically structured but one in which every member is free to contribute his or her own insights. The bishops with the Pope guide the people of God but this is not a function which is exercised by the Pope in isolation from the episcopal college.

Humanae Vitae, which was issued by the Pope alone and not in conjunction with the bishops, was an attempt to settle the birth control controversy, by an exercise of authority in the old mode. It manifestly failed. Reformers in the Church today, and here they differ sharply from the sixteenth-century reformers, are not challenging the Roman Primacy as such, but its manner of exercise and are seeking to redefine its scope. They are trying to shift the emphasis on the papal role away from that of power towards service, a process initiated by Pope John. 'He revealed,' writes Hans Küng, 'a new or rather a very old idea of Petrine ministry, and instead of seeing the primacy as a more or less dictatorial sovereignty over spiritual subjects, he saw it as a discreet call to serve his brethren inside and outside the Catholic Church, which must be inspired by love and understanding for mankind in the modern world and subject to the true Lord of the Church.'[1]

This book is presented in the Joannine tradition as a contribution to the dialogue in a free and open Church. It is intended to heal and not to wound, to reconcile and not to create division, and is free, I hope, from that schismatical spirit which is displayed by some Ultramontanes. Neither is it intended to be mischievous in the manner Newman thought he detected in Simpson, the nineteenth-century editor of the Catholic review *The Rambler*, whom he saw as riding along the high-road 'discharging pea-shooters at cardinals who happen by bad luck to look out of the window'.[2] What it sets out to do is to show how Christians can best bring their influence to bear on a vital contemporary social problem not to dominate others but to serve them.

At this moment of time one cannot know what the ultimate attitudes of the Catholic Church will be to contraception. One must look for that to the historical process itself and to the mysterious life of the Church as the main body of Christians assimilating some ideas as consonant with Christian teaching and throwing off others as incompatible. Meanwhile, Catholics can at least seek to discuss the issues rationally, ridding themselves of that spirit of exclusiveness and intolerance which identifies opposition with treason and criticism with disloyalty, an attitude of mind which, however appropriate in a dissenting sect, should not be the mark of the Universal Church.

---

[1] *The Church* (London, 1968), p. 450. See also *Structures of the Church* (London, 1964), p. 203, by the same author.
[2] Meriol Trevor, op. cit., p. 228.

CHAPTER I

Birth Control – A Brief History

Almost the only uncontroverted fact about birth control is that there is nothing very new about it. Over the centuries techniques of birth control have been greatly improved especially in modern times but from the earliest times man seems to have attempted to control conception. Anthropologists have established that both magical and rational methods were employed by primitive tribes.[1] Among the civilised nations of antiquity, the Egyptians, the Jews, the Greeks and the Romans all possessed knowledge of contraception. An Egyptian papyrus dated 4,000 years ago mentions a plug of crocodile's dung used as a primitive type of diaphragm. Since this dung is now known to be alkaline and therefore to some extent spermicidal its use is not as bizarre as appears at first sight. In ancient Greece abortion and infanticide were used as means of family limitation and magical methods such as the use of amulets were also employed, but by scientific research Greek physicians and medical writers improved existing contraceptive techniques.[2] Soranos of Ephesus (98–138) made the greatest single contribution and knew about the sterile period but failed to establish the correct dates: indeed he fixed the moment of sterility as immediately after menstruation which we now know to be the most fertile one. In Aristotle's *History of Animals* we read:

[1] See Norman E. Himes, *Medical History of Contraception* (Baltimore, 1936), and John T. Noonan, *Contraception, a History of its Treatment* (Harvard, 1965).
[2] One method of amulet contraception was to wear a charm made from the womb of a lioness or the liver of a cat. The tooth of a child was also thought to have contraceptive properties.

'Wherefore, since if the parts be smooth, conception is impeded, some anoint that part of the womb on which the seed falls with cedar oil, ointment of lead, or frankincense and olive oil.' Greek discoveries were utilised by the Romans but while contraceptive techniques were known in sophisticated circles among medical writers, physicians and scholars, contraceptive knowledge was not necessarily widespread. The point is one of dispute among scholars. It is even more obscure whether contraception as such was condemned or approved in the Graeco-Roman world. Roman law, however, accepted that the main purpose of marriage was procreation and under the Emperor Augustus in the first century laws were passed penalising those who were childless.

Christianity came into a world where contraception was known and certainly tolerated by law and showed a hostility to contraception which was part of its rejection of the lax sexual standards of the Roman Empire. Roman medicine made no great advance on Greek knowledge and with the fall of the Empire and the coming of the Dark Ages medical research came to a standstill. When medical learning was revived in the Middle Ages the inspiration came from Islam and the Middle East which in turn relied on Greek sources. An influential medical textbook of this period was Avicenna's *The Canon of Medicine* which originated in eleventh-century Damascus and was translated into Latin in the middle of the following century. Avicenna deals with a number of contraceptive methods and points out the contraceptive properties of certain plants. Among the methods of contraception recommended is for the woman to jump backwards from seven to nine times after sexual intercourse. Given the primitive medical knowledge of the period and the hostility of the Church to contraception it is not surprising that virtually no medical advance in the contraceptive field was made during this period.

It was not in fact until the sixteenth century that a new element came into the situation with the publication in 1564, two years after his death, of Gabriele Fallopio's *De Morbe Gallico*, a treatise on venereal disease. This treatise contained the first published account of the condom or sheath, which Fallopio claimed to have invented. The condom was employed during the eighteenth century, both in England and on the Continent, being mainly used in brothels, but also sold in shops in London and elsewhere.[1] At the end of the century contraceptives were still associated with immorality and vice but by the close of the nineteenth century this position had been deeply undermined and the way prepared for the general acceptance of contraception which has been so marked a feature of our own time.

Thomas Malthus, an Anglican curate was the unwitting founder of the modern birth control movement, by means of his famous *Essay on the Principle of Population* published in 1798. His thesis was simple. Both population and food supplies tend to increase, but since population increases faster than means of subsistence, the majority of the human race is doomed to perpetual poverty and malnutrition. Disease and war act as natural checks and so prevent a universal cataclysm. In the first edition of his book Malthus offered no way of escape from this dreadful treadmill, but in 1803 the second edition of his *Essay* included recommendations for 'moral restraint'. By this Malthus did not mean that sexual intercourse should be restrained in marriage, but that marriage should be postponed to a late age or complete celibacy embraced. Far from advocating any means of contraception, he expressly condemned recourse to 'improper arts'.

Radical reaction to Malthus's pessimistic and conservative doctrine was sharp. Generally accepted, it would put an end to all efforts at social reform, for by his hypothesis these were automatically condemned to failure. Godwin wrote two ineffective replies to refute Malthus, but it was left to Francis Place, a free-thinking radical, in his *Illustrations and Proofs of the Principle of Population*, published in 1822, to suggest that in the use of artificial contraception lay the answer to population problems.[2] If, he wrote, 'it were once clearly understood, that it was not disreputable for married persons to avail themselves of such precautionary means as would, without being injurious to health, or destructive of female delicacy, prevent conception, a sufficient check might at once be given to the increase of population beyond the means of

---

[1] An early reference to the condom is found in a letter of Mme de Sévigné, written to her daughter in 1671 as 'a bulwark against enjoyment, and a cobweb against danger'. Condoms were first designed for women and later for men.
[2] Jeremy Bentham had advocated the use of birth control to reduce the poor rate as early as 1797.

subsistence; vice and misery, to a prodigious extent, might be removed from society and the object of Mr Malthus, Mr Godwin and of every philanthropic person, be promoted, by the increase of comfort of intelligence, and of moral conduct in the mass of the population.'[1] Place supplemented his argument by distributing among the working classes a series of 'diabolical handbills' recommending contraception. Despite their outlining a particular method of contraception – the use of a sponge and attached ribbon – they were not legally suppressed. The young John Stuart Mill (17), who was recruited by Place to distribute his leaflets and plunged into his task with enthusiasm did not fare so well. He handed out leaflets to the wives and daughters of 'mechanics and tradesmen' and even to maids scrubbing steps in areas. An indignant crowd hauled him off to a magistrate. Mill expressed his support for contraception in an article in *The Black Dwarf*. 'By checking population,' he wrote, 'no pain is inflicted, no alarm excited, no security infringed. It cannot therefore, on any principles, be termed immoral. . . . if it tends to elevate the working people from poverty and ignorance to affluence and instruction I am compelled to regard it as highly moral and virtuous.'[2] Among the disciples of Place were Richard Carlile, Richard Hassell, and William Campion, who enjoyed legal immunity for their publications but were bitterly attacked by other radicals. Cobbett, for example, described Place as 'a monster' and Carlile as 'nearly a madman'. Their attitude was not dissimilar to those in underdeveloped countries today who regard the attempt to spread knowledge of birth control as a Western plot to keep the poor of the world in permanent subjection by restricting their numbers.

Place's influence spread to the United States, where Robert Dale Owen, who had been born in Glasgow in 1801, was emboldened in 1830 to publish the first American booklet on birth control entitled *Moral Physiology*. This went through several editions within a year and had achieved an Anglo-American circulation of 75,000 by 1877, the year of Owen's death. Two years later, Dr Charles Knowlton, a Massachusetts physician, published

[1] London edition of 1930, p. 165.
[2] See Peter Fryer, *The Birth Controllers* (London, 1965), p. 80.

anonymously a further treatise on contraceptive methods, curiously entitled *Fruits of Philosophy*. This little book was destined to become one of the most influential tracts on birth control during the nineteenth century, despite the lack of critical attention on its appearance in 1832. It took the *Boston Medical and Surgical Journal* eleven years to notice it and then only to say: 'the less that is known about it by the public at large, the better it will be for the morals of the community'. Knowlton eventually served three months hard labour for his part in publishing the book and later it was the subject of a famous English trial. By 1881 it had sold over 277,000 copies in England and the United States.

During the 1840s, partly because of the dominance of Chartism, propaganda for birth control was muted but Malthusian contentions were revived by George Drysdale in his *Elements of Social Science*, published in England in 1854, in which he advocated 'preventive sexual intercourse'. In the 1870s came a decisive battle with the trial of Charles Bradlaugh and Annie Besant, the English freethinkers, for publishing an English edition of *Fruits of Philosophy*. Up to this point Malthusian prophecies and their suggested remedies for population crisis were known and discussed in educated circles but the general public was still ignorant of contraception and the arguments for its use. Birth control literature was considered obscene and dealt with by the law governing obscene libel. The sensational trial made contraception a subject debated throughout the country and among all classes. The case really began in 1876 with the prosecution of a Bristol bookseller for selling the book, which had been freely available in England for forty years. Charles Bradlaugh and Annie Besant who had formed the 'Free Thought Publishing Company', decided to republish it in London minus the illustrations which had been added without authorisation and which may have prompted the original prosecution. Their trial opened at the Old Bailey on 18 June 1877. Mrs Besant utilised a golden opportunity to spread the good (or bad) Malthusian news, speaking at inordinate length and spending much of her time addressing the public on the laws of Malthus and the necessity for birth control, rather than defending herself against the charge of publishing an obscene libel. 'Better not to produce children than to produce them only to be destroyed by starvation, disease and death,' she declared at the end of the first day of the trial and at this point the court adjourned. *The Times* wearily commented: 'Mrs Besant intimated (though she had spoken several hours) that she had not yet nearly finished her address and when she has concluded Mr Bradlaugh is to follow.' Both defendants were found guilty but the following year the conviction was set aside for a defect in the indictment.[1] As the judge at the first trial, Sir Alexander Cockburn, declared: 'A more ill-advised and more injudicious prosecution never was instituted. Here is a work which has been published for more than forty years and which appears to have got into general circulation and which by these injudicious proceedings has got into large circulation so that the sale has suddenly risen by thousands.' The judge was right since the circulation of *Fruits of Philosophy*, which before the trial had averaged a thousand a year, rocketed skywards. Knowledge of contraceptive methods spread and the work was carried forward by the Malthusian League, founded in 1878 with Annie Besant as its first secretary.[2]

Of itself the Bradlaugh–Besant trial would probably not have resulted in a popularisation of contraception, but it came at a moment peculiarly favourable to the cause. Industrialisation and the fall in the death rate had resulted in a vastly increased population, the great depression of 1873–96 led to a widespread dislocation in agriculture and industry, women were becoming more emancipated and unwilling to bear the burden of unrestricted families, while legislation forbidding child employment had reduced the value of children as income-earning assets. Shortly after the trial, in 1880, education for the first time was made compulsory in England, and this increased the financial burden of large families. Technological advance was also being exploited and the discovery of the process of vulcanising rubber by Goodyear and Hancock in 1843–4 made possible the production of a cheap, reliable condom.

Contraception had still to win general social acceptance but after 1878 few attempts were made to suppress bona fide birth

[1] For a fuller account of the trial see Norman St. John-Stevas, *Obscenity and the Law* (London, 1956).
[2] It is fair to point out that Mrs Besant renounced her views of contraception when she became a theosophist in 1891.

control propaganda by law.[1] The way was thus opened for a flow of publications advocating birth control. In 1879 Annie Besant published her own treatise *The Law of Population*. By 1891 it had sold 175,000 copies in England alone, at the low price of sixpence each. English law had become quiescent apart from the occasional, sporadic prosecution (two are recorded in the 1890s) but private opposition to birth control was still strong. Thus in 1887 Dr Henry Allbutt's name was erased from the medical register by the General Medical Council for publishing a popular work on birth control, *The Wife's Handbook*. By 1913 the Malthusian League was able for the first time to published a practical handbook on birth control, *Hygienic Methods of Family Limitation*, and put it in general circulation without legal incident.

Meanwhile events in the United States had taken a parallel course. Dr Knowlton was succeeded by other medical writers advancing the cause of birth control, including A. M. Mauriceau, J. Soule, Edward Bliss Foote, and his son Edward Bond Foote. John Humphrey Noyes founded the Oneida colony in New York and advocated his own particular method of birth control.[2] In 1873 the birth control movement suffered a severe setback when, thanks to the efforts of Anthony Comstock, Congress enacted a statute excluding contraceptives and contraceptive information from the mails, declaring them obscene.[3] Many states followed suit and passed statutes banning the sale and distribution of contraceptives. These laws were enforced with varying degrees of efficiency in different parts of the country but undoubtedly hindered the acceptance of birth control by the community. Between 1873 and 1882 Comstock's New York Society for the Suppression of Vice was responsible for obtaining 700 arrests, 333 imprisonments and fines totalling $62,256 for obscene offences, including the sale of contraceptives and the imparting of information.[4] After the passing of Comstock the law was not enforced with such zeal but the legal battles continued in the United States long after they had finished in England. The

---

[1] Edward Truelove, a bookseller, was tried and sent to prison in 1878 for publishing birth control tracts and his publications finally ordered to be destroyed in 1879, but these latter proceedings were connected with those of 1878.
[2] *Coitus reservatus:* intercourse which stops short of ejaculation.
[3] Section 211 of the Penal Code. [4] See Peter Fryer, op. cit., p. 193.

medical profession supported Comstock and in 1890 Dr John Reynolds in his presidential address to the American Gynaeco- logical Society spoke on birth control and warned his hearers that they 'should have nothing to do with the nasty business'. President Theodore Roosevelt (1859–1918) was a strong opponent of birth control warning the nation against 'race suicide' and the 'willfull sterility' that 'inevitably produces and accentuates every hideous form of vice'.[1]

Things however began to change before the First World War. In 1912 Dr Jacobi in his presidential address to the American Medical Association came out in favour of contraception although only in veiled language. In that same year Margaret Sanger, a New York nurse, started her life's work as a zealot for birth control. She began studying the subject and gave her first public lectures. In 1914 she undertook publication of a new monthly magazine, *The Woman Rebel*, and was arrested and indicted under the Comstock law. She fled to Europe and the following year her husband was imprisoned for a short term for handing out a copy of her pamphlet on *Family Limitation*. Mrs Sanger returned to the United States and on 16 October 1916 opened the first birth control clinic in the United States in Brooklyn. The clinic was raided and closed by the police, Mrs Sanger and her sister both being sentenced to thirty days' imprisonment in 1917. Neverthe- less, she continued her work and propaganda, basing her appeal on the suffering caused to women by unlimited child-bearing rather than on Malthusian arguments. In 1917 the National Birth Control League was founded and Mrs Sanger began publication of the *Birth Control Review*. National and international conferences were held and in November 1921 Mrs Sanger had a major clash with the Catholic authorities in New York, when Cardinal Hayes secured police intervention to close down her mass meeting on the subject 'Birth Control, is it moral?' That year however saw the opening of the New York Birth Control Clinical Research Bureau.

Mrs Sanger and another pioneer, Mary Ware Dennet, cam- paigned for the repeal of the anti-birth control legislation but split on what the law should in fact do. Mrs Sanger was content with the objective of removing legal fetters from the medical profession

[1] See H. F. Pringle, *Theodore Roosevelt* (London, 1932), p. 172.

so that they could give birth control advice freely, but Mrs Dennet had the more ambitious objective of securing the repeal of all the restrictive legislation. These two firm-minded, crusading ladies became bitter rivals. In 1929 the New York clinic was raided and its director and assistant arrested. They were later discharged and the clinic continued its work. Public opinion gradually began to favour birth control. The gynaecological section of the American Medical Association had passed a motion in 1925 recommending the altering of the law to allow physicians to give contraceptive advice: in 1931 the Federal Council of the Churches of Christ published a report favouring birth control; support also came from the American Neurological Association, the Eugenics Society, and the Central Conference of Rabbis. In 1936 the Court of Appeals upheld a ruling of the district court that contraceptives imported for a lawful purpose did not come within the restrictions of federal law. In 1937 the American Medical Association unanimously agreed to accept birth control 'as an integral part of medical practice and education'.

In the post-Second World War period birth control became both generally accepted in the United States and also big business.[1] Campaigns against the remaining birth control statutes were mounted and a signal success secured in 1965 when the Connecticut statute penalising 'the use' of a contraceptive was struck down as unconstitutional by the United States Supreme Court in the case of *Griswold* v. *Connecticut*.[2] In the international field the United States modified its policy of neutrality on contraceptive programmes and in January 1965 President Johnson came out in support of American aid for such projects.[3] In 1969 President Nixon sent a special message to Congress asking members to approve an enlarged programme for birth control and family planning within the United States.[4]

---

[1] In April 1958 Robert Sheehan estimated that the contraceptive trade in the United States grossed $200 million a year. See 'The Birth Control Pill', *Fortune Magazine*, April 1958.
[2] 381 U.S. 479 (1965).
[3] For a fuller treatment of this subject see Chapter VII of this book and Norman St. John-Stevas, 'United States Population Policy: An Ethical Appraisal', *Dublin Review*, Autumn 1967, pp. 206–21. Also *World Population and U.S. Government Policy and Programmes*, ed. Franklin T. Bayer (1968), pp. 4–5.
[4] See *The Times*, 19 July 1969. See also pp. 302–3 below.

The birth control cause has made even more spectacular progress in England. After the First World War, the social restrictions on dissemination of birth control information dissolved. Marie Stopes began a campaign in England similar in many ways to that of Margaret Sanger. In 1918 she published her book, *Married Love*, which was frank about sex but contained little on birth control as such and followed this up with *Wise Parenthood* published the same year, which dealt specifically with the subject of contraception and recommended and described methods of birth prevention. Significantly enough the book was not challenged by the law: the era of legal intervention had come to an end. Mrs Stopes was not a woman to be content with legal immunity: like Mrs Sanger she was imbued with converting zeal and in 1920 she communicated a message to the Anglican bishops assembled in London for the Lambeth Conference which counselled the acceptance of birth control and which, she maintained, had come directly to her from God. The bishops ignored this divine message.

More to the point was the opening in 1921 of the first birth control clinic in London and the founding by Mrs Stopes of the Society for Constructive Birth Control. Mrs Stopes appeared to be carrying all before her when she ran into trouble with the Roman Catholic Church. In 1922 she was attacked by Dr Halliday Sutherland, a Catholic physician, in his book *Birth Control: A Statement of Christian Doctrine against the Neo-Malthusians*. Mrs Stopes began a libel action against Dr Sutherland which lasted for nearly two and a half years and which she finally lost in the House of Lords by a majority of three to one. Despite his victory, Dr Sutherland found himself responsible for legal costs of £10,000 which were met by English Catholics. Cardinal Bourne led the appeal with a donation of £400 and a declaration that he would stand by him to the end. Mrs Stopes made a riposte some years later in 1933 when she chained a copy of her book *Roman Catholic Methods of Birth Control* to the font in Westminster Cathedral.

Marie Stopes remained active in the birth control movement until her death in 1958. Other prominent workers in this field were Harold Cox, Julian Huxley, Norman Haire, Dean Inge, and Lord Dawson of Penn. In 1921 Lord Dawson of Penn, then physician to George V, had given a notable fillip to birth control by announcing his support for the cause when he addressed a lay Church congress in Birmingham. The dispute continued in the medical profession throughout the 1920s but by the 1930s the birth controllers had effectively carried the day. Voluntary family planning clinics were opened all over the country but in the 1920s birth control advice could not be obtained at the maternity centres run by local authorities. In 1922 a health visitor was dismissed from the service for giving this advice instead of referring the patient to a doctor or a hospital. In 1924 the Conference of Labour Women passed a resolution declaring that the Ministry of Health should permit local health authorities to provide birth control information to those who wanted it and not to withhold grants from local authorities which did so. The Ministry of Health went some way to meet this demand in 1930, with a circular allowing contraceptive advice to be given in maternal and child welfare clinics to those married women for whom a pregnancy would be detrimental to health.[1] Birth control advice to the unmarried was not to be given, nor was advice to be preferred on other than health grounds. These restrictions continued to operate under the National Health Service Act of 1948.[2] Local authorities were however allowed to open contraceptive clinics, provided the Minister approved and advice was confined to nursing mothers requiring it on medical grounds. They could also with ministerial consent give grants to family planning associations. The most tangible and important way, however, in which local authorities assisted family planning was by allowing these organisations to conduct their clinics on their premises or those of regional hospital boards. By 1963 seven out of eight family planning association clinics were located on local authority or hospital premises and 184 authorities were making grants. In addition 118 local health authorities were running family planning clinics of their own.[3] In 1966 the Minister of Health in a circular asked local authorities to provide family planning services free of charge for women to whom pregnancy would be detrimental to health.[4]

[1] Memorandum 153, *Birth Control*, 1930.   [2] See s. 28.
[3] See Peter Fryer, op. cit., p. 264.
[4] See *Daily Telegraph*, 20 February 1966. The Catholic Doctors' Guild condemned the circular but Cardinal Heenan, Archbishop of Westminster, refused to comment.

This position was thought by many to be too restrictive and in 1967 a Bill was introduced into the House of Commons by a private member, Mr Edwin Brooks, to make further provision for setting up contraceptive clinics under the National Health Service. It received the Royal Assent on 28 June 1967.[1] The Act provides that local health authorities *may* with the approval of the Minister of Health, and to such extent as he may direct, *shall*, provide facilities for the giving of contraceptive advice and the provision of contraceptives. The local health authority may 'with the approval of the Minister of Health, recover from persons to whom advice is given under this section or substances or appliances supplied thereunder or from such persons of any class or description such charges (if any) as the authority consider reasonable, having regard to the means of those persons.' The Act is thus mainly permissive and not mandatory but the Ministry of Health has made it clear that the Government favours its vigorous implementation. The Act removed the limitation that contraceptive advice could only be given to avoid detriment to health but left the local health authorities free to charge for advice and the provision of contraceptives if these were given on non-medical grounds, subject to ministerial approval. In a circular issued in July 1967 the Minister clarified the position.[2] Local authorities were told that while they might charge for contraceptives prescribed in non-medical cases they were not to charge for advice given in such cases. Neither advice nor contraceptives were to be charged for in medical cases. The Minister also threw some light on the position of minors and the unmarried under the Act. The

---

In 1966 the Ministry of Health authorised the charging of a fee by doctors for advice or prescription of contraceptives on social grounds. This led to a government debate in the House of Commons. See *Hansard*, 24 May 1966, Column 421, when the circular was criticised by Mr Leo Abse, M.P.

[1] *National Health Service (Family Planning) Act*, Chapter 39 of 1967. The Bill received an unopposed second reading in the Commons and Lords and in the Commons only one M.P. criticised it. In form a private member's bill it received the direct support of the Government. The Minister of Health had prepared the way for the Bill in February 1966 when he issued a circular to local authorities accepting that family planning was necessary and encouraging local authorities to use fully the powers they then possessed. Circular 5/66, 17 February 1966. The Act applies only to England and Wales, but similar provisions are made for Scotland under the *Health Services and Public Health Act*, 1968.

[2] Circular 15/67.

Act makes no distinction between the married and the unmarried and the Minister makes none as such either. He does however state: 'In the case of unmarried persons under the age of 21 authorities, will, no doubt, wish to apply the same rules relating to requests for parental consent as they apply to the provision of other services. In so far as they may consider it desirable to provide services for persons under 16, authorities would be well advised to seek the consent of the parents of such persons.'[1] The Minister requires prior consultation with the woman's general practitioner before oral contraceptives are supplied or intra-uterine devices fitted.

Some dissatisfaction has been expressed at the speed with which the Act has been implemented by local authorities.[2] According to a Family Planning Association survey published in October 1968, thirty-nine out of the 204 local health authorities in England and Wales have taken no action at all. Only thirty-four are providing a full service while over half provide only a limited service. Often there are no facilities for unmarried women.[3] Moral and financial considerations have contributed to this tardiness but it is too early to say whether the Minister would be justified in using his mandatory powers under the Act, which was designed to take into account variations in local reactions.[4]

General practitioners within the National Health Service are today free to give contraceptive advice and make out prescriptions for contraceptives. They may advise on contraception for medical or social reasons and may not make any charge for these services. When issuing prescriptions for oral contraceptives or making arrangements for the fitting of appliances a distinction is made between medical and social indications. While no charge is to be

[1] On 4 November 1968, in the House of Commons I endeavoured to secure clarification of this ambiguous formula from the Minister for Social Services but did not succeed. See *Hansard*, Volume 772: col. 477.
[2] See *Hansard*, 16 July 1968, Volume 768: col. 1236.
[3] See *Sunday Times*, 13 October 1968. In December 1969 Mr Richard Crossman, Secretary of State for Social Services, sent a letter to all regional hospital boards urging them to set up family planning bureaux for women patients. See *Daily Telegraph*, 16 December 1969. It was not intended that clinics should be set up by hospitals but that doctors in hospitals should give advice on family planning and issue prescriptions.
[4] In 1970 vasectomy, the male sterilisation operation, became available under the National Health Service on grounds of potential ill health to a husband *or wife*.

made for contraceptives prescribed on medical grounds, a fee may be charged for the provision of contraceptives on social grounds. This fee is not to be a heavy one.[1] It can be seen that the National Health Service has now accepted the recommendation of the Royal Commission on Population that all restrictions on giving contraceptive advice to married women under public health services should be removed. Public authorities, said the Commission, should not view the furnishing of advice as a concession but as a positive duty. This accords with the view it expressed that 'public policy should assume, and seek to encourage, the spread of voluntary parenthood'.[2] The triumph of the planned parenthood movement in Britain has been virtually complete.[3]

In the United States movement has been in the same direction, but owing to the lack of a comprehensive national health service the issue has not been so simply disposed of as in Britain.[4] Attitudes towards state-sponsored contraception have, however, radically altered in the past decade. In the 1950s the giving of contraceptive advice in tax-supported hospitals or as part of public health services was heavily restricted. In a number of Southern states, where Roman Catholics are few, such advice was freely given, and similar practices were followed in other regions, but in many municipally financed hospitals in the North, West, Midwest and East it was forbidden. Towards the close of the 1950s the controversy grew more intense and centred on proposals in certain states to include birth control advice as part of relief programmes for the poor and the indigent. The form the struggle took varied in different states but there was a basically similar pattern.

The state of New York provides a good example of how the power struggle was fought out. The issue came to a head in New York City in 1958 where for many years city hospitals had followed an unwritten rule that advice on birth control should not be given. In July 1958, a Protestant physician employed at King's County Hospital announced that he was going to fit a Protestant patient

---

[1] See the advice of the B.M.A. in the *British Medical Journal*, 28 January 1967, p. 29.
[2] Report of the Royal Commission, Cmd. 7695 (1949), paras 434 and 557.
[3] On 23 February 1971 the rate support grant for local authority family planning in England was trebled. *Hansard* 812: 313–14.
[4] See Frederick S. Jaffe, 'The United States: A Strategy for Implementing Family Planning Services', in *Studies in Family Planning* (17 February 1967).

with a contraceptive diaphragm but was forbidden to do so by the New York City commissioner of hospitals. A public controversy followed with Protestants and Jews demanding that the ban be lifted in the interests of accepted therapy and preventive medicine and the Roman Catholic chancery office stating: 'It would be extremely unfortunate if our hospitals and medical faculties, aimed for the preservation of life should be perverted to seek for the prevention of life.' In September 1958, the full hospital commission reversed the ban. The board ordered that municipal hospitals 'should provide such medical advice, preventive measures and devices for female patients under their care whose life and health in the opinion of the medical staff may be jeopardised by pregnancy and who wish to avail themselves of such health services.' They required a certificate of medical necessity signed by two physicians to be issued, the consent of the patient and that of her husband obtained if possible, and the board recommended that the woman should confer with her spiritual adviser. Physicians, nurses, and other employees with religious or moral objections to contraceptive procedures were excused from participation. The New York Department of Welfare adopted a similar policy later the same month.[1]

Although an advance on the previous position this policy was still severely restrictive and was subject to criticism, but it reflected reasonably accurately the state of public opinion in the 1950s. By the end of the 1960s there had been a radical alteration in opinion

[1] For an account of this incident see *New York Times*, 17, 18, and 23 September 1958. A similar controversy broke out in Chicago (Cook County) in 1963 concerning provision of birth control advice to those on welfare. For an account of this see Norman St. John-Stevas, 'Birth Control: Morals, Law and Public Policy', in *Religion and the Public Order* (Chicago, 1965), p. 55. Other disputes have taken place in California, Wisconsin, and Colorado.

After the issue of *Humanae Vitae*, Dr Edward O'Rourke, New York's Health Commissioner, stated that family planning 'by whatever method the family chooses' would remain a high health service priority in spite of the Encyclical. Dr O'Rourke, a Roman Catholic, said: 'As a public official, I am an American first. Without effective family planning for everyone, most of our other health programmes would be in deep trouble. We cannot give good public health if we have to deal with unwanted babies.' See *The Times*, 2 August 1968.

The New York Commissioner for hospitals eventually accepted that other than mere physical factors could justify dissemination of birth control information and treatment and authorised doctors to act on the W.H.O. definition of health, 'A state of complete physical, mental and social well being and not merely the absence of disease or infirmity.'

as to the provision of contraceptive services as part of domestic
health programmes, but the initiative for this change had come
not from state sponsoring of domestic programmes, rather it had
sprung from the changed attitude of the United States in sponsoring birth control programmes abroad. When the Draper committee, appointed to study the foreign aid programme, submitted
its third interim report to the President in July 1959, it recommended that when requested by aid-receiving nations the United
States should help to formulate programmes 'to deal with the
problem of rapid population growth and should support research
leading to better understanding of this problem'. In November
the Roman Catholic bishops denounced this suggestion as a
'morally, humanly, psychologically, and politically disastrous
approach to the population problem'. President Eisenhower
weighed in with the declaration that he could not 'imagine anything more emphatically a subject that is not a proper political or
governmental activity or function or responsibility'. Such was the
status quaestionis in 1959, but six years later came President
Johnson's statement in his state of the Union address: 'I will seek
new ways to use our knowledge to help deal with the explosion in
world population and the growing scarcity in world resources.'[1]
In June 1965 it was revealed that even President Eisenhower had
moved on. He declared in a letter to Senator Gruening that 'if we
now ignore the plight of those unborn generations which, because
of unreadiness to take constructive action in controlling population growth, will be denied any expectations beyond abject
poverty and suffering, then history will rightly condemn us'. The
duty of the United States to promote policies of international
family planning was thus recognised and what was held to apply
in the international sphere could hardly be held irrelevant in the
domestic one. The change in attitude can best be seen by looking
at figures for the growth in tax supported family planning programmes. In 1963 only thirteen states supported such projects
but by mid-1966 they were to be found in over forty states. The
number of publicly financed birth control clinics had increased in

---

[1] 4 January 1965. While avoiding the use of the controversial word 'contraception',
the effect of President Johnson's declaration meant that the administration would in
fact be prepared to help with contraceptive programmes.

the same period from 400 to over 700.[1] In January 1966 the Department of Health and Welfare issued a declaration of policy stating that it would support programmes making family planning information and services available on request.[2] In December 1970 Congress passed the Family Planning Services and Population Research Act which authorised a three-year budget of $236 million, the biggest item to be used for grants to non-profit organisations to establish and expand family planning clinics. These clinics would offer medical advice and contraceptives on request, especially to low income groups. An office of Population Affairs in the Department of Health, Education and Welfare will be set up under the Act to disburse grants for research into birth control. Abortion is excluded.[3]

This position was not reached without struggle. There had been fierce controversy in New York in 1964 when it was announced that a birth control service would be made available to recipients of state relief. When the District of Columbia announced in March 1964 an appropriation of $25,000 to distribute birth control information and devices at health department clinics, the action was vigorously denounced by the Catholic archdiocese of Washington, and the Archbishop set up his own clinic to provide instruction in the rhythm method. In October 1965 Governor Scranton of Pennsylvania approved the first federal anti-poverty programme in his state providing for birth control information and services. The following year, however, the Catholic Conference of Pennsylvania organised a campaign which succeeded in modifying the programme. A compromise was reached by which caseworkers were not to initiate discussions on birth control and services were not to be made available to the unmarried. Federal funds from the anti-poverty programme had also been made available in Texas earlier in 1965 at Corpus Christi. The policy

---

[1] See C. Thomas Dienes, 'Moral Beliefs and Legal Norms: Perspectives on Birth Control', 11 *St. Louis University Law Journal*, 536 (Summer 1967). Nevertheless it was estimated in 1966 that while half a million women were receiving some form of public assistance on family planning, 'as a minimum, five million fertile medically indigent women in the United States are unable to afford contraceptive services'. See G. W. Perkin and D. Radel, 'Current Status of Family Planning Programmes in the United States', *Population Programme* (Ford Foundation, 1966).

[2] H.E.W. report on Family Planning (September 1966).

[3] *Time* magazine, 21 December 1970.

of the Office of Economic Opportunity on the matter was stated by Mr Sargent Shriver at a press conference in March 1964: 'We say that if a community has a comprehensive plan . . . and family planning is a part of that plan and meets with the consensus of approval in that community, we will be willing to underwrite such programming. On the other hand we are not going to go out from Washington and try to force that type of family planning on anybody.'[1] This compromise policy did not appease the Catholic bishops who in November 1966 called upon 'all – and especially Catholics – to oppose vigorously and by every democratic means, those campaigns already under way in some states and at the national level towards the active promotion, by tax supported agencies, of birth prevention as a public policy, above all in connection with welfare-benefit programmes.'[2] Despite a hard core of resistance the opposition to government sponsoring of birth control programmes within the United States is clearly lessening and is likely to diminish further in the future.[3] As early as autumn 1965 an opinion poll showed that 63 per cent of Americans favoured the proposition that the United States Government should give aid to states and cities for birth control programmes if they requested it. Fifty-nine per cent of Roman Catholics also approved of such policies.[4]

One agent behind such revolutionary changes in attitude has undoubtedly been the birth control pill which has popularised contraception throughout the English-speaking world.

Progesterone, a hormone which among other things inhibits ovulation was first isolated in 1934. All later developments of 'the

---

[1] See report referring to this speech in the *New York Times*, 6 January 1965. $295,200 was granted to Corpus Christi and of this amount $12,580 was earmarked for birth control information and mobile clinics. Other cities such as Milwaukee and Philadelphia have followed the example of Corpus Christi in applying for funds for this purpose.

[2] See *Statement on the Government and Birth Control*: adopted by the Roman Catholic bishops of the United States on 14 November 1966.

[3] In July 1970 the United States Senate voted unanimously without debate to launch a five-year programme costing nearly a billion dollars to teach birth control methods to the nation's poor and to supply contraceptives to anyone seeking them. See *Catholic Herald*, 24 July 1970.

[4] See C. Thomas Dienes, op. cit. The attitude of Communist countries has varied in relation to birth control but it now seems to be in favour. Thus in the 1950s in China contraception was frowned upon but returned to favour in the 1960s and today is actively encouraged. See *The Times*, 23 January 1970.

pill' have been basically combinations of synthetic forms of female hormones – progesterone and oestrogen – which inhibit the maturation and release of the egg in the female ovary and thus prevent its fertilisation. Oestrogen – the collective name for other female hormones – and the male hormone, testosterone, have similar effects to progesterone. In 1940 a new stage was reached when an American research worker Russell Marker devised a process of making a synthetic progesterone. Ten years later in 1950, Dr Gregory Pincus began his pioneer work on behalf of the Planned Parenthood Federation of America who requested him to try to develop a simple and safe mode of birth control which would be more effective and acceptable than the methods currently in use. At this time Professor John Rock, a gynaecologist in charge of a fertility clinic in Boston and a Roman Catholic, began his experiments in this sphere. While treating women for infertility he had discovered that although the use of progesterone stimulated fertility after it had ceased to be used, during the actual period of use it prevented ovulation. Dr Rock used combinations of oestrogen and progesterone in his treatment. Professor Rock and Dr Pincus then combined their researches and developed progesterone further as an oral contraceptive, but it was not entirely satisfactory since it worked in only 85 per cent of the cases, had undesirable side effects, such as bleeding, and had to be taken in very large amounts by injections. Taking through the mouth was not effective. They then developed a synthetic form of progesterone, known as progestin, and employed it effectively as an oral contraceptive in Puerto Rico in 1955. This, too, had undesirable side effects but when oestrogen was added these were found to be greatly diminished. A commercial oral contraceptive then became a possibility and was introduced into Britain in 1961. Since then the growth in the use of oral contraception has been phenomenal. Today there are about 20 million women in the world taking the pill, including 1 million in Britain and 8·5 million in the United States.[1] In Britain there are today over twenty varieties of the birth control pill on sale to the public. The Family Planning Association in Britain revealed in 1968 that 44 per cent

[1] The figure for the United States refers to early 1970. That in Britain to early 1968. See *Daily Telegraph*, 8 February 1968, and *The Times*, 22 January 1970.

of its clients were prescribed oral contraceptives.[1] This growth in
the use of oral contraception has been paralleled all over Europe.[2]
When one considers that the pill was only introduced into
Britain in 1961, the rate of growth in use can be seen to be very
high.[3]

The advantages of the pill as a method of contraception are
considerable. It is easy to take and does not interfere with the
physical nature of the sexual act. On the other hand, it is relatively
expensive for the less well off and this limits its use among the
poor.[4] The most serious objection to the pill is, however, its
possible harmful side effects. Too little is known about these to be
absolutely certain as to what these effects are ultimately likely to
be. In December 1968 the Family Planning Association in Britain
announced that a fifteen-year study into the effects of the contraceptive pill would start the following year. The Association and
Medical Research Council will investigate 10,000 women who
have taken the pill and 10,000 who have not. They will be married
women aged between twenty-five and thirty-nine.[5]

[1] See *The Times*, 15 November 1968. The total number of patients at the F.P.A.'s
clinics approaches 500,000.
[2] The increased sale of contraceptive pills in Catholic countries has been very great.
The figures for 1966–7 are as follows:

Country	Catholics	Sales Increase
Austria	80%	87·6%
France	80%	122·7%
Italy	80%	45·3%
Belgium	90%	34·5%
Spain	90%	98·8%
Portugal	90%	87·3%
Brazil	80%	33·4%

Taken from *The Pope, the Pill and the People* (Daily Mirror Books, 1968). The birth rate
in eleven Roman Catholic countries of Europe averages 18·1 per 1,000 per year and
in non-Catholic countries 18·0.
[3] For a full and useful account of the development of the pill and its effects, see *Living
with the Pill*, a paperback published by The Times Newspapers in 1968. See also
Ernest Havemann, *Birth Control*, published by Time Magazine in 1967. See also the
relevant sections of *Contraceptives*, a special supplement of *Which?*, published by the
Consumers Association in 1966, and *The Pill on Trial*, by Paul Vaughan (London,
1970).
[4] The pill may be prescribed under the National Health Service, but only if the doctor
considers a further pregnancy would be detrimental to the woman's health. Otherwise
it has to be privately prescribed.
[5] See *The Times*, 11 December 1968.

Meanwhile what are the risks involved in taking the pill?[1] The most frequent side effect – estimated to affect one woman in five – is subsequent nausea. In addition there may be such effects as putting on weight, cramp, and tiredness. These usually disappear after a period of use, and can sometimes be eliminated by switching to a different brand of pill. Taking the pill may also aggravate asthma and varicose veins. On the other hand, taking the pill can have beneficial effects, such as relief from tension, improvement in the condition of the hair and skin, etc. In certain cases asthma may be relieved.

More serious is the possibility of diabetes, thrombo-embolism and cancer resulting from the use of the pill. With regard to diabetes, there is a possibility – no more – that this may be precipitated in certain women. As far as thrombo-embolism or blood clotting is concerned, there seems no doubt that a connection has been established between this condition and the taking of the pill. If a clot is formed the danger is that it may lodge in an artery and cause death. In England the Committee on Safety of Drugs (the Dunlop Committee) began an investigation on the effects of the pill in 1964. It does not expect to have its final results available until the early 1970s. Meanwhile public anxiety continues to be aroused by cases reported from time to time in the newspapers concerning the death of women from thrombosis who have been using the pill.[2] In November 1965 the Dunlop Committee

[1] For an authoritative review of the effects of the pill see Richard Doll, 'The Long-Term Effects of Steroid Contraceptives', *J. Biosoc. Sci.* (1970), **2**, pp. 367–89. Professor Doll reaches an agnostic conclusion: 'From the review one thing at least emerges clearly: that we are not yet in a position to weigh accurately the advantages and disadvantages attributable to the use of the drugs', at p. 381. See also the report of the meeting of the Central Medical Committee of the International Planned Parenthood Federation held in New York in April 1970 to discuss the side effects of steroidal contraception – *Comments on Steroidal Contraception* (London, 1970).

[2] e.g. see *Daily Telegraph*, 12 August 1965. A mother of two, Mrs Jean Rowley (34), died suddenly of an embolism after she had been taking the contraceptive pill for six months. An open verdict was recorded. The Coroner stated: 'We cannot say definitely that the pills did not take any part in her death. No one can say at this stage.' Cf. another case reported in *The Times*, 14 February 1967, and another on 21 January 1969. In the latter case Dr Brian Jones, pathologist, stated of a mother of three who died of thrombosis: 'It would be so unlikely for clotting to occur in the pelvic veins of an otherwise fit and non-pregnant woman that in my opinion the oral contraceptive was almost certainly responsible.' See also case of death of a woman by blood clotting after taking the pill, reported in the *Guardian*, 13 November 1968, and another in *Daily Telegraph*, 7 February 1969.

published an interim report. This stated that in the year ending 31 August 1965 sixteen women in Britain died from 'thromboembolic episodes'. During this period 400,000 women were known to be taking the pill and the Committee stated that it could be expected that thirteen women between fifteen and forty-five years of age could normally be expected to die from cerebral, heart, lung, and other internal thrombosis or embolism during this period. The Committee was thus unable to reach any final conclusion. In 1966 further evidence came to light from a research team working at Withington Hospital in Manchester. They reported a rise in 'factor VII', one of the thirteen medically recognised clotting factors, among women taking the pill. In June 1966 the Dunlop Committee ordered a series of rigorous tests on existing pills being marketed and ruled that no new pills should be introduced until 1969 so that tests could be undergone. The Committee stated that it expected the results of the experiments on existing pills to be available by June 1970.[1] In August of the same year the United States government announced, through an expert medical committee appointed by the Food and Drug Administration, that a ten months' study of oral contraceptives pointed to their safety and that there was no need to set a time limit on their continuous use. This conclusion accorded with an earlier report of the World Health Organisation.[2] The Committee however was careful to point out that no dogmatic conclusion could be reached, especially about blood clots or cancer until much longer and more comprehensive epidemiological studies had been made. In April 1967 a further report came from the Dunlop Committee. The Committee concluded that women taking oral contraceptives incur a slightly increased risk of thrombosis, but the risk is less than that incurred in normal pregnancy and childbirth. The Committee did not, therefore, recommend withdrawal of the drug.

Three further reports on the risk involved in taking birth control pills were published in May 1967.[3] The first, published by the Royal College of General Practitioners, was based on relatively small numbers. The survey covered only 147 women. The doctors

[1] *The Times*, 17 June 1966.
[2] *Guardian*, 16 August 1966.
[3] See *Daily Telegraph*, 5 May 1967, and also Dr Alfred Byrne, 'Long-Term Consequences', in *Living with the Pill*, p. 48.

found a statistically significant excess of blood clot disorders in women taking the pill. 'It could be said,' states the report 'that being pregnant or puerperal is associated with a quadrupling of the rate of thrombo-embolic disorders, and using an oral contraceptive with a doubling of the rate.' The Committee of the Medical Research Council under the chairmanship of Lord Platt studied twenty-nine patients admitted to London hospitals and concluded that women who take the pill are nine times more likely to be admitted to hospital for thrombo-embolism than those who do not. A recent report of the Dunlop Committee estimates that oral contraceptives are likely to cause the deaths from thrombo-embolism and various kinds of thrombosis of 1·3 healthy women aged 20–34 and 3·4 aged 35–44 out of every 100,000 users each year. On the other hand they did not find enough evidence to say that oral contraceptives cause coronary thrombosis, although this seems to be somewhat more common in women using the pill than in those who are not.

In December 1969 the Dunlop Committee issued a strong warning that certain pills might cause thrombosis. In a preliminary report the Committee let it be known that in their opinion preparations containing a high oestrogen content probably carry a greater risk of a blood clot developing.[1] Professor Eric Scowen, chairman of the committee, stated that if he was a doctor his advice would be to make a switch as quickly as possible.

[1] The Times, 12 December 1969. There are about thirty contraceptive pills available in Britain. Nine with low dosage oestrogen content are: Anovlar 21, Gynolar 21, Minovlar, Minovlar E.D., Norinyl 1, Norlestrin 21, Orlest 28, Volidan, and Volidan 21. The committee recommended two pills containing no oestrogen – Normenon and Verton. Normenon has however been ordered to be withdrawn in the United States. Normenon had been launched in England with the claim that it eliminated any risk of thrombosis. However, the manufacturers admitted that it had 'slightly lesser efficiency' in preventing pregnancy than other pills. The Family Planning Association refused to recommend the pill claiming that it was 50–100 times less effective than other oral contraceptives.

See The Times, 28 May 1969. The difficult choice has to be made between effectiveness and safety. The Government has declined to ban fertility drugs pending further research to lessen the risk of multiple births. See The Times, 28 June 1970.

For a full discussion of the position regarding oral contraceptives see 'Risks of Family Planning' in The Times, 15 December 1969. The author, the paper's medical correspondent, concludes: 'What it all therefore would appear to boil down to is that the pill is not the end-all and be-all of family planning. It has played, and is still playing, a useful part, but it is not the final answer. Meanwhile, for those who prefer it to the alternative available methods, it can be commended provided it is used with care and caution.'

The manner in which this warning was given, to the industry and public before the medical profession, was the subject of sharp criticism in the House of Commons.[1] The Ministry of Health was asked in the House of Lords in January 1970 to ban all contraceptive pills but the Minister declined to do so.[2] The Dunlop warning led to repercussions in the United States where early in 1970 the Food and Drug Administration asked doctors to make their patients fully aware of any risks involved in the use of the pill for birth control. The F.D.A. also required new labelling on oral contraceptives including the words: 'An increased risk of thromboembolic disease associated with the use of hormonal contraceptives has now been shown in studies in both Great Britain and the United States. Other risks such as those of heightened blood pressure, liver disease and reduced tolerance to carbohydrates have not been quantitated with precision.'[3]

Does taking the pill cause cancer? There is no hard evidence of this. In the United States the Food and Drug Administration was consulted on the subject in April 1965 and concluded: 'There is no bona fide evidence that these pills will produce cancer'.[4] Despite this, some doctors are uneasy at the prospect of a woman taking hormone substances for long periods in case they affect the natural balance of the body and create conditions favourable to malignancy. There is particular cause for concern as the breast

[1] See *Daily Telegraph*, 16 December 1969.
[2] See *The Times*, 23 January 1970. The request was made by Lady Summerskill on the grounds that Normenon had been banned in the U.S.A. and therefore all pills were likely to be dangerous. In late January 1970 the English manufacturers of Normenon and Verton announced that they had 'suspended' production. See *The Times*, 29 January 1970.
[3] *San Francisco Chronicle*, 20 January 1970. Women belonging to blood group 'A' are more than twice as likely to suffer from thrombosis if taking oral contraceptives than those of blood group 'O', according to an article in the *Lancet*, of 30 January 1971. The reason is that they have more 'antihaemophilic globulin' in their blood and hence are more likely to form blood clots. See also *The Times*, 1 February 1971.
[4] In January 1970 a Senate sub-committee on small business monopoly headed by Senator Gaylord Nelson of Wisconsin took evidence on the effects of the pill. Dr Hugh Davis of Johns Hopkins Hospital warned that it might cause breast cancer that could not be detected for 20 years. Dr Roy Hertz also drew attention to the dangers of oestrogen. On the other hand Dr J. W. Goldheizen gave evidence to the effect that driving a car or smoking was more dangerous than taking the pill. See *Los Angeles Times*, 15, 16, and 23 January 1970. In an article in *Los Angeles Times*, 19 January 1970, Mr Max Lennen concludes: 'My own vote, if I were a woman, would be on balance against the pill, until we know a good deal more about it than we now know.'

and the uterus are especially affected by hormones. A further point is that taking the pill may mask signs of cancer. A frequent sign of cancer is bleeding between periods or after the menopause and this could be hidden by use of the pill. It seems reasonable to conclude that there is a definite risk to health in taking the pill but it is not a high one and may well be thought worth taking by women who wish to avoid pregnancy.[1] It is equally clear that both short-term and long-term research is needed in order to throw further light on this difficult subject.[2]

An increasingly popular method of contraception is the intra-uterine device. This had been known in a crude form to the Bedouins in the desert who are said to have inserted pebbles into the wombs of their camels to prevent them conceiving while crossing the desert. A human intra-uterine device was not, however, developed until the early years of this century when a German gynaecologist, Grafenberg, invented a ring of coiled silver wire which was then implanted in the uterus. Work on developing these devices continued spasmodically in Israel, England, and Japan, but it was not until 1959 that they became popular. In 1966 it was estimated that four million devices were in use throughout the world and in 1968 the Family Planning Association in Britain reported that 14 per cent of their clients were fitted with an intra-uterine device.[3] Today these devices can be made of plastic and in a number of shapes, including loops, bows, and spirals. It is not known with any certainty how they work. One theory is that they set up muscular movements which force the egg into the womb before it is in fact ready to be implanted. It has not reached the right stage of development by the

[1] The risks of taking the pill are assessed in *Textbook of Contraceptive Practice*, by John Peel and Malcolm Potts (Cambridge, 1969). They point out that one cigarette is three times more dangerous to life than a single pill and that an amateur cricketer or footballer is more likely to be killed playing weekend sport than is his wife to die from taking the pill.

[2] Early in 1970 the Food and Drugs Administration in the United States announced that packages of birth control pills in America would in future have to contain, like packets of cigarettes, a warning of possible health hazards. See *Daily Telegraph*, 5 March 1970. The mini pill was also withdrawn from the market in early 1970. See *Sunday Times*, 25 January 1970.

[3] *The Times*, 15 November 1968. These are popular because they can be introduced into the uterus without pain in the majority of cases and remain there indefinitely. In 1966 a new device 'the polygn' made of polythene and containing a magnet to indicate that the device is in place was marketed in Denmark.

time it reaches the inside of the uterus and therefore cannot implant itself. Another view is that the devices somehow prevent the walls of the womb from accepting the egg, so that even if fertilisation has occurred, the egg cannot develop in the womb. The question arises whether use of such devices is a method of contraception or of abortion. Because of the lack of knowledge on how these devices work a final answer to this point cannot yet be given, although there is increasingly strong evidence that they destroy the blastocyst. The great advantage of intra-uterine devices is that they are easy and cheap to acquire and that once put in place they require little further attention. They are thus particularly suited for use in primitive countries.

Undoubtedly new methods of contraception and developments of old ones will take place in the future. A new kind of oral contraceptive which is simpler to use and safer in effect than the existing pill is being tested by doctors in Mexico.[1] This new pill consists of only one hormone, a progestin, such as chlormadinone acetate, which achieves its effect without interfering with ovulation, pregnancy being prevented by diminishing the production of mucus in the cervix.[2] Thus it avoids many of the side effects caused by the pill and is free from those features of interference with the activity of the pituitary or ovarian hormones which causes many people concern. Another possible contraceptive of the future is the 'morning after' pill, which is already the subject of experimental use. This would be a form of oestrogen taken after rather than before intercourse. As in the case of the intra-uterine devices it is not known exactly how it works but in some way it prevents the fertilised egg from being implanted in the wall of the womb. At the moment the 'morning after' pill has to be taken from four to six consecutive days after intercourse, and some varieties have caused disagreeable side effects. The 'morning after' pill could be open to the objection that it is a form of abortion which destroys human life. Whether this is so or not will depend whether human life is considered to begin when the egg is fertilised or only when it becomes implanted in the wall of the

[1] See *Sunday Times*, 9 July 1967.
[2] Chlormadinone has however been withdrawn by the manufacturers at the request of the F.D.A.

womb and begins to develop into an embryo.[1] Another possible development of the future is the use of chlormadinone as a mini pill. This pill, which already exists in experimental form, would not be taken twenty times a month, like the present ones, but every day of the year. The advantage of this is that it is not necessary to keep a track of the days. It consists of a very small dose of progestin but with nothing else added. It is not known at the moment exactly how it works.

Yet another possible development is a 'long-term' pill. Such a pill would contain enough mini doses of hormone stored in a single pill (which would only be taken once) to provide protection against pregnancy for many years. A capsule could, for example, be implanted under a woman's skin and remain there until she wished to have it removed. Yet another possibility is that women may at some time in the future be vaccinated against pregnancy just as they are vaccinated today to prevent smallpox and other diseases. The vaccination would work by making the body immune to sperm. Research is also proceeding into the possibility of developing a pill for men which would make conception impossible, by either preventing development of sperm or making it incapable of uniting with the egg.[2] Such research has not so far yielded successful results. One effect of a male contraceptive pill that has been in experimental use has been to reduce alcoholic tolerance in the individual taking it.[3] This and other male

[1] In February 1969 it was reported from Prague that a drug had been discovered which prevented conception in rats if administered after copulation. It must be administered within seven days of intercourse. In the few cases where conception did occur the foetus was normal. See *The Times*, 17 February 1969.
[2] In April 1969 Lord Arran asked in the House of Lords whether the Government would pronounce in favour of a safe and proved contraceptive pill for men and with their limited financial capacities encourage the production of such a device. Lady Serota, Minister of State for Health, declined to take action. See *The Times*, 24 April 1969.

In January 1970 the hearings of the Senate sub-committee, already referred to, were brought to a halt by a score of long-haired, mini-skirted women demanding: 'Why isn't there a pill for men?' See *Los Angeles Times*, 24 January 1970.
[3] An American truck driver who took the pill subsequently took a glass of beer. The effect produced was that of drinking a large quantity of high proof alcohol in a short period. See report in *The Times*, 16 November 1968. Another effect could be that the sperm might not be destroyed but damaged, and so be capable of fertilising an ovum and producing an abnormal child. Yet another anti-fertility drug for men has the effect of reddening the whites of the eyes. Other drugs experimented with are effective

contraceptive pills possess marked liver toxicity and the likelihood of an immediate scientific breakthrough seems unlikely.

Finally there is the possibility of developing a pill which will regularise periodicity in women. Such a pill would be of particular interest to those women who have no regular periods and it would enable all women to pinpoint the moment of ovulation. Here again though research is proceeding there seems no likelihood of a breakthrough in the immediate future.

------

as contraceptives but reduce the sex drive. Experiments involving cyprotetenone acetate have been carried out on male rats in the United States but the results are not conclusive. See *The Times*, 8 August 1969.

CHAPTER II

The Law in England and the United States

ENGLISH LAW

Traditionally the law in England followed the Prayer Book in recognising the procreation of children as the primary purpose of marriage. Thus, in an early nineteenth-century case, Sir John Nicholl referred to the procreation of children as 'the primary and most legitimate object of wedlock'.[1] The continued operation of the doctrine was illustrated by a Court of Appeal case of 1946, where it was held that a man who had consistently refused to have intercourse without employing a contraceptive against the wishes of his wife had wilfully refused to consummate the marriage, thus entitling her to a decree of nullity.[2] 'We are of opinion,' said Lord Justice du Parcq, 'that sexual intercourse cannot be said to be complete where a husband deliberately discontinues the act of intercourse before it has reached its natural termination or when he artificially prevents the natural termination, which is the passage of the male seed into the body of the woman. To hold otherwise would be to affirm that a marriage is consummated by an act so performed that one of the principal ends, if not the principal end, of marriage is intentionally frustrated.'[3] Two years later, the

[1] *Brown* v. *Brown* (1828), 1 Hagg. Ecc. 523 at p. 524. Cf. *G.* v. *M.* (1885), 10 A.C. 171 at p. 204 per Lord Fitzgerald: 'The procreation of children being the main object of marriage, the contract contains by implication, as an essential term, the capacity for consummation.' See also *D.* v. *A.* (1845), 1 Rob. Ecc. 279 at p. 298 per Dr Lushington.
[2] *Cowen* v. *Cowen* (1946), p. 36.
[3] *Cowen* v. *Cowen* (1945), 2 All E.R. 197 at p. 199.

House of Lords abandoned the principle.[1] 'It is indisputable,' said Lord Jowitt, with remarkable confidence, 'that the institution of marriage generally is not necessary for the procreation of children; nor does it appear to be a principal end of marriage as understood in Christendom, which as Lord Penzance said in *Hyde* v. *Hyde* (1866) L.R. 1 P & D 130, 135, "may for this purpose be defined as the voluntary union of one man and one woman to the exclusion of all others".'[2] Accordingly, a spouse has no matrimonial remedy at English law if the other spouse insists that intercourse shall only take place with the employment of a contraceptive.[3]

As has been noted, contraceptive information was in the nineteenth century classified as obscenity, and sale of contraceptives doubtless came within the common law offence of publishing obscene matter, but this is no longer the case. Books are no longer considered obscene if they advocate or describe methods of birth control. 'It cannot be assumed,' said the Home Secretary in answer to a question in the House of Commons in 1922, 'that a court would hold a book to be obscene merely because it deals with the subject referred to.'[4] Sale of contraceptives is not subject to common law or statutory restriction save for certain by-laws which restrict the sale of contraceptives from slot-machines in public places.[5] Advertisements for contraceptives are not *per se* considered obscene. This lack of legal restraint is not surprising, since it accords with prevailing English opinion on the subject, summed up by the Royal Commission on Population when it

[1] *Baxter* v. *Baxter* (1948), A.C. 274. Refusal of a nullity decree to a husband whose wife declined intercourse unless the husband took contraceptive precautions. He agreed under protest.

[2] Lord Penzance, when defining marriage *for this purpose*, was referring not to procreation but to the effect of polygamous marriages.

[3] The effect of *Baxter* v. *Baxter* will largely depend on whether it is confined strictly to the category of 'wilful refusal to consummate' as a ground for a nullity suit, or whether this type of consummation is accepted as valid in all matrimonial causes. Lord Jowitt's dictum on the purpose of Christian marriage has been much criticised. See the Report of the Commission appointed by the Archbishops of Canterbury and York in 1949 to consider *The Church and the Law of Nullity of Marriage* (London, S.P.C.K., 1955).

[4] St. John-Stevas, *Obscenity* . . . , p. 70.

[5] The by-laws were suggested by the Home Secretary in a circular of 22 October 1949, after public controversy over sale of contraceptives from slot machines. He circulated a model by-law, suggesting this was the appropriate remedy since the practice was an evil only in some public places. For a discussion of what constitutes a *public place* see *The Justice of the Peace and Local Government Review*, 7 January 1950, p. 114:4.

stated: 'Control by men and women over the numbers of their children is one of the first conditions of their own and the community's welfare, and in our view mechanical and chemical methods of contraception have to be accepted as part of the modern means, however imperfect, by which it can be exercised.'[1]

Formerly advice on birth control under the National Health Service could only be given in restricted circumstances. Thus the Minister of Health allowed contraceptive advice to be given in maternal and child welfare clinics but only to those married women for whom a pregnancy would be detrimental to health.[2] Contraceptive appliances were not obtainable on National Health Service prescriptions but if a patient needed them, payment could be authorised by a local authority medical officer or hospital consultant. As has been noted in the previous chapter these restrictions have been removed by the Family Planning Act of 1967.[3]

The Act has not, however, been vigorously implemented and whereas the Abortion Act is well known there is little knowledge of the Family Planning Act. Sir John Peel, former President of the Royal College of Obstetricians and Gynaecologists commented on the situation in an address to the Royal College in February 1968. 'We still,' declared Sir John, 'have no properly formulated national policy on family planning and expert advice ... is not as readily available as it should be. A country that appears to want abortion free and easy and contraception expensive and difficult has its priorities curiously awry.'[4]

One controverted legal problem of some practical importance is whether a doctor is liable for an action in damages if he gives a married woman contraceptive advice or provides her with contraceptives without her husband's consent. The view of the Medical Defence Union, having taken counsel's opinion, is that in general a doctor is entitled to give and a woman to receive instruction on methods of contraception which she herself can

---

[1] Cmd. 7695 (1949), par. 427. The Commission hoped that voluntary parenthood would become universal (p. 430).
[2] See Ministry of Health Memorandum 153 of 1930 *Birth Control*. Circular 1208 of 1931. Circular 1408 of 1934. Circular 1622 of 1937.
[3] See pp. 23–5 above.
[4] See 'Prevention Better than Cure' by 'Notero', 16 May 1968, *New Law Journal*, 118:480.

apply, without the husband's consent. In such cases the ultimate decision to employ the contraceptive is hers and the doctor is not involved. Special considerations however are thought to apply to the pill and the intra-uterine device. Both of these can be used secretly by a woman without the knowledge of her husband. The Medical Defence Union is of the opinion that a husband might have a right of action in damages against a doctor who fitted an intra-uterine device or prescribed pills, either without the husband's prior consent or knowing that the husband opposed his wife using any method of contraception, unless the insertion or prescription was reasonably necessary in the interests of the wife's health. The element of secrecy is thought to alter the situation and in the case of the intra-uterine device there is also an operation performed by the doctor. The Medical Defence Union accordingly advises its doctors to obtain a husband's consent in the above cases. The Family Planning Association requires it where fitting intra-uterine devices are concerned, but not when the pill alone is involved.[1]

UNITED STATES LAW

Federal Law
Federal law restricts the distribution of contraceptives in several ways. Knowingly to deposit any contraceptive in the mails or to take such articles from the mails for the purpose of distribution is a felony under federal law.[2] The ban extends to any information as to where contraceptives may be obtained, and any written or printed matter telling 'how or by what means conception may be prevented'. A further federal felony is constituted by depositing contraceptives or information where they may be obtained with an

[1] These views are based on a conversation with officers of the Medical Defence Union. The Union holds that an operation to sterilise a man is lawful provided the patient gives full and valid consent. In the case of a married patient the written consent of both spouses should be obtained and the Union has prepared a model form of consent to the operation. (See *The Times*, 24 June 1966.) Despite the Union's view I feel that the law in respect of sterilisation is doubtful. See the chapter on sterilisation in my book *Life, Death and the Law* (London, 1961). I conclude then that in regard to voluntary sterilisation that therapeutic sterilisation is lawful, contraceptive sterilisation unlawful, and the position of eugenic sterilisation doubtful. I fully concede that opinions have changed since then and that these conclusions may well no longer be valid, especially in view of the passing of the Abortion Act of 1967.
[2] 18 U.S.C.A. 1461.

express company or other common carrier. Books on contraception are not specifically mentioned, but obscene books are included in the ban. To import contraceptive articles or obscene books is also a felony and prohibited by federal statute.[1]

Read literally, these statutes impose an absolute and universal ban, and many attempts have been made to modify their scope by legislation. All have failed.[2] They have, however, been modified by judicial interpretation. A first step was taken in 1930, when Judge Swan stated: 'The intention to prevent a proper medical use of drugs or other articles merely because they are capable of illegal uses is not lightly to be ascribed to Congress.'[3] Without deciding the point, he suggested that the Criminal Code should be interpreted as requiring an intent on the part of the sender that 'the articles mailed or sent by common carrier be used for illegal contraception or abortion or for indecent or immoral uses'. This reasoning was applied in *Davis* v. *United States* (1933), when an intent to use the articles for illegal purposes was held necessary for a conviction under the postal and transport statutes.[4] The decision permitted manufacturers of contraceptives and others in the trade to dispatch their wares to druggists, jobbers, and physicians. These decisions led logically to that of *United States* v. *One Package* in 1936, when Dr Hannah Stone was allowed to import a package of vaginal pessaries into the United States.[5] Judge Augustus Hand conceded that the Tariff Act of 1930 exempted only those articles excepted by the Comstock

---

[1] 18 U.S.C.A. 1462 (transport and import). 19 U.S.C.A. 1305 (import). The penalties are fines of not more than $5,000 or not more than five years imprisonment, or both, for a first offence; and fines of not more than $10,000 or ten years imprisonment, or both, for a second offence. The higher penalties also apply to customs officers who aid or abet such offences (18 U.S.C.A. 552).

[2] For full list see Alvah H. Sulloway, *Birth Control and Catholic Doctrine* (Boston, 1959), p. 190, n. 20.

[3] *Youngs Rubber Corporation* v. *Lee*, 45 F. 2d, 103 (2d Cir.) (1930) at p. 108. The case arose from an action for trademark infringement by a manufacturer of prophylactics, the defence being that redress was contrary to public policy since the federal statutes were being violated in carrying out the business. 'We conclude,' said Judge Swan, 'therefore . . . that a manufacturer of drugs or instruments for medical use may in good faith sell them to druggists or other reputable dealers in medical supplies, or to jobbers for distribution to such trade.' (p. 109.)

[4] 62 F. 2d, 473 (6th Cir.) (1933). Two charges were involved: (*a*) mailing circulars on contraception contrary to 18 U.S.C.A. 334, and (*b*) transporting articles for preventing conception contrary to 18 U.S.C.A. 396.

[5] 86 F. 2d, 737 (2d. Cir.) (1936).

Act of 1873, but he went on to say that the court was satisfied 'that this statute, as well as all the Acts we have referred to, embraced only such articles as Congress would have denounced as immoral if it had understood all the conditions under which they were to be used. Its design, in our opinion, was not to prevent the importation, sale, or carriage by mail of things which might intelligently be employed by conscientious and competent physicians for the purpose of saving life or promoting the well being of their patients.'[1] Judge Learned Hand was clearly uneasy about these verbal gymnastics but contented himself with observing that people had changed their minds about such matters in recent years, and he concurred in the judgement.

Books on contraception are specifically banned from the mails by the postal statute, but the section restricting imports mentions only 'obscene' books. It is now established that a book on contraception is not *per se* considered obscene by the federal courts.[2] Dismissing a charge against *Contraception* by Marie Stopes in 1931, Judge Woolsey stated: 'It is a scientific book written with obvious seriousness and with great decency, and it gives information to the medical profession regarding the operation of birth control clinics and the instruction necessary to be given at such clinics to women who resort thereto.' Such a book, he held, was not obscene, 'for the reading of it would not stir the sex impulses of any person with a normal mind'.[3]

[1] p. 739. Judge Augustus Hand stressed that all the federal statutes should be interpreted by a common standard, since they were intended to constitute a single moral code.

[2] For a first suggestion of this see *United States* v. *Dennett*, 39 F. 2d, 564 (2d Cir.) (1930). See also *U.S.* v. *One Obscene Book entitled 'Married Love'*, 48 F. 2d, 821 (S.D.N.Y.) (1931), where the book by Marie Stopes was declared admissible at any port in the United States.

[3] *U.S.* v. *One Book Entitled 'Contraception'*, 51 F. 2d, 525 (S.D.N.Y.) (1931), at pp. 527–8. See also *U.S.* v. *Nicholas* 97 F. 2d, 510 (2d Cir.) (1938). A book for Nicholas and some magazines for Himes coming from abroad through the mails were seized under the Tariff Act. 'We have twice decided,' said Judge Learned Hand, 'that contraceptive articles may have lawful uses and that statutes prohibiting them should be read as forbidding them only when unlawfully employed. . . . Contraceptive books and articles are of the same class and those at bar were therefore lawful in the hands of those who would not abuse the information they contained.' The magazines were sent on to Himes as editor and, therefore, an appropriate person to receive them. The book was detained in the post office pending an application by the addressee. 'Only the addressee can prove whether he is among the privileged classes; he ought at least to go forward with the evidence, even if the burden of proof is not eventually on him.' (Judge Learned Hand at p. 512.)

The federal statutes are accordingly by no means dead letters, but contraceptives intended for bona fide medical use, for the treatment or prevention of disease, and contraceptive books and pamphlets which are not written in obscene language may be freely imported, transported, and mailed. In practice this means that contraceptives must be going to or coming from doctors or other professional persons, or anyone acting at their discretion or under their supervision. Druggists, jobbers, and dealers, provided they are legitimate traders, thus enjoy immunity. This rule applies to contraceptive books and pamphlets going through the mails, but not to the importation of such books or to their transport in interstate commerce.[1] Under the customs law, only obscene books are excluded, and, as has been noted, bona fide contraceptive manuals are not any longer within this category. To secure a conviction under the statutes an intention to use the materials illegally must be established by the prosecution. However, for administrative purposes, consignments may be stopped by the authorities temporarily, pending the production of prima facie evidence by the addressee that he is a privileged recipient. The Family Planning Association makes it a practice to consign contraceptives and information under a doctor's signature and thus obviate vexatious delays. Private persons importing, mailing, or transporting contraceptives purely for the purpose of preventing conception, with no medical intention for their employment, would still, at least theoretically, be caught by the statutes.[2]

The Law of the States

State law on the subject of contraception has varied greatly in the past from state to state and still to a considerable extent does so today. Many states have no legislation and never have had. Some have had restrictive statutes in the past but have recently repealed them.[3] Others prohibit traffic in contraceptives but exempt doctors, pharmacists, or others operating under special licence from the

[1] 18 U.S.C.A. 1462, the section dealing with inter-state transportation and import does not ban books on contraception as such, but only those 'giving information directly or indirectly where or how they (contraceptives) may be obtained or made'.
[2] Such persons could import or transport contraceptive books, provided they did not violate the provision in n. 1 above, but presumably could not mail them except subject to restrictions on mailing contraceptives.
[3] e.g. Colorado, Indiana, Kansas, and Minnesota.

statutory prohibition.[1] Yet others have no law against contraception but restrict or prohibit its advertisement, some allowing an
exception for medical journals and textbooks, etc.[2] Other states
regulate the trade by requiring contraceptive information to be
accurate and prohibiting the sale of articles which do not comply
with certain defined standards. In certain states the sale of contraceptives from slot-machines is forbidden: in others sale to the
unmarried is restricted.[3] In the past, five states, Connecticut,
Kansas, Massachusetts, Mississippi, and Nebraska have prohibited both the sale and advertisement of contraceptives. Prohibition of the sale or advertising of contraceptives or the dissemination of information on birth control has consistently been held
to be within the police power of individual states.[4] Until 1938
none of the cases had included a qualified physician as party to
the proceedings, or else the statute under review contained a
clause exempting physicians from its operation. In that year,
however, in Gardner's case, a statute imposing an unconditional
ban was upheld by the Massachusetts courts, and an appeal to
the United States Supreme Court was dismissed.[5]

The actual effect of these laws has varied in different areas.
In the majority of states their effects have long been marginal.
Exemptions for doctors and other qualified persons have been
broadly interpreted or exemptions authorising the distribution of
contraceptives for the prevention of disease have been provided
legislatively or read into the statutes by interpretation. The states
in which most litigation has occurred over birth control statutes
have been Connecticut, Massachusetts, and New York. The
Connecticut law, around which controversy raged for years, was

[1] States adopting this approach are Arkansas, Delaware, Idaho, Iowa, Montana,
Ohio, Oregon, Wisconsin, Wyoming, and New York.
[2] See law in the states of Arizona, California, Hawaii, Louisiana, Maine, Michigan,
Nevada, Pennsylvania, and Washington.
[3] See the law of Wisconsin.
[4] That the police power may be exercised to protect public morals, health, and safety
is firmly established. See e.g. *Peterson* v. *Widule*, 157 Wis. 641; 147 N.W. 966 (1914)
(Physical examination required for issue of marriage licence). Cases on birth control
include *McDonnell* v. *Knoxville*, 110 S.W. 2d, 478 (Tenn., 1937); *State* v. *Arnold*, 217
Wis. 340; 258 N.W. 843 (1935); *Barretta* v. *Barretta*, 182 Misc. 852; 46 N.Y.S. 2d, 261
(1944).
[5] *Cw.* v. *Gardner*, 300 Mass. 372; 15 N.E. 2d, 222 (1938). An appeal to the U.S.
Supreme Court was dismissed *per curiam* 'for want of a substantial federal question'.
Gardner v. *Mass.*, 305 U.S. 559 (1938).

finally struck down as unconstitutional in 1965 in a case which has already had wide repercussions on the law governing birth control in other states, and is likely to have an effect on the law governing morality in a number of other fields. The Connecticut situation, therefore, must be examined in more detail.

Connecticut. The Connecticut statute forbidding birth control dated from 1879, when it was dealt with as part of the obscenity statute, but in 1887 it became a separate enactment. 'Any person who shall use any drug, medicinal article or instrument for the purpose of preventing conception shall be fined not less than 50 dollars or imprisoned not less than 60 days nor more than one year or be both fined and imprisoned.'[1] The statute was unique in that it prohibited not merely the sale, but the *use* of a contraceptive. In 1940 a campaign against the statute began which was to succeed a quarter of a century later. Two physicians and a nurse, indicted for counselling a married woman to use a contraceptive, contended that the statute was unconstitutional unless it was interpreted to except the medical profession. The Supreme Court of Errors rejected this argument, which had been accepted by the lower court, and upheld the statute.[2] The court confined its decision to situations where the 'general health' of the woman would be endangered by lack of contraception and left open the question whether an exception existed where 'pregnancy would jeopardize life'. This loophole was closed in 1942. In that year a doctor sought a ruling whether the statute would apply where pregnancy would entail specific dangers to health because of high blood pressure, tuberculosis, or three pregnancies within twenty-seven months. The court held (3–2) that it did apply, and that abstention in such predicaments must have been considered by

---

[1] Connecticut, Statutes (1958), c. 53, s. 32. Also c. 54, s. 196: 'Any person who shall assist, abet, counsel, cause, hire or command another to commit any offence may be prosecuted and punished as if he were the principal offender.'
[2] *State* v. *Nelson*, 126 Conn. 412, 11 A 2d, 856 (1940). Decision taken 3–2. In a companion case to *State* v. *Nelson*, the Connecticut Supreme Court held that the contraceptive materials seized in connection with this case were not subject to seizure under a Connecticut statute authorising search for and seizure of articles used generally for gambling, notwithstanding that the statute also provided for seizure of articles used for the violation of any of the criminal laws of Connecticut. *State* v. *Certain Contraceptive Materials*, 126 Conn. 428; 11 A 2d, 863 (1940).

the legislature as an alternative to the use of contraceptives, when passing the statute.[1]

The attempt to modify the statute by court action appeared to have met the same fate as attempts to modify it through the legislature.[1] In 1958 however a series of cases began which were to lead to a different ending and the downfall of the statute. Between May 1958 and 1959, nine plaintiffs sought declaratory judgements as to the constitutionality of the Connecticut birth control statute. These plaintiffs included a Dr Buxton and a number of his patients. Five of the cases reached the courts. The cases were dismissed in the Court of First Instance in New Haven County and were then taken on appeal to the Connecticut Supreme Court where once again they were dismissed.[3] This decision was reached by Chief Justice Aldwin acting unanimously with four other judges. Undeterred the plantiffs appealed to the United States Supreme Court in 1961. The Supreme Court of the United States declined to hear the case at all, holding that no case or controversy existed as there would in fact be no prosecutions under the statutes. The plea of the American Civil Liberties Union that the statute violated the 14th amendment by arbitrarily invading the privacy of the appellants and unreasonably interfering with Dr Buxton's right to practise his profession was dismissed. So was the contention of sixty-six doctors, all heads of departments in medical schools, who claimed that the overwhelming majority of doctors held that contraception was both advisable and necessary when a pregnancy would be harmful to health. The Supreme Court held that it could not render an opinion if no case or controversy existed. 'This court,' declared Judge Frankfurter, 'cannot be umpire to debates concerning harmless, empty shadows.' What proved fatal to the plaintiff's case was the reply to those justices who asked whether the law in Connecticut was really being enforced. They were told that there had been no

[1] *Tileston* v. *Ullman*, 129 Conn. 84; 26 A 2d, 582 (1942). An appeal was taken to the Supreme Court and dismissed, the physician being held to lack standing to raise a constitutional issue. *Tileston* v. *Ullman*, 318 U.S. 44 (1943).

[2] Attempts to alter the law by legislative action had been frequent since the 1920s e.g. 1923, 1925, 1927, 1929, 1935, 1954-7. These bills either repealed the law or inserted an exception for doctors when counselling married women for health reasons. Although sometimes passed in the House, all were defeated in the Senate.

[3] *Buxton* v. *Ullman*, *Poe* v. *Ullman*, 147 Conn. 48; 156 A 2d, 508 (1959).

prosecution since the year 1879, except in the case of *State* v. *Nelson* (1940). They were also told that contraceptives were readily available in the state and that doctors were in fact giving birth control advice. In fact, the Supreme Court may have exaggerated the non-effect of the statute, and there may well have been other prosecutions besides Nelson's case, although accurate information about them does not seem to have been available.[1]

The Planned Parenthood League of Connecticut and the Planned Parenthood Federation of America welcomed the recognition that the law in Connecticut had become a nullity. They thereupon outlined plans to contravene the Connecticut statute by distributing information on all contraceptive techniques, including the opening of a clinic in New Haven, which would have a budget of $45,000 per year and between 2,500–3,000 patients annually. In November 1961 the clinic opened and was visited by the police. A complaint was then lodged with the police that the clinic was passing out 'immoral literature and breaking the law' and detectives visited the clinic questioning the director, Mrs Griswold, for two hours, as well as Dr Buxton, the medical director. A week later the police returned with warrants for the arrest of Mrs Griswold and Dr Buxton and the clinic was closed. Mrs Griswold and Dr Buxton were released on bail. Their trial opened on 24 November, both pleaded not guilty and a hearing was postponed until 8 December. In January 1962 the trial court delivered judgement and found the defendants guilty, fining them $100 each. The judge commented that the statute represented 'a constitutional exercise of the police powers of the State of Connecticut'. In January 1963 the Appellate Division of the Circuit Court affirmed the convictions and the defendants' appeal to the Connecticut Supreme Court was also dismissed,[2] the court rejecting the contention of the defendants that they could not be punished as accessories because the prosecution of the principals would be unconstitutional. Finally they appealed to the United States Supreme Court which ruled that they had a justiciable issue to argue on its merits. Professor Thomas Emerson of the

[1] The decision was reached 5–2 with Judge Frankfurter and Chief Justice Warren joining the majority and Judges Douglas and Harlan dissenting.
[2] *State* v. *Buxton, State* v. *Griswold*, 151 Conn. 544; 200 A 2d, 479 (1964).

Yale Law School acted as counsel for the appellants. Their appeal was upheld and in 1965 the Connecticut statute was struck down. It was held that the statute invaded the right of privacy.[1]

The Supreme Court, which has nine members, reached its decision by a majority vote of 7–2. The opinion of the court was written by Judge Douglas: Judge Goldberg wrote a concurring opinion and was supported by Chief Justice Warren and Judge Brennan. Concurring and separate opinions came from Judges Harlan and White. Judges Black and Stewart dissented. With so many different opinions and a subject-matter so vague as the right to privacy, the *ratio decidendi* of the case can only be ascertained with some difficulty; the judges of the majority were agreed about the existence of the right but divided as to which sections of the constitution were relevant. The case in fact involved a whole panorama of conflicting rights: the rights of the individual claiming a right to liberty, those of the theologian demanding that moral standards should be enforced by law, those of the doctor seeking to practise his profession freely and so heal and help, and the rights of the state to exert its influence in the interests of public health and morals by the exercise of the police power.

The question the court had to decide was whether the banning of the use of contraceptives was such an invasion of the right of privacy of married couples as to be unconstitutional. The court first held that the appellants had standing to assert the constitutional rights of married persons since they were in a professional relationship with them. Judge Douglas held that although the state had a general legitimate interest in the matter, the law infringed a right of marital privacy protected by what he called the 'penumbras of the 1st, 3rd, 4th and 9th amendments, as applied to the states by the 14th amendment'.[2] He added that the

[1] *Griswold* v. *Connecticut*, *Buxton* v. *Connecticut*, 381 U.S. 479 (1965).
[2] The relevant amendments to the Constitution read as follows.

First Amendment. 'Congress shall make no law respecting an establishment of religion, or prohibiting the free exercise thereof; or abridging the freedom of speech, or of the press; or the right of the people peaceably to assemble and to petition the Government for a redress of grievances.'

Third Amendment. 'No soldier shall, in time of peace be quartered in any house, without the consent of the owner, nor in time of war, but in a manner to be prescribed by law.'

Fourth Amendment. 'The right of the people to be secure in their persons, houses, papers and effects, against unreasonable searches and seizures, shall not be violated

statute was offensive to 'the sacred precinct of marital bedrooms'. It invaded the zones of privacy created by the penumbras of specific guarantees of the Bill of Rights and formed by 'emenations from those guarantees that help give them life and substance'. Thus, according to Judge Douglas, the rights protected by the Constitution are not limited to those specifically mentioned in the Constitution and the Bill of Rights, but must be shown to be connected with them in some way. A whole range of peripheral rights can be said to exist to secure the specific rights guaranteed by the Constitution. The judges of the majority laid great stress on the 9th amendment to the Constitution which states: 'the numeration in the Constitution, of certain rights shall not be construed to deny or disparage others retained by the people.' Judge Douglas stated that since the state could achieve its declared purpose of deterring illicit sexual behaviour by means that would not impinge on a protected right, e.g. the regulation of the sale and manufacture of contraceptives, the law could not stand. Judges White and Harlan stressed that the Connecticut statute violated the due process clause of the 14th amendment. Judge White held that the law seriously interfered with the family planning and at times the health of married couples. He and Judge Harlan agreed that the applicable standard for reviewing a state statute is found not in the Bill of Rights, but in a 'concept of ordered liberty'. This idea of a 'concept of ordered liberty' seems to be similar to that contained in Judge Douglas's phrase concerning 'penumbras'. Judge Goldberg supported Judge Douglas's opinion and laid additional stress on the 9th amendment. 'To hold,' he declared 'that a right so basic and fundamental and so deep rooted in our society as the right of privacy in marriage

---

and no Warrants shall issue, but upon probable cause, supported by Oath or affirmation, and particularly describing the place to be searched, and the persons or things to be seized.'

Ninth Amendment. 'The enumeration in the Constitution of certain rights, shall not be construed to deny or disparage others retained by the people.'

Fourteenth Amendment. 'Section I. All persons born or naturalised in the United States, and subject to the jurisdiction thereof, are citizens of the United States and of the State wherein they reside. No State shall make or enforce any law which shall abridge the privileges or immunities of citizens of the United States; nor shall any State deprive any person of life, liberty or property, without due process of law; nor deny to any person within its jurisdiction the equal protection of the laws.'

E

may be infringed because that right is not guaranteed in so many words by the first eight amendments to the Constitution is to ignore the 9th amendment and to give it no effect whatsoever.' The dissenting judges, Black and Stewart, described the Connecticut statute as 'uncommonly silly' and 'offensive', but maintained that the court had no authority to invalidate it. They stated that no constitutional right of privacy was created by the first eight amendments to the constitution, neither was one conferred by the 9th amendment which merely limited the Federal Government's power in relation to the states. None of the judges passed on the arguments put forward on behalf of the American Civil Liberties Union that the statute violated the equal protection clause of the Constitution by prohibiting contraception by 'devices' while allowing it by other methods, e.g. rhythm; by discriminating against married women compelling them to have children and so preventing them from developing a career; and was discriminatory by punishing the users of devices but not the manufacturers or sellers. The American Civil Liberties Union had also suggested that the statute violated the article of the Constitution guaranteeing the separation of Church and State.

The Griswold case thus rests upon the declaration of a natural right to privacy in the case of married couples, which is presupposed or else incorporated by 'penumbras' in the Bill of Rights of the Constitution. Judge Douglas declared: 'We deal with a right of privacy older than the Bill of Rights – older than our political parties, older than our school system. Marriage is a coming together for better or for worse, hopefully enduring, and intimate to a degree of being sacred. The association promotes a way of life, not causes; a harmony involving political faiths; a bilateral loyalty, not commercial or social projects. Yet it is an association for as noble a purpose as any involved in our prior decisions.'[1]

The case had an immediate effect on other birth control laws. In New York, for example, the statute was amended to eliminate a total prohibition against sale and distribution of contraceptives and to permit contraceptives to be dispensed by prescription. In Chicago the day after the decision was reached, counsel for the City Council of Chicago declared that the decision provided

[1] *New York Times*, 8 June 1965.

ample legal basis for approving the City's contract to purchase contraceptive supplies for the Board of Health.[1] Massachusetts liberalised its law banning contraception.[2] Other states have since repealed or amended their birth control laws and the Federal Department of the Interior initiated a programme of advice and service with regard to birth control including the dispensation of contraceptive devices.[3]

Certain possible effects of the Griswold decision should be noted. First, its influence could spread out to invalidate all prohibition of dissemination of birth control information to adult married persons, since it could be argued that if there is a marital right to use contraceptives, then there is also a right to obtain expert guidance on how to use them. Again a possible argument based on similar grounds could be advanced to invalidate statutes prohibiting the sale of contraceptives. On the other hand, it could equally be argued that the effect of such a prohibition would be too remote to violate any right to privacy and so these statutes can be distinguished from the Connecticut statute.[4] The effects of Griswold's case may also be felt on other statutes which may be attacked for invading the right to privacy in matters which have no substantial bearing on the life of the community. Thus statutes prohibiting miscegenation, sodomy between married persons, and fornication might be declared invalid.[5]

New York. New York law prohibits distribution of contraceptives and birth control information, but contains a number of modifying provisos. First of all the law provides 'an article or instrument, used or applied by physicians lawfully practising, or by their direction or prescription, for the cure or prevention of disease is not an article of indecent or immoral nature or use, within this article.

---

[1] *Chicago Sun Times*, 9 June 1965.   [2] *New York Times*, 8 June 1965.
[3] *New York Times*, 20 June 1965.
[4] This argument draws support from the statement of Judge Douglas in the Griswold case that since the state could achieve its declared purpose of deterring illicit sexual behaviour by means that would not impinge on a protected right, e.g. the regulation of sale and manufacture of contraceptives, the law could not stand. This indicates that the sale of contraceptives comes into a different category.
[5] Nineteen states in fact have miscegenation statutes. Other matters which could be affected by the notion of the right to privacy are electronic eavesdropping, loyalty oaths, and the penalising of homosexual relations.

The supplying of such articles to such physicians or by their direction or prescription is not an offence under this article.'[1] In 1917 Margaret Sanger was sentenced to thirty days' imprisonment for violating the statute. Her appeal was dismissed, but the judge gave a liberal interpretation to the section. It protected, said the court, the physician who 'in good faith gives such help or advice to a married person to cure or prevent disease'. 'Disease' was not limited to venereal disease, but defined as 'an alteration in the state of the body, or some of its organs, interrupting or disturbing the performance of the vital functions, and causing or threatening pain and sickness; illness; sickness; disorder'.[2]

Following on the Griswold decision in Connecticut the New York law was amended further.[3] The amended law allows the sale or distribution by duly licensed pharmacists to persons of sixteen or over of contraceptives for the prevention of conception.

Massachusetts. Connecticut apart, birth control legislation has been the cause of more dissent in Massachusetts than in any other state of the Union. Publication of any printed matter containing birth control information and distribution of instruments and articles for preventing conception are prohibited by a statute dating from 1879.[4] The statute was upheld as constitutional and applied in 1917 when certain pamphlets containing birth control information were held to be obscene.[5] In 1938 the courts rejected a plea that physicians were exempt from the operation of the statute when prescribing for health reasons.[6] In 1940, however, it was held that the

[1] *New York Consolidated Laws* (1944), s. 106, 1145.
[2] *People* v. *Sanger*, 222 N.Y. 192; 194–5 (1918), 118 N.E. 637 (1918). In *People* v. *Byrne*, 163 N.Y.S. 680 (1916), the statute had been held constitutional. 'Nor is it to be doubted, in my opinion, that the legislature have the power to declare that articles should not be used to prevent conception by married women, except in cases where attending physicians believe that pregnancy would be dangerous to the health of the woman.' (Judge Crosprey.)
[3] Penal Law 1142 effective 1 September 1965.
[4] Massachusetts, *Annotated Laws* (1956), c. 272, s. 20–1. Whether information on the sterile period would be construed as 'contraceptive advice' is dubious. In 1934 the Customs allowed Mrs Hazel Moore to import a book on rhythm but seized others on artificial contraception. See Sulloway, Alvah, H., *Birth Control and Catholic Doctrine*, Boston, 1959 at p. 29.
[5] *Cw.* v. *Allison*, 227 Mass. 57; 116 N.E. 265 (1917).
[6] *Cw.* v. *Gardner*, 300 Mass. 372; 15 N.E. 2d, 222 (1938). An appeal to the U.S. Supreme Court was dismissed *per curiam* 'for want of a substantial federal question'. *Gardner* v. *Mass.*, 305 U.S. 559 (1938).

distribution of prophylactics, which could also be used for contraception, did not come within the statute, unless it could be proved that the distributor intended to prevent conception rather than venereal disease or knew that such unlawful use was intended by the buyer.[1] As in Connecticut, unsuccessful attempts were periodically made to modify the law. In 1930 a Bill was introduced into the legislature to give licensed physicians the right to provide information to married couples, but it was later withdrawn. The following year a petition for change was signed by 7,000 laymen, 1,300 doctors, and 400 ministers of religion, but it failed to secure implementation. An amendment to the same effect was defeated in the House of Representatives in 1941 by 133 votes to 77 and in the Senate by 18 to 16. Referendums in 1942 and 1948 also failed to alter the law. Both referendums concerned an Act 'to allow physicians to provide medical contraceptive care to married persons for the protection of life or health'. It was only after the Griswold case in 1965 that Massachusetts finally took action which led to a liberalisation of the contraceptive law.[2]

In 1966 the Massachusetts law was substantially amended by legislation creating exceptions to the operation of the statute restricting publication of birth control information and the distribution of contraceptives.[3] The amendment provides: 'A registered physician may administer to or prescribe for any married person drugs or articles intended for the prevention of pregnancy or conception. A registered pharmacist actually engaged in the business of pharmacy may furnish such drugs or articles to any married person presenting a prescription from a registered physician. A public health agency, a registered nurse, or a maternity health clinic operated by or in an accredited hospital may furnish information to any married person as to where professional advice regarding such drugs or articles may be lawfully obtained.'[4] Three years later a test case involving the

---

[1] *Cw.* v. *Corbett*, 307 Mass. 7; 29 N.E. 2d, 151 (1940); *Cw.* v. *Werlinsky*, 307 Mass. 608; 29 N.E. 2d, 150 (1940).
[2] See *New York Times*, 8 June 1965, p. 1.
[3] Annotated Laws (1965) c. 272. This law has been referred to at p. 56.
[4] Section 21 of c. 272 was amended by St. 1966, c. 265, paragraph 3, in para. 21a.

interpretation of the amended statute came before the State Supreme Court, *Commonwealth* v. *Baird*.[1]

Mr William Baird, a strongly individualist opponent of the state birth control statute, gave an address on contraception to an audience of some 2000 students in the Hayden Auditorium of Boston University on 6 April 1967.[2] In the course of his address he displayed and explained the use of various contraceptive devices, pointing out that he was breaking the law and invited arrest. At the end of the lecture he invited members of the audience to come to the stage and to help themselves to contraceptive articles. He personally handed to one young lady a package of Emko vaginal foam, a contraceptive substance. At this point a police officer told Mr Baird to call his attorney to the stage and to 'wind it up'. Mr Baird was then taken to police headquarters. At the subsequent trial the judge held that there had been a breach of the statute. He then reported the case to the Supreme Court with the consent of both parties. The Court gave its opinion in April 1969.

The Supreme Court upheld the constitutionality of the statute by a majority of four to three. Giving the conclusions of the majority Chief Justice Wilkins first pointed out that the Griswold decision and the subsequent Massachusetts amending statute had swept away the ground of the decision in Gardner's case, but went on to add that there had been no repeal of the prohibition against laymen imparting information on contraception and that the group entitled to receive such information had not been enlarged: 'unmarried individuals are still excluded'. The Chief Justice ruled that the lecture in itself was not obscene: 'we are of opinion that delivery of the lecture was an exercise of free speech which has first amendment protection'. The exhibition of the contraceptives was incidental to the lecture and therefore was also constitutionally protected. In so far as the state law purported to prevent this it was unconstitutional. The Chief Justice, however, went on to hold that the prohibition against distribution of

[1] 354 Mass. (1969): 246 N.E. 2d, 574 (1969).
[2] Mr Baird was not considered entirely *persona grata* by the official planned parenthood association in Massachusetts and had no mandate from them to become involved in a criminal case. It would in fact have been better for the petitioner to bring an action for declaratory judgement concerning the constitutionality of the law.

contraceptives fell into a different category and was constitutional. 'The Commonwealth,' he stated, 'has a legitimate interest in preventing the distribution of articles designed to prevent conception which may have undesirable, if not dangerous, physical consequences.' Distribution 'added nothing to the understanding of the lecture and was not an exercise of a right guaranteed under the first amendment'. The Chief Justice added that 'the legitimacy of the purpose depends upon a distinction as to the distributor and not as to the marital status of the recipient'.

Three of the seven judges of the court registered their dissent from this opinion. They agreed that the exhibition of the contraceptives was lawful but dissented from the view that their distribution was not. Two of the judges held that the law on contraception had been so much eroded over the past fifty years that it had become 'unconstitutionally vague'. Furthermore it was 'uncertain' what legislative purpose the prohibition served. 'There seems to us,' they concluded, 'to be no rational basis using what little is left of a statute designed to prevent all assistance of all birth control merely to deter non-marital intercourse.' The third judge, Judge Spiegel, dismissed the argument that the law served some social purpose in these words: 'The serious risk of an undesired pregnancy and the unwanted child, disastrous alike to the married as to the unmarried parents and to society as a whole, is utterly disproportionate in harm to any slight public benefit to be gained from a probably ineffective attempt to discourage fornication.' Despite this weighty dissent the statute was upheld and Mr Baird was subsequently sentenced to three months' imprisonment by the Suffolk Superior Court, which had deferred passing sentence until the decision had been taken on the legal point in the Supreme Court.[1]

Mr Baird then sought the intervention of the United States Supreme Court on a writ of *certiorari*. The Court refused to hear the matter, giving no reason for its decision, which it is under no obligation to do. Mr Justice Douglas was of the opinion that *certiorari* should have been granted.[2] Mr Baird's attorney attempted to secure his release in March 1970 by going to the Federal Court

[1] *New York Times*, 20 May 1969.
[2] *Baird* v. *Massachusetts* (January 1970), 396 U.S. 1029, 90 S.Ct. 580.

on a writ of *habeas corpus*. This petition was denied, the Court holding that: 'The legislature of Massachusetts has a legitimate purpose in safeguarding the health of citizens.'[1]

This, however, was not destined to be the end of the story. Mr Baird appealed to the United States Circuit Court of Appeals which quashed his conviction on 6 July 1970. The Massachusetts law was held to be an 'infringement of basic human rights'. Prohibiting the sale or delivery of contraceptive articles to *unmarried* persons was unconstitutional since it was justified neither on grounds of morality or public health.[2] The State of Massachusetts promptly appealed to the United States Supreme Court where Mr Robert H. Quinn, the State Attorney-General, argued strongly for the statute's constitutionality. 'What radical change,' he asked the Court, 'has occurred in the society in which we live to make such a law not constitutional? Have people acquired rights to extra-marital relations free of any public and criminal responsibility? If so, what becomes of our laws against fornication and adultery?' Mr Quinn went on to argue that the statute's purpose to protect 'purity and chastity' was still viable in 1970.[3] The Supreme Court has not yet handed down its decision and it will be of considerable interest and importance when it does so, since twenty-five states make it a crime to give contraceptives to unmarried persons.

LEGAL ISSUES IN THE FUTURE

Surveying the history of the law in the United States and in particular developments over the past decade, it seems clear that blanket legislative banning of the sale of contraceptives or the dissemination of contraceptive information is no longer a serious issue. Legal questions remain important but they are of a less comprehensive character. The questions which seem likely to be raised in the future fall into two groups. First there are those which are of a regulatory kind. Should contraceptives be sold to minors?

[1] *Baird* v. *Eisenstadt* (March 1970) U.S. District Court for Massachusetts, 310 F. Supp. 951.
[2] *Baird* v. *Eisenstadt* (1 Cir. 6 July 1970). Summoned at 56 A.B.A.S. 1101 (November 1970).
[3] *National Catholic Reporter*, 16 October 1970.

Ought contraceptive advice to be available to the unmarried? What restrictions should there be on advertising contraceptives in the interests of public morality? Should the sale of contraceptives from slot-machines be allowed? All these questions presuppose that contraception is accepted in contemporary society as a normal adjunct to family life.

The second important group of questions centre round the provision of contraceptive advice and contraceptives themselves as part of federal, state, and local health services. There seems little doubt that the provision of such ancillary services on a public basis is constitutional. Twenty-nine states provide contraceptive advice as part of their health services, and state-supported centres are found in many large cities. A new departure came in 1965 when the Department of the Interior became the first federal agency to offer direct birth control services and advice, including the supply of contraceptives, to sections of the American public. The Secretary of the Interior, Mr Stewart Udall, authorised three departmental agencies to offer birth control guidance. This was to be made available to American Indians on reservations, to the inhabitants of the Pacific Trust Territories, and to Indians, Eskimos, and Aleuts in Alaska. The programmes authorised physicians employed by the Office of Territories 'to offer appropriate birth control advice and services to their patients, consistent with the patient's culture and conscience'. It further authorised social service workers to refer those who might decide that pregnancy should be avoided to the appropriate public or private medical service.

The question of the provision of birth control services by the state is closely linked with the wider issue of population policy. If the state should have a population policy what should be its limits? On 1 April 1965, Senator Gruening of Alaska introduced a Senate bill which called for the creation of an office for population problems to be set up as a government agency. The purpose of the office would be to develop and clarify the aims of population policy, to keep federal and state employees advised of their duties in this respect, and to seek the co-operation and assistance of private institutions, groups, etc. Clearly such a programme could present a danger to civil liberty. There could be invasions of the right of privacy and such policies could be discriminatory towards the poor. They could find themselves without full freedom in relation to state-sponsored family planning programmes. These bad results could be avoided by legal insistence on the maintenance of the voluntary principle. Detailed legal discussion is needed as to how the voluntary principle can best be preserved both in theory and in practice.

CHAPTER III

Christian Attitudes

THE OLD TESTAMENT

The early Christian Church depended heavily on Judaism for its moral teaching and attitudes to sexuality and marriage. The Jewish and indeed the whole Oriental tradition stressed the importance of woman as a child-bearer. In Jewish culture the domestic virtues were exalted while at the same time there was a built in idea of the essential inferiority of the woman to the man. Another important feature of the Jewish approach to sexuality was a stress on the importance of fruitfulness and child-bearing. In the Book of Genesis after the creation of Man and Woman God blesses them and declares 'be fruitful and multiply, and replenish the earth, and subdue it; and have dominion over the fish of the sea, and over the fowl of the air, and over every living thing that moveth upon the earth'.[1] Clearly for a nomadic tribe like the Jews who also thought of themselves as the Chosen People the continuance of the race and the keeping up of numbers was of prime importance. Fertility was stressed very much more than love and a woman who was childless was regarded in some sense as cursed. Jewish culture also regarded sex as tainted in some way with impurity, hence the custom of purification after childbirth which later even the Virgin Mary herself submitted to.[2]

No text in the Old Testament refers exclusively to contraception. The nearest approach is in the Book of Genesis where the sin of Onan is visited with death. The text reads: 'and Judah said

[1] Ref: Gen. 1:28.   [2] Luke 14:22-4.

unto Onan, go in unto thy brother's wife and perform the duty of
an husband's brother unto her, and raise up seed to thy brother.
And Onan knew that the seed should not be his; and it came to
pass, when he went in unto his brother's wife, that he spilled it on
the ground, less he should give seed to his brother. And the thing
which he did was evil in the sight of the Lord: and he slew him
also.'[1] Scholars have not been agreed about the interpretation of
this text. One interpretation has been that the text is an explicit
condemnation of contraception. Another which has gained
adherents in modern times is that Onan was punished not so much
for indulging in *coitus interruptus* as for breaking the Levirate law
which required a man to raise children to his brother's widow so
that she should not be left without a child and the tribe would
continue. There are, however, difficulties in the way of accepting
this interpretation. John Noonan points out in his book *Contraception*, that the law refers to a situation where the father is dead,
and the brothers are holding land in common.[2] Thus the duty of
begetting offspring arises in order to maintain the share of the
deceased brother by allowing his widow's son to take his place.
In the Genesis story the situation is distinguishable because the
father is alive. There is the further point that the punishment for
breach of the Levirate marriage law is laid down elsewhere in the
Old Testament.[3] Death is a more severe penalty than that of
the public infamy which is laid down. The fairest judgement on the
text seems to be that Onan was punished for a number of delin-
quencies, disobedience to his father, lack of concern for the family
and for indulging in a form of contraception. Whatever view one
may take of this, the influence of the text on the Church Fathers
was very considerable and it was interpreted as a condemnation of
contraception. Thus St Augustine declares that 'intercourse even
with one's legitimate wife is unlawful and wicked where the conception of the offspring is prevented. Onan, the Son of Judah, did
this and the Lord killed him for it.'[4] It is worth noting that in the

[1] Gen. 38:8–10.
[2] *Contraception* (Cambridge, USA, 1965), pp. 33–6.
[3] Deut. 25:7–10: 'The woman shall come to him before the ancients, and shall take
off his shoe from his foot, and spit in his face, and say: "So shall it be done to the man
that will not build up his brother's house" and his name shall be called in Israel, the
House of the Unshod.'
[4] *De adulterinis conjugiis* II. xii.

encyclical *Humanae Vitae* there is no reference to the sin of Onan. One other Old Testament text could be relevant. It has been suggested that the slaying of Sarah's seven husbands by the Devil was a punishment for their employment of contraception, but this seems unlikely, since the Angel, when overcoming the reasonable reluctance of Tobias to marry her, and so risking the same fate, refers to Sarah as a virgin.[1]

THE NEW TESTAMENT

In the New Testament the emphasis is upon the law as the law of love. Virginity is exalted but the New Testament also contains a high doctrine of marriage. St Paul, for example, emphasises its holy state, and compares the union of the spouses with the relationship of Christ to his Church.[2] Furthermore it is stated in the Epistle to Timothy that woman will be saved through 'childbearing'.[3] Certainly no clear condemnation of contraception can be found in the New Testament and any such condemnation has to be induced by inference.

It should be remembered that the pagan world in which the infant Church found itself was one of lax moral standards, widespread sexual perversions and promiscuity. Christian reaction to this decadence and permissiveness was to proclaim strict sexual standards. At the same time there was a reaction against promiscuity within the pagan world itself. The Stoics, for example, emphasised the need for the rational control of sexual desires. Christianity adopted this Stoic attitude and baptised it in order to meet the objections of the Gnostics who were hostile to all forms of procreation. If the Church Fathers stressed the importance of procreation in sexuality, it was not for imperialist reasons but as a means of avoiding sexual excesses. Christianity also reacted against the low value placed upon human life by many in the

[1] Tobias 3:8; 6:22. The reason given for the death of the husbands is that they were among those 'Who in such manner receive matrimony, as to shut out God from themselves, and from their mind, and to give themselves to their lust, as the horse and mule, which have not understanding, over them the Devil has power.' (6:17). For a discussion of the text see Michael J. Gruenthaner, *Catholic Biblical Quarterly*, VIII (1946), 98, who concludes that the text does not refer to contraception.
[2] Eph. 5:25–33.
[3] 1 Tim. 1:15. The authenticity of this Epistle (1 Timothy) is however doubtful.

pagan world. Medical knowledge did not allow for a clear distinction between contraception and abortion and contraception accordingly was often denounced as a form of homicide. Indeed St John Chrysostom in a sermon delivered about the year 390, declared that contraception was worse than murder. 'I do not know what to call it,' he declared, 'for she does not kill what is formed, but prevents its formation.'[1] St Jerome also castigates contraception as a form of murder.[2]

ST AUGUSTINE

It was St Augustine, however, who formulated the Christian attitude to contraception which was to have such influence on succeeding generations of theologians and writers. St Augustine was the doughtiest opponent of the Manichean heresy which dismissed the world as wholly evil, but in some ways he never fully escaped from his own Manichean past. He further suffered from guilt over sexual matters arising from the illicit union which he enjoyed outside of marriage for many years until he was separated from his lover by the influence of his mother, Monica. St Augustine roundly condemned all forms of contraception, including the use of the sterile period. In his book *The Morals of the Manichees* he writes: 'Is it not you who used to warn us to watch as much as we could the time after purification of the menses when a woman is likely to conceive and at that time refrain from intercourse, lest a soul be implicated in the flesh? From this it follows that you consider marriage is not to procreate children, but to satiate lusts. Marriage, as the marriage tablets themselves proclaim, joins male and female for the procreation of children. Whoever says that to procreate children is a worse sin than to copulate thereby prohibits marriage; and he makes the woman no more a wife but a harlot, who, when she has been given certain gifts, is joined to man to satisfy his lust. If there is a wife there is matrimony. But there is no matrimony where motherhood is prevented; for then there is no wife.'[3]

[1] Homily 24 on the Epistle to the Romans, p. 60: 626–7.
[2] See Noonan, op. cit., pp. 100–1.
[3] *The Morals of the Manichees*, 18.65, pl. 32:1373.

In his letter against Faustus written in 400, Augustine repeats his condemnation of contraception.[1] In his book on marriage *The Good of Marriage* written in the same year, St Augustine gives a more positive teaching on marriage and upholds it as an actual good. The triune ends of marriage are set out as offspring, fidelity, and solemn obligation. (Proles, fides, sacramentum.) He does not, however, make any reference to love between husband and wife. Refraining from the sexual act is held out as a good, and spouses improve themselves by abstention by mutual consent. St Augustine treats intercourse without a procreative purpose as a sin. Nevertheless, he allowed one spouse to give a response to another even though the intention of the demanding spouse might not be procreative. Such a response was not sinful since it was required in returning the conjugal debt. In other circumstances sexual intercourse undertaken for mutual enjoyment would be sinful.

St Augustine's thought on sexuality was clearly inadequate, and in parts actively misleading, but it would be virtually impossible to overestimate the influence of his thought on the Church in the West. In *Marriage and Concupiscence* he explicitly condemns contraception in words which influenced subsequent writers for centuries and also played a part in the formulation of canon law. 'It is one thing,' writes Augustine, 'not to lie except with the sole will of generating: this has no fault. It is another to seek the pleasure of the flesh in lying, although within the limits of marriage: this has venial fault. I am supposing that then, although you are not lying for the sake of procreating offspring, you are not for the sake of lust obstructing their procreation by an evil prayer or an evil deed. Those who do this, although they are called husband and wife, are not; nor do they retain any reality of marriage, but with a respectable name cover a shame . . . sometimes this lustful cruelty or cruel lust, comes to this, that they even procure poisons of sterility, and, if these do not work, extinguish and destroy the fetus in some way in the womb, preferring that their offspring die

[1] 'They take wives according to the laws of matrimony by tablets announcing that the marriage is contracted to procreate children; and then, fearing because of your law, lest they infect a particle of God with the foulness of their flesh, they copulate in a shameful union only to satisfy lust for their wives. They are unwilling to have children, on whose account alone marriages are made.' (*Against Faustus*, 15.7.)

before it lives, or if it was already alive in the womb to kill it before it was born.'[1] St Augustine is saying that unless there is a subjective desire to procreate there is venial sin in sexual intercourse, and if procreation is positively and objectively excluded then the sin becomes mortal. He does not, however, condemn contraception as homicide and distinguishes between abortion and contraception. St Augustine clearly regarded sexual intercourse with suspicion, treating it as tainted by concupiscence and needing to be justified by procreation.

CATHOLIC THOUGHT AFTER AUGUSTINE

St Augustine's view of the place of sexuality in marriage was developed over the following seven centuries by the monks. In the sixth century, for example, St Caesarius, who was both monk and bishop, was forthright in his condemnation of contraception. Another condemnation was provided by St Martin of Braga who died in 579. At Rome Pope Gregory the Great (590–604) developed an austere doctrine on marital intercourse. Pope Gregory was of the opinion that pleasure in intercourse constituted a minor sin. 'This pleasure cannot be without fault, for not of adultery nor of fornication, but of lawful marriage was he born who said, "behold I was conceived in sins, and in delights my mother bore me".'[2] Pope Gregory did not explicitly condemn contraception as such, but the condemnation by implication is clear. The monks exercised their influence through the Penitentials, works made up of lists of sins together with the penances prescribed for them. Contraceptive acts are always treated in the Penitentials as being serious sins. These books exercised considerable influence, but they did not constitute part of the official teaching of the Church.[3]

A new stage was reached with the publication of Gratian's compilation of laws in 1140, which contained an explicit condemnation of contraception. Gratian's work, known as the Decretum, became part of the basic canon law of the Church.[4] Ecclesiastical

---

[1] 1.15.17.   [2] Epistles II.64.
[3] On the other hand it should be noted that medieval medical writers gave contraceptive remedies in their books mainly without comment. Some of them afterwards became bishops, e.g. Arandel of Chichester.
[4] *The Decretum*, 2.32.2.7. 'They are fornicators not spouses who procure poisons of sterility.'

emphasis on the importance of procreation in marriage was in part a defence against the views of the Bogomils, who opposed procreation, and whose views on sex were similar to the Manicheans, and in part a reaction to the Troubadors who exalted love between man and woman and separated it from marriage. In the thirteenth century Raymond of Pennaforte compiled a collection of decrees under papal direction which became the basis of canon law in the Catholic Church for the following seven centuries. His compilation contains an explicit condemnation of contraception: 'If anyone to satisfy his lust or in meditated hatred does something to a man or a woman or gives something to drink so that he cannot generate, or she conceive, or offspring be born, let hem be held a homicide.'[1]

By far the most influential writer of the thirteenth century was St Thomas Aquinas (1225–74) whose thought on contraception ranks with that of St Augustine in the influence it exercised over the Church. St Thomas discusses and develops the idea of the natural law, and it is against this background that his thought on sexuality must be considered. For St Thomas the natural law is that part of the law of God which can be known by human reason. Man is a rational being and is able to order his inclinations by reason so that they accord with the will of God. By reason he perceives that sex is intended for the conservation of the species so that it is wrongly used when this purpose is frustrated. Any act of sexuality not directed towards generation is wrong as a sin against nature.[2] St Thomas reinforced this general and abstract view of the purpose of sexuality with a very particular but equally abstract notion about the nature of male semen. Semen, St Thomas points out, is necessary for generation, and exists for the purpose of continuing the race – semen thus has a special significance and any misuse of it is gravely sinful. He goes so far as to maintain that in this class of sin only murder is worse because murder destroys actual human nature, whereas misuse of seed destroys human nature in potential.[3] Rigorously applying this principle, he concludes elsewhere that masturbation is worse than fornication or adultery since in the latter whatever the social effects generation

[1] *Decretals*, 5.5.12.   [2] See *Summa Theologica*, 2.2.154. 1 and 2.
[3] *Summa Contra Gentiles*, 3.123.

F

is not *ipso facto* excluded.[1] St Thomas's whole approach is concerned with human nature, not with human beings as such, and the personal factors of love and affection are barely considered any more than they are in the thought of St Augustine. The purpose of insemination is all important. From this starting-point, he goes on to draw conclusions about the right mode of sexual union, the correct position of man and woman in the act of coitus, etc. – none of these should be altered by man at will.

St Thomas had emphasised the overriding importance of procreation in intercourse. Its intentional and objective exclusion was mortally sinful, and he held that to avoid venial sin in sexual union there must be at least some subjective intention of procreation. In the centuries which followed, the first position was maintained but the second was substantially modified. Professor Noonan selects the publication of Martin Le Maistre's book *Moral Questions*, as a turning-point. Le Maistre, a professor at the University of Paris, was born in 1432 and died in 1481, but his book was not published until after his death in 1490. In the book Le Maistre writes that 'not every copulation of spouses not performed to generate offspring is an act opposed to conjugal chastity. . . . I say that someone can wish to take pleasure, first for love of that pleasure, secondly to avoid tedium and the ache of melancholy caused by the lack of pleasure.' The view also gained ground and eventually became dominant that non-procreative use of marriage was lawful in order to avoid fornication. This view had been known in medieval times but had been supported by only a minority of theologians. Cardinal Bellarmine and other Jesuit moralists in the seventeenth century stressed that man's sexual tendencies were in themselves both natural and good, although they were marred by a tendency towards lust in the individual. These views did not go unchallenged, and the Jansenists, for example, insisted that intercourse was sinful if it was embarked upon with other than a procreative purpose. This latter view received support in Rome, and on 2 March 1679, the Holy Office under Innocent XI condemned the proposition that 'a marital act exercised for pleasure alone lacks entirely any fault and any defect'. The argument was continued at various levels, but by the

[1] *Summa Theologica* 2.2. 154.12.

mid-eighteenth century there was a widespread rejection of St Augustine's view that intercourse was only justified for a procreative purpose. This influence is seen in the writings of St Alphonsus Ligouri (1697–1787), who quotes in his book *Moral Theology* the view that there is no sin in intercourse 'to avoid danger of incontinence in oneself or one's partner'. He went on to state that it was clearly established that one purpose of marriage was to provide an outlet for the sexual impulse.

Despite these modifications, the condemnation of contraception as such remained. Indeed, the view that contraception was homicide was surprisingly revived in the Bull Effraenatam issued by Sixtus V in 1588. Fierce penalties were laid down in the Bull against those 'who proffer potions and poisons of sterility to women and offer an impediment to the conception of a foetus, and who take pain to perform and execute such acts or in any way counsel them, and the women themselves who knowingly and voluntarily take the same potions'. This Bull equated the use of contraceptives with murder from the point of view of canon law. The severity of this decree owed much to the austere character of Sixtus V, and it was revoked by his successor, Gregory XIV.

The traditional position might have been re-evalued had it been challenged by the Reformation theologians, but both Calvin and Luther on this subject, at any rate, held to the traditional views. Nor was there any pressure for reform coming from technological developments during this period. It is true that the sheath was developed during the seventeenth century, but no method of providing a cheap and efficient contraceptive was discovered. Nevertheless, by the second half of the eighteenth century there had been considerable shifts in the analysis of the evil of contraception. It was viewed, not so much as homicide, but rather as a violation of the general purposes of marriage. Moralists, like the Jesuit Paul Laymann, argued that contraception was prohibited for the practical reason of avoiding sexual excess, thus shifting the argument away from absolute to relative considerations.

NEW DEVELOPMENTS

The stage was now being set for important developments which would have a profound effect on the Church's traditional attitude to contraception. In France in the closing decades of the eighteenth century the French birth rate declined sharply, and the population of France was consequently reduced, the most likely cause being the spread of birth control. In England, on the other hand, population was on the increase, but this led to fear of excessive population growth and food shortage, as has been noted in Chapter I, and in the early part of the nineteenth century to the open advocacy of birth control. By mid-century, the vulcanisation of rubber had at last made possible the cheap mass-production of contraceptives.

Moral theology within the Catholic Church at this time, was at a low ebb, but these developments did provoke reactions at Rome and elsewhere. The pastoral reactions at Rome were not, in the event, excessively stringent. When Bishop Bouvier, a French bishop, inquired about contraception in Rome in 1842, an instruction was issued by the Penitentiary.[1] The Penitentiary ruled that if a husband insisted on using a contraceptive, co-operation by the wife might be tolerated, and did not insist on instructing the penitent in the confessional on the evil of contraception in all cases. In May 1851 the Inquisition under Pius IX gave a more rigorous ruling. It condemned the propositions that for serious reasons it was lawful for spouses to use marriage in the way that Onan used it, and also the view that such use of marriage was not prohibited by the natural law. The Inquisition condemned these views as erroneous, although they were not sigmatised as heretical. The view at Rome at this period seemed to have been that contraception was a form of Onanism. There was not however at this stage a developed argument against contraception. This was to come later.

Meanwhile, the birth control movement was making progress, especially in England and the United States, but Malthusian leagues were formed in other countries, including Germany (1889), Spain (1904), Sweden (1911), and Italy (1913). Roman reaction to the situation was still not sharp. In February 1880, Leo XIII issued a major encyclical on marriage under the title

---

[1] The Pentitentiary is the Roman tribunal which deals with questions arising from the administration of the sacrament of penance.

Arcanum Divinae Sapientiae. It contained no express condemnation on contraception.

In the absence of a strong lead from Rome, reactions took place among the various national Roman Catholic hierarchies. In 1909, for example, the bishops of Belgium ordered their clergy to initiate inquiries about the use of contraception and to instruct penitents against Onanism. In 1913, the German bishops issued a pastoral letter condemning the spread of contraception. They were followed by the French bishops who, in May 1919, issued a pastoral letter on the whole subject. 'The principal end of marriage,' declared the French bishops, 'is the procreation of children; for this God honoured the spouses by associating them in His creative power and paternity. It is to sin seriously against nature and against the will of God to frustrate marriage of its end by an egotistic or sensual calculation. The theories and practices which teach or encourage the restriction of birth are as disastrous as they are criminal. The war has forcefully impressed upon us the danger to which they expose our country. Let the lesson not be lost. It is necessary to fill the spaces made by death, if we want France to belong to Frenchmen and to be strong enough to defend herself and prosper.' The nationalist motivation behind this condemnation is clearly evident, and was to lead to a banning in France of contraception. In 1920, nationalist and Catholic deputies combined to pass a law forbidding the dissemination of contraceptive propaganda. The law was effective in preventing the opening of birth control clinics. The United States hierarchy also issued a pastoral letter in 1919 condemning contraception. Thus, while the birth control movement was making headway in various parts of the world, the hostile reaction of the Roman Catholic Church was not in doubt.

PROTESTANT AND ANGLICAN ATTITUDES

This hostility towards contraception was at the beginning of the twentieth century shared by all Christian denominations, and they condemned it as immoral or unnatural and contrary to divine law. Today there has been a complete revolution in attitudes, and the changes in non-Catholic religious and theological attitudes towards contraception can best be illustrated by tracing developments in the Church of England. The first Anglican position was a clear-cut condemnation of contraception as a threat to both Church and State. The Lambeth Conference of 1920 issued a solemn warning against 'the use of unnatural means for the avoidance of conception' and stressed that the primary purpose of marriage was the procreation of children.[1] This judgement was echoed by the House of Bishops of the Protestant Episcopal Church meeting at Portland, Oregon, on 15 September 1922. The Lambeth Conference of 1930 again declared that the primary purpose of marriage was the procreation of children but conceded that in certain limited circumstances contraception might be morally legitimate.[2] In a resolution, passed by 193 votes to 67, the Conference declared: 'Where there is a clearly felt moral obligation to limit or avoid parenthood, the method must be decided on Christian principles. The primary and obvious method is complete abstinence from intercourse (as far as may be necessary) in a life of discipline and self-control lived in the power of the Holy Spirit. Nevertheless, in those cases where there is such a clearly-felt morally sound reason for avoiding complete abstinence, the Conference agrees that other methods may be used, provided that this is done in the light of the same Christian principles. The Conference records its strong condemnation of the use of any methods of conception-control from motives of selfish-

[1] The first Lambeth Conference met in 1867. Its resolutions are not theologically binding but are taken to express the mind of the Anglican Church. The 1908 Conference, like its successor of 1920, condemned contraception. The resolution of 1920, No. 68, reads: 'The Conference, while declining to lay down rules which will meet the needs of every abnormal case, regards with grave concern the spread in modern society of theories and practices hostile to the family. We utter an emphatic warning against the use of unnatural means for the avoidance of conception, together with the grave dangers – physical, moral, and religious – thereby incurred, and against the evils which the extension of such use threatens the race. In opposition to the teaching which, under the name of science and religion, encourages married people in the deliberate cultivation of sexual union as an end in itself, we steadfastly uphold what must always be regarded as the governing considerations of Christian marriage. One is the primary purpose for which marriage exists, namely the continuance of the race through the gift and heritage of children; the other is the paramount importance in married life of deliberate and thoughtful self-control.' Resolution 70 called for a campaign against the open or secret sale of contraceptives. See *The Lambeth Conferences, 1867–1930* (London, 1948).

[2] Resolution 13, on the purpose of marriage; Resolution 15, on contraception. *The Lambeth Conferences, 1867–1930.*

ness, luxury, or mere convenience.[1] In 1958 the Lambeth Conference gave unanimous approval to contraception, passing a resolution in the following terms: 'The Conference believes that the responsibility for deciding upon the number and frequency of children has been laid by God upon the consciences of parents everywhere: that this planning, in such ways as are mutually acceptable to husband and wife in Christian conscience, is a right and important factor in Christian family life and should be the result of positive choice before God. Such responsible parenthood, built on obedience to all the duties of marriage, requires a wise stewardship of the resources and abilities of the family as well as a thoughtful consideration of the varying population needs and problems of society and the claims of future generations.'[2]

The change in attitude from 1920 to 1958 was brought about partly by social changes. In 1920 there was widespread fear of underpopulation, while in 1958 prospects of overpopulation aroused anxiety, especially in India, Africa, and the West Indies, all strongly represented at the Conference. A second factor influencing the decision was the modern development of knowledge of the safe period, showing that nature provided her own method of birth control. Equally important was the theological development of the doctrine of Christian marriage which had taken place since 1920. The Conference of that year had been unequivocal in stressing procreation as the primary purpose of marriage, and this had been repeated in 1930. The 1958 Conference, on the other hand, did not stress the reproductive end of

[1] In the report accompanying the resolutions, 'The Life and Witness of the Christian Community', it is pointed out that contraception is not condemned in the New Testament, nor by any Ecumenical Council of the Church. The Protestant Episcopal Church again followed the lead of Lambeth. On 9 October 1934, the Bishops passed a resolution by 44–38 approving 'the efforts now being made to secure for licensed physicians, hospitals and medical clinics, freedom to convey such information (on birth control) as is in accord with the highest principles of eugenics and a more wholesome family life wherein parenthood may be undertaken with due respect for the health of the mother and the welfare of the child.' See *Journal of Social Psychology*, VIII (May 1936), p. 229.

[2] *The Lambeth Conference, 1958* (London, 1958), Resolution 115. Cf. the Report on 'Responsible Parenthood and the Population Problem', the conclusions of a study group appointed by the World Council of Churches which met at Mansfield College, Oxford, 12–15 April 1959. The twenty-one members were drawn from the main confessions represented on the World Council. With the exception of the Orthodox members they reached similar conclusions to the Lambeth Conference on the use of contraceptives. *The Ecumenical Review*, XII (October 1958), pp. 85–92.

marriage in this way. Biblical revelation, it was agreed, did not limit the function of sexuality and the family to the reproductive process but stressed equally the companionate purpose of marriage. These two ends are not separable in importance, 'are not subordinated one to the other; they are not directly related to one another; their relationship, in the developing experience of Israel, is to be found in yet a third area – that of the place of the family in giving responsible security to the children born of the love of husband and wife.'[1] Procreation of children and promotion of the mutual love of the spouses are thus accepted as co-equal ends.

A parallel development in Anglican theology has been the increasing stress on *henosis*, the union of man and wife in one flesh that takes place within the marriage relationship.[2] Christ himself stressed this aspect of marriage, and St Paul developed the doctrine.[3] The act of *coitus*, far from being a merely physiological device to perpetuate the race, has a quasi-sacramental character of the highest importance in developing the personal and spiritual life of the married couple. Traditional theology is inadequate in stressing the procreative purpose of marriage and underestimating the intrinsic importance of the sexual act. Some writers have gone so far as to suggest that it is *henosis* that is primary in marriage and not procreation. Thus Canon Warner writes: 'The unitive achievement of sexual intercourse precedes procreation and is primary in time sequence as well as in its inner constitutive nature as *object*.'[4] He adds that the traditional doctrine is right in the sense that procreation must not be totally excluded from marriage, but it is not the primary end of every act of *coitus*, nor is it its object.[5]

---

[1] *The Lambeth Conference, 1958*, II, p. 143.
[2] See, for example, D. S. Bailey, *The Mystery of Love and Marriage* (London, 1952).
[3] Matt. 19:6. St Paul, Ephesians 5:23–33.
[4] 'Theological Issues of Contraception', *Theology*, LVII (January 1954), 8–14 at p. 11. Canon Warner means by *object*, 'that at which the action aims and in which it naturally results, and with the attainment of which it is completed'. R. C. Mortimer, *Elements of Moral Theology*, p. 63. Procreation is thus the possible result of *coitus* but not its object. 'We are left, then, with the act of *coitus* which, in its natural functioning, has one "object" in uniting (or deepening the union of) man and woman, and an *occasional* end (among others) of fertilising the ovum.'
[5] The reason for this is that the act of procreation is necessarily associated with the act of union in the natural order. The writer seeks to save himself from inconsistency by invoking the natural order at this point by stressing that the use of contraceptives must not be judged in relation to isolated acts of intercourse, but in the context of actual or prospective family life.

Given that the ends of marriage are co-equal, may the parties separate them at will or are they restricted for separation to the periods of natural infertility? Anglican theologians have given different answers to the questions, but the consensus appears to be that at least in certain circumstances the use of contraceptives is legitimate. Contraception may be a positive good. It extends man's rational control over his own nature, the children born are desired and welcomed, and sexual intercourse can be regulated according to the needs of a personal relationship and not controlled by decisions about the desirability of conception. But may the couple manipulate natural processes at their own will? If one regards the biological pattern as something 'given', which a couple are required by God to submit themselves to in order to receive the blessing of matrimonial union, the answer will be negative. Man may use his reason to fulfil the biological pattern more completely but not to supersede it. *Coitus* accompanied by the use of a contraceptive is ontologically and morally distinct from *coitus* without such a device. If on the other hand one regards *coitus* as a purely spatio-temporal event without metaphysical implications, then contraceptives may be freely employed.

With these considerations in mind, the anonymous author of the first of three articles on contraception in the authoritative Anglican publication, *The Family in Contemporary Society*, concludes that the Church should not give its approval to contraception as a positive good. 'It is, to say the least,' he observes, 'suspicious that the age in which contraception has won its way is not one which has been conspicuously successful in managing its sexual life. Is it possible that, by claiming the right to manipulate his physical processes in this matter, man may, without knowing or intending it, be stepping over the boundary between the world of Christian marriage and what one may call the world of Aphrodite – the world of sterile eroticism against which the Church reacted so strongly (perhaps too strongly) in its early days? For one of the characteristics of the latter world was (and is) the exercise of unlimited self determination in sexual activity.'[1] Despite this condemnation in general, the writer points out that it is possible to conclude that contraceptives may be used in particular

[1] (London, S.P.C.K., 1958), p. 135. The first contribution is found at pp. 132–7.

circumstances, for although the act will be ontologically distinct, it may be morally equivalent, as the best symbol of love and union available in the circumstances. The justifying circumstances are not specified.

The second contributor concludes that contraception may be used legitimately as a normal part of married life.[1] It represents a responsible use of human freedom in the interests of personal relationship or the needs of the community as a whole. The conclusion is identical with that in Canon Warner's article, where he writes: 'In general it is morally legitimate to use a material agent in order to forward the well-being of man in his personal relations in society; e.g., wearing glasses or deaf aid. If on moral grounds the unitive object of an act of *coitus* must be achieved without involving the procreative end, then there is nothing in principle wrong in using a material agent, for the agent is forwarding the personal relational factor essential for marriage, and good marriages are essential for society and the welfare of children.[2] Both these latter theologians reject the view that the spiritual effects of *coitus* are dependent on its conforming to certain empirical physiological features. But what then is the criterion by which the morality of physical sexual acts between man and woman is to be judged? The conclusion is ineluctable that there is no objective criterion, but that the rightness or wrongness of using contraceptives will depend on the integrity of the parties' assessment of the circumstances and the purity of their motives. How, then, one may legitimately ask, is one to distinguish between use of a contraceptive and other sexual actions, such as sodomy, which have a relational value but which are condemned by Christian moralists. Perhaps it might be answered that whereas the use of a contraceptive preserves the physical structure of the act, a perversion

---

[1] pp. 137–47.
[2] *Theology*, LVII, p. 12. Canon Warner concludes that complete abstention is morally wrong, as is the exclusive use of the safe period. *Coitus interruptus* and *reservatus* are neither procreative nor unitive in the full sense and must therefore be condemned. The use of a condom is illegitimate as it impairs 'unitive orgasm'. Diaphragms and suppositories are legitimate. On oral contraceptives he writes: 'We have here an interference with the actual function of an organ (the ovary) by which the biological processes are prevented from achieving their "object".' (p. 14). Their use is not justified if a contraceptive is available which does not radically inhibit a physiological function.

such as sodomy destroys it altogether, but this is not wholly convincing. At any rate, neither of the writers disposes of the difficulty.

The theologians whose views have just been described criticise the terms of traditional moral theology and question their applicability at the present time, but they adopt them in modified form for their own use. They are writing within the Catholic tradition. Other contemporary theologians have considered the problem from the Protestant viewpoint. Reinhold Niebuhr has not dealt with the subject at great length, but he indicated his views briefly in the course of the first series of Gifford lectures for 1939.[1] 'The prohibition of birth control,' he said, 'assumes that the sexual functions in human life must be limited to its function in nature, that of procreation. But it is the very character of human life that all animal functions are touched by freedom and released into more complex relationships. This freedom is the basis of both creativity and sin.' In place of the Catholic idea of the law of nature, he suggests the substitution of the Lutheran notion of the 'order of creation', giving as an example natural bisexuality. 'It is not possible to escape the natural fact that the primary purpose of bisexuality in nature is that of procreation. But it is not easy to establish a universally valid "law of reason" which will eternally set the bounds for the function of sex in the historic development of human personality.' Dr Niebuhr, while drawing no immediate concrete conclusions, is here asserting the transcendence of the personal and rational over the purely biological, while taking the latter into account. It would thus seem that given certain circumstances man may morally use contraceptives in sexual intercourse.[2] What those circumstances are must be left to the Christian insight

---

[1] *The Nature and Destiny of Man* (New York, 1949), vol. 1, pp. 281–2.
[2] Cf. Joseph Fletcher: 'With the medical technology of contraception, parenthood and birth control become matters of moral responsibility, of intelligent choice. We are able to control our fertility. No longer do we have to choose between reproduction and continence. Sex is no longer a helpless submission to biological consequences. Nor is the only alternative a denial of sexual love, either *in toto* or according to lunar calculations in a sophisticated and doubtful rhythm mathematics. When such calculations enter in, the spontaneity of love goes out. Rhythm is a denial of freedom; it offers only an alternation of necessities, not a method of true control.' *Morals and Medicine* (Princeton, 1954), p. 96. See also Paul Ramsey, 'Freedom and Responsibility in Medical and Sex Ethics: A Protestant View', *New York University Law Review*, XXXI (1956), p. 1194.

of the individual, an approach commended in the third of the articles appearing in the Anglican publication already referred to.[1]

This approach is at first sight identical with that of utilitarians and libertarians who assert that conception of children should be the full voluntary choice of the parents.[2] The difference lies in the motivation determining the choice, for utilitarians would lay no claim to Christian insight. Karl Barth is another Protestant theologian who has discussed contraception at rather greater length.[3] Having conceded that family planning is generally accepted by theologians as desirable, he goes on to discuss the legitimacy of the means that may be employed. Abstinence he characterises as an 'heroic' course, which is not wrong in itself but may be psychologically dangerous. The safe period might seem the ideal expedient, but the anxiety caused by its unreliability, as well as its check on the spontaneous nature of sexual expression, are grave objections to its use. *Coitus interruptus* is fraught with psychological dangers and its practice may well imperil marital union. There remains the last alternative of contraception, the use of mechanical devices which are not evil in themselves. If, says Dr Barth, human interference with the natural act of *coitus* is regarded as wrong in itself, then all four methods must be rejected without distinction. If, on the other hand, family limitation is recognised as desirable, then it should be recognised that all the methods are open to some objection, and this is the price to be paid for an extension of freedom. In making the choice between the various methods certain considerations apply. The choice must be made in faith and with a free

---

[1] *The Family in Contemporary Society*, pp. 149–54. Cf. the second article: 'The fact that man in his freedom stands above nature and is therefore at liberty to interpret sex in terms of personality and relation and to use it for personal and relational ends, leads to the conclusion that contraception is morally right in certain circumstances.' (p. 145.)

[2] See Horace M. Kallen: 'I similarly appraise the right of men and women to full knowledge of all that the sciences of nature and man have established regarding sex and reproduction, and to decide for themselves upon the number of children they want and the intervals at which they want them.' 'An Ethic of Freedom: A Philosopher's View', *New York University Law Review*, XXXI (November 1956), p. 1167. Cf. Glanville Williams, 'The Control of Conception', in *The Sanctity of Life and the Criminal Law* (New York, 1957), pp. 34–74.

[3] *Die Kirchliche Dogmatik*, III, pp. 300–11.

conscience, and it must be a joint decision of husband and wife taking into account the significance of their joint life together and the whole purpose of the matrimonial union. These Protestant approaches are similar in that they offer no binding principle which can be universally applied but rather state that in certain circumstances the informed Christian conscience can conclude that contraception is lawful without the incurring of sin.

Official acceptance of birth control by Protestant churches has kept pace with theological developments. In March 1931 the Federal Council of Churches of Christ in America approved of artificial methods of birth control by a vote of 24–4.[1] Since then numerous other Protestant churches and sects have followed suit.[2] In 1954 the Synod of the Augustana Lutheran Church, at its meeting in Los Angeles, endorsed birth control.[3] The Methodist Church took unanimous similar action at its General Conference in 1956.[4] In England, Methodists have expressed similar views.[5] Typical of numerous Protestant statements is the following by the Rev. James L. Novarro: 'We Baptists definitely consider fertility and conception as providential and a power given to man to be

---

[1] See Margaret Sanger, *My Fight for Birth Control*, p. 344.
[2] These include the Connecticut Council of Churches; the American Unitarian Association; the General Council of Congregational and Christian Churches; the Protestant Episcopal Church (House of Bishops and House of Deputies); the Quakers, Baptists, Disciples, and Jehovah's Witnesses leave the matter to be decided by the individual. For various statements of Christian views see *The Churches Speak Up on Birth Control*, published by the Planned Parenthood Federation of America, New York. The pamphlet quotes a statement of the Federal Council of Churches: 'The public has a right to expect guidance from the church on the moral aspects of birth control. As to the necessity for some form of effective control of the size of the family and spacing of children, and consequently of control of conception, there can be no question. It is recognized by all churches and physicians. There is general agreement that sex union between husbands and wives as an expression of mutual affection without relation to procreation is right. This is recognized by the Scriptures, by all branches of the Christian church, by social and medical science, and by the good sense and idealism of mankind'. The General Assembly of the Church of Scotland has been advised by its Committee on Temperance and Morals to approve the practice of contraception provided it is not resorted to for selfish motives. See *The Times*, 5 May 1960.
[3] But not all Lutherans accept this; the Missouri Synod of the Lutheran Churches, for example, has condemned it as sinful.
[4] *New York Times*, 4 May 1956. See 17 October 1956, for acceptance by United Lutheran Church Convention.
[5] See welcome of Norman H. Snaith, President of Methodist Conference, to the Lambeth Report, *The Times*, 27 August 1958.

properly utilised. Fertility and conception should not be left up to accident, but should be well planned, thereby contributing to the moral, spiritual, and physical health of all concerned.'[1] Baptists, however, like many Protestant sects, have not officially supported birth control but leave it to the consciences of individual members of their congregation to decide for themselves. It seems beyond question that the overwhelming weight of Protestant opinion favours artificial birth control at least to some degree.

JEWISH ATTITUDES

Judaism has developed no agreed opinion on birth control. The Central Conference of American Rabbis, as well as individual Jews, have supported contraception, but Orthodox Judaism has taken a different stand. The Rabbinical Alliance has stated: 'Orthodox Judaism does not condone any artificial birth control measures by the male spouse, under any circumstances. Only in cases where the health of the female is jeopardised are certain birth control measures allowed and then only through direct consultation between the medical and rabbinic authorities.'[2]

The Jewish approach to contraception is more flexible than is immediately apparent from the statement of the Rabbinical alliance. There is no question of considering contraception as intrinsically evil. It becomes a question of balancing various 'mitzvot' (religious commandments) which may be in conflict. Thus procreation is a mitzva, but so is the preservation of health, and so is marital sex used as an instrument of love and conjugality. It is best to fulfil all the mitzvot but if this is not possible it is better to carry out some than none. Hence abstinence does not figure as an acceptable alternative in the Jewish scheme of things. The value given to the promotion of love between the spouses is high so that in certain circumstances it can override the 'evil' of non-conception. At the same time Jewish law has a high respect for the integrity of the sex act: the seed must be cast within the

---

[1] See *Simple Methods of Contraception* (New York, 1958), p. 43.
[2] See *Planned Parenthood News*, No. 22 (Fall 1958), p. 4. See also Rabbi Emanuel Rackman, 'Morality in Medico-Legal Problems: A Jewish View', *New York University Law Review*, XXXI (November 1956), p. 1207.

body of the woman. When contraception is permitted it must not be by means of an improper emission of the male seed.[1]

PIUS XI AND CASTI CONNUBII

While the non-Roman churches, with the exception of Orthodoxy, were softening their condemnation of contraception, Rome itself remained adamant, and in December 1930, prompted in part by Lambeth's qualified acceptance of contraception the previous August, the Pope, Pius XI, issued his encyclical on Christian marriage, *Casti Connubii*. In October, Cardinal Francis Bourne, Archbishop of Westminster, had declared that the Anglican bishops by their decision had forfeited any claim to be 'authorised organs of Christian morality'. He was backed in Rome by the Belgian Jesuit theologian, Arthur Vermeersch (1858–1936). Vermeersch had been a strong opponent of contraception for many years and had already influenced the Belgian bishops in their condemnation of contraception. His appears to have been the dominating influence in the Encyclical. Like Cardinal Bourne, he was strongly critical of the Lambeth Conference decision. Other factors influencing the Pope to issue the Encyclical were certain developments in Catholic thought in Germany challenging the traditional formulations on Christian marriage, and it was felt that a strong statement was needed from Rome to quell dissidence and to prevent the rot from spreading.

The Encyclical dealt with the whole of Christian marriage, and restated traditional doctrines: it dealt shortly with contraception, but its condemnation was in forthright terms. After a reference to the Anglican decision, the Encyclical states: 'The Catholic Church, to whom God himself has committed the integrity and

[1] For a full discussion of the Jewish approach to birth control see David M. Feldmann, *Birth Control in Jewish Law* (New York, 1968). See also an article by the same author 'Birth Control in Jewish Law', in *The Jewish Chronicle*, 23 August 1968. There is also a discussion of the Jewish position in *Blackfriars*, 50 (November 1969), p. 760 in another article 'Birth Control in Jewish Law' by David M. Cohen. Dr Feldmann concludes: 'Procreation is an imperative that must be heeded; certain contraceptive devices are objectionable; but contraception at any given moment with proper means and proper motivation is acceptable.' (See article in *Jewish Chronicle*.) This approach is remarkably similar to that of Anglicans and liberal Catholics but differs sharply from the traditional Christian view.

decency of morals, now standing in this ruin of morals, raises her voice aloud through our mouth, in sign of her divine mission, in order to keep the chastity of the nuptial bond free from this foul slip, and again declares: any use whatever of marriage, in the exercise of which the act by human effort is deprived of its natural power of procreating life, violates the law of God and nature, and those who do such a thing are stained by a grave and mortal flaw.'[1] The Encyclical stresses that contraception is intrinsically against nature, and adds: 'Since therefore the conjugal act is destined primarily by nature for the begetting of children, those who in exercising it deliberately frustrate its natural effect and purpose, sin against nature and commit a deed which is shameful and intrinsically vicious.'[2]

The Encyclical thus restates and synthesises the traditional Catholic attitude to contraception. It is based on the thought of St Augustine and St Thomas, and on the nineteenth-century interpretation of the nature of the sin of Onan. Its language is unambiguous, but has given rise to dispute about its scope and authority. Some have interpreted its condemnation of contraceptives as being limited to those used in the actual exercise of the marriage act. This would leave the question of the legitimacy of the use of drugs open. Sterilisation is not dealt with by the Encyclical in the section dealing with contraception, but it condemns self-mutilation in general, and makes a specific condemnation of compulsory sterilisation. Subsequently, Pius XII made a specific condemnation of sterilisation in an address to the Italian Catholic Midwives in October 1951. 'Direct sterilisation', said the Pope, 'that is, that which seeks as means or end to render procreation impossible, is a serious violation of the moral law.'[3]

As to the status of the Encyclical, it is clearly intended as a solemn utterance from the Pope, and its language is strong and, indeed, might be described as violent. Some have maintained that it ranks as an infallible statement. Certainly the statement was addressed to the whole Church on a matter of morals and the Pope was using his apostolic authority, but this does not end the matter. Others have argued that contraception is not a matter on

---

[1] *Acta Apostolicae Sedis.* (Hereafter referred to as *A.A.S.*), 22: 560.
[2] *A.A.S.*, 22:559.   [3] *A.A.S.*, 43:843.

which it is possible for an infallible statement to be made. Which-
ever view is right, the effect of the Encyclical is clear. It confirmed
traditional attitudes and prevented their being openly challenged
for a quarter of a century. It impeded the work of the German
theologians, who had been attempting to move away from the
somewhat stark Augustinian–Thomist approach to marriage with
its emphasis on social and procreative purpose, and to give greater
stress to the personal factors of friendship and love between the
partners, which had been virtually disregarded.[1] These writers
wished to see stress laid on the personal aspects of marriage, its
role in increasing mutual love and perfecting the personalities of
the spouses. To further this aim, they wished to abandon the
traditional terminology of 'primary' and 'secondary' ends of
marriage. Dr Herbert Doms in his book *The Meaning of Marriage*
denied that the constitution of marriage consists in a subservience
to a purpose outside the spouses themselves for which they marry.
'It consists in the constant, vital ordination of husband and wife to
each other until they become one. If this is so, there can no longer
be sufficient reason from this standpoint, for speaking of procreation as the primary purpose (in the sense in which St Thomas used
the phrase) and for dividing off the other purposes as secondary.'
The meaning of marriage is the community of life between the
spouses, of which the child is the fruit and visible embodiment.
This approach, claim its supporters, does not diminish the importance of the child in marriage, but stresses it in a different way. It
is peculiarly apposite at a time when many seek to explain man in
purely physiological terms, and it brings theology up to date
by taking into account a whole range of biological and psychological data of which scholastic theologians were unaware. It is
helpful in disposing of the problems raised by sterile unions, virgin
marriage, and the practice of periodic continence.

The Encyclical *Casti Connubii*, in certain sections, seems to have
foreshadowed this view. The Pope wrote: 'This mutual interior
moulding of husband and wife, this determined effort to perfect
one another, can in a very real sense as the Roman catechism
teaches, be said to be the chief reason and purpose of matrimony,
provided matrimony be looked at not in the restricted sense as

[1] See Dietrich von Hilderbrand, *Die Metaphysik der Gemeinschaft* (Munich, 1930).

G

instituted for the proper conception and education of children, but more widely or as a blending of life as a whole, and the mutual interchange and sharing thereof.' While retaining the traditional doctrine of the ends of marriage, the Pope is taking into account the motives of the parties, which in most cases will be based on mutual love rather than on a desire to have children. Dr Doms and his followers have had a profound influence on contemporary writing on marriage, and have concentrated the attention of religious writers on the hitherto neglected 'secondary' ends of marriage, of the complexity of which theologians are now much more aware. They did not, however, secure immediately the abandonment of the traditional terminology. Indeed, Dr Doms's book was censured by the Vatican, and a categorical reassertion of the primary and secondary ends of marriage was made in a decree of 1944.[1]

PIUS XII AND THE STERILE PERIOD

The one important development which took place in Catholic teaching on contraception during the Pontificate of Pius XII concerned the legitimacy of the use of the sterile or safe period. For centuries doctors had speculated about the possibility of a sterile period in women, but it was not until 1930 that the researches of two doctors, Dr Ogino of Japan and Dr Knaus of Austria, working independently, enabled the incidence and length of the period to be calculated accurately. A woman's menstrual period is normally twenty-eight days, and during this time ovulation occurs only once, the ovum or egg being discharged from an ovary into the fallopian tubes. Conception can only take place when the egg is present. Thus, if the date of ovulation can be accurately calculated, the commencement of the sterile period can be ascertained. The latest research based on the finding of Ogino and Knaus indicates that ovulation takes place on the fifteenth day before the onset of menstruation; by avoiding inter-

[1] The following question was addressed to the Holy Office. 'Can the opinion of certain recent writers be admitted, who either deny that the procreation and education of offspring is the primary end of marriage, or teach that secondary ends are not essentially subordinated, but equally principle and independent?' Reply: negative. *A.A.S.*, 36:103 (April 1944).

course on certain days conception can be avoided. Allowance has to be made for the irregularities in the cycle, and for the period in which male sperm can survive in the female genital tract, approximately two to three days and for the period for the life of the ovum, one day. Thus, in the case of a woman with an absolutely regular cycle of twenty-eight days the fertile period will be five days. Various methods have been developed of pinpointing the day of ovulation, including charts and the taking of basal body temperature. Directly after ovulation, the basal or lowest normal daily temperature rises, and remains at the higher level until shortly before the next period of menstruation. Yet another method of fixing the time of ovulation is the use of a piece of chemically prepared tape which can be held against the neck of the womb and which changes colour if an egg is present. A period of four days' abstention after the tape shows green is advised. Experiments are also proceeding to develop a drug which will stabilise the menstrual period, and this would be especially helpful for women with highly irregular periods. So far no such drug has been successfully synthesised.

Various studies have been undertaken to ascertain the effectiveness of the rhythm method of birth control in practice. In an investigation carried out by the St Louis University Department of Sociology, two-thirds of the doctors who replied to a questionnaire thought the method was not too complicated for most women. As to effectiveness opinion was very divided, ranging from estimates of 5 per cent to 100 per cent, the midpoint in the distribution of estimates being 71 per cent.[1] Other doctors have estimated that if the rules are strictly observed, the percentage of failure is 3 per cent.[2] The most recent research into the effectiveness of rhythm (employing the calendar) has been carried out by medical scientists at the University of Georgetown, Washington. Three medical scientists from the University's Institute of Population Studies carried out the investigation among women in the United States and Canada. The project affecting women with

[1] G. S. Schnepp and J. Mundi. 'What Doctors think of the Rhythm Method', *American Ecclesiastical Review*, 123:111 (July–December 1950). The questionnaire was sent to 523 physicians of whom 273 replied. Catholic doctors comprised 39 per cent.
[2] S. Fleck, E. F. Snedecker, and J. Rock, 'The Contraceptive Safe Period', *New England Journal of Medicine*, 223:1005–9 (1940).

ages ranging from fifteen to forty-four was undertaken in 1963–4 and the researchers established that the calendar rhythm method was unreliable for 70 per cent of more than 2,000 women whose menstrual cycles they charted over two years. Dr Franklin T. Brayer, Director of the Institute, suggested that this method of birth control was too risky for the woman who did not want a child or who might suffer physical harm from pregnancy. 'If a woman is lucky enough to have fairly regular ovulation cycles, varying by eight days or less', stated Dr Brayer, 'she can use this method very efficiently. But only 30 per cent of the women we studied had cycles limited to that variation.'[1]

From the medical and other evidence available, one may reasonably conclude that while the safe period as a method of birth control does not merit the contempt with which it has often been dismissed by those advocating use of appliances, it is by no means foolproof and exaggerated claims on its behalf are not supported by fact. No contraceptive is wholly reliable, but in the present state of knowledge the margin for error is greater in rhythm than in appliance control. The conclusions of Dr Tietze and others seem justified when they write that the rhythm method offers a satisfactory degree of protection against unwanted pregnancy to 'rigorously selected and carefully instructed wives, who with their husbands, are intelligent and strongly motivated. For others and for those to whom pregnancy would be dangerous, the effectiveness of the method in preventing conception is not considered adequate.'[2]

Use of the infertile days as a method of avoiding conception had been condemned by St Augustine, but in the intervening centuries his opinion had been challenged. The point remained academic until the discovery of a means of establishing the safe period with reasonable accuracy. In *Casti Connubii* Pius XI made only a passing reference to the matter. Intercourse during the safe period, held the Pope, was lawful 'provided always the intrinsic

---

[1] *Tablet*, 19 April 1969, p. 401. See subsequent comment by Dr John Marshall, 'Birth Control: Medical Reflections', in *Tablet*, 26 April 1969, p. 412. Dr Marshall expressed surprise that American researchers, etc. 'should have clung to calendar rhythm for so long'. Use of the basal temperature method was preferable.

[2] C. Tietze, S. R. Poliakoff, and J. Rock, 'The Clinical Effectiveness of the Rhythm Method of Contraception', *Journal of Fertility and Sterility*, 2:444 (1951).

nature of that act is preserved, and accordingly its proper relation to the primary end'. The Pope did not deal with the point whether it was lawful to use the infertile period as a systematic method of family planning. Debate about the licitness of the use of the sterile period to plan families continued among theologians, and a variety of views were expressed. In 1950 the Fourth National Convention of Italian Catholic Physicians approved the use of rhythm in particular cases. In the following year on 29 October 1951, Pius XII in an address to the Italian Catholic Midwives dealt with the whole question. He returned to the subject a month later in an address to the National Congress of the Family Front.[1] In these addresses, Pius XII made it clear under circumstances of maximum publicity that the safe period could be used as a method of family planning provided there was serious reason for it. To have intercourse and avoid procreation without such reason would be a sin. The serious reasons might be medical, eugenic, economic, and social. Pius XII said: 'The matrimonial contract which confers upon the parties the right to satisfy the inclination of nature, constitutes them in a state of life, the state of matrimony. Now upon the parties who make use of this right by the specific act of their state, nature and the Creator impose the function of providing for the conservation of the human race. . . . It follows from this that to enter upon the state of matrimony, to make constant use of the faculty proper to it and only in matrimony allowable, and on the other hand consistently and deliberately, and without serious reason, to shirk the primary duty it imposes would be a sin against the very meaning of married life.'[2]

Following upon the papal statements the general consensus of theologians appears to be that the deliberate use of the safe period as a means of family planning is morally indifferent, and that the morality of its employment will depend on the motives for which it is used. Two indispensable conditions are that both parties to the marriage freely agree to its use and both are able to bear the strain which it may impose. It is ironical to reflect that the one advance in the official papal teaching on contraception during

[1] See 'Address to Italian Catholic Union of Midwives', *A.A.S.*, 43:835 (9 October 1951) and 'Address to National Congress of the Family Front', *A.A.S.*, 43:855–60 (26 November 1951).
[2] *A.A.S.*, 53:835–54.

this century was achieved by Pius XII who is looked on by many as the arch-reactionary. The significance of the papal statement lay in the fact that it finally repudiated the views of St Augustine on recourse to rhythm and went beyond the cautious suggestions for its employment which confessors had made in the nineteenth century to a full sanctioning of its use. Catholic attitudes to contraception seemed to have reached a final point, but the truth, despite appearances, was quite otherwise, and the stage was being set in the 1950s for a series of convulsions from the effects of which the Roman Catholic Church is still suffering. The new stage of development was triggered off by the invention of the birth control pill and this, and other developments, will be dealt with in the next chapter.

CHAPTER IV

The Catholic Revolution

As has been noted, research into the development of a contraceptive pill began in the early 1950s – less than ten years later a
reasonably efficient, commercially viable pill was on the market.
The existence of this new form of birth control caught the public
imagination: widespread interest was aroused and subsequent
theological discussion, although in fact ranging far wider was,
as far as the public were concerned, a discussion of the merits of
the pill. Was its use legitimate or was it not? In fact, although the
pill stimulated the theological dialogue within the Catholic
Church, discussion rapidly broadened to take in the whole traditional teaching on contraception. By the mid-1960s the founda-
tions for a possible Catholic revolution had been laid.

The first contraceptive pill to be developed was hesperidin. This
pill affected the semen and so prevented the fertilising of the
ovum. The next pill invented was the progesterone pill, taken
orally by a woman over a period of days, and which prevented
conception. It was not, and is not, entirely clear how this pill
works, since it produces a number of different effects. The principal effect, however, is the inhibition of ovulation; the pill
prevents the egg from being released from the ovaries. It also
appears to render the cervical mucus hostile to sperms. A third
effect seems to be the rendering of the inner lining of the womb
unfavourable to the implantation of the egg. From the theological
point of view, the second effect would probably be classified as

contraceptive, and the third as abortive. Theological discussion in fact has centred on its first effect. The question asked was whether an anovulant, which inhibited ovulation, was merely another form of contraception, or was it something quite different, the legitimacy of which needed to be re-examined?

The first reactions of Catholic theologians to the use of the pill were unanimously negative.[1] In 1953, André Snoeck, a professor at Louvain, held the use of hesperidin to be a form of sterilisation.[2] The French Jesuit, Stanislas de Lestapis passed a similar judgement.[3] Progesterone was also subjected to theological analysis. Theologians concluded that use of these pills for limited purposes would not be immoral. One justification for their use would be a medical rather than a contraceptive motive, e.g. relief from pain caused by menstruation, when their employment would be justified on the principle of double effect. Use of the pills to regularise a woman's menstrual cycle would not be contrary to Catholic teaching.[4] American theologians condemned the anovulants as contraceptive and sterilising. Francis Connell held that use of the pill was 'a grave sin'. Two other theologians, Gibbons and Burch, thought that the pills were sterilising agents and, therefore, not acceptable.[5] Pius XII gave his support to these views in an address to the Congress of Haematologists on 12 September 1958. The Pope allowed the indirect use of the pills for medical reasons, but went on: 'but one provokes a direct sterilisation and therefore an illicit one, whenever one stops ovulation in order to preserve the uterus and the organism from the consequences of a pregnancy which they are not capable of supporting. Certain moralists assert that it is permitted to take drugs to this end, but this is a mistake. It is equally necessary to reject the opinion of several doctors and moralists who permit their use whenever a medical indication

---

[1] See *American Ecclesiastical Review*, CXXII (1950), p. 225, and CXXXVII (1957), p. 50; John J. Lynch, 'Fertility Control and the Moral Law', *Linacre Quarterly*, XX (1953), p. 83.
[2] See *Nouvelle Revue Théologique*, 75 (1953), p. 702.
[3] See *La Limitation des Naissances* (Paris, 1960), p. 182.
[4] For a discussion of the moral problems raised by birth control pills, see Dennis Callaghan, 'Fertility Control by Hormonal Medication', *Irish Theological Quarterly*, XXVII (January 1960), pp. 1–15.
[5] See Connell, 'The Contraceptive Pill', p. 50, and Gibbons and Burch, 'Physiologic Control of Fertility', *American Ecclesiastical Review*, 138 (1958), p. 262.

renders an early conception undesirable, or in other similar cases which it would not be possible to mention here; in these cases the use of medication has as its end the prevention of conception by preventing ovulation. They are instances, therefore, of direct sterilisation.'[1] The occasion for this papal utterance was not a particularly solemn one, but it was of importance as the only Vatican statement on the subject. As such, over the next four years it exercised a restrictive influence on theological speculation. Nevertheless a number of theologians continued to argue that the pills might be used to perfect the menstrual cycle. Use of the pills to ensure sterility during lactation was also considered by some to be legitimate. The difficulty of holding use of the pill to regularise the cycle by suppressing ovulation to be legitimate, was that it was not clear why it should not be used to suppress ovulation independent of the cycle. Furthermore, could it not be argued that it could be used to create new cycles? A way was sought out of this dilemma by concluding that its use was only legitimate within the twenty-five to thirty-five day cycle which was the natural variety for most women. Yet another exception admitted by the theologians was that the pill might be taken before a possible rape. This case was distinguishable in that no alternative of abstention from sexual intercourse existed. Suppression of ovulation was justified in order to avoid harm to the body as a whole. It was not direct sterilisation since the essence of this was the attempt to deprive the voluntary exercise of the sexual function of its procreative potentiality. Taking the pill was a safeguard against the effects of an unjustly enforced act of intercourse.

A number of theologians were nevertheless dissatisfied with these scholastic gymnastics. They, and other writers, were unhappy with the old formulations on contraception, yet they seemed to be stuck with them; they seized upon the pill as offering a new way out. In 1958 Louis Janssens, a professor at Louvain, concluded that not only was the indirect use of anovulants legitimate, but it was also lawful to use them to produce sterility during lactation. The normal period of lactation was nine months, during which nature herself inhibited ovulation. Janssens concluded that if nature failed to provide this check an artificial

[1] *A.A.S.*, 50:735-6.

one could be substituted. This article prompted the condemnation of Pius XII referred to above.[1]

A turning-point in the discussion came in 1963 when John Rock, the Catholic doctor who had first developed the pill, published his book entitled *The Time has Come*, in which he argued that there was no difference between the safe period as established by nature and that established by the pill. There was no mutilation or damage to any natural process. If nature herself inhibited ovulation during pregnancy in order to protect the child in the womb, why should not this situation be artificially created for the benefit, for example, of other existing children of the family? Dr Rock's point of view was challenged by a number of American theologians and was rejected by Cardinal Cushing of Boston, but his thesis was given wide publicity and his arguments appealed to an increasing number of Catholics.[2]

Meanwhile in Europe criticism of the condemnation of the pill was stirring among continental theologians. On 21 March 1963, Bishop Bekkers of Hertogenbosch in the Netherlands, became the first bishop to criticise by implication the traditional teaching of the Church on birth control. In a television broadcast, the bishop stated that the essence of marriage was a loving personal relationship accompanied by a sense of mutual responsibility for offspring and the already existing family. 'The Christian,' declared the bishop, 'should draw his own conclusions from this view of marriage regarding the difficult question of birth regulation. Each technique for that purpose is somehow unsatisfactory since it contains the danger that the right view of marriage will become obscured, that it may endanger mutual love and faithfulness. . . . We realise, too, that there may be certain situations in which it is impossible to be mindful of all and every Christian and human value at the same time.' The bishop was evidently hinting that the choice of means of birth regulation should be left to the informed consciences of the married partners.

In August 1963 the Dutch bishops issued a statement about the

---

[1] See Louis Janssens, 'Is the Inhibition of Ovulation Morally Lawful?', *Ephemerides, Theologicae Lovanienses*, 34 (1958), p. 360.

[2] See Cardinal Cushing's statement published in *Pilot*, 9 May 1963. The statement itself was made on 30 April 1963.

use of the pill. 'At the very time when so many new views on man, the meaning of life, the purpose of sex, and the notion of love in marriage are being expressed,' declared the bishops, 'there has been a remarkable development in biological and biochemical means of regulating and limiting human fertility. The Church is now confronted with questions which arise from conditions which are continually changing. It is impossible to provide one ready made solution for every problem in a situation which is rapidly evolving. The new contraceptive pill now being advertised can be no more acceptable as the answer to the problem of married people than the contraceptive instruments hitherto in use. But moral theologians are discussing whether there are any special circumstances in which the use of these pills could be justified.' Here the bishops were making a bridge statement avoiding any general approval of use of the pill, but at the same time leaving the way open for theological discussion on possible legitimate uses. The bishops expressed the hope that the whole matter would be fully discussed at the Vatican Council.

This hope of open Council discussion was never in fact realised, but the theological dialogue was, in fact, intensified. A vitally important article was published by Fr Louis Janssens in the autumn of 1963.[1] Two other seminal articles appeared at this period, one written by William van der Marck, a Dutch Dominican from Nymegen,[2] the other by Bishop Joseph Reuss, auxiliary bishop of Mainz, which appeared in the journal of the Catholic Theological Faculty at the University of Tübingen.[3] All three articles were of prime importance but the views of Fr Janssens were those destined to be most widely disseminated.[4] Canon Janssens stressed in his article the importance of a generous attitude towards procreation. He also emphasised the importance of respecting the natural structure of the sexual act. But he went on to elaborate the

---

[1] 'Conjugal Morality and Progestins', *Ephemerides, Theologicae Lovanienses*, 4 (October–December 1963), p. 787.
[2] 'Fertility Control: an attempt to answer a still open question', *Vruchtbaarheidsregeling*.
[3] 'Marital Sacrifice and Procreation', *Tübingen Theologische Quartalschrift*, 143 (1963), p. 454.
[4] For example, I wrote an article 'Catholics and Birth Control' in the *Observer*, 3 May 1964, a few days before the English hierarchy's statement on the subject was issued. My article set out Fr Janssens's thesis.

proposition that the pill is not a contraceptive in the normal sense of the word since it leaves the essential, given, structure of the sexual act unimpaired. Neither does it constitute sterilisation since the function of ovulation is merely postponed; the ova remains in the ovaries ready for future fertilisation. He further justified the use of the pill by drawing a parallel between it and the use of the sterile period as a means of family planning. The use of either device to exclude children from marriage for selfish reasons would be wrong, but the employment of either prudently for serious reasons would be lawful. Use of the pill, argued Canon Janssens, was essentially indistinguishable from periodic continence, and since use of the sterile period was not regarded as sterilisation neither should utilising the pill.

Similar arguments were advanced by Fr Van der Marck, although he presented them in rather a different way. Fr Van der Marck redefined the act of birth regulation. The act to be analysed was the use of hormonal compounds to regulate fertility. Such an act was intrinsically good, not evil. 'The typical quality of the human act,' he stated, 'is precisely that the physically separated elements can, by human giving of meaning, become one by reason of the intended end.' The objective act being good, all that was required was a subjective good intention, e.g. using regulation for serious or adequate reasons. Bishop Reuss's argument proceeded from the basis that biological and physiological acts are not immune from interference, and this is true of sexual acts, the act of coitus itself being excepted. It is not, however, for the theologian to lay down details about sexual intercourse, he can 'merely say that the intervention must be made in such a way as to safeguard the personal dignity of the couple'. Bishop Reuss argued that revelation confined itself to the command that marriage should be fruitful. The sexual union was one means of establishing harmony between the parents which in itself conduced to the good of the children. It was not right to prohibit intercourse in marriage, and at the same time it was not right to have children who could not be adequately supported. The only alternative, therefore, was intercourse which was not in itself fruitful. This could be brought about by the use of the infertile days, but other means might also be legitimate. The Bishop distinguished between interventions which do not leave intact the processes of the act and those made *in view* of the fulfilment of intercourse, and which like the selection of certain days, leaves absolutely intact the process of the act. The Bishop concluded that there was an obligation on married couples first of all to see if use of the sterile period would meet their needs, but if this were not so, they were free to resort to other interventions consonant with their personal dignity. These articles, important as they undoubtedly were, represented merely the tip of the iceberg. Spoken speculation was widespread and much more daring than most of what was committed to print, theologians in this sphere being chary of taking risks and prejudicing their careers.

THE ENGLISH REACTION

In England little had been written by Catholics about birth control in theological journals or the Press, one reason being fear of ecclesiastical censure. Nevertheless, in the 1960s in periodicals such as the *Spectator*, the *New Statesman* and the *Catholic Herald*, there were signs of an emergent dissatisfaction among Catholics with the teaching on birth control, although nothing of major theological importance was published.[1] One bizarre but revealing incident of this period concerned the opening by Dr Anne Bieżanek, a Roman Catholic doctor, of a birth control clinic in Wallasey in Liverpool. Dr Bieżanek opened the clinic in September 1963 and dedicated it to St Martin de Porres, a black South American saint. In her clinic she provided advice on all means of birth control for Roman Catholics and others. In December 1963 she was refused Communion by her parish priest, who was supported in this by the Bishop of Shrewsbury, who maintained that she was causing scandal by carrying out activities contrary to the Church's teaching. In May 1964 Dr Bieżanek informed Cardinal Heenan that she would come to receive Communion at Westminster Cathedral on 31 May. The Cardinal wisely refrained

[1] A typical article appeared in the *Spectator*, 30 August 1963, entitled 'Catholics and Birth Control'. It appeared under a pseudonym of 'Catholic parent', but was in fact written by Mr Bruce Cooper. The article stressed the difficulties of applying Catholic theories on birth control in practice, and subsequent correspondence showed the deep diversity of views among Catholics. Cf. an article on birth control in the *New Statesman*, 17 January 1964, and subsequent correspondence.

from interference and she was able to approach the altar rails without incident. Some Catholics condemned her, but others supported her and the incident showed once again the division among Catholics over the question of birth control.[1]

The Anne Bieżanek episode was always something of a side-show, and the storm only broke in England in April 1964 with the publication of an article on birth control in the Catholic periodical *Search*.[2] Archbishop Roberts started his article by saying that he personally did not find the traditional Catholic ethical argument condemning birth control a convincing one: 'I have lectured in a good number of universities and often enough to doctors. I have on these occasions admitted that I personally cannot follow what is called the ethical argument. It does not seem to me to be conclusive. If I were not a Catholic, I would accept the position taken by the Lambeth Conference, namely that there are cases where conscientious thought by the parties concerned would entitle people to practise contraception. How you can destroy the position by reason alone is not clear to me.' Archbishop Roberts went on to state that this being the case he could only fall back on the Church's authority. But he then raised the further question as to whether as far as authority was concerned there was not the possibility of a change in the attitude to contraception as there had already been in the case of the Church's attitude to usury. The Archbishop also pointed out that the Fathers at the Vatican Council had given statements on freedom of conscience a few months previously, which were extremely difficult to reconcile with the Syllabus of Errors of Pope Pius IX. He ended his article by dealing with the situation in India. 'The Protestant missionary suggests that nature did not give sex organs only for the production of children, but also, even independently, for the expression of married love. He offers a contraceptive not as an ideal solution but as a lesser evil than sterilisation, than abortion, than the hunger of his children, than the death of his wife or the death of their married life. It is that advice that we Catholics must condemn as "unnatural". Those of us who can't see why or

[1] For a full account of the whole incident, see Anne Bieżanek, *All Things New* (London, 1964).
[2] *Search* was a private subscription periodical edited by Michael de la Bedoyère, a former editor of the *Catholic Herald*, with a small but influential readership.

how to convict of crime the millions who see contraception as a right or duty in marriage – we certainly may and must press for the acceptance by the General Council of the "challenge" to justify by reason our own challenge to the world made in the name of reason.'

Archbishop Roberts had refrained from giving explicit approval to contraception, but there was no doubt where his sympathies lay. The Archbishop was making a powerful plea for the revision of Catholic teaching. Dr Bieżanek could be dismissed by Cardinal Heenan as an eccentric hardly worth making a fuss about, but an Archbishop was clearly another matter. The Archbishop's article had received wide publicity in the Press, and on 25 April 1964, Fr Maurice O'Leary, Chairman of the Catholic Marriage Advisory Council, made a statement on the Church's teaching on contraception which was evidently 'inspired'.[1] Fr O'Leary declared that there was no uncertainty about the Catholic teaching on contraception. Having quoted *Casti Connubii* and also Pius XII, he stated: 'We have this certainty from the teaching of the Church, that contraception is intrinsically immoral and no opinion to the contrary may be followed.' Fr O'Leary's statement was but a preliminary shot, and on 7 May the hierarchy of England and Wales issued a solemn statement. The statement was the joint responsibility of all the bishops, but the Press attached it to the name of Cardinal Heenan who issued it as President of the Hierarchy. The statement discussed the difficulties faced by Catholic couples in marriage. These difficulties, it went on, 'are only increased when it is irresponsibly suggested that the Council may produce a new moral code for married people. It has even been suggested that the Council could approve the practice of contraception. But the Church, while free to revise her own positive laws, has no power of any kind to alter the laws of God.' The bishops went on to quote Piux XI and St Augustine as well as Pius XII. They expressed their 'fatherly compassion' for Catholic couples: 'We know that sometimes there can be an agonising choice between natural instincts and the law of God. Our hearts are full of sympathy but we cannot change God's law.' The bishops called in aid the statement of the Dutch bishops on the

[1] See *Tablet*, 25 April 1964 – I mean inspired by the hierarchy, not by the Holy Spirit!

pill, and hinted that the Council might approve a pill to make the time of ovulation predictable. Contraception itself, they added: 'is not an open question for it is against the law of God'.

The hierarchy statement could hardly have been in more uncompromising terms. That evening I appeared on B.B.C. television and was asked my opinion of the effect of the statement. I replied that as the hierarchy had spoken out in such a way the debate among Catholics would, in all probability, cease and the directive would be obeyed. I was swiftly proved wrong. Far from ending the conflagration the statement of the bishops merely added fuel to the flames. Archbishop Roberts himself defended his attitude in an article published in the *Evening Standard* on 19 May. He was particularly irate about the charge of advocating pagan solutions and leading the Catholics astray which had been made in the bishops' declaration. Archbishop Roberts and the hierarchy were both supported and criticised in the Press. Catholics wrote to *The Times*, the *Guardian* and the *Daily Telegraph*, expressing different points of view. A lively correspondence took place in the columns of the *Spectator*. The controversy also raged in Catholic papers, such as the *Tablet* and the *Catholic Herald*. It was pointed out that the hierarchy statement contained some serious inaccuracies. They had, for example, quoted St Augustine as saying: 'Intercourse is unlawful and wicked where the conception of the offspring is prevented.' A correspondent in *The Times* drew attention to the fact that what St Augustine had in fact written was: 'Where the conception of offspring is *avoided* (divatur).' This was significant since his words would include in his condemnation the use of the rhythm method of birth control. Others pointed out that the views of the Dutch hierarchy had not been fully presented since the reference to the discussion by Catholic moral theologians as to whether the pill's use could be acceptable in certain circumstances had been omitted.[1]

[1] There was some confusion caused by two translations of the Dutch bishops' statement. The first translation appeared in the *Universe*, 2 May 1964: 'The new contraceptive pill now being advertised can be no more acceptable as the answer to the problem of married people than the contraceptive instruments hitherto in use. But moral theologians are discussing whether there are any special circumstances in which the use of these pills could be justified.' The *Tablet* for 30 May 1964, on the other hand, translated the Dutch statement as follows: 'Though the now advertised oral, chemical means of preventing conception can be no more accepted as the generally used solution

One of the most significant Catholic contributions was published in the form of a letter in *The Times* signed by a number of
young Catholic married couples. They declared that the hierarchy statement was 'not only untimely, but basically unjustifi-
able'. They stated that as the mind of the Universal Church had
not been made up on the issue, the English bishops had no authority
to lay down what they called 'the laws of God'. They went on to
state that there was no warrant in scripture for an infallible
condemnation of responsible family planning and no infallible
statement on the issue by the Church. The acceptance of the
'safe period' method of birth control had moved the controversy
'away from the realm of fundamental principles into that of
academic hairsplitting'. The case of the nuns in the Congo who
had been authorised to take the pill when in danger of rape had
'removed the validity of an absolute ban once and for all'. The
letter concluded by looking forward to a revised theology of
marriage differing radically in concept and tone from the existing
one. 'It will contain a new emphasis on the importance of intention, and on the responsibilities of each married couple to decide
the means towards the success of their marriage, on which, since
this is their chosen vocation, they will ultimately be judged. We
trust in the wisdom of the Church and because of this we can only
consider that the hierarchy's statement is contrary to the present,
and essential, spirit of the Church, and should be at least officially
modified in several important respects. Authority alone, in the
present state of the Church's teaching on this vital matter, cannot
compel our obedience.'[1] This fierce reaction astonished the bishops
among others and showed the depth of feeling on the issue which
existed in the Catholic community. It provided a kind of dress
rehearsal for the English reaction to the papal encyclical *Humanae
Vitae*, when it was published four years later. It represented a
new development in Catholic life in England. Hitherto public

---

to matrimonial distress than the already long known instrumental means, Catholic
moral theologians are discussing the question whether these means could be acceptable
in certain circumstances.'
[1] The letter was signed Paul Burns; Penelope Burns; Adam Broadbent; Sarah Broadbent; Michael Ryan; Giustina Ryan; P. J. Sheahan; M. C. Sheahan; Patrick Tickell;
Diana Tickell.

H

controversy among Catholics had been minimal and confined to the Catholic papers. For the first time Catholics in England were using the secular news media as a means of expressing their views. This was to prove of vital importance when the papal encyclical came to be discussed.

The birth control controversy in England remained largely a domestic affair, although echoes of the dispute reached the United States. One Continental theologian was, however, drawn into the maelstrom, Fr Bernard Häring, one of the foremost Catholic moral theologians and Professor of Moral and Social Theology at the Lateran University in Rome.[1] In an interview with Mr George Armstrong, published in the *Guardian* on 9 May 1964, Fr Häring stressed that the pill presented quite a new issue since Pius XII spoke on the matter in 1958. 'It would seem to me,' said Fr Häring, 'that the statement of Archbishop Heenan bears the date of that year not 1964.' There followed a controversial passage: 'Surely we must make distinctions between these pills and other forms of contraceptives, and I am sure there will be developments along that line in Catholic doctrine. I think the British bishops erred in this in their statement.' The English hierarchy were not unreasonably dismayed by this report, and contacted Fr Häring. Fr Häring denied that he had said that the British bishops had 'erred' in their statement.[2] He reaffirmed the essential point that he considered a new situation had arisen which needed further discussion before definite answers could be given. In an article published in the *Catholic Herald* on 29 May 1964, Fr Häring declared again that no final judgement could be expressed on the subject. He concluded cautiously: 'In my

[1] Cardinal Ottaviani also unintentionally became involved. A magazine interview with the Cardinal published on 3 June was interpreted by some commentators as a rebuke to the English hierarchy for making a premature pronouncement on birth control. Cardinal Heenan at once got in touch with Rome and a bulletin was issued from Archbishop's House, Westminster, on 18 June 1964 containing a clarification by Cardinal Ottaviani in which he denied that what he had said had any reference to the English hierarchy but to the 'danger of voicing new theories which foster newfangled opinions'. See *The Times*, 19 June 1964.

[2] *Guardian*, 14 May 1964. The confusion had apparently arisen from a misreading by Mr Armstrong of the tape used for the interview with Fr Häring. Monsignor Worlock, secretary for the Council to the English hierarchy, telephoned Fr Häring in Rome and a clarifying statement from Fr Häring was issued from Archbishop's House, London. See *Tablet*, 16 May 1964, for the full text of the statement and an account of the incident, p. 564.

opinion it is too soon yet for married people to conclude from current discussions that the pill is a positively acceptable method of birth regulation, raising no difficulties or problems from the moral point of view. We must have patience, and await further developments in the weighing of all the pros and cons.'[1]

THE SITUATION IN THE UNITED STATES

In the post-war decades down to nearly the end of the 1960s, Catholic opposition in the United States to any form of state-sponsored family planning programmes on the national or international level remained strong.[2] Catholics were also prominent in resisting any attempts to liberalise or repeal state laws restricting the provision of contraceptive information or penalising their sale or distribution. When in November 1959 the Catholic bishops announced that they would fight any attempt to use foreign aid funds to promote 'artificial birth prevention programmes' in underdeveloped countries, their statement caused a political storm.[3] Bishop James A. Pike, the Protestant Episcopal Bishop of California, condemned the statement and asked whether it was binding on candidates for public office. The reference was clearly to Senator Kennedy, one of the aspirants for the Democratic nomination in 1960, who replied that he thought such policies would be mistaken since they would be interpreted as discriminatory. The United States had never urged them, either at home or in western Europe.[4] If faced with a bill embodying such a programme, he stated he would judge the measure by whether 'it would be in the interests of the United States'. If it became law he would uphold it.[5]

[1] In February 1965, another English 'incident' occurred when Fr Joseph Cocker (26) of the Portsmouth diocese publicly opposed the official Catholic teaching on birth control. His priestly facilities were withdrawn. Fr Cocker refused to withdraw his views, expressing himself in sympathy with Fr Arnold MacMahon, another English priest, who had recently been called to Rome to explain his opposition to the Catholic position on contraception. See *The Times*, 26 February 1965 and the *Daily Telegraph*, ibid.

[2] Chapter I, pp. 26–30.   [3] Chapter I, p. 28.

[4] Mr Stevenson and Senator Humphrey were in favour of providing information on request, only Senator Symington expressing himself unequivocally in favour of birth control. See *Economist*, 5 December 1959.

[5] *Time*, 7 December 1959. Senator Kennedy's replies were both judicious and constitutionally correct.

In July 1960 a special report which I had written for the Center for the Study of Democratic Institutions at Santa Barbara, California, entitled 'Birth Control and Public Policy' was published in the United States and aroused wide interest; it was the subject of news reports and editorial comment throughout the United States. A principal conclusion reached by the report was that if an act was believed to be contrary to the natural law this did not imply that it should be forbidden by the law of the state. 'Whether such legislation is desirable is a jurisprudential rather than a theological question which must be decided in relation to the conditions prevailing in a given community. While Roman Catholics in a democracy have every right to work for legislation outlawing the sale and distribution of contraceptives, the conclusion is reached that the Roman Catholic community in England and the United States would be wise not to attempt to secure a total legislative ban on contraceptives, but should limit its efforts to securing a policy of state neutrality on the issue and the passing of measures to preserve public morality, commanding the general support of the community.' The report stated that a statute such as that then in force in Connecticut which forbade the *use* of contraceptives violated Catholic principles of jurisprudence. This conclusion seems mild enough today, but at that time it was considered revolutionary.

It was not until four years later that the Catholic theological position was openly challenged by Catholic writers. In 1964, Fr John L. Thomas, S.J., Professor of Sociology at St Louis University, addressed the Planned Parenthood World Population Convention in Dallas, Texas, the first time a priest in the United States had taken part in a national meeting sponsored by the birth control agency. The central issue for theologians over the contraceptive pill, stated Fr Thomas, 'is to determine how far man may go in regulating, controlling or correcting the sterility–fertility cycle of the generative system. Since they may not fully agree on the arguments derived from reason showing why human intervention in the generative system is wrong, there is room for theological discussion when new means of intervention must be evaluated'.[1] At the same time, the Catholic laity in the United

[1] See *Tablet*, 16 May 1964.

States began to make their voice heard. Writing in the magazine *Commonweal*, on 14 February 1964, Michael Novak declared: 'The layman's strong point in discussing marital questions is that he alone has a connatural, empirical grasp of the nature of Catholic marriage. His weak point is that he has been silent for so long that he lacks a language for expressing himself. . . . Catholic laymen, it seems, would do well to begin breaking through the vicious circles of most public discussions of these questions, by speaking as frankly and as clearly as they can of what Catholic marriage is as they have come to know it. If every Christian state has its own proper charisma, then it is laymen who should be writing the authentic and prophetic books on the sacrament of marriage as it is lived.' Lay Catholics in the United States had earlier asked for an investigation of the natural law basis of Catholic teaching on birth control, but they had been content that the investigation should be left to the theologians.[1] The significance of Michael Novak's article was that he was making the important and novel point that the layman's contribution to the theology of marriage was an essential one. This was followed by a number of books in which married couples gave their views on the morality of contraception.[2]

1964 also saw the publication by Louis Dupré, Professor of Philosophy at the Jesuit University of Georgetown, of an important article in *Cross Currents*, 'Towards a Re-examination of the Catholic Position on Birth Control', which made a radical attack on the traditional Catholic view.[3] Professor Dupré criticised Catholic thought for isolating the act of *coitus* from any general spiritual or marital context, and treating it as though it were an absolute value in itself. Biological nature had been confused with human nature, and insufficient allowance made for man's essential

[1] See 'Birth Control and Public Policy', *Commonweal*, August 1963, and subsequent correspondence.
[2] See *The Experience of Marriage, Thirteen Married Couples Report*, ed. Michael Novak, 1964. The couples expressed different views on the desirability of rhythm and the use of contraceptives but the important fact was that they were giving open though anonymous testimony for the first time. See also: *What Modern Catholics think about Birth Control*, ed. William Birmingham, 1964. This book contains the testimony of fifteen Catholic men and women on the subject of birth control and contraception.
[3] See: *Cross Currents*, XIV (Winter 1964), p. 63. Professor Dupré later expanded this article into a book, *Contraception and Catholics, a New Appraisal*, 1964.

freedom which enables him to transcend natural facts and gives scope for constant development. Professor Dupré concluded tentatively that even the use of contraceptives could be justified. The important thing, he maintained, was not that every act of sexual intercourse should be directed to procreation, but that in the context of the whole marriage relationship the general procreative purpose should be maintained. If the spouses found that the value of procreation conflicted with other values in the marriage, such as the upbringing and education of existing children, the resort to the use of the sterile period or even to contraceptives as a means of family planning could be justified, although use for personal pleasure alone would never be legitimate. The significance of these contributions to the debate, apart from their intrinsic arguments, was that they showed that for the first time a real freedom of discussion of the birth control issue had been achieved by Catholics.[1]

THE COUNCIL AND THE VATICAN

The calling of the Second Vatican Council, which was to prove a major turning-point in the history of the Catholic Church, was announced by Pope John XXIII in January 1959, three months after he had been elected to the Chair of Peter in succession to Pius XII.[2] After more than three years of preparation the Council was finally opened on 29 September 1962. One of the issues that clearly would need to be discussed was the Church's attitude to birth control, but the Pope and his advisers were not anxious to have it discussed in open session as being too 'delicate' a topic. Accordingly, Pope John appointed a small commission of six clerics and laymen to consider certain limited aspects of the question with particular reference to population problems.[3] Pope

[1] 'Contraception and Holiness', the title of a book published in the United States in 1964, containing a number of theological and other contributions on birth control and introduced by Archbishop Roberts, S.J., illustrated the shift taking place in Catholic opinion. Such a title would have been unthinkable a few years earlier.
[2] Pius XII died in the early hours 9 October 1958, the Conclave opened in Rome on 25 October, and at 4.45 p.m. on 28 October the white smoke coming from the Vatican gave the first indication that Cardinal Roncalli had been elected Pope.
[3] The six original members of the Commission were Fr Henri de Riedmatten, O.P. (Geneva); Fr Stanislas de Lestapis, S.J. (Paris); Fr C. Mertens, S.J. (Belgium); Dr P. van Rossum (Belgium); Professor J. Mertens de Wilmars (Belgium); and Dr John Marshall (England).

John died before this commission could report, but it continued its work after his successor, Cardinal Montini, ascended the papal throne as Paul VI in June 1963. Early in 1964 Paul VI expanded the membership of the commission to include eighteen members. He added various theologians representing different schools of thought, together with a number of other experts. The Commission held a meeting in March 1964 but nothing of great note seems to have taken place. It met again in June 1964 and at that point Dr Marshall has testified that in his estimation 'sixteen of the eighteen members, whatever their internal doubts, had not sufficiently formulated their ideas as seriously to challenge the traditional teaching'.[1] Nevertheless the Commission's interim report seems to have contained sufficient expression of doubt on the teaching of the Church to have alarmed the Pope. Speaking to the College of Cardinals on 23 June, the Pope said: 'We will soon give the conclusions of it [the Commission] in the form which will be considered most adapted to the subject and to the aim to be achieved. But meanwhile, We say frankly that We do not have sufficient reason to regard the norms given by Pope Pius XII in this matter as surpassed and not therefore binding; they must therefore be considered valid, at least until We feel in conscience bound to modify them. In a subject of such seriousness it certainly seems that Catholics want to follow a single law, such as the Church authoritatively proposes; and it therefore seems opportune to recommend that no one should, for the time being, take it upon himself to pronounce himself in terms differing from the norm in force.' Undoubtedly, the Pope's intention was to bring public discussion to an end, but the phraseology he used was calculated to stimulate rather than to stifle speculation. Dr Marshall has said that he found the declaration 'startling', and indeed there was something startling in the implication that what had always been presented as a matter of natural law could, in fact, be subject to revision.

In September 1964 the Council reassembled for its third session, and in October began discussion of the controversial report 'The Church in the Modern World', known as Schema XIII.

[1] See 'Papal Commission's Theological Doubts', by John Marshall, *The Times*, 3 August 1968.

Paragraph 21 of this report dealt with the Church's teaching on marriage and the family. Before this paragraph was reached, the session had been enlivened by a hard-hitting speech from Archbishop Heenan. He criticised severely various omissions in the document, including its silence on the question of the contraceptive pill. Married couples were told by the document that they must act according to the teaching of the Church. 'But,' asked the Archbishop, 'this is precisely what married people want to be told – *what is* now the teaching of the Church? To this question our document gives no reply. For that very reason it could provide an argument from our silence to theologians after the Council who wish to attack sound doctrine. . . . When our children ask us for bread, we should not give them a stone.'[1]

On 29 and 30 October, the Council had a short but dramatic debate on paragraph 21 of the schema. The section was remarkable for its strongly personalist approach to marriage. While it stressed the procreative end of marriage, it abandoned the terminology of primary and secondary ends concerning procreation and relationship between the spouses which had been traditionally used. In an appendix, the schema stated: 'The ultimate decision and practical application of universal principles belongs to the spouses themselves. However, they should act according to a conscience formed in accordance with the teaching of the Church.' It was this vagueness about the 'teaching of the Church' which had been criticised by Archbishop Heenan, but since the Pope had expressly reserved to his own Commission any statement on birth control the criticism was not entirely fair.

The discussion on marriage was opened by Archbishop Dearden of Detroit. The Archbishop stressed that couples could 'for sufficiently grave reasons' regulate the number of their children, but

[1] I happened to be attending the Council on 22 October, and heard Archbishop Heenan's speech. It caused a sensation among the Council Fathers. The Archbishop made a strong attack on the experts in a well-turned Latin phrase, 'timeo peritos adnexa ferentes' which can be translated: 'I fear specialists when they are left to explain what the bishops meant.' Some interpreted the Archbishop's speech as a tit-for-tat against Fr Häring for his criticism of the English hierarchy. I saw Fr Häring immediately after the speech had been made and, while the point had not escaped him, he seemed unperturbed. The reference to 'sound doctrine' in the Archbishop's speech indicates that at this stage he was still strongly opposed to any revision of the traditional teaching.

they were not authorised to use any means to do so: 'Nothing can be permitted which is opposed to the natural orientation of the marital act, or which destroys the conjugal act's expressiveness of personal and marital love.' The Archbishop's words were carefully chosen, so as not to exclude any possible solution, but they did not add anything very new to the discussion. This omission was soon remedied in three notable speeches delivered by Cardinal Léger, Archbishop of Montreal, Cardinal Suenens, Archbishop of Brussels, and Patriarch Maximos IV Saigh, who despite his eighty-seven years of age made the most revolutionary contribution of all. These three speeches brought into the Council at the highest level the doubts and questions about the traditional teaching of the Church on birth control existing in the minds of millions of Catholics.

Cardinal Léger stressed the need for the renewal of the whole theology of marriage. 'Conjugal love,' he stated, 'is good and holy in itself and it should be accepted by Christians without fear . . . in marriage the spouses consider each other not as mere procreators, but as persons loved for their own sakes.' 'It must also be stated,' went on the Cardinal, 'that the intimate union of the spouses also finds a purpose in love. And this end is truly the end of the act itself, lawful in itself, even when it is not ordained to procreation.'

Cardinal Suenens then rose to speak, and called for the appointment of a conciliar commission on marriage probems to work in collaboration with that already appointed by the Pope. The Cardinal wondered whether a perfect balance had been achieved in all aspects of the teaching of the Church on marriage. 'It may be,' he declared, 'that we have accentuated the gospel text, "increase and multiply" to such a point that we have obscured another text, "and they will be two in one flesh". These two truths are central, and both are scriptural; they must illuminate each other in the light of the full truth that is revealed to us in our Lord Jesus Christ.' Cardinal Suenens went on to ask whether 'the classical doctrine, especially that of the manuals' took sufficient account of the new knowledge achieved by modern science, for example, in relation to 'the complexity with which the real or the biological interferes with the pyschological, the conscious with the sub-conscious. New possibilities are constantly being discovered in man, of his power to direct nature.' 'I beg of you,' he said, 'let us avoid a new "Galileo affair". One is enough for the Church.' At the conclusion of Cardinal Suenens's speech the assembled Fathers burst into applause.[1]

The third and most outspoken contribution came from Patriarch Maximos. The Patriarch got to the root of the matter straight away declaring there was a conflict between the official doctrine of the Church and the contrary practice of the vast majority of Christian couples. He added that demographic pressures prevented any increase in the standard of living of hundreds of millions of human beings, and condemned them to 'unworthy and hopeless misery'. Warming to his theme, the Patriarch asked whether, perhaps, 'a bachelor psychosis' was responsible for certain positions. 'Are we not, perhaps unwillingly, setting up a Manichean conception of man and the world, in which the work of the flesh, vitiated in itself, is tolerated only in view of children?' The Patriarch stressed that the collaboration of married Christians in considering the problem was necessary, as well as a dialogue on the subject with other Christian Churches and even with those of the non-Christian religions. Cardinal Alfrink came in to support the three previous speakers. He pointed out that there was 'honest doubt' among married people and among scientists and some theologians regarding at least the arguments used to prove that the only legitimate form of birth control was complete or periodic continence. Cardinal Alfrink wanted a permanent commission on the whole subject.

A contrary view was put to the Council by Cardinal Ottaviani, the Secretary of the Holy Office. In a moving and eloquent speech, he pointed out that he was the tenth of a family of twelve children, and that his father had been a labourer in a bakery. 'I purposely say labourer, not the owner of a bakery.' Despite difficuties, his parents had never doubted the ways of providence. 'I am not pleased,' said the Cardinal, 'with the statement of the text that

[1] Not everyone was enthusiastic about the Cardinal's intervention. A few days later, he took the unprecedented step of 'clarifying' his statement on marriage. This neither added nor detracted from anything he had said earlier. Speculation was rife at the time as to why he should have thought this necessary, and the most probable explanation is that he had displeased the Pope.

married couples can determine the number of children they are to have. This has never been heard of before in the Church.' Cardinal Ottaviani was speaking extempore, and a more considered contribution came from Cardinal Browne. Cardinal Browne set out, once again, the classical scholastic doctrine on the primary and secondary ends of marriage. 'The primary end of marriage,' declared the Cardinal, 'is procreation and the education of the children. The secondary end is, on the one hand, the mutual aid of the spouses, and on the other a remedy for concupiscence.' He declined to say anything on the question of the pill, since the Pope had reserved this issue to himself. Eight speakers then addressed the Council, four being in support of the progressive Cardinals, and four being against. At 11.15 a.m. on 30 October, Cardinal Agagianian, the President for the day, suddenly called for a vote to close the debate on Article 21, and this was carried. The debate had been a short one, but it had brought the fundamental issues before the Council.[1]

The Council finished its first debate on 'the Church in the Modern World' on 10 November 1964, and the document, together with suggested amendments, then went back to be considered by the Conciliar Commission. At the fourth and final session of the Council in September 1965, the revised schema came up for debate on 21 September, when the discussion was initiated by Archbishop Garrone.[2] The debate on the sections dealing with marriage opened on 29 September, and the text had been little changed from its original version. It skirted round birth control, since the Pope had reserved this issue to himself, but stressed the importance of conjugal love and reproduction as vital ends of marriage without subordinating one to the other. Despite the objections of Cardinal Ottaviani, the declaration that parents were responsible for deciding on the number of their children remained in the text. The debate was neither particularly lively nor controversial although significant speeches were made. Cardinal Suenens called for scientific research in the area of sexual life. This should be directed to 'man himself in all his complexity,

[1] Sources for this account of the debate include: Xavier Rynne, *The Third Session* (London, 1965), and *The Times*, 30 and 31 October 1964.
[2] The revised schema was much longer than the version considered the previous year and had expanded from 27 to 80 pages.

particularly on the sexual and conjugal level. We must have a better understanding of the laws of human fecundity as well as the psychological laws of self-control. . . . The efforts made thus far are insufficient.' Cardinal Colombo, Archbishop of Milan, speaking on behalf of thirty-two Italian bishops stated: 'We can accept the schema's fully human and personalist perspective without any reservation. However, we cannot accept anything that vitiates conjugal relations. The schema should eliminate any equivocation about this. . . . We need not seek the justification of this moral law in the fact that the physical integrity of the conjugal act constitutes a moral value in itself, but rather in the fact that the physical perfection of the relation is an intrinsic and inseparable element of the will to love one another and procreate.' This intervention foreshadowed the later dramatic developments when the Pope sought to have the schema modified. Another important contribution came from Bishop de Roo of Victoria, Canada. He placed a high value on conjugal love: 'Married couples tell us that conjugal love is a spiritual experience of the most profound kind. It gives them their deepest insight into their own being, into what they mean to each other, into their mutual communion in unbreakable union. Through this love they grasp as in a synthesis the mysterious purpose of their life as one, as well as the bonds that link them to God the Creator. In an almost tangible way they commune in God's love and through their activity as spouses they see intuitively that God is the source of life and happiness. . . . They provide the new members who increase the Body of Christ. They become instruments for the redemption of humanity and for the progress of the universe.' The Council approved the schema and forwarded it with the oral and written interventions to the sub-commissions of the Mixed Commission who started their work of revising the text. The chapter on marriage was dealt with on 25 October.

All appeared to be going smoothly until a papal bombshell burst upon the Commission on 24 November, when it was meeting to consider the schema's text. Cardinal Ottaviani asked the Secretary of the Commission, Father Tromp, to read a communication from the Secretary of State, Cardinal Cicognani, to the members. 'I announce to you,' said the letter, 'that the August

Pontiff desires that you, by reason of the office and authority which are yours, inform the Commission . . . that there are certain points which must of necessity be corrected in the text which is to be proposed to the General Session of the Ecumenical Council, Vatican II, with regard to the section which treats 'of promoting the dignity of marriage and the family''.' The letter went on to demand explicit mention of the encyclical *Casti Connubii* and of the address of Pius XII to the midwives, both of which have been referred to earlier. 'Secondly,' went on the letter, 'it is absolutely necessary that the methods and instruments of rendering conception ineffectual – that is to say, the contraceptive methods which are dealt with in the Encyclical Letter *Casti Connubii* – be openly rejected; for in this matter admitting doubts, keeping silence, or insinuating opinions that the necessity of such methods is perhaps to be admitted, can bring about the gravest dangers to the general opinion.' Enclosed with the letter were four amendments to bring about the modifications in the text.[1] The amendments would also have had the effect of restating the doctrinal position of the primary and secondary ends of marriage which had been rejected by the Council. The missive threw the Commission into understandable confusion. The effect of following it would have been to undo the work of the Council, which had specifically wished to leave the whole question of contraception open, and would also have preempted the work of the papal Commission on birth control which had still not presented its report. Since the sections on marriage had received overwhelming votes in their favour and an absolute majority on 16 November, their text could not be substantially changed according to the Council rules.[2]

The conservatives on the Commission were naturally delighted: '*Christus ipse locutus est* – Christ himself has spoken,' Cardinal Browne is alleged to have exclaimed. Others were less enthusiastic. Archbishop Dearden questioned the authenticity of the letter in the sense of its expressing the mind of the Pope. Cardinal Léger made a strong statement deploring the proposed

---

[1] This letter and a following letter of 25 November, were reproduced in J. C. Ford and J. J. Lynch, 'Contraception: a Matter of Practical Doubt', *Homiletic and Pastoral Review*, April 1968, p. 563.
[2] The sections concerning marriage had been approved by 2,052 to 91 votes, and by 2,011 to 140 votes.

amendments, and saying that if they were adopted the prestige and reputation of the Holy See might be irreparably damaged. The meeting broke up in confusion and Cardinal Léger left hurriedly in order to see the Pope. Despite the oaths of secrecy, news of the intervention spread rapidly throughout Rome that day and an account of what had taken place was printed the following morning in the newspaper *L'Avvenire d'Italia*.[1]

The Commission met again the following morning, Friday, 26 November. In the interval various people had hurried to the Pope's apartments, including Cardinal Colombo; representations had also been made to the Pope by the lay auditors. Cardinal Ottaviani asked Father Tromp to read a second letter from the Secretary of State. The letter stated that the previous instructions should be considered: 'as the counsels [concilia] of the Supreme Pontiff in this matter of such great importance. With regard to the manner of expression, however, they do not contain anything definitive, and therefore need not necessarily be adopted word for word. The Commission, can, therefore, propose other formulations also, which, however, should take account of these counsels and satisfy the desires of His Holiness. These new formulations will be carefully weighed by the Holy Father and can indeed be approved, if they appear to him to agree with his mind.'[2] The Commission seized upon the opportunity offered by this letter of reformulating the wording and adding words of their own, and as a result the schema emerged substantially unchanged. The amendment which called for the condemnation of 'contraceptive practices' was changed into 'illicit practices against human generation'. A wording was devised to preserve the equality of the ends of marriage so that conjugal love was not subordinated to procreation. The references to *Casti Connubii* and the address of Pius XII were not included in the text but were placed in a footnote coming after an amended passage declaring: 'Sons of the Church may not undertake methods of regulating procreation which are found blameworthy by the teaching authority of the Church in its

[1] Once again I happened to be in Rome at this critical moment, and was able on 26 November to discuss the situation which by this time was public knowledge with Cardinal Suenens, Professor Hans Küng, and Father Claude Leetham, I.C. a *peritus* (expert) advising on Schema 13.
[2] The letter was dated 25 November 1965.

unfolding of the divine law.' This wording in the text still left the question open, and the Commission succeeded in adding after the references to Pius XI, Pius XII, and Paul VI (the address of 23 June 1964) the following additional matter. 'Certain questions which need further and more careful investigation have been handed over, at the command of the Supreme Pontiff, to a Commission for the Study of Population, Family, and Birth, in order that, after it fulfils its function, the Supreme Pontiff may pass judgement. With the doctrine of the *Magisterium* in this state, this Holy Synod does not intend to propose immediately concrete solutions.' So ended the last attempt at what can only be described as a 'railroading' of the Council. The schema was approved overwhelmingly by the Council on 4 December: the section on marriage securing 2,047 favourable votes with only 155 against.[1]

The short section on marriage in the schema set the seal of Conciliar approval on the new theology of marital relations. Its whole approach to marriage stresses the idea of the creation of a community of love, as well as the purpose of procreating and educating children. This authentic love between the spouses is caught up into divine love and enriched by it. In a passage which sounds the death knell of Catholic Manicheanism, the schema declares: 'This love is uniquely expressed and perfected through the marital act. The actions within marriage by which the couple are united intimately and chastely are noble and worthy ones. Expressed in a manner which is truly human, these actions signify and promote that mutual self-giving by which spouses enrich each other with a joyful and a thankful will.'

THE PAPAL COMMISSION

Meanwhile, as the deliberations of the Council and its Commission were proceeding, the papal Commission was continuing its work. Its membership was expanded during 1964 and early 1965 and eventually reached a total of sixty-four. The Commission's

---

[1] References to speeches and proceedings at the Council are taken from Xavier Rynne, *Fourth Session* (London, 1966), and *Pope and Pill*, ed. Leo Pyle (London, 1968).

composition was international in character, members coming from the United States, France, Germany, Belgium, Italy, Canada, England, India, Japan, the Netherlands, Spain, Brazil, Chile, Jamaica, Madagascar, the Philippines, Senegal, Switzerland, and Tunis. By disciplines the members included theologians, demographers, economists, doctors, and representatives of the married laity including five women. The enlarged Commission held its first meeting in Rome from 25–28 March 1965. There was no doubt after this meeting, according to Dr Marshall, 'that there was serious doubt about the basis of the Church's teaching'.[1] This was all the more serious in that the Pope had instructed them on 27 March 1965, to answer the question as to what form and according to what norms married couples ought to exercise their love for each other. In February 1966, the Commission was further enlarged by the addition of sixteen cardinals and bishops.[2] Cardinal Ottaviani of the Holy Office was appointed President of the Commission, and Cardinal Heenan of Westminster and Cardinal Doepfner of Munich joint Vice-Presidents. In fact, Cardinal Ottaviani does not seem to have played a prominent part in the Commission's deliberations, and the effective presidency was exercised by Cardinal Heenan and Cardinal Doepfner. The Commission divided itself into various working parties to consider the problems raised by theology, medicine, pastoral requirements, and demographic and social issues. A critical stage was reached on 23 April when the four theologians of the Commission backing the traditional teaching acknowledged that they could not demonstrate the intrinsic evil of contraception on the basis of natural law and rested their case on authority. 'For me,' writes Dr Marshall, 'this was certainly the crisis point in a slow and painful evolution, for if the Church held that contraception was intrinsically evil because it was contrary to natural law, it seemed that able and sincere theologians who earnestly believed in the evil of contraception and had worked

[1] See *The Times*, 3 August 1968.
[2] These were: Cardinals Ottaviani (Holy Office), Heenan (Westminster), Doepfner (Munich), Suenens (Brussels), Shehan (Baltimore), Gracias (Bombay), Lefebvre (Bourges); and Bishops Dupuy (Albi), Binz (St Paul, U.S.A.), Dearden (Detroit, U.S.A.), Reuss (Mainz), Zoa (Cameroons), Woztyla (Cracow), Morris (Cashel), Mendoz (Venezuela), and Colombo (the Vatican).

hard at the problem should be able to demonstrate this with some degree of conviction.'[1]

Fifteen theologians, on the other hand, were in favour of a revision of the traditional teaching. During this session the rival groups of theologians produced conflicting working papers, and eventually on 6, 7, and 8 June 1966, the Commission met in full session to prepare its final report. This was then submitted to a meeting of fifteen of the sixteen cardinals and bishops who had been appointed to the Commission, and who met in Rome from 19–26 June. The cardinals and bishops were assisted by twenty experts, ten theologians, and ten non-theologians. On 21 June, the bishops asked for a draft of a theological report from the theologians, but only those representing the majority view were willing to undertake this. They presented their draft to the cardinals and bishops on 23 June and the text was amended on a number of points. On 24 June, three questions were put to a formal vote. The answer to the fundamental question, namely, 'Is contraception intrinsically wrong?' was 'Yes' – 2; 'Yes, with reservation' – 1; abstained – 3; 'No' – 9. Voting on two other questions which concerned the means of contraception and the wisdom of making a public pronouncement on the issue were of a similar proportion. The theologians, who were members of the Commission, voted 15 to 4 against contraception being considered intrinsically wrong. The final report consisted of an introductory pastoral document drawn up by Monsignor Dupuy, Bishop of Albi, and the theological statement. The report was dated 26 June 1966, and was officially ratified by the Commission on 28 June. It was then taken to the Pope by Cardinal Doepfner and Father de Riedmatten, General Secretary of the Commission.[2] The report of the Commission evidently did not please the Pope, and in the autumn of 1966 he appears to have set up an unofficial commission of six to eight members, dubbed a 'mini commission', to

[1] See *The Times*, 3 August 1968.
[2] These facts have been taken from Jan Grootaers, *Mariage Catholique et Contraception* (Paris, 1968). The way individual cardinals and bishops voted is not known, but it is thought that Cardinal Ottaviani, Bishop Colombo, and Archbishop Morris were against the report and three, Cardinal Heenan, Cardinal Gracias, and Archbishop Binz were doubtful. It is thought also that Cardinal Ottaviani presented a personal document to the Pope outlining his views, dated 1 July 1966, but this document never came before the Commission.

I

give him further advice.[1] The exact composition of this commission is not known, but Bishop Colombo, the Pope's personal theologian, was a member and another member is thought to have been Monsignor Lambruschini. Much of its time seems to have been spent considering a document drawn up by Bishop Colombo which may have been intended as the basis of a draft encyclical. This was never issued owing, it is thought, to the intervention of Cardinal Suenens and Cardinal Doepfner.[2]

Speculation and discussion continued despite the Pope's desire for silence, and the whole controversy was given a new stimulus in April 1967 when the *National Catholic Reporter* in the United States and the *Tablet* in England published what they called the majority and minority reports of the birth control commission together with a 'position paper' setting out the arguments in favour of reform. This nomenclature was, in fact, misleading. What was called the majority report was, in fact, the full report of the Commission. There was never any minority report as such and what appeared under this title was a working paper drawn up by the four theologians of the conservative view and discussed by the Commission. The document called 'The Argument for Reform' was a reply to the working paper and was approved by the sixteen theologians who took the majority view. The first working paper was dated 23 May 1966, and the second 27 May 1966. The full report was dated 26 June 1966, and it was preceded by a fourth document, a pastoral introduction, which was not, in fact, published until 1968. The three documents published in 1966 had been obtained from a private source and there is no doubt that they are genuine.[3]

[1] Cardinal Heenan had evidently expected an early statement by the Pope. In his Trinity pastoral letter issued before the meetings of 6–8 June he had stated: 'Towards the end of the month the meetings of the full commission will be held. Then after prayerful deliberation the Pope will give us the guidance he has promised.' The Cardinal seemed to be hinting that some change or development in the teaching was possible. He wrote: 'The modern outlook is very different from that of 100 years ago. Physical science has revealed new facts about nature. Medicine and psychology have made discoveries about human life itself. Although truth remains the same, our knowledge of it is always increasing. Some of our notions of right and wrong have also undergone change.' See *Guardian* and *Daily Mail*, 6 June 1966.

[2] For an account of this commission, see *On Human Life: an examination of 'Humanae Vitae'* (London, 1968), pp. 23–4.

[3] For an account of the documents see *On Human Life*, pp. 162–9.

The introductory document 'Pastoral Approaches' declares that it was the Council's realisation of the freedom and responsibility of human beings and the experience of married couples which had led the assembled fathers to reaffirm the importance of joint, responsible and generous parenthood. It stresses that what the Church had condemned in the past was rejection of procreation as a purpose of marriage. 'In the past, the Church could not speak other than she did, because the problem of birth control did not confront human consciousness in the same way. Today, having clearly recognised the legitimacy and even the duty of regulating births, she recognises too that human intervention in the process of the marriage act for reasons drawn from the finality of marriage itself should not always be excluded, provided that the criteria of morality are always safeguarded.' The document goes on to give some criteria for lawful means of family planning. These are effectiveness, regard for health, respect for the personal dignity of husband and wife, attention to any possible psychic consequences, and avoidance of any means which would hinder 'expression of an increasingly close union between two persons'. This attitude, says the document, is not a turning back on traditional values but a deepening of them, and adds hopefully, 'the whole of this developed doctrine can only appear to those who reflect on it as an enrichment, in full continuity with the deep, but more rigorous, moral orientations of the past.'[1]

The theological report of the Commission starts off by stressing the essential freedom of man: 'In creating the world, God gave man the power and the duty to form the world in spirit and freedom and, through his creative capacity to actuate his own personal nature.'[2] Yet there are limitations on this freedom, and within marriage what strengthens the union of the two spouses must 'never be separated from the procreative finality which specifies the conjugal community'. The fundamental requirement of a married couple's mission is responsible parenthood: 'they will make a judgement in conscience before God about the number of children to have and educate according to the objective criteria indicated by Vatican Council II.' If they are to observe and

[1] See *On Human Life*, pp. 216–23.
[2] For the text of the report, see *Tablet*, 22 April 1967.

cultivate all the essential values of marriage, 'married people need decent and human means for the regulation of conception'. The report continues that the morality of sexual acts between married people takes its meaning first of all 'from the ordering of their actions in a fruitful married life, that is one which is practised with responsible, generous and prudent parenthood. It does not then depend on the direct fecundity of each and every particular act. An egoistical, hedonistic, and contraceptive way, followed arbitrarily can never be justified.' The document goes on to say that this attitude is not contrary to 'the genuine sense' of the Church's tradition. New factors have come into play including 'social changes in matrimony and the family, especially in the role of the woman; lowering of the infant mortality rate; new bodies of knowledge in biology, psychology, sexuality and demography; a changed estimation of the value and meaning of human sexuality and of conjugal relations; most of all, a better grasp of the duty of man to humanise and to bring to greater perfection for the life of man what is given in nature.'

Coming to the 'objective criteria of morality' which must regulate the choice and the use of birth control methods, the document places the main burden on the consciences of the couples themselves acting together: 'It is impossible to determine exhaustively by a general judgement and ahead of time for each individual case what these objective criteria will demand in the concrete situation of a couple.' A couple will have to take into account the whole complex of values involved by their own welfare and that of their children. Abortion must always be ruled out. Sterilisation should 'generally be excluded'. With regard to the criteria for choosing methods the report states: 'The action must correspond to the nature of the person and of his acts so that the whole meaning of the mutual giving and of human procreation is kept in a context of true love.' Criteria of effectiveness, health, and economics are also relevant. 'Therefore,' concludes the report, 'not arbitrarily, but as the law of nature and of God commands, let couples form a judgement which is objectively founded, with all the criteria considered.'

The working paper of the conservative theologians sets out a very different view.[1] The paper starts off by asking the central question whether contraception is always 'seriously evil'. It defines contraception, as understood by the Church, as 'any use of the marriage right in the exercise of which the act is deprived of its natural power for the procreation of life through human intervention'. The teaching of the Church as shown by the declarations of the bishops and the documents of the papal *magisterium* has consistently taught the intrinsic evil of contraception. In support of this statement, the document refers to the Encyclical *Casti Connubii* of Pius XI: the *Address to Midwives* of Pius XII (1951); and the Encyclical *Mater et Magistra* of John XXIII (1961).[2] The traditional teaching of the Church has dealt with contraception as being analogous to homicide and as an offence against the negative precept 'one may not deprive the conjugal act of its natural power for the procreation of new life'. Certain acts have been treated as 'in some way specially inviolable precisely because they are generative'.

The document then asks why the Church cannot change her teaching. It replies that the teaching cannot be changed because it is true, and seeks to demonstrate its truth by pointing out that the Church instituted by Christ could not have erred during so many centuries on such an important matter. Furthermore the consequences of changing the teaching on the authority of the Church's *magisterium* would be disastrous: 'If the Church could err in such a way, the authority of the ordinary *magisterium* in moral matters would be thrown into question. The faithful could not put their trust in the *magisterium*'s presentation of moral teaching, especially in sexual matters.' Again it would have to be admitted that over long periods of time the Holy Spirit had not been assisting the Catholic Church. 'If contraception were declared not intrinsically evil, in honesty it would have to be acknowledged that the Holy Spirit in 1930, in 1951 and 1958,

[1] For text of the paper, see *Tablet*, 29 April 1967. The paper was subscribed to by four theologians, Fr John Ford, of the Catholic University, Washington, Fr Jan Visser, of the Urban University, Rome, Fr Marcelino Zalba, of the Gregorian University, Rome, and Fr Stanislas de Lestapis. The official report was supported by nineteen theologians.

[2] It might be maintained that the references in *Mater et Magistra*, are not sufficiently specific to be taken as referring to contraception and refer rather to abortion. (See paras. 189, 193, and 194.)

assisted Protestant Churches, and that for half a century Pius XI, Pius XII and a great part of the Catholic hierarchy did not protest against a very serious error, one most pernicious to souls; for it would thus be suggested that they condemned most imprudently, under the pain of eternal punishment, thousands upon thousands of human acts which are now approved. In this matter the Holy Spirit would be found guiding the Anglican Church rather than the Catholic Church. Once the teaching was abandoned that "each and every conjugal act of its very nature has a certain *specific, intrinsic, proper order,* inasmuch as by its nature it is both ordered to the whole reality of procreation, and in that way is ordered as an act of *bestowing life*", the way would be open to all sorts of abuses, it would no longer be possible to condemn extra-marital sexual relationships, or any sexual act in marriage which the parties approved of, e.g. anal or oral intercourse, nor could masturbation be condemned nor sterilisation, nor 'homosexuality.'

These points were answered in a working paper of the majority group.[1] The paper states that *Casti Connubii* does not constitute a true doctrinal definition and that its argument from reason is both vague and imprecise. It constitutes evidence of a tradition, but the essential part of the tradition is not an understanding of the natural law which is inadequate, but a constant concern for protecting the goodness of procreation. The teaching of the Church has been in constant evolution in matrimonial matters and new factors have come into play. Furthermore, the mind of contemporary man has altered: 'He feels that he is more conformed to his rational nature, created by God with liberty and responsibility, when he uses his skill to intervene in the biological processes of nature so that he can achieve the ends of the institution of matrimony in the conditions of actual life, than if he would abandon himself to chance.' In the traditional position, the simple biological conformity of the acts has been adhered to as the determining criterion of morality, but a whole complex of values is now considered. Prominent among these is the obligation of parents to

[1] Published in the *Tablet*, 6 May 1967 under the title 'The Argument for Reform'. It was signed by Fr Joseph Fuchs, S.J., of the Gregorian University, Canon Philippe Delhaye, of the Catholic University of Lille, and Fr Raymond Sigmond, O.P., of the Angelicum, Rome, and approved by a majority of the theologians of the Commission.

educate their children. An obligation of conscience exists for not generating, it springs from the rights of an already existing child or the rights of a future child: 'Therefore the procreative end is substantially and really preserved even when here and now a fertile act is excluded; for infecundity is ordered to a new life well and humanly possessed.' As to the point about opening the way to abuses, the document points out that abortion is an entirely different matter from contraception since it concerns a human life already in existence and such things as oral intercourse are ruled out because they are not consistent with the dignity of love nor that of the spouses. Extra-marital relations are of a different order since they lack the possibility of normally accepting and educating children. Again contraception can be distinguished from masturbation since birth control preserves the inter-subjectivity of sexuality while masturbation denies it.

The Pope was reported to be extremely distressed over the publication of the birth control documents, the more so as those on the Commission had been bound by a personal oath of secrecy to himself.[1] Publication may have been prompted by a desire to pressure the Pope into making a statement, or by fear that the report would be suppressed entirely and never see the light of day. In the event the leaking of the report seems to have delayed the issue of the papal statement which was not issued until fifteen months later.

THE POPE'S POSITION

On 27 March 1965, Pope Paul VI addressed the enlarged birth control Commission. When the Pope did eventually issue his encyclical, he disappointed many, but an examination of his public statements in the period of uncertainty shows that apart from the somewhat ambiguous statement of June 1964, already referred to,[2] he gave no indication that he personally favoured a revision of the traditional teaching. Such indication as he did give of the state of his mind showed that if anything he favoured the maintenance of the *status quo*. That these hints were ignored or

---

[1] See *Catholic Herald*, 21 April 1967.　　[2] See p. 107 above.

explained away by others is an interesting psychological phenomenon. It shows the intensity of their desire for a modification of the traditional attitude, but the Pope said little to encourage them in their hopes.

In his address to the enlarged Commission on 27 March 1965, the Pope outlined their task as follows: 'In the present case, the problem posed can be summed up like this: in what form and according to what norms ought married couples, in exercising their love for each other, to fulfil this life giving function to which their vocation calls them? The Christian answer will always be inspired by an awareness of the duties of the married state, of its dignity – the love of the Christian spouses being ennobled by the grace of the sacrament – and of the grandeur of the gift bestowed upon the child who is called to life.' He then did give a hint of some development when he said: 'If very difficult problems have arisen – the very ones that We are asking you to examine calmly and with full liberty of mind – then doesn't the thorough-going study to which We have just alluded serve as a harbinger of solutions to some problems that at the present day seem so difficult to solve? We like to think so, and to hope so.' The perplexity of the Pope over the whole issue was clearly shown in an interview which appeared in the *Corriere della Sera* on 4 October, of the same year. In what must be regarded as a very untypical papal utterance, he said: 'The world is wondering what We think and We must give an answer. But, what? The Church has never in her history confronted such a problem. This is a strange subject for men of the Church to be discussing, even humanly embarrassing. The Commissions are in session and mountains of reports are piling up. There is a good deal of study going on; but We have to make the decision. This is our responsibility alone. Deciding is not as easy as studying. But We must say something. What? ... God must truly enlighten us.'[1]

The day after the *Corriere* interview had appeared, the Pope made history by appearing before the General Assembly of the United Nations in New York and addressing it on the occasion of its twentieth anniversary. The address made a deep impression

[1] It is perhaps not unfair to comment that most Popes have found it easier to decide than study, rather than the reverse.

on all those who heard it.[1] The Pope was principally concerned with peace, but he also touched upon the question of birth control. 'You proclaim here,' said the Pope, 'the fundamental rights and duties of man, his dignity, his freedom – and, above all, his religious freedom. We feel that you thus interpret the highest sphere of human wisdom and, we might add, its sacred character. For you deal here above all with human life. And the life of man is sacred; no one may dare offend it. Respect for life, even with regard to the great problem of the birth rate, must find here in your Assembly its highest affirmation and its most reasoned defence. You must strive to multiply bread so that it suffices for the tables of mankind, and not rather favour an artificial control of birth, which would be irrational, in order to diminish the number of guests at the banquet of life.' This passage aroused some unfavourable comment, but it was explained by some that the Pope was merely restating the traditional teaching of the Church and was not pre-empting the decision of his birth control Commission. Others pointed out that the statement still left the issue of the legitimacy of the pill open since it might not be classified as an 'artificial' means of birth control.

The next major statement by the Pope on birth control came on 29 October 1966, when he addressed the delegates to the Italian Society of Obstetrics and Gynaecology. After a rather lyrical passage exalting the role of woman, the Pope passed on to the 'delicate' question of the regulation of birth. 'We will only recall here,' said the Pope, 'what we said in our discourse of 23 June 1964 – that is: the thought and the norm of the Church are not changed; they are those in force in the traditional teaching of the Church. The Ecumenical Council recently held brought out certain elements of judgement which are most useful for the integration of Catholic doctrine on this most important subject. But they were not such as to change its substantial elements. Rather they were moved to illustrate it and to prove with authoritative arguments the very deep significance the Church attaches to questions concerning love, matrimony, birth and the family'.

[1] I was present at the address to the United Nations and the Pope gave an impression both of great authority and deep humility. The experience of seeing the tiny white clad figure walking to the rostrum through the ranks of representatives of almost every state in the world was one which I shall never forget.

'The new pronouncement awaited from the Church on the problem of the regulation of births is not thereby given, because we ourselves, having promised and having reserved the matter to ourselves, wanted to consider carefully the doctrinal and pastoral applications which have arisen regarding this problem in recent years, studying them in relation to scientific and experiential data which have been presented to us from every quarter, especially from your medical field and from the field of demography, in order to give the problem its true and worthy solution, which can only be one which is integrally human, that is, moral and Christian. We believe we have taken up the study of these applications and elements of judgement objectively. That seemed to be our obligation; and we have sought to fulfil this obligation in the best way possible, appointing a broad, varied and extremely skilled international Commission.'

The Pope went on to say that the Commission had presented its report but the conclusions could not be considered 'definitive'. It was necessary, he said, to undertake a supplementary study and this was being done. This was why a papal statement had been delayed.

He then went on to deny that there was any doubt in the Church's attitude in a passage which gave rise to some lively comment: 'Meanwhile, as we have already said in the above-mentioned discourse, the norm until now taught by the Church, integrated by the wise instructions of the Council, demands faithful and generous observance. It cannot be considered not binding as if the *magisterium* of the Church were in a state of doubt at the present time, whereas it is rather in a moment of study and reflection concerning matters which have been put before it as worthy of the most attentive consideration.' This distinction between 'a state of doubt' and a 'moment of study and reflection' was not immediately obvious to all.[1]

In March 1967, the Pope issued his encyclical *Populorum*

---

[1] See, for example, the editorial by Charles Davies, *Clergy Review*, December 1966. He explained the papal statement about 'doubt' as excluding a state of doubt in a juridical sense which means that the Pope did not recognise a sufficient degree of uncertainty to allow the law on birth control to be regarded as a doubtful law and therefore not binding. Cf. 'Contraception: A Matter of Practical Doubt', by J. C. Ford, S.J. and J. J. Lynch, S.J., *Homiletic and Pastoral Review* (April 1968), p. 563.

Progressio on the developing world and the relationship between the rich and the poor nations. The Encyclical gave its approval to family planning and its promotion by the state, but it warned that there was a 'temptation' to check the demographic increase by means of radical measures. The Encyclical declared that it was for parents to decide 'with full knowledge of the matter, on the number of their children, taking into account their responsibilities towards God, themselves, the children they have already brought into the world, and the community to which they belong. In all this they must follow the demands of their own conscience enlightened by God's law authentically interpreted, and sustained by confidence in Him.' This, to quote a currently fashionable phrase, left all the options open.

OTHER EVENTS

A number of other events of importance in the development of the Catholic debate may conveniently be grouped together and noted here. In 1965 Professor John Noonan published his definitive study of the treatment of the question of birth control by Catholic theologians and canonists over the centuries.[1] The book clearly showed the strength and tenacity of the Catholic condemnation of contraception from early times, and as such was seized upon by upholders of the traditional position.[2] Professor Noonan, himself however, drew other lessons from his researches and concluded that the maintenance of the essentials of the Catholic traditional position was not incompatible with revision of the ban on contraception.

Other members of the laity made important contributions to the discussion. In October 1964 a private address on the subject of family problems signed by an international group of 120 laymen was submitted to the Pope and the Council. It called for a reappraisal of the teaching on family life in general and of birth control in particular.[3] In May 1966 a second memorandum

[1] *Contraception* (Harvard, 1965).
[2] In the working paper of the conservative theologians on the papal birth control Commission, there is a reference to 'the excellent work of Professor John T. Noonan'.
[3] In March 1965 a conference of thirty-nine American Catholic scholars (including twenty-six priests) meeting at Notre Dame University drew up a statement explaining

on the *magisterium* of the Church and family problems was sent to the Pope and all Catholic archbishops. The document, compiled in four languages (French, Italian, German, and English) was signed by 550 laymen from eighteen countries. The signatories included doctors, sociologists, demographers, population experts and others. It expressed concern that the doctrine of marriage formulated by the Council was not finding full expression in the moral, theological, and pastoral fields due to certain reactionary influences. It pointed out that methods of birth control, based on continence, were 'particularly unsuitable remedies for the great demographical problems'. In more technically advanced countries, the great majority of married couples were forced, often to their regret, to practise some form of birth control during the greater part of their married life. 'The Church,' stated the memorandum, 'cannot take the responsibility before history of minimising one of the main problems which humanity must face, let alone of constituting an obstacle to general research into real solutions: humanity expects a positive moral contribution from one of the great spiritual forces of the world.' In present conditions, it continued, it was no longer possible to consider the total preservation of the biological order as a *sine qua non* condition of human integrity. The laymen expressed their anxiety about tendencies suggesting that the problem should be solved on the disciplinary and pastoral level simply by maintaining old directives, which had become doubtful. They concluded by calling for a spirit of open inquiry and intensified research.[1]

The theme was returned to by the Third World Congress for the Lay Apostolate Meeting in Rome from 11–18 October 1967. The Congress passed a resolution which drew attention to 'the very strong feeling among Christian lay people that there is a need for a clear study by the *teaching authorities of the Church* which would focus on fundamental, moral and spiritual values, while leaving the choice of scientific and technical means for achieving responsible

---

why they found the Catholic Church's 'conventional position' on birth control 'unconvincing'. A majority of the group found that 'contraception is not intrinsically immoral'. These findings were sent to the papal birth control Commission and eventually reached its members. See *Catholic Herald*, 15 October 1965.
[1] See *Herder Correspondence*, September–October 1966.

parenthood to parents acting in accordance with their Christian faith and on the basis of medical and scientific consultation.'[1]

In the same month, the first Synod of Catholic Bishops met in Rome, but were prevented from discussing birth control which was excluded from their agenda.

One other development should be noted. On 4 December 1966, Fr Charles Davis, editor of the *Clergy Review*, and one of England's leading theologians, decided to leave the Catholic Church. One factor leading to his decision was the papal statement of 29 October 1966, which has already been referred to. Mr Davis accused the Pope of making a false statement 'to protect the authority of the Holy See and out of fear of the consequences, both theoretical and practical, of admitting that the teaching authority of the Church was uncertain in such a matter'.[2] In an article published in the *Observer* on 1 January 1967, Mr Davis wrote: 'One who claims to be the moral leader of mankind should not tell lies.' Mr Davis's remark was somewhat uncharitable and gave offence to many Catholics. He subsequently explained that he did not leave the Church because he thought Paul VI was a sinner and a dishonest man, but referred to the statement because it 'so vividly illustrated the defects of the social structure of the Church and its lack of credibility as the embodiment of Christian faith and love'.[3]

[1] The resolution was voted on by the heads of delegations and was passed by 67 'for' to 31 votes 'against' with 10 abstentions. On hearing the result the 3,000 delegates broke into spontaneous applause.
[2] See Charles Davis: *A Question of Conscience* (London, 1967), pp. 96–7. Chapter IV is devoted to 'The Pope and Birth Control'.
[3] Op. cit., p. 98.

CHAPTER V

The Encyclical and its Aftermath

In the first six months of 1968 sporadic rumours came from Rome that the Pope was about to issue a definitive statement on birth control, but these rumours had circulated so many times before without any concrete result that they were given little credence. In July they became more insistent, and over the weekend of 27 to 28 July it became clear in Rome that the issue of a statement was imminent. This took the form of the encyclical *Humanae Vitae*, which was in fact published on the morning of Monday, 29 July – the long period of suspense was at an end.[1]

There have been many reports of the actual genesis of the Encyclical but in the nature of things it is impossible at this point to establish definitively the truth of the matter. It is believed that the final draft of the Encyclical was written by the Pope, or at any rate amended by him. His principal consultant in the drafting was Bishop Carlo Colombo, his personal theologian. Fr Gustave Martelet, the French Jesuit is also believed to have played a leading part in the drafting. There seem to have been a number of

[1] The text was never available before the last week in July outside a small circle of papal advisers but it appears that some attempts were made to dissuade the Pope from publishing it. It is understood that Cardinal Suenens had written to the Pope, although he had not seen the text, requesting him not to issue an encyclical on his own authority but to make it a collegial act of all the bishops. It has also been reported that Cardinal Doepfner of Munich and Cardinal Koenig of Vienna also intervened with the Pope. The members who had put forward the majority report of the Commission were not consulted. Fr Häring has stated, 'We had no possibility to approach the Pope. In my eyes he was walled in.' See *Tablet*, 31 August 1968.

drafts, and one already existed at the time of the meeting of the Synod of Bishops in Rome in October 1967. The Encyclical was evidently finally finished in the first half of July and handed over to translators and then to the secret section of the Vatican Press. The *Tablet* has reported that the first copies of the Encyclical were sent out to papal representatives on 20 July with instructions that the text was to be released to the bishops on 27 July.[1]

The Encyclical, which is not a lengthy document (it runs to only thirty-eight pages of large type in the official English translation), opens with a declaration that the duty of transmitting human life belongs to the married couples who are the free and responsible collaborators with God the Creator, and that this has been a source of great joy as well as of difficulty. It then sets out the various changes which have taken place in modern times. It points out that the world population is growing more rapidly than available resources, that modern living conditions have made the education 'of an elevated number of children' difficult, that woman's place in society has changed, and that there has been a re-evaluation of the place of conjugal love. It stresses that man has made great progress in dominating and organising the forces of nature. These changes raise the question whether, in fact, the time has not come for modern man to trust his reason and his will rather than the biological rhythms of his organism in the task of regulating birth. The Encyclical states that it is the duty of the teaching authority of the Church to answer this question. The Pope explains that in order to assist him to reach a decision in this matter he had appointed a Commission of experts and consulted a number of bishops, and he expresses to them his sense of 'our lively gratitude'. Despite the value of these conclusions and recommendations the final decision of necessity rested with the Pope, the more so because 'within the Commission itself, no full concordance of judgements concerning the moral norms to be proposed had been reached, and above all because certain criteria of solutions had emerged which departed from the moral teaching on marriage proposed with constant firmness by the teaching authority of the Church'.

The Encyclical goes on to describe conjugal love, which has its

[1] See *Tablet*, 17 August 1968.

origin in God. Marriage is not the effect of chance or evolution but the wise institution of the Creator to realise in mankind his design of love. Conjugal love, states the Encyclical, is human, total, faithful, exclusive, and fecund. It is destined to raise up new lives. It requires from husband and wife an awareness of their mission of 'responsible parenthood'. 'In relation to the biological processes responsible parenthood means the knowledge and respect of their functions; human intellect discovers in the power of giving life biological laws which are part of the human person.' Responsible parenthood can be exercised either by the decision to raise a numerous family, or by one 'made for grave motives and with due respect for the moral law, to avoid for the time being, or even for an indeterminate period, a new birth'.

The Encyclical, in paragraphs 11 and 12, then comes to the heart of its teaching. It first states that the acts by which the husband and wife are united and by means of which human life is transmitted are noble and worthy, 'and they do not cease to be lawful if, for causes independent of the will of husband and wife, they are foreseen to be infecund, since they always remain ordained towards expressing and consolidating their union'. God has provided natural laws and rhythms of fecundity which cause a separation in the succession of births. 'None the less the Church calling men back to the observance of the norms of the natural law, as interpreted by her constant doctrine, teaches that each and every marriage act (*quilibet matrimonii usus*) must remain open to the transmission of life.'

This teaching is based upon 'the inseparable connection willed by God and unable to be broken by man on his own initiative, between the two meanings of the conjugal act: the unitive meaning and the procreative meaning. Indeed by its intimate structure, the conjugal act, while most closely uniting husband and wife, capacitates them for the generation of new lives, according to laws inscribed in the very being of man and of woman.'

Applying these principles, the Encyclical states: 'We must once again declare that the direct interruption of the generative process already begun, and, above all, directly willed and procured abortion, even if for therapeutic reasons, are to be absolutely excluded as licit means of regulating birth.' It condemns perpetual or temporary sterilisation, either of the man or of the woman! Similarly excluded is any action which 'either in anticipation of the conjugal act, or in its accomplishment, or in the development of its natural consequences, proposes, whether as an end or as a means, to render procreation impossible'. Contraception, says the Encyclical, is 'something which is intrinsically disorder, and hence unworthy of the human person, even when the intention is to safeguard or promote individual, family or social well being'.

The Encyclical, however, does allow 'the use of those therapeutic means truly necessary to cure diseases of the organism, even if an impediment to procreation, which may be foreseen, should result therefrom, provided such impediment is not, for whatever motive, directly willed'. The Church also allows the use of the natural rhythms in the generative functions to space out births provided this is done for serious motives. This is quite different from contraception: In the former, 'the married couple make legitimate use of a natural disposition; in the latter, they impede the development of natural processes.'

Humanae Vitae goes on to warn of the consequences of using contraceptives. A wide and easy road would be opened up towards conjugal infidelity and a general lowering of morality. It is also to be feared, states the Encyclical, 'that the man, growing used to the employments of anti-conceptive practices, may finally lose respect for the woman and, no longer caring for her physical and psychological equilibrium, may come to the point of considering her as a mere instrument of selfish enjoyment, and no longer as his respected and beloved companion.' It would also open the way for governments to impose any method of contraception which they pleased.

The final section of the Encyclical is concerned with 'pastoral directives'. These concede that the observance of the law laid down in the Encyclical is difficult, especially in the modern world where the media of social communications lead 'to sense excitation and unbridled customs, as well as every form of pornography and licentious performances . . . vainly would one seek to justify such depravation with the pretext of artistic or scientific exigencies'. The Pope appeals to rulers not to 'permit that by legal means

K

practices contrary to the natural and divine law be introduced into that fundamental cell, the family'. The Encyclical reverts to the population problem, but stresses that it may not be alleviated by unlawful means. The Pope appeals to men of science to provide 'a sufficiently secure basis for a regulation of birth, founded on the observance of natural rhythms'.

The Encyclical then addresses itself to married couples, and appreciates the difficulties which face them. 'If,' it declares, 'sin should still keep its hold over them, let them not be discouraged, but rather have recourse with humble perseverance to the mercy of God, which is poured forth in the sacrament of penance.' The Pope then appeals to priests to 'expound the Church's teaching on marriage without ambiguity'. He asks them to set an example 'of loyal internal and external obedience to the teaching authority of the Church'. The Encyclical ends with an appeal to the bishops, to Catholics, and 'to all men of good will' to observe the laws 'written by God in human nature'.

Humanae Vitae was launched at a Press conference in Rome by Monsignor Lambruschini. He made it clear that the Pope did not intend the Encyclical to be an infallible document: 'Most of the theologians, while admitting that the *magisterium* can define infallibly some of the aspects of natural law, explicitly or implicitly contained in Revelation, consider that this has not yet come to pass in the field of morals. Attentive reading of the Encyclical *Humanae Vitae* does not suggest the theological note of infallibility; this is also shown by a simple comparison with the Profession of Faith proclaimed on 30 June during the solemn rite in St Peter's Square.'[1] Monsignor Lambruschini went on to demand obedience to the teaching of the Encyclical: 'Those who in recent times uncautiously believed, even in good faith, that they could teach the lawfulness of using artificial contraceptive practices for the regulation of births and behave accordingly in pastoral directives and in the ministry of confession, must change their views and give the example by full adhesion to the teachings of the Encyclical.' This appeal was given piquancy by the fact that Monsignor

[1] See *Pope and Pill*, p. 103. It is understood that in one of the drafts presented to the Pope the words 'ex infallibile auctoritate' were contained, but the infallible reference was struck out by the Pope.

Lambruschini himself had been one of those who had supported the majority recommendations of the Papal Commission.[1]

WORLD REACTIONS

The Encyclical was the subject of comment throughout the world within hours of its appearance. Some welcomed its issue, but the overwhelming majority of secular comment was hostile to its conclusions. Catholic opinion was divided, some giving the Encyclical wholehearted support and others condemning it. The timing of the issue of the Encyclical at the end of July at the opening of 'the silly season', when there is a world-wide shortage of news, meant that it was to dominate the front pages for many days until it was driven off them by the Soviet invasion of Czechoslovakia.

THE POSITION OF BRITAIN

Interest in Britain in the Encyclical was intense. It became the subject of comment and correspondence in the daily papers, especially *The Times*, the *Guardian*, and the *Daily Telegraph*, as well as in the weeklies such as the *Economist* and the *New Statesman*. These papers were virtually unanimous in their rejection of the Encyclical. The *Economist* described the Encyclical as 'a tragedy for the world and a disaster for the Roman Catholic Church'. It conceded that it would not have been reasonable to have expected the Pope to give a blanket approval to contraception, but then it was not reasonable either to expect a flouting of the majority report of his own Commission. 'What was reasonable to anticipate was a moderate and balanced restatement of Catholic general principles on marriage and childbearing, leaving it to individual Catholic theologians, scientists and doctors to work out in practice their application in the changed conditions of the modern world.' Instead of this there had come a rigorous restatement without modification or qualification of any kind of the old scholastic position that contraception is intrinsically evil. Low churchmen, suggested the *Economist*, would regard the claim of an 'Italian

[1] He was subsequently rewarded for his loyalty by being raised to the episcopate.

bachelor' to be the voice of God on matters of human sexuality as a manifestation of 'the sin against the Holy Ghost'.[1]

The first Catholic reaction came in a 'Panorama' television broadcast on the evening the Encyclical was issued. Five Catholics, the Bishop of Leeds, Lady Antonia Fraser, the President of the National Board of Catholic Women, Dr Edward Larkin, a psychiatrist, and myself, were assembled to give our opinions. Lady Antonia said that she was 'passionately disappointed', and regretted the Encyclical's male-orientated approach. The President of the Catholic Women, on the other hand, was profoundly relieved that the Pope had spoken. Nevertheless she conceded that a certain number of her members would be disappointed and that the young would be very angry. I expressed my strong condemnation of the Encyclical, saying: 'I have lived as a Catholic, and pray God I shall die as a Catholic. And I have never uttered a word of criticism of the Pope in public, but I should be failing in my duty, both to my fellow Catholics and to the people of Britain, if I concealed my opinion of this document, which I have studied closely, and which today I have read three times. I feel, and this is my considered judgement upon it, that it is extreme, that it is partial, at the same time it is inadequate, and by the violence of its language, it will create more problems than it solves. It would have been better, I think, for the Church if such a document had never been issued.'[2] Bishop Wheeler expressed his support for the Encyclical and praised it for its wise counsel to bishops and priests. In a hundred years' time the world not just the Church would thank the Pope for what he had said. At the same time the bishop stated that a person must always follow his own conscience, even when it was an erroneous one. Therefore the laity 'will do right to follow their conscience, if it leads them elsewhere, though

---

[1] See *Economist*, 3 August 1968. The use of the phrase 'Italian bachelor' and the rest of the article aroused *L'Osservatore Romano* to fury. It attacked the *Economist* denouncing the article and the personal reference to the Pope, as worse than the lowest type of journalism produced in the days of the Weimar Republic. It was not clear however whether it was the adjective that was objected to or the noun. It was rumoured in London that I was responsible for this inappropriate and ill-judged phrase but this was not true, although I had some influence in the article.

[2] Rereading this statement two years later, I would not modify it in essentials but I feel that I rather underestimated its compassion and would not today have referred to its language as 'violent'. 'Archaic' would be a more suitable word.

objectively speaking I don't think it would be a true conscience'.[1]

The division among English Catholics seen in the 'Panorama' broadcast was reflected in the attitudes of the Catholic Press. The *Tablet*, the most influential Catholic paper, and the *Catholic Herald* were critical of the Encyclical, while the *Universe*, the most popular Catholic paper, supported it. In a leading article, the *Tablet* insisted that the debate should go on, the Pope's words had a dominant place in the debate but had not brought it to an end. 'Loyalty to the Faith and to the whole principle of authority now consists in this,' declared the *Tablet*, 'to speak out about this disillusion of ours, not to be silenced by fear.'[2] The *Catholic Herald* published two articles from different points of view, one by Archbishop Murphy of Cardiff and the second by myself. The Archbishop of Cardiff gave the fullest support to the Encyclical, which he claimed would be hailed 'as the Magna Carta, not merely of all women but of all men and all children'. The Archbishop went on to state: 'If this Encyclical has proved anything, it has proved in these matters of interpreting the natural law that all honesty, all compassion, all erudition, all theological acumen is of little account.' Far from undermining the position of women, the Encyclical had consolidated it: 'The Pope has refused to bow to the compassionate plea of those who in a sincere desire to strip woman of her anxieties would strip her of all dignity and status and reduce her to a mere chattel of her lord.'[3] In my article I wrote that because of the theological emptiness of the Encyclical and its begging of so many questions that, while it might 'ask for obedience' it could not command intellectual assent. I concluded that the Encyclical had shown that in the modern world the papal centralised system of government needed to be radically reformed and collegiality translated from a theory to a fact: 'A way must be found of associating the laity at every level with the government of the Church.' That week a group of Catholics,

[1] After this broadcast I received very many letters which were 30–1 in favour of my views. Asked by some whether they should leave the Church I replied: 'No, you must remain and follow your conscience'. One correspondent hailed me as 'the "Dubcek" of the Catholic Church', but I had mixed feelings about another who wrote: 'Enoch Powell has saved us from domination by the Blacks and you have saved us from subjugation by something worse than Communism, namely Catholicism.' See *The Times*, 5 August 1968.

[2] 3 August 1968.   [3] *Catholic Herald*, 2 August 1968.

including myself, sent a letter to the Pope through the Apostolic Delegation taking the view that despite the Encyclical the question remained an open one and discussion should continue: 'We believe that it continues to be the responsibility of individual Christians to come by the light of conscience and reason, to their own decisions concerning the manner and mode of family planning.'[1] No comment on the Encyclical came from the English bishops as such at this stage, indeed in the manner in which it had been sprung upon them it was hardly possible for them to make a considered statement, and Cardinal Heenan contented himself with a terse declaration that the Encyclical was 'clear enough. This is no snap decision. Pope Paul consulted every possible authority.'[2]

Catholics did not confine themselves to expressing their opinions in the Catholic Press but used all the secular media of communications to make their views known. For weeks a correspondence raged in *The Times*. It opened on 31 July with a letter from Dr John Marshall, a member of the papal Commission on birth control. 'I feel compelled,' said Dr Marshall, 'to dissociate myself from the statement in the papal Encyclical that artificial birth control opens a wide and easy road towards conjugal infidelity and general lowering of morality, and may cause men to consider their wives as a mere instrument of selfish enjoyment.' There was no scientific evidence to support this assertion which moreover cast 'a gratuitous slur which I greatly regret on the countless responsible married people who practise contraception, and whose family life is an example to all.' A letter of mine published the same day made a broader criticism of the Encyclical. 'All reasonable men will sympathise with the Pope's dilemma', I wrote, 'but sympathy, or even loyalty to the Pope, must not blind one's judgement to the theological barrenness of the Encyclical, to its lack of reality, and its imprudence. To call upon public authorities in our contemporary pluralist society to place a ban on contraception shows a divorce from the facts of the contemporary world which is both incredible and alarming.' Catholics, I went on, do not require compassion in the confessional as had been

---

[1] So far as I know, no reply was ever received to this letter.
[2] Bishop Gordon Wheeler set out his views in 'The Case for the Encyclical', *Spectator*, 2 August 1968. I replied to this, see *Spectator*, 9 August.

suggested by the Bishop of Leeds but freedom and responsibility. I stressed once again the need for the establishment in the future of a genuine system of shared counselling and responsibility, in which case the 'sad Encyclical' might even do some good.[1]

The Times received letters on the Encyclical at the rate of a thousand a week, and at times so great was the flood of correspondence that the entire leader page, apart from the editorial articles, was given over to the expression of various points of view. Some correspondents wrote maintaining that the Pope was upholding the plain teaching of Christ in the Encyclical. Others thought it misguided, but stated their intention of remaining within the Church and raising their voice in order to secure a change from within. Problems raised by population growth were stressed by others. The delay in issuing the Encyclical was criticised. One correspondent asked for guidance as to whether or not he should leave the Church. Mr Malcolm Muggeridge, writing as a 'dubious Christian', paid tribute to the Pope's 'noble statement on birth control'. Obviously, Mr Muggeridge continued, 'his words are not going to be heeded by large numbers of his co-religionists, who are clearly resolved to join in the pursuit of happiness, American style – a Gadarene slide which will infallibly take them, as it has the rest of us, towards acceptance of easy divorce, promiscuity and abortion.'[2] A former priest wrote to say that those who possessed an 'erroneous conscience' on a moral issue were not obliged to live outside the Roman Catholic Church. Fr Peter de Rosa declared that while the Pope's teaching on contraception was not infallible it was authoritative, but added that only time would show if it were Catholic. 'Gregory XVI has proved that a teaching is not Catholic simply because a Pope proposes it. The Catholic people and their hierarchies have yet to express the Catholic mind in its fullness.' One correspondent,

---

[1] A later correspondent, Mr Ronald Flaxman, writing in The Times on 1 August, characterised my letter as 'insolent'. I replied on 5 August: 'To be insolent is to be insulting in some way and the assumption that because one disagrees with the Pope one is insulting him is radically false. Slaves prostrate themselves before their masters: sons, when they are of age, sometimes stand up in the household and contradict their father. That is not a mark of insolence but maturity. That is the heart of the present dispute. The laity of the Church have come of age, they are expressing their minds to the Holy Father. This is an act of love and trust not of contumely and insult.'
[2] The Times, 2 August 1968.

Fr T. A. McGoldrick, Catholic chaplain to the University of Liverpool, suggested the summoning of a Council, and a new point was reached on Monday, 5 August, when Fr Brocard Sewell, a Carmelite of Aylesford Priory, called for the resignation of the Pope. 'The present Pope,' wrote Father Sewell, 'a few years ago made a significant pilgrimage to the tomb of San Celestine. If he would now resign his See, as did St Celestine, and make it possible for one of the Oriental Patriarchs to succeed him, the Latin Church might yet be saved from an ignominious dissolution. In the meantime, until we are censured for doing so, many of us who have pastoral responsibilities of one kind or another will continue to bear in the mind the maxim: *'Impossibili nemo tenetur'*.

Father Richard Incledon, Catholic chaplain at Cambridge, wrote to say that he intended to allow married couples to approach the sacraments: 'If conscience directs them to use methods not permitted by the Encyclical *Humanae Vitae*, they can communicate freely without regarding the practice as sinful or even speaking of it in the confessional. I intend to go on giving this advice to anyone who seeks my counsel.'[1] All this was too much for the Vicar of Dagenham, the Rev. E. P. C. Paterson, who wrote a brief letter: 'Sir, – Article 37 of the National Church, the Church of England, states: "The Bishop of Rome (i.e. the Pope) hath no jurisdiction in this Realm of England." One has some sympathy with the Vicar.

Meanwhile various other priests were making their views known. On 3 August, Monsignor Anthony Reynolds, of the diocese of Southwark, published an open letter to the Pope which he sent to the Apostolic Delegate protesting against the Encyclical. The letter was sent 'on behalf of the suffering people of my parish'. He said that as doubt still remained people were still free to follow their own consciences in the matter.[2] On Sunday, 4 August, Dr

---

[1] In fact no action was taken against Fr Incledon, possibly because the chaplain at Cambridge is appointed by the entire hierarchy and not by an individual bishop.
[2] A week later Monsignor Reynolds apologised for his 'impetuosity'. He stated: 'Further reflection makes me realise that there is a third way: that the teaching of the Pope will gradually become accepted by all. . . . May I give my advice to priests who find they cannot give intellectual assent to the Encyclical. They are official spokesmen for the Pope and their bishop, and can in good conscience promulgate such teaching.' See *The Times*, 10 August 1968. Almost exactly a year later, Monsignor Reynolds announced that once again he had changed his opinion. He had reverted to his original rejection of the Encyclical. See *The Times*, 26 July 1969.

P. J. Fitzpatrick, a priest of St Cuthbert's, Hartlepool, Durham, announced that he was the author of a book on birth control severely criticising the Catholic official position which had been published under a pseudonym two years earlier.[1] In a sermon preached on the Sunday, Dr Fitzpatrick declared: 'That the use of contraception is a matter for decision for a married couple', and regretted the turning of the Pope into 'an oracle'. In a statement to *The Times*, Dr Fitzpatrick gave his opinion: 'In any crisis there are two ways of going about things. Diplomacy is one, but it has its limitations. There comes a time when diplomacy is not enough and when a way must be taken of publishing a manifestation of one's opinions, because if we remain silent we are acquiescing in a position we believe to be wrong, and failing to show the extent of diversity of opinion which exists in the Church.'[2] Another priest to make his views known was Fr Thomas Corbishley, a leading Jesuit, who stated: 'I think it is very sad for the image of the Church throughout the world. In many ways Pope Paul has tried to bring the Church up to date but he has set us back several centuries.'[3] Archbishop Roberts declared that people had been making their own decision on the matter and would continue to do so.

Another form of criticism of a less radical variety concentrated on the translation of the Encyclical. This, according to the *Guardian*, had aroused the indignation of both Cardinal Heenan and Archbishop Cardinale, the Apostolic Delegate. The Apostolic Delegate was reported as intending to take up the matter with the Vatican. The Catholic Truth Society commissioned another translation to be undertaken by Monsignor Alan Clark.[4]

[1] The book was 'Birth Regulation and Catholic Belief', by G. Egner. Dr Fitzpatrick explained that the word 'Egner' was a simple pun on *Gegner* the German word for adversary. 'My reason for doing this was not to secure anonymity – I gather the authorship has become an open secret in ecclesiastical circles. It was to avoid a confrontation with episcopal authority before it was absolutely necessary.'

[2] See *The Times*, 5 August 1968. Fr Fitzpatrick was in difficulties with the bishop after this statement, but on giving an undertaking not to preach on this subject the bishop allowed the matter to rest.

[3] *Catholic Herald*, 2 August 1968.

[4] See the *Guardian*, 17 August 1968, whose news item opened with the words 'Move Over Norman'. Mgr Clark, a strong supporter of the Encyclical was created auxiliary Bishop of Northampton in 1969. The criticisms of the Vatican English version seem to be justified since the language is certainly tortuous and rather grates on English

Reactions of Other Churches in England

By an ironical coincidence the Lambeth Conference which had by its liberal attitude to birth control in 1930 provoked the previous Encyclical *Casti Connubii*, was once again in session in London when *Humanae Vitae* was issued. The Archbishop of Canterbury in a statement to a special meeting of the steering committee of the Conference on 30 July stressed that the teaching in the Encyclical was quite different from that of the Anglican Communion. In a personal comment the Bishop of Cariboo, the Secretary of the Conference said: 'I think it will cause great disappointment to many people – Roman Catholics, of course. We feel the deepest sympathy with millions of lay people and a not inconsiderable number of clergy and bishops who will be equally disappointed.' Bishop Moorman, the Bishop of Ripon, and a leading ecumenist, stated that the papal announcement was not a setback to talks between the two Churches.[1] Later the Lambeth Conference reaffirmed the teaching formulated in 1958, but speakers refrained from any sharp criticism of the Pope although some, like the Bishop of Western Missouri, stressed their belief that contraception enhanced marriage. Thanks to the Conference's restraint relations between Rome and Canterbury were not embittered by the issue of the Encyclical.[2]

---

ears, e.g. the reference to the education of 'an elevated number of children'. One sentence in the English translation does not appear in the Latin at all, namely the statement: 'Though we are thinking also of all men of goodwill, we now address ourself particularly to our sons from whom we expect a prompter and more generous adherence.' This precedes the section on pastoral directives. Probably what happened was that this passage was cut from the Latin text and the necessary emendation of the English translation was then overlooked.

[1] See *Church Times*, 2 August 1968.

[2] For speeches at the Lambeth Conference, see *The Times*, 6 and 7 August 1968. A group of Catholics, including myself, asked the Lambeth Bishops for their prayers, as well as making this request of the British Council of Churches and the World Council of Churches. When Cardinal Heenan was preaching from the pulpit at St Paul's Cathedral at a united service on 22 January 1969 he thanked the Anglicans for their forbearance. 'They issued no criticism or condemnation. Our Community, embarrassed by attacks on the Pope from some of its own members, was grateful beyond measure for the forbearance and compassion shown by the Anglicans. I have deliberately awaited this opportunity of speaking in St Paul's Cathedral to express our appreciation of this act of friendship', *The Times*, 23 January 1969. What the Cardinal did not add was that the Anglicans of course having thrown off the jurisdiction of the Pope at the Reformation had no need to criticise him. They were not directly affected by the Encyclical because it had no authority for them. Catholics owing allegiance to Rome were in a very different position.

The British Council of Churches gave a firm assurance of its sympathy and prayers to Catholics standing out against the Pope's Encyclical. This was in reply to the letter sent to the Council by myself and others. The Secretary of the Council, Bishop Kenneth Sansbury, said he had felt it right to respond to the signatories with 'a firm assurance that their request would be met'. 'No wonder,' commented the Bishop, 'many are openly rebellious, believing that the decision is mainly due to the desire to preserve traditional authority, while others are taking refuge in the fact that the Encyclical is not an infallible utterance and are treating the issue as still open.' The Greek Orthodox Archbishop, Athenagoras, Head of the Orthodox Church in the British Isles and Scandinavia, in a letter to his priests pointed out that within the Orthodox Church a system of co-operation was practised to solve marriage problems involving the couples themselves, the priest confessor and the family doctor. He said that the Encyclical contained elements that were 'praiseworthy and which must attract the attention of all conscientious Christians'.[1]

Further Developments in England
Meanwhile the English laity organised their own protests led by a specially formed *Ad Hoc* group of lay men and women.[2] They set aside Saturday, 17 August, for prayer demonstrations and Catholics were asked to attend their local cathedrals and to say special prayers at noon.[3] Sunday, 18 August, was also set aside as a special day of prayer. On that same Sunday at the National Pilgrimage of Catholics at Walsingham in Norfolk, the Abbot of Downside, Dom Wilfrid Passmore, rebuked critics of the Encyclical. 'Do you want the Pope to give his judgement as the Vicar of Christ?' asked the Abbot, 'or do you want the Pope to approve

[1] See *The Times*, 9 August 1968.
[2] Prominent members of this group which was later to develop into the *Renewal Movement*, were Mr and Mrs Patricia Worden, Mr and Mrs Anthony Spencer, Dr Oliver and Mrs Pratt, Dr Monica Lawler. I was never a member of this group but remained in close touch with it.
[3] I attended the 'Pray-In' at Westminster Cathedral with my aunt, a convert from Anglicanism who announced that she was 'all for the Pope'. When approached by an organiser saying that they were praying for freedom of conscience, she replied: 'I have never heard such nonsense in all my life.' These remarks were subsequently reported in the *Observer*, 18 August 1968.

your own private views? That is the issue and don't run away from it.' The same day a former Abbot of Downside, Bishop Butler, auxiliary Bishop of Westminster, upheld the rights of conscience in a sermon preached at Guildford Anglican Cathedral. 'The rights of conscience (a conscience which has tried to instruct itself adequately) are absolute', declared the Bishop. 'And wherever conscience is aroused, there is bound to be heart searching and fierce debate; all the more when what is involved is not only happiness but the basic conditions of human existence and social life.'[1] On Monday, 19 August, a further sensation was caused by the news that Fr Brocard Sewell, who had written to *The Times* calling for the Pope to resign, had been suspended from preaching and hearing confessions.

Fr Sewell lived in the diocese of Southwark, and trouble had already arisen there over priests who had publicly criticised the Encyclical. The controversy centred round Fr Paul Weir of St Cecilia's, North Cheam. In the absence of the Archbishop of Southwark on holiday, the Vicar-General, Monsignor Gibney, stated that he could not allow Fr Weir to preach or hear confessions. His other public priestly functions were allowed to continue.[2] On 18 August, a group of young people from Fr Weir's parish marched in protest from Westminster Cathedral to St George's Cathedral, Southwark. They carried banners, one of them declaring: '1968 youth need 1968 priests'. The procession of more than a hundred, including children and babies in perambulators, was orderly throughout.

The suspension of certain priests who had made their views known in criticism of the Encyclical convinced me that something further needed to be done to hold the position. The laity protest had been spontaneous and to a certain degree effective, but if priests were not able to speak their minds it was clear that the

[1] See *Tablet*, 24 August 1968.
[2] Another priest suspended in the diocese of Southwark was Fr David Payne of St Joseph's, New Malden, Surrey. Like Fr Weir, Fr Payne was a curate. Mgr Gibney, the Vicar-General of the Archdiocese caused much controversy by his statement concerning Fr Weir. 'He does not know it, but when he is out of the parish he will not matter any more.' Fr Weir's parishioners were incensed by their pastor's suspension and a group organised what was intended to be an all-night 'sit-in' at St George's Cathedral, Southwark on Friday, 16 August. The 'sit-in' was brought to an end when the Administrator of the Cathedral, Mgr Canon Bogan, called the police. The protestors then left the cathedral.

battle would be lost. Accordingly, in company with a number of sympathisers, I launched a Freedom of Conscience Fund on 3 September 1968 in order to provide support for those priests who were suffering want because of the stand they had taken.[1] The problem was a very real one, since Catholic priests in England rarely have private means or large savings. I also felt that the existence of such a fund would discourage those bishops who were inclined to take a hard line from proceeding to extreme courses. The trustees of the Fund, apart from myself, were Lady Asquith, Dr Anthony Boyle, and Mr Anthony Spencer.[2] At the time the Fund was launched eleven priests were under suspension for opposing the Encyclical in various parts of England. The existence of the Fund had two beneficial side-effects: it slowed down the suspension of other priests and led the bishops to make financial provision for those who had been suspended, a course which I think it improbable they would have taken had the Fund not been in existence. Contributions of over £700 were received by the trustees, who were able to assist a number of priests in want.

Such was the situation in England one month after the Encyclical had been issued.[3] Battle had been joined and the struggle was to continue over the next twelve months. The story will be taken up later in this chapter, but it is necessary to look now at foreign reactions to the Encyclical in order that the English situation can be seen in a wider setting.

Some Foreign Reactions
The fiercest response to the Encyclical took place in England, but the conflict was sharp throughout the world. Even in Ireland,

[1] An 'Association of Ex-Clergy' was formed independently about this time. See *Catholic Herald*, 25 October 1968.
[2] Lady Asquith, although over eighty and with no particular sympathy for Catholicism, immediately agreed to be a trustee of the fund and entered into its activities with the greatest enthusiasm and skill. She proved the most prescient of our trustees and never missed a meeting until shortly before her death.
[3] On 4 October, seventy-six lay members of the Catholic Church in Britain published a statement criticising the Encyclical. They included Mr Graham Greene, Lady Albermarle, Mr Michael Fogarty, and Dr Anthony Coady of the Catholic Marriage Advisory Council. The statement rejected the distinction made by the Encyclical between rhythm and contraception and maintained that the choice of means of birth control lay with the married couple and was 'not a matter for confession'. See *The Times*, 4 October 1968.

probably the country with the strongest emotional loyalty to Rome, the reception was mixed. Archbishop McQuaid, of Dublin, described the Encyclical as an essential document which set forth once again the teaching of the Church. As soon as the Encyclical was published, he telegraphed the Pope expressing his support. Fr James Good, Professor of Theology at University College, Cork, on the other hand, described the Pope's statement as 'a major tragedy in the Church'.[1] Subsequently Dr Good was suspended from his priestly functions. He thought that most theologians and lay people would reject it. The Irish laity were divided and many dismayed. Some doctors expressed their determination to proceed with prescribing the pill. Cardinal Conway, Primate of all Ireland, declared in Armagh Cathedral on Sunday, 4 August, that he gratefully believed the majority of Irish Catholics would accept the Encyclical 'not just in a spirit of loyalty but a spirit of faith'. The Encyclical represented the authentic views of the Church, but some would accept it with pain and no one was more sensitive to this realisation than the Pope. He appreciated that it would create some human personal problems.[2]

In Holland four leading Dutch Catholics, including Monsignor Ruygers, Vicar-General of Breda, and Monsignor Van Laarhofen, Vicar-General of Den Bosch, declared that the Encyclical was not to be regarded as an infallible pronouncement. They stated that it was 'against the majority position of the papal birth control Commission, against the majority position of the moral theologians, against the majority position of the International Lay Congress, and against the position of a great part of the world's bishops'. 'Therefore,' they concluded, 'the discussion remains completely open.'[3] Cardinal Alfrink, Archbishop of Utrecht, asked if the papal ban might lead to a schism, said that 'the time of schisms is passed. After the latest Council, the position of the Pope is clear.' A less sybilline utterance came from Bishop Zwartkruis of Haarlem who warned that 'the faithful are due to give approval in a very particular way to the authentic teaching authority of the Pope, even when he does not speak *ex-Cathedra*'.[4]

[1] *The Times*, 30 July 1968.   [2] The *Daily Telegraph*, 5 August 1968.
[3] *Tablet*, 3 August 1968.   [4] Ibid.

In the United States conflict was also evident in the immediate reactions. While Cardinal Cushing, Archbishop of Boston, contented himself with saying, 'Rome has spoken. For the time being, at least, the cause is settled', a spokesman for Archbishop Cooke of New York declared that those who would publicly teach against the directive 'would at least be guilty of disobedience and a violation of faith'. Cardinal McIntyre, Archbishop of Los Angeles, welcomed the Encyclical 'as a positive expression of fundamental principles of morality' which was 'refreshing'. On the other hand, the Rt Rev. George Schlichte, Rector of the Pope John XXIII National Seminary in Western Massachusetts, supported by seven faculty members, called the edict 'most disappointing', and the 'expression of a minority view'. They felt that it reflected a view 'which according to recent scholarship is neither biblical, theological, nor truly historical'. The strongest criticism of the Encyclical was made in Washington where a group of eighty-seven Catholic theologians, led by those with teaching posts at the Catholic University of America, issued a statement upholding the rights of married Catholic couples to practise birth control. This statement became one of the factors in the continuing conflict with the Archbishop of Washington, Cardinal O'Boyle.[1]

Conflict was again evident in South Africa where Cardinal McCann, Archbishop of Cape Town, declared: 'The Holy Father has spoken and people will accept his decision.' Quite a different view came from Archbishop Hurley of Durban: 'A great number of the faithful and of their priests will experience an agonising conflict between their loyalty to Pope Paul and their difficulty in accepting his decision.' With the publication of the Encyclical, the Church was entering 'an extremely critical phase in its crisis of authority'.

In Spain the Encyclical was hailed as one of the most important decisions taken by the Catholic Church during the twentieth century. Archbishop Morcillo Gonzalez of Madrid said the Encyclical represented an 'advance' in Catholic doctrine in that it 'exalted the woman in her personal dignity as a "wife" ' and called upon scientists to devise a safe birth control system using the rhythm method. He added that the Government and industry

[1] This conflict is examined in greater detail at pp. 177–85.

should ensure that the workers' wages increased as their families grew. On the other hand, the Young Workers' Catholic Action Movement (Y.O.C.) maintained a significant silence.

In Germany the reaction of the bishops was cautious. Cardinal Doepfner, Archbishop of Munich and Chairman of the German Bishops' Conference, stated that it was not going to be easy for the Church to convey a closer understanding of the Pope's teaching. The bishops would have to decide how best they could help the laity to interpret the Encyclical.

Support for the Pope came from Brazil, where a spokesman for Cardinal De Barros Camara, Archbishop of Rio de Janeiro, said that the Pope's decision must be accepted as law by all Catholics and that no further comment was necessary. Archbishop Helder Camara of Olinda was a little more pessimistic and said that the Pope's words would be difficult to fulfil but he added: 'We now have the guide that all the world was waiting for.'[1]

Strong backing for the Pope came from Portugal and Malta. In Lisbon, Cardinal Cerejeira, the Patriarch, in a television interview, gave his support to the most rigid interpretation of the Pope's Encyclical. He said that on the question of the obligation to accept the teachings of the Encyclical, no Catholic conscience could hesitate. The Pope had spoken with the authority of Christ, and whoever disdained that disdained Christ. The Portuguese Press carried several articles approving of the Pope's decision, and excerpts from foreign papers were confined to those which supported the Encyclical. In Malta, Archbishop Gonzi sent a cable to the Pope thanking him for the Encyclical and expressing his full support. Even the Cana Movement, which advises on marriage problems, and had recently organised courses in family planning, pledged its support.[2]

Support for the Pope also came from Archbishop Athenagoras, Patriarch of Constantinople, who made it clear that he agreed with the Pope's Encyclical. The Pope, he stated, was 'strictly

---

[1] For these statements and preceding quotations see *Tablet*, 3 August 1968. Bishop Mendez Arceo of Cuernavaca in Mexico issued a statement in support of the Encyclical as did Bishop Maldonado in Venezuela. See *Tablet*, 10 August 1968. In Colombia the Foreign Minister, Signor Hernandez, resigned after declaring in Lima that he disagreed with the Pope's Encyclical. See *Tablet*, 17 August 1968.

[2] See *Tablet*, 17 August 1968.

following the path drawn up by our Holy Bible'. In an interview with the Anatolian Newsagency, the Patriarch said he believed birth control devices were contrary to the principles of Christianity. 'The Pope could not do otherwise,' declared the Patriarch. All scriptures, including the Moslem Koran contain 'almost the same principles regarding the family and family life'.[1]

A voice expressing considerable misgivings about the Encyclical was that of Dr Hans Küng, the noted theologian from Tübingen. In a broadcast on Swiss television on 3 August, Dr Küng pointed out that though the Encyclical was authentic teaching, it was also fallible. Dr Küng stressed that the debate should continue. The conscientious decision of the Pope should be taken seriously, but his arguments should be fully discussed. 'We shall not, therefore, suppress but express our misgivings, in order to help ourselves and the Church to reach clarity; and at the same time we shall not indulge in mutual condemnation, but try to understand one another.' Those who after serious, mature reflection 'come to the conclusion that, for the sake of maintaining their love and of the continuance and happiness of their marriage, they must act in a way differently from what the Encyclical lays down: these are bound in accordance with traditional teaching, of the Popes also, to follow their conscience. They will, therefore, not accuse themselves of sin when they have acted in good faith. But, calmly and secure in their conviction, they will share in the life of the Church and of her sacraments. They may certainly rely on the understanding of their priests.[2]

Strong criticism of the Encyclical was made by a number of individuals in Australia. Fr Nicholas Crotty, for example, a Passionist father and Professor of Moral Theology, published two lengthy articles rejecting the arguments of the Encyclical and advising Catholics to follow their own consciences. As a result, he was deprived of his priestly faculties by the Archbishop of Melbourne. Other protests came from twenty-seven tutors and students at St John's College, the Catholic Residential College at the University of Sydney, who signed a letter disagreeing with it. At a public meeting at Sydney University a resolution urging all

[1] See *Catholic Herald*, 16 August 1968.
[2] See Hans Küng: *Truthfulness, the Future of the Church* (London, 1968), pp. 238–40.

Catholics to unite behind the Pope was carried by one vote, 114 votes to 113. The *Catholic Worker*, an independent monthly published by laymen in Melbourne, attacked the Encyclical. The Australian bishops, on the other hand, backed the Encyclical unitedly, declaring that refusal to accept the Pope's decision would be a grave act of disobedience.[1]

Jesuits throughout the world seem to have been as divided as everyone else over the merits of the Encyclical. In a letter dated 15 August, but not in fact made public until 23 September, the General of the Society, Father Pedro Arrupe, urged every Jesuit to support the Encyclical. 'Every Jesuit,' declared the General, 'must take action to enter and to help others to enter a line of thought which so far may not have been his, but of which he will find the sound foundation, overcoming his own convictions.' He went on, however, to state that to obey 'is not to stop thinking, nor to parrot the Encyclical word for word in a servile manner'. The type of obedience required was 'faithful, firm, open and truly creative'. The letter caused further confusion among Jesuits, and another missive was sent out by the Secretary of the Society, Father Correia Alfonso, on 4 October. In it he explained that 'the obedience that the Father General expects is an active obedience, one which is intelligent, discerning and open to further investigation. He in no way demands the rejection of a conscience formed in accordance with traditional principles.' The difficulty had been in part occasioned by the fact that the Jesuits take a special fourth vow of loyalty to the Holy See, but this vow is a vow to go 'on missions and does not of itself imply a doctrinal position'. While public discussion by Jesuits does seem to have been curtailed by this missive, a number of members of the Society by interpretation seem to have been able to retain a certain amount of *de facto* freedom in expressing their views on the Encyclical.[2]

---

[1] See *Tablet*, 17 August and 31 August 1968.
[2] See *Tablet*, 16 November 1968. Fr Alfonso's letter seems to have been occasioned by an article in the German weekly, *Der Spiegel*, containing some gibes about 'programmed Jesuits'. Two German Jesuit Provincials travelled to Rome to seek clarification of the letter and also of their position resulting from the fourth vow. They declared as a result of their visit that: 'The Father General by no means wished to suppress by his letter informed discussion of those questions provoked by the Encyclical, for he is of the opinion that this discussion, if pursued seriously, will gradually lead to a general acceptance of the disputed statements of the Pope in the Encyclical'. For a parallel

THE ENGLISH BISHOPS

The public attitude of the English bishops to the Encyclical went through three distinct phases. The first, which lasted through August 1968, consisted in a number of individual reactions to the Encyclical, but no effort was made to act as a collegiate body. The second phase began in September when it was realised that the bishops had to act together, and after a meeting in London a joint statement was issued. This was of a mild character. The third phase came a month later in October when the bishops once again acted jointly but this time took a much tougher line with dissident priests. This was enforced rigidly by the Bishop of Nottingham but in this he was isolated in the hierarchy, who modified the rigours of their own declaration in individual cases.

The early reactions of Cardinal Heenan and Archbishop Murphy have already been noted. Archbishop Murphy had supported the Encyclical in language which the *Daily Telegraph* described in a leading article as more suitable to the reign of James II than to the present day, but Archbishop Heenan had not made his position so clear. Clarification came on Sunday, 4 August, when a pastoral letter was read from the pulpits of Catholic churches in his Archdiocese. Westminster Cathedral in London was crowded as the Cardinal's letter was read out. The Cardinal accepted the Pope's decision and pointed out that he was pro-President of the final birth control Commission which reported to the Pope. No member of that Commission had thought that the problem could be resolved by a majority vote. 'We were asked to sift evidence and present the Pope with our findings. It

interpretation by two leading American Jesuits, see *The National Register* (U.S.A.), 29 September 1968. Fr Bernard Cooke, S.J., interpreted the letter as meaning that an individual should re-examine his opinion: 'You may have been wrong,' he said, 'but it might be that you were not wrong.' Fr Burkhardt said: 'As I see it, Fr Arrupe is appealing to Jesuits, on the basis of the special Jesuit commitments to the Holy See, which places on a Jesuit a particular obligation to try to see papal directives and papal teaching as the Pope sees them. In this context, he seems to ask for an initial disposition, an attitude favourable to papal directives and teaching, a disposition or attitude which is more likely to lead to intellectual agreement than an objective, critical, disposition would do.' Fr Burkhardt of Woodstock College, Maryland, was one of those who had earlier signed a statement disagreeing with the Encyclical. Fr Cook had stressed the right of Catholics 'to form responsibly their own conscience on the question of birth control'.

was always understood that the decision must be by him alone, as Christ's vicar.' 'The law of God cannot be decided by a majority vote.' When he came to actual pastoral directives, the Cardinal's attitude was flexible. Addressing those who had become accustomed to using contraceptives, he stated that they might not be able all at once to resist temptation, but should not despair over this. 'Above all,' he added, 'they must not abstain from the sacraments. However often they fail, they must ask God's grace to find the strength to obey his law. May God grant us all the wisdom and humility to accept the guidance of the Head of the Church on Earth. May God bless every family in the diocese and lead each priest to guide his people with gentleness, prudence and love.'[1] The letter represented a considerable shift in the Catholic position in England on birth control. No threats were made against the 'sinner' and those practising birth control were not apparently to be barred from Holy Communion. The Cardinal's point was ambiguous on this as it was not clear whether he meant that they should go to confession first or not. The eirenic tone of the Cardinal's declaration was widely welcomed. In a statement I said: 'Cardinal Heenan has made a major contribution towards maintaining Church unity. There is still a grave danger of a split, but by saying that you must continue to take the Sacraments, the Cardinal has avoided sharpening the position.'[2] The Cardinal also held out the hope that the invention of a pill to provide 'a secure basis for the rhythm method of birth control would solve all difficulties.'

[1] *Daily Telegraph*, 5 August 1968.
[2] *Observer*, 4 August 1968. In an article in the same issue Charles Davis pointed out the flaw in the Cardinal's approach. He attacked 'the seemingly compassionate leniency for those who cannot all at once follow the papal teaching. They are exhorted to continue their efforts and go to the sacraments. What this means is that Catholics, while accepting the papal teaching that they are committing sin in practising contraception, should solve the problem of their inability to follow the law by constantly confessing their sin and receiving absolution. They are told in effect that they will receive every consideration, however often they fail, provided they admit their guilt and promise to continue the struggle. This is to preserve intact the papal teaching at the cost of fostering permanent guilt feelings in people. The policy is psychologically destructive, and it undermines the sincerity of personal conscience.' Mr Davis's logic cannot be faulted and I was aware of the point at the time, but felt that the overriding need was to avoid a possible schism and therefore, while not abandoning my own position, I thought it wise to put as mild and charitable interpretation on the Cardinal's pastoral as possible.

The following week the Archbishop of Liverpool, Dr Beck, also issued a pastoral letter. Dr Beck, who had originally been a strong upholder of the traditional position, had nevertheless allowed free discussion of the matter in his Archdiocese and divergent practice. The issue of the Encyclical resolved his own doubts, but he realised that not everyone could be expected to make such an immediate adjustment. He stressed that the Pope was speaking in the name of Christ and with apostolic authority, since the apostles had been constituted 'as guardians and authoritative interpreters of the moral law'. Archbishop Beck stressed the compassionate nature of the Encyclical and its urging of married couples who had difficulty in accepting it 'to persevere in prayer, to seek grace and charity in the Eucharist, not to be discouraged, but to rely on the mercy of God which is poured out in the sacrament of penance'. Dr Beck thought the Encyclical displayed 'far-sighted and noble vision'.[1] In his pastoral, the Archbishop had not directly dealt with the question of conscience, but in an interview subsequently given in the *Catholic Herald*, he stated that in a moral crisis of this kind: 'I think the only thing one can tell people is that they must do what they think is right. Really this is what I meant by saying they must follow their own consciences.'[2] The Archbishop also stated that the debate was still open 'in the sense that discussion is essential in order to help people to form their consciences . . . what is needed now, more than ever, is dialogue among laity, priests and the episcopate and the Holy Father so that this fashioning of the mind of the Church may come about.' Archbishop Beck returned to the theme of the need for moderation in a letter sent to teachers in his diocese in September. 'In the present circumstances,' he stated, 'it would be unwise to take up too rigid a position on either side until the implications of the Holy Father's teaching have been clarified.'[3]

Very different was the tone of the pastoral letter of Archbishop Cowderoy of Southwark, which was issued at about the same time. He rebuked Catholics who had publicly disassociated themselves

[1] *The Times*, 9 August 1968.
[2] *Catholic Herald*, 23 August 1968. Archbishop Beck had been quoted as saying earlier that those who could not accept the Encyclical in conscience 'must do whatever they think is right'.
[3] *Universe*, 6 September 1968.

from the Encyclical and added: 'Some of our poor, simple people have been misled by disobedient priests who did not heed the command of the Holy Father that the traditional rules must be followed until and unless he made a change. They, like other priests, were told not to confuse their people with the specious argument that the law was in doubt, when the Pope said it was not in doubt. In spite of this they have disobediently broken silence, and it is not to be wondered at that simple people having been given the impression that a change was coming and, especially, that the pill would be allowed, are now very disappointed. We can sympathise with them. But their bitterness would be better directed to these false and devious advisers who gave them unfounded hope, and not to the Holy Father who has never held out any hope that he was about to alter the traditional teaching of the Church.' At the same time the Archbishop asked for sympathy and kindness towards those facing difficulty in their married lives and the avoidance of rash judgement: 'Generally, we know absolutely nothing about the personal, intimate married lives of other people, and it is certainly not for us to judge them.'

The following week yet another difference of emphasis was given in a pastoral letter issued by Bishop Worlock of Portsmouth. The Bishop declared that the Pope's statement demanded 'deep study and reflection by the whole Church'. The Bishop recognised the conscientious difficulties which some Catholics found themselves in, but stated that it was his duty to point out that the Holy Father's words constituted 'a definite directive'. He went on to give a narrow interpretation to Cardinal Heenan's plea for married couples practising contraception to go to the sacraments and seemed to envisage their going to confession before receiving Communion. He recognised that 'certain difficulties of conscience' could remain for some and expressed the wish that they should discuss these matters frankly with their priests, and with absolute honesty of conscience.[1]

These differing statements of the bishops caused further confusion. An insight into their difficulties was given on 4 September, when *The Times* published the text of a covering letter from Cardinal Cicognani, Papal Secretary of State, which had been sent

[1] *Tablet*, 24 August 1968.

with the text of the Encyclical in August and which urged the bishops to ensure that the papal teaching was understood and obeyed. As *The Times* pointed out in a leading article, not only bishops but priests were in a difficult position since they held a teaching office and were being called on to teach what had been decided.[1]

In these circumstances Cardinal Heenan, President of the Hierarchy, called an extraordinary meeting of the Bishops of England and Wales to meet in London on 17 September. This meeting took place against a background of rising lay and clerical criticism and protest against the Encyclical. On Friday, 13 September, the London Circle of the Newman Association, a group of Catholic graduates, arranged a 'teach-in' at the Central Hall, Westminster. The hall was packed, and eight speakers debated the Encyclical, four supporting it and four dissenting.[2] The 'teach-in' represented a new departure in Catholic life in England and set a pattern for further 'teach-ins' in other parts of the country. It proved to be both lively and orderly. Fr de Rosa spoke of his optimism for the future: 'I see a Catholic clergy and laity more mature and more personally responsible than ever before, and bishops everywhere not least in England, realising, with due love and respect for the Holy Father and his Office, that they too are true shepherds of their flocks and not just Vatican sheep-dogs, obedient to every whistle and snarling and snapping at the heels of wayward sheep.'[3]

[1] *The Times*, 4 September 1968. On 6 September, the Archbishop of Cardiff wrote to *The Times* protesting at the heading, 'Secret Letter before Encyclical' as misleading. He pointed out that the letter had not even been marked 'confidential', and had been cyclo-styled (badly) including the signature. Dom Benet Innes also wrote to point out that every priest in the diocese of Clifton had received a copy of it and it was not labelled 'secret' – *The Times*, 6 September. Nevertheless the revelation of the existence of the letter caused wide controversy, particularly in the United States. It was called by Mr John Deedy, Managing Editor of the Catholic magazine, *Commonweal*, 'a typical Church device to manage opinion' – (*The Times*, 5 September).

[2] Those supporting the Encyclical were Fr Leonard Whatmore, Mr Douglas Woodruff, Fr Clement Tigar, and Mr Christopher Derrick. Those dissenting were Dr John Marshall, Fr Peter de Rosa, Mr Anthony Spencer, and Fr David Woodward. I had been invited to participate but was unable to do so as I was fulfilling an engagement in New York.

[3] *The Times*, 14 September 1968. *The Times* also reported that a group of Catholic priests and monks had appealed to all clergy and religious organisations throughout the country to support them in 'the open Church in which discussion should take place without fear'. Signatories of the appeal including the Abbot of Caldey, The Rt Rev. J. R. Wicksteed, and the Prior of Blackfriars, Oxford, the Very Rev. Guy Braithwaite.

When the bishops met on 17 September, they had before them among other documents, eight searching questions from the Laity Commission, which had been set up by the hierarchy to advise the bishops on matters affecting laymen and which had been published earlier in *The Times*.[1] The meeting started at 11.30 in the morning and lasted until well into the evening. Three strands of opinion were represented among the bishops, those demanding a total assent to the Encyclical and the suspension of dissenting priests; those who viewed the Encyclical as an ideal to which immediate adherence could not reasonably be demanded; and those who gave a liberal interpretation to the document. The statement eventually issued on 25 September was evidently a compromise. It stressed that the Encyclical was not concerned only with contraception but with the whole institution of Christian marriage, and that it came from 'the Vicar of Christ'. Its lack of collegiality could not be invoked as a reason for refusing assent. Skating over one of the principal problems raised by the Encyclical, it declared that parents were entitled to decide how many children they should have in the light of the moral considerations laid down in the Encyclical. It then went on: 'One of these considerations is that "each exercise of the marriage act must remain in itself open to the transmission of life" although, as the Pope points out, in fact "not every conjugal act is followed by a new life", nevertheless it is against the plan of God to take positive steps to destroy the possibility of the transmission of life. The use of marriage during infertile periods, on the other hand, does not destroy the act's "openness to the transmission of life".' The statement went on to concede that many wives and husbands, anticipating the promised statement of the Pope, had come to rely on contraception in a conscientious manner and after seeking pastoral advice. It conceded further that they might well be unable to see that for them personally contraception was wrong. It alluded also to the particular difficulty facing 'those who after serious thought and prayer cannot as yet understand or be fully convinced of the doctrines as laid down'. Others because of ill-

[1] *The Times*, 13 September 1968. The questions concerned the authority of the Encyclical, questioned some of its factual statements, probed a number of ambiguities, and asked for clarification.

health or some other obstacle would be involved in a serious conflict of duties.

The statement supported the Encyclical, but added a gloss in the following words: 'It must be stressed that the primacy of conscience is not in dispute. The Pope, bishops, clergy and faithful must all be true to conscience. But we are bound to do everything in our power to make sure that our conscience is truly informed. Neither this Encyclical, nor any other document of the Church takes away from us our right and duty to follow our conscience.'[1] In a leading article *The Times* described the statement as mild and inconclusive. It recognised that it had not resolved a number of contradictions between the demands of the Encyclical and the demands of conscience: 'It does not propose an unquestioning adherence as the only licit response to the teaching of the Encyclical. But neither does it clarify the right of conscientious dissent.' Nevertheless *The Times* welcomed it as an indication that 'no very strenuous attempt will be made to enforce the closure by ecclesiastical authority'. The *Catholic Herald* took a similar line, pointing out that while its reasoning would hardly satisfy some modern theologians, it was 'a hopeful, sane, adult and compassionate document. Perhaps even the vagueness is a point in its favour. At a time of stress and anguish the fewer boundaries drawn on the map of conscience the better.'[2] The *Tablet* was more critical, but pointed out that the document respected conflicting views and made no attempt to enforce mandatory solutions. 'At least the possibility of dialogue is kept open and deadlock is not a foregone conclusion.' At the same time, the *Tablet* criticised the statement on a number of points, for its partial quotation of the statement of the Belgian bishops, for its identification of the Church with ecclesiastical authority, and its failure to resolve crucial points. It stressed, however, that there was 'no mandate in this document for persecution of conscientious priests who are unable in all honesty to accept the Encyclical *au pied de la lettre*'.[3]

On the following day, Cardinal Heenan held a Press conference at Archbishop's House, Westminster, to discuss the statement. He pointed out that priests were not at liberty to contradict the

[1] *The Times*, 25 September 1968.
[2] *Catholic Herald*, 27 September 1968.   [3] 28 September 1968.

Pope in his public teaching: 'They had no right to denounce the Pope from the pulpit. There was a great difference between their duty as priests – to present the teaching of the Church – and their own views in private conversation. The priest had to say: "this is the teaching of the Vicar of Christ in the Encyclical". He could then say: "For my part personally, I do not agree." It was important to distinguish between their duty as priests and their duty to their consciences.'[1] The Cardinal went on to put the matter in proportion by stating: 'Condemnation of artificial contraception is not the central tenet of the Catholic religion.' Asked by a reporter whether he believed that the Pope knew of the feelings of Catholics in England, or whether reports had been intercepted by the Vatican civil service, the Cardinal replied that he had written to the Pope the day before and marked his letter 'ad manus proprias' – 'into his own hands'. 'There is no doubt that the Pope will know what is going on.'

If the statement was intended to bring public controversy among Catholics to an end, it was not notably successful. One unexpected result was the withdrawal from the exercise of his priestly duties of the Rt Rev. Anselm Thatcher, parish priest of Broadstairs, Kent, and titular Abbot of Faversham. In a letter to the Press, he attacked the bishops' statement, writing: 'In my opinion they have succeeded in doing what three hundred years of persecution failed to do – destroy papal authority among the Catholics in this country.' We are told, went on the Abbot scornfully, that priests 'must follow the official party line in public. In private, and in the confessional, they may air their own views, even if contrary to the direct teaching of the Encyclical.'[2] A distinguished group of over seventy lay men and women, all leaders in professional or public life, also issued a statement that the choice of methods of birth control was one to be made by the husband and wife 'not in an arbitrary manner but in a conscientious exercise of their responsibility before God to uphold and foster a creative love; the choice thus conscientiously made is not a matter for confession'. The signatories maintained that the

---

[1] *The Times*, 26 September 1968.
[2] See *The Times*, 30 September 1968. The letter was originally published in the *Daily Telegraph*.

use of rhythm as a method of birth control was as artificial as the use of a chemical or mechanical device.[1]

The statement, however, which effectively hit the headlines, was contained in a letter to *The Times*, published on 2 October and signed by fifty-five priests. It read: 'We respect the decision on birth control made by our Holy Father the Pope according to his conscience. We realise the possible grave dangers that can result from the indiscriminate use of artificial means of birth control. We deeply regret, however, that according to our consciences we cannot give loyal internal and external obedience to the view that all such means of contraception are in all circumstances wrong. As priests we feel that our duty towards Catholic people compels us to bear witness to the truth as we see it.' Three of the signatories of the letter, Fr Kenneth Allan, parish priest of Coulsdon in the Archdiocese of Southwark, Fr Peter de Rosa, lecturer in theology at Corpus Christi College, Bayswater, and Fr Nigel Collingwood, Catholic chaplain to Essex University, held a press conference the same day to explain the signatories' views. The priests had been somewhat alarmed by the headline in *The Times*: 'Fifty-five priests defy the Pope' and Fr de Rosa stressed: 'I must emphasise that none of the fifty-five signatories considers himself to be a rebel against authority, whether vested in the Pope or the bishops of the Church. This letter is intended to be, and I hope it will be received as, a straightforward expression of conscience.'[2]

Unhappily, the bishops did not see it quite like this, and there is reason to think that publication of the letter was a tactical error since it played some part in encouraging the bishops to move on to a new stage and adopt a more rigorous attitude towards dissenting priests.[3] At a meeting held in late October they decided to take a firmer line against these priests, and their decision came out in the form of letters by the individual bishops to their clergy, the first of which from Cardinal Heenan was published on 25 October.[4] 'The Bishops of England and Wales have no wish to inhibit

[1] See *Tablet*, 5 October 1968.
[2] *The Times*, 3 October 1968.
[3] The letter appears to have been drawn up some weeks before its publication and may well have been overtaken by events. Owing to the delay in publication some of the signatories were under the impression that it had been decided not to make it public.
[4] See *Catholic Herald*, 25 October 1968.

reasonable discussion,' wrote the Cardinal, but he then went on to detail conditions in relation to priests which seemed to contradict this assertion. 'It was, therefore, unanimously decided at a hierarchy meeting last week,' continued the Cardinal, 'that each bishop would speak personally to those of his priests who maintain opposition to the Encyclical. Now that the bishops have had time to see the dissident priests it is opportune to publish the conditions laid down. Priests are required in preaching, teaching, in the Press, on radio, television or public platforms, to refrain from opposing the teaching of the Pope in all matters of faith and morals. If a priest is unwilling to give this undertaking the bishop will decide whether he can be allowed without scandal to continue to act in the name of the Church. Although he need not be required to cease celebrating mass, a priest may not normally hold faculties to hear confessions without undertaking to declare faithfully the objective teaching of *Humanae Vitae* in the confessional and when giving spiritual guidance.' The Cardinal gave an undertaking that priests unwilling to accept these conditions would be maintained by the diocese and added that religious superiors had been invited to make similar proposals to those of their members who had publicly rejected the Encyclical

This statement precipitated a new crisis. The *Tablet* published a critical leading article.[1] The *Ad Hoc* committee of laymen issued a strong statement deploring 'the negative and repressive terms in which the bishops proposed to bring their clergy into line and the brutal and vindictive manner in which some conscientious priests have been presented with these terms.'[2] The statement upheld the right of priests to make known their views in public, and their right to follow their consciences in giving pastoral counsel. I also issued an independent statement as follows: 'I have every sympathy with Cardinal Heenan and the Roman Catholic hierarchy in the dilemma in which they find themselves over the status and rights of priests in the birth control controversy. I welcome the fact that priests are to remain free to counsel the laity privately in accordance with their own consciences as well as in accordance with the papal Encyclical. While it is reasonable to ask priests to refrain from expressing their conscientious views in

[1] 2 November 1968.   [2] *Daily Telegraph*, 26 October 1968.

the pulpit and from making any personal criticism of His Holiness the Pope, it is unreasonable and may well be unconstitutional, to forbid them to take any part in the public dialogue on an issue in which the whole Church, and indeed the whole world, is intensely concerned and interested, unless they express a particular point of view. British priests are members of the Catholic Church, but they are also citizens of this country. The constitutional rights of free speech apply to them equally with all citizens and they cannot, and should not be, taken away by ecclesiastical superiors however well intentioned.'[1] I had assumed in my statement that priests were to be free in counselling and in the confessional, having stated the view of the Pope, to give their own conscientiously held views, but this was by no means absolutely clear in the statement and subsequently different bishops interpreted this part of the statement in different ways.[2]

THE POSITION OF PRIESTS IN ENGLAND

After the issue of the second episcopal statement, the birth control crisis in England entered a new and decisive phase. If the statement could be made effective and enforced uniformly throughout England then those working for liberalisation would have sustained a massive defeat. In the event, the second statement, like the first, received different interpretations in different dioceses and a uniform practice was not established. Cardinal Heenan and the majority of the bishops gave a liberal and moderate interpretation to their own statement, influenced by the sharp reaction of sections of the laity including that of the *Ad Hoc* group, the stand taken by the trustees of the Freedom of Conscience Fund, and their own common sense. Cardinal Heenan clearly did not want a showdown with priests in his diocese and adopted a policy of

[1] See *Catholic Herald*, 1 November 1968. The two statements were made quite independently and there is an obvious difference of tone. Unfortunately some newspapers confused the two and amalgamated them as though they were a joint statement. See, for example, the *Daily Mail*, 26 October 1968. I corrected this misapprehension in letters to *Daily Mail* (29 October 1968) and to the *Tablet*.

[2] In an article in the *Catholic Herald* I raised the question and stated that if priests were not free to give their own views, as well as those of the Pope, that it was 'difficult to see how the sacrament of penance and counselling is to avoid being reduced to the status of a spiritual slot machine. Spiritual healing is a personal encounter, not the mechanical application of a rule.' See *Catholic Herald*, 1 November 1968.

peaceful co-existence, making it plain that he was not seeking a confrontation with dissidents. There was an ambiguity in this policy, as indeed there had been in Cardinal Heenan's attitude throughout the controversy, which did not recommend it to theologians or intellectuals but had the effect of preventing a split in the Church. It also enabled him to keep his options open, since if there was a decisive swing of opinion one way or the other he would not be left stranded. This diplomatic approach was seen elsewhere, notably in Liverpool in the North, and eventually in Southern dioceses such as Portsmouth and Arundel and Brighton.[1]

Bishop David Cashman of Arundel and Brighton, had difficulties with a number of priests and it was not clear at first what line he would take. Five priests in the diocese expressed their opposition to the Encyclical. One of them, Fr Andrew Beer, of St Dunstan's, Woking, while expressing his conscientious objection to the Encyclical, added: 'I hope desperately that I do not have to leave the priesthood which means more to me than anything else in the world. But I cannot exercise it in bad faith.' Fr Beer was temporarily suspended from preaching and hearing confessions by his bishop. Another priest, Fr Anthony Burnham, curate at Englefield Green, Surrey, informed parishioners in a newsletter that he was unable to accept the Pope's teaching on contraception. A third priest, Fr Michael Winter, of the Beda College, Rome, declined to read a pastoral letter from Bishop Cashman at the parish church at Godalming where he was temporarily supplying.[2] Bishop Cashman asked the priests to spend a period in meditation and prayer free of pastoral duties and no sanctions were invoked against them. Fr Beer was subsequently appointed assistant Catholic chaplain at Sussex University. Fr Beer made it clear that the only undertaking he had given on accepting his new appointment was that he would not preach against the Encyclical from the pulpit.[3] No action was taken by the Bishop of Northamp-

---

[1] Bishop Worlock of Portsmouth had all along taken a moderate line as was instanced in the treatment of Fr Henry Clarke of Petersfield who had described the Encyclical as 'disastrous'. Fr Clarke undertook not to preach against the Encyclical, but was not required to retract. See *The Times*, 14 August 1968.

[2] See *The Times*, 12 August and 19 August 1968.

[3] See *The Times*, 11 and 12 November 1968. Restrictions on the pastoral work of Fr Michael Winter were also raised. See *The Times*, 14 November 1968. According to *The Times*, Fr Winter was dismissed from his teaching post at the Beda College.

ton against Fr David Woodward, parish priest of Burnham, Buckinghamshire, and his two curates, the Rev. Nicholas Lash and the Rev. Vincent McDermott, who shared responsibility for a sermon preached in criticism of the Encyclical in early August. The priests subsequently held a 'talk-in', discussing the Encyclical paragraph by paragraph with their congregation.[1]

Two diocesan bishops on the other hand, Archbishop Cowderoy of Southwark, and Bishop Ellis of Nottingham, took a harder line. The suspension of Fr Paul Weir, of Southwark, has already been referred to.[2] He was among eight priests of the diocese who had declared their opposition to the Encyclical.[3] Fr Weir's position attracted national publicity and his became something of a test case. He had been interviewed by the Archbishop in September and stated subsequently: 'A complete retraction was required that in no circumstances would I counsel anyone, however hard the case, that they might exercise freedom of conscience and not necessarily follow the Pope's ruling.'[4] The other priest around whom the Southwark situation revolved was Fr Kenneth Allan, who, like Fr Weir, was highly respected in the diocese, but unlike Fr Weir was a parish priest. In the event, Fr Allan's turned out to be the key case. He had already made his views on the Encyclical known when the second episcopal statement was issued on 25 October. The day before he had been interviewed by Archbishop Cowderoy at Archbishop's House, Southwark, and later described his four-minute interview. 'The Archbishop said I had given great scandal to the Church by my letter to *The Times* and by giving a Press conference and appearing on television.' Fr Allan added: 'He then read me the conditions and asked if I accepted them. I said that I could not do so without clarification in writing. The Archbishop replied that he would write nothing.' Fr Allan then said he could not give an answer and Dr Cowderoy declared that he would interpret silence as a refusal to accept the conditions.

[1] See *The Times*, 19 August 1968.   [2] See p. 144 above.
[3] Fr Daniel Futter was suspended.
[4] *The Times*, 19 September 1968. Dissenting priests in the Archdiocese received different treatment and this aroused comment. *The Times* on 14 October reported the official explanation: 'A spokesman for the Archbishop, explaining the situation, said that Fr Weir and Fr Futter had expressed their dissent in writing, leaving the Archbishop no choice but to suspend them. The other two priests spoke about their views, and it was felt that this left sufficient latitude for a more lenient and sympathetic stand.'

'He said he would remove my faculties and suspend me. I said that he could not do so because my faculties derived from my office and that he would have to dismiss me,' stated Fr Allan. 'The Archbishop said he would dismiss me from office and offered me £500 a year. I said I had consulted a canon lawyer and said he could not dismiss me without stating my crime, and that I could not think of any crime. I told the Archbishop that he would have to state my crime in writing and initiate judicial procedure. He said he would think over what I had said.' The interview then ended.[1]

It was this interview with the Archbishop that led to my statement on the bishop's second ruling: I had wished to avoid comment but, in view of the treatment of Fr Allan, something clearly needed to be done. The strength of Fr Allan's position was that he was in possession of his parish as a parish priest and was strongly supported by his parishioners.[2] He refused to accept his dismissal by Archbishop Cowderoy as being valid, and the Freedom of Conscience Fund took counsel's opinion to ascertain the position of the Catholic clergy in general in this situation and Fr Allan's status in particular.[3]

The legal position of the Roman Catholic Church in England, it appears, does not depend upon statutory enactments but it ranks as a private and voluntary religious society resting upon a consensual basis. Its members, like members of any other communion, may adopt rules for enforcing discipline within their body which are binding on those who expressly or who by implication have assented to them. The English courts will not take cognizance of questions relating purely to matters of religious doctrine or discipline, but where the exercise of discipline has temporal consequences they will intervene to ensure that the rules of the Church are complied with. They would thus intervene to enforce any relevant provisions of canon law which had not been observed. English courts will also require voluntary organisations to observe

[1] See *The Times*, 25 October 1968.
[2] More than 500 of 660 people attending the morning Masses at Fr Allan's church on Sunday, 27 October, signed a letter to *The Times* expressing support for their parish priest. See *The Times*, 28 October 1968.
[3] At this time the Freedom of Conscience Fund had made grants of £445 to eight priests suffering hardship. The Fund knew about the attitudes of 220 priests at this time. See the *Guardian*, 26 October 1968.

the rules of natural justice. These require that a person, against whom sanctions are sought, must be given reasonable notice of anything alleged against him, that he must be given a reasonable opportunity of defending himself, and that anyone deciding an issue must act fairly and impartially in reaching the decision. This duty of a bishop to observe the rules of natural justice cannot be taken away by any provision of the code of canon law. Provisions of the code of canon law, which limit the powers of the bishop, must, on the other hand, observe the minimum requirements of fairness and impartiality.

The position then appeared to be that the Archbishop of Southwark, or any other bishop, could not deprive a parish priest of his parish summarily since this would be contrary to canon law, and the procedures for deprivation had to be adhered to. In Fr Allan's case, this would probably have necessitated a judicial process on the grounds that Fr Allan had committed a delict.[1] Without this process, Fr Allan could not be deprived of the exercise of the powers of his priesthood since these derived from the office he held and not from the will of the bishop.[2] One further point of importance is that according to canon law, recourse to the lay courts to impede ecclesiastical jurisdiction is punishable by excommunication at the special instance of the Holy See. According to English law, however, once civil proceedings have been commenced any threat of excommunication would be a criminal contempt of court, and anyone making it would be liable to imprisonment. There would even be a possibility of proceedings for contempt in the event of an excommunication being pronounced after any proceedings had been terminated.

The situation was accordingly perilous, and at one time it seemed as if a head-on collision between the civil courts and the ecclesiastical authorities was likely. Fortunately this did not come about as wiser counsels prevailed. No more was heard about the dismissal of Fr Allan and the whole matter, as far as he was concerned, was allowed quietly to drop into oblivion.

[1] Although it would probably also have been possible to 'suspend' Fr Allan by episcopal decree if it could be shown that a 'delict' had been committed.
[2] Here again an episcopal decree 'suspending' Fr Allan from the exercise of his powers of priesthood might have been valid if it could be shown that he had committed a 'delict'.

M

Two other priests of the diocese, who had been penalised, were given new posts at the end of October, Fr John McNamara, one of the priests who had signed the letter to *The Times* opposing the Pope's teaching, and Fr David Payne of New Malden, Surrey, who had been relieved of his duties as a curate after writing to a local newspaper. They did not retract their position and their appointments were not made conditional on silence.[1] The situation in the Southwark Archdiocese was clearly improving, but the position of Fr Weir who remained suspended continued anomalous. In January 1969, I wrote to the Archbishop of Southwark on Fr Weir's behalf and received a courteous reply. Fr Weir was himself in touch with the Archbishop, and at the end of January he was reinstated.[2] Fr Weir stated that he had not changed his feelings about the Pope's ruling but that he would not be preaching about it. Asked how he would advise people who put birth control problems to him he replied: 'Any teaching must be presented in the light of the theological and personal considerations governing each case.' Monsignor Gibney, Vicar-General of Southwark, said: 'The Archbishop has not laid down any new requirements, but he is satisfied that Fr Weir will be prudent regarding criticisms of the Pope's teaching.'[3] So ended the Southwark crisis.[4]

The Nottingham situation was not so happily resolved, and at the time of writing it remains intractable. Bishop Ellis had issued a pastoral letter on 11 August 1968, in which he gave strong support to the Encyclical. Dealing with the question of conscience he wrote: 'There is a specious appeal to conscience, but a silence as to

[1] See *The Times*, 30 October 1968. Monsignor Gibney, Vicar-General of the Southwark archdiocese, had compared Fr Payne favourably with Fr Weir: 'Father Weir caused a lot of trouble. Father Payne has kept very quiet.' *Observer*, 18 August 1968.
[2] See *The Times*, 31 January 1969.   [3] *Catholic Herald*, 7 February 1969.
[4] 'Archbishop Cowderoy,' I wrote, in an article published the week of Fr Weir's reinstatement, 'is a man of deep faith and strongly held views and holds high office in the Church. It is difficult for any leader to move from an entrenched position and for a Church leader perhaps most difficult of all, but Archbishop Cowderoy has succeeded in doing this without loss of authority or dignity. His status in his own diocese will be greatly increased by the charitable magnanimity with which he has supplemented his firm stand on principles.' See *Catholic Herald*, 8 November 1968. I have long enjoyed Archbishop Cowderoy's friendship and admired his selflessness and pastoral zeal and hence was personally distressed at being in any way in conflict with him. We were fully reconciled at the Hierarchy Low Week reception on 15 April 1969.

the duty of informing that conscience according to God's law. Followed to its logical conclusion, it implies that when, for example, a husband in so called good conscience is attracted to another woman, he may quite rightly have intercourse with her. In accordance with such ideas, Our Lord would not have said to the adulterous woman: "Go and sin no more", but: "you have followed your conscience and therefore you have no sin. You may continue so to act".[1] In October–November 1968, three priests were suspended by Bishop Ellis because of their attitude to *Humanae Vitae*. They were Fr James Kilkenny, parish priest of St Patrick's, Leicester, Fr Aquinas Furlong, master at the Becket School, Nottingham, and Fr Joseph Calnan, priest-in-charge of the new parish of Clown, Derbyshire. A fourth priest, Fr John Keane, curate at the Good Shepherd Church, Woodthorpe, Nottingham, was later also suspended. It seems that 'suspension' was the fate of these priests, but since the Bishop declined to put anything in writing there remains some doubt about their status. Fr James Kilkenny had written to the Bishop in October to say that he could not present a teaching which he regarded as wrong. Fr Kilkenny, who had been a priest for nineteen years, saw the Bishop later in the month, and was dismissed from his parish. A few weeks' later, Fr Murdoch, the dean of the area, publicly stated: 'Fr Kilkenny has not been suspended, he simply asked to leave.'[2] Fr Kilkenny denied this story of resignation in a letter in the paper of the same date. The Bishop had told him that he would be sending a priest to take over his parish, and the priest arrived on 31 October. Fr Kilkenny then left the parish.[3] A number of Fr Kilkenny's parishioners protested in a petition to the Bishop but, owing to his departure and the fact that he had only been in the parish a few weeks, little organisation took place.

[1] A full account of the Nottingham situation is contained in a pamphlet 'Four Honest Men' published in September 1969 by a committee of the Nottingham Catholic Renewal Group. The pastoral letter is quoted on page 18. For another account of the Nottingham crisis, see three articles by John Horgan, *Irish Times*, 6–8 January 1969.
[2] See *Leicester Mercury*, 28 November 1968.
[3] It is doubtful whether the Bishop's action was valid either canonically or at English law, but since Fr Kilkenny complied with the verbal order there has never been any means of testing this. It was also put about that Fr Kilkenny had inherited a fortune from a rich uncle in the United States, but there was no truth in this.

On 14 November, the Press reported that forty-eight priests of the diocese were reliably known to be unhappy about the Encyclical. A week later, on 21 November, all the priests of the City of Nottingham, concelebrated Mass at the Cathedral as a common prayer for the solution of their difficulties, but at the mass a sermon, reported in the Press, was preached by one parish priest who represented the mass as being a gesture in support of the Bishop. *The Times*, in response to this, reported that sixteen of the thirty-eight Nottingham city priests were in fact opposed to the Encyclical. The following day, a meeting was called of the thirty-eight priests in order to pass a resolution to be sent to *The Times* and repudiate the report, but there was no agreement at the stormy meeting. A resolution was put to the vote that the priests 'unanimously accept the teaching of *Humanae Vitae*', but in a secret ballot sixteen of the thirty-eight voted against it. Some of the clergy said that they would be prepared to accept the resolution if it included the words 'as interpreted by the universal *magisterium*'. This, too, raised objections and twelve voted against it. As a result no agreed statement could be sent to *The Times*.

A few days later, a meeting of all the diocesan clergy was called to hear an address by Mgr McReavy, a staunch upholder of the Encyclical and a discussion of limited duration ensued. In a letter to the *Nottingham Evening Post*, the deans of the diocese declared that the clergy present were free to express their views and 'gave not the slightest indication of doubt or unrest'.[1] The following day, however, a letter appeared from Fr Mark Swaby, the Rector of the diocesan junior seminary, which gave a different account. 'I saw,' wrote Fr Swaby, 'considerable indications of doubt and unrest. Were the deans misled I wonder by the calm politeness with which questions were raised?'[2] The diocesan council of priests had also discussed the Encyclical at an earlier meeting and there had been divergent views expressed. Further controversy was caused by a somewhat emotional letter sent to various clergy of the diocese by the *Ad Hoc* group in London, calling upon them to stand firm, not to leave their parishes if requested to do so by the Bishop but to stand on their rights and to get in touch with

[1] 3 December 1968.
[2] *Nottingham Evening Post*, 4 December 1968.

a canon lawyer. This letter aroused the ire of the deans of the diocese who on 3 December published a letter in the Press denouncing the *Ad Hoc* communication as 'an attempt to incite a perfectly loyal and devoted clergy to rebel against and to defy their own Bishop and all ecclesiastical authority'.[1] A 'teach-in' on the Encyclical was held under lay auspices in Nottingham in November.

In December, Fr Keane wrote to the Bishop saying that while he was entirely willing to remain silent in public about the Encyclical, and indeed had always done so, he could not convince himself of its truth. He felt it his duty to confide what he thought to the Bishop. On going to see the Bishop, he was told to leave his parish, but not until after Christmas as there was no one to take his place until then. The parishioners thereupon organised a petition signed by over a thousand in a parish of which the total adult population is 1,500. A subsequent parish meeting appointed a delegation of eight to present the petition to the Bishop, and were able to do so after a number of delays. After a second parish meeting, and a meeting with the Bishop at which no progress was made, the parishioners appealed to the Apostolic Delegate and to Cardinal Heenan to intervene, but neither was able or willing to help. At the time of writing, the four priests remain suspended and are all outside the diocese, and on 30 August 1969, it became known that a fifth priest had been suspended, although his name was kept secret.[2] Throughout 1969 sporadic attempts were made to secure the reinstatement of Fr Keane, efforts coming mainly from his parishioners, but also from the Nottingham Catholic Renewal Group. Their difficulties were increased by the unwillingness of the Bishop to receive delegations or to comment on the situation publicly. As the Bishop's Secretary stated early on in the controversy, it was the Bishop's 'unyielding policy never to comment on such matters'.[3] Today Nottingham is the only English diocese in which priests remain under penalties for their attitude to the Encyclical.

[1] *Nottingham Evening Post*, 3 December 1968.
[2] See *The Times*, 30 August 1969.
[3] I wrote to the bishop on 19 December 1968, asking him to reconsider his attitude to the suspended priests 'at this time of charity and goodwill' but never received a reply.

THE DEVELOPING SITUATION IN ENGLAND

Certain other developments in the English situation need to be recorded. Cardinal Heenan's position in the controversy retained throughout an element of ambiguity which was certainly not dispelled by an incident which occurred on 6 December 1968 during an interview with Mr David Frost.[1] The Cardinal stressed that the rights of conscience were paramount, and that it was a basic teaching of the Church that everyone must follow conscience. He went on: 'Now it's the duty of a Catholic to inform his conscience. But it could happen easily, particularly after this long period of dispute and doubt, it could happen that a couple might say conscientiously I'm quite sure that this is the right thing for me to do. And if that can be said conscientiously, this is what I must do, then of course they must follow their conscience. There is no dispute about this.' Pressed by Mr Frost to answer the question, 'What should the priest say in this?', the Cardinal replied: 'God bless you. If they're really following their conscience then in the sight of God, which is all that matters – the priest, the bishop, the Pope doesn't matter compared with God – if every person is really dealing with Almighty God.' The Cardinal also made it clear that in such circumstances the priest should not refuse to admit the couple to the sacraments. In one sense it is true that the Cardinal had said nothing new, but the manner in which it was said, the setting, the degree of explicitness about admission to the sacraments, gave his words an impact which was new. When Mr Frost commented that previously the Cardinal had not spoken out as clearly or as forthrightly, His Eminence replied: 'I didn't have Mr Frost to help me to express myself.' The phrase, 'God bless you', is of course an ambiguous one and is open to different interpretations, but the broadcast was generally interpreted as a more liberal approach to the problem from the Cardinal than had previously been seen.[2]

[1] Quotations which follow are taken from the transcript of the interview kindly supplied by London Weekend Television. The interview was widely reported in the Press, and extracts from it also appeared in *The Times*, 7 December 1968.
[2] Following the broadcast and comments in the Press, Cardinal Heenan stated that his remarks on television were not to be taken to mean that he had told Catholics to ignore the Pope's Encyclical on birth control. See *The Times*, 9 December 1968. News

The Cardinal came into controversy again later in the same month when he wrote a letter to *The Times* protesting against what he called 'over-exposure' of the Roman Catholic Church in England in the newspaper. Having criticised a headline about Catholic theologians calling for a charter of their rights which appeared in *The Times* on 18 December, the Cardinal came to the main point of his letter: 'I have left until last my chief reason for writing this letter. May I put in a plea for your non-Catholic readers? They must be growing very tired of the extensive coverage given to any item of news concerning the Church of Rome. Every day they are told of priests who disagree with the Pope, or regret their vow of chastity, of laymen who allegedly speak in the name of their enlightened brethren to express contempt for the bishops and all in authority in the Church. I think that the majority of your readers would be glad of some respite. I can assure you that my community is beginning to suffer from over-exposure.'[1] This provoked a sharp reply from Professor C. J. Hamson of Cambridge who stated that the tension within the Church concerned a great issue, the conciliation of liberty with authority and the balance of the rights of the individual with the legitimate demands of the community. Accordingly, the events in England had an importance far transcending the immediate scene. Professor Hamson went on to praise *The Times* for giving publicity to important matters which the Church authorities would have preferred to keep secret. He concluded: 'I note that His Eminence the Cardinal Archbishop of Westminster complains that, so doing, you have over-exposed a community which he describes as his. I do not for my part claim as mine the community of which I trust I may be reckoned a member; but I do venture to assure you that there has certainly been no over-exposure. You have caused a chink of

---

of the Cardinal's broadcast flashed round the world, and I happened to be in St Louis, Missouri, giving a lecture at the University on theological contributions to the solving of world population problems, when news of the Cardinal's broadcast arrived. Wireless and television programmes were interrupted with a news flash. I had been stressing the primacy of the rights of conscience and some at the Conference believed that I had synchronised my remarks with those of the Cardinal. This was not so. Most people interpreted the remark, 'God bless you', in a liberal sense, but some took a different view. The Apostolic Delegate in Britain, Archbishop Cardinale, for example, told me, that what the Cardinal had meant was 'God help you'.

[1] See *The Times*, 19 December 1968.

light to penetrate into the secretive dark in which the ecclesiastical authorities have long accustomed themselves to operate. This they find, understandably enough, painful and distressing. It is, however, evidently desirable that their established practices should in this manner continue to be disturbed. Long may you continue so to disturb them.'[1]

In January of the following year, the Cardinal was once again involved in a clash with *The Times* over its reporting of Catholic news. The incident arose from the reporting of the circumstances of the resignation of Fr Benedict Sketchley, Headmaster of St Michael's School, Stevenage. Fr Sketchley was a priest of radical views who had been one of the signatories of the September priests' letter to *The Times*. During a speech at the school on 26 January, the Cardinal denied the report in *The Times* that the primary reason why Fr Sketchley was asked to resign was that he had signed this letter. The Cardinal then went on: 'In passing I would warn you to be very careful in reading *The Times* when things of Catholic interest are reported. There is a member of the staff of *The Times* who is a Catholic – I am not referring to Mr Rees-Mogg (the Editor) – who seeks every opportunity to produce slanted news which is not trustworthy. And this is a very good example, because any reporter who really wanted to know the truth could have discovered whether or not the signing of the letter to *The Times* had anything to do with the resignation of Fr Sketchley.' This, of course, was a serious accusation and damaging to the member of the staff concerned although the Cardinal had not named him. The Cardinal evidently realised that his statement had not been fair and retracted it in the course of an article dealing with the problem of publicity and the Church, published in *The Times* on 19 February.[2]

Meanwhile, rival organisations within the Church rallied their forces for the struggle. Before the issue of the Encyclical, Fr

[1] *The Times*, 24 December 1968.
[2] In the article the Cardinal stated that he had become over-sensitive about the reporting of Catholic news in *The Times* and had come to regard it as slanted. 'I said as much in a speech which – alas! – *The Times* reported without any slant. In the course of this speech I mistakenly attributed a biased report to one reporter. In fact this journalist was not responsible for the story. I have since privately expressed regret if I was unjust to *The Times* and to the journalist. It is well to confess publicly that it is sometimes the Church and not the Press which is at fault.'

Flanagan, the parish priest of Polegate in Surrey, had founded an organisation of Catholic priests *Cephas* with the task of combating 'neo-modernism in the Church'. The organisation was called *Cephas* (the name being chosen to indicate that the society like the Church was founded on a rock) but unfortunately the rock split. Some members of the society, finding Fr Flanagan's views too extreme, went off under the leadership of Mgr Clark and formed a new society called *Kephas*.[1] *Cephas*, as such, eventually went out of existence and became the Catholic Priests' Association with its lay auxiliary *Unitas*. Both these organisations strongly supported the Encyclical.

The *Ad Hoc* movement had sprung into existence to challenge the Encyclical, and in January 1969 was transformed into the Renewal Movement under the Chairmanship of Mr Peter Worden.[2] The aim of the Renewal Movement was to renew the Catholic Church in the spirit of the Second Vatican Council, and so had a wider purpose than the old *Ad Hoc* committee. In a manifesto issued after its second national meeting in March, it called for co-responsibility in the Church, for the observance of truth and justice, and for a complete openness in communication. 'Authority', declared the manifesto, 'should be an expression of the mind of the whole Church and not imposed from above. The principle of collegiality should be extended so that all bishops have a proper part in the central government of the Church with the Curia subject to them: this sharing of responsibility should be expanded to include other levels of the Church, clergy and lay, so that all members of the Church are fully able to use their talents in the service of the Gospel.' Groups of Renewal members were set up in the different dioceses in England and also in Scotland. Although concerned with wider issues, the Renewal Movement played a prominent part in organising discussion of the Encyclical.[3]

[1] In Matt. 16:18, Christ speaks of founding his Church upon a rock. He makes a pun on the name Peter. Peter's name in Greek was 'Petros' and the Greek for rock is 'Petra'. Christ, of course, did not speak Greek but Aramaic. The Aramaic for rock is 'Kepha'.

[2] See *The Times*, 22 January 1969.

[3] For example, on 7 March 1969, the Movement organised a 'teach-in' 'The Church and responsible Parenthood' in Leicester where the speakers were myself, Dr John Marshall, Mrs Worden and a priest. On 8 June 1969, the Scottish Renewal Movement organised another 'teach-in' at Glasgow where the principal speakers were myself and Fr Enda McDonagh.

Not all the laity were happy with these activities and a manifestation of the opposing point of view, stressing obedience to the
Pope, occurred in July 1969, when a group of laity sent a declaration of loyalty to the Pope. The declaration, not only professed
its loyalty to the Pope, but made a sharp attack on those who were
working for a more open Church.[1]

THE POSITION IN THE UNITED STATES

The first reactions to the Encyclical in the United States have
been noted.[2] The division among Catholics was similar to that
which had been shown in England but the conflict, partly
because of the continental nature of American society, the great
distances separating Catholics, and their different cultural
and ethnic backgrounds, did not have the concentrated national
character it assumed in England. Individual voices were raised in
protest. In New York, for example, Fr Robert Johann, a leading
Jesuit philosopher at Fordham University, said artificial birth
control was 'not only permissible but obligatory in certain circumstances'. He said it would be a sign of hope if Roman Catholics
ignored the Encyclical. Senator Eugene MacCarthy also let it be
known that he was 'not a very strong supporter' of the Pope's
pronouncement.[3] Dr John Noonan strongly criticised the Encyclical in an article appearing in the *National Catholic Reporter*.[4]
Another critic was Fr Bernard Häring the moral theologian who
was lecturing at Santa Barbara, California. 'We appeal to the
Pope,' declared Fr Häring, 'urgently to use all the resources of
collegiality in order to come to a broader consensus which is
worked out by the whole Christian community. This will surely

[1] The memorial to the Pope stated that it was made in grateful acknowledgement of
his decision to convene an extraordinary synod to assist the Church in passing through
its present period of difficulty, but added two other reasons of a more polemic
character, namely: 'In appreciation of the profession of faith by which in closing
the year of faith your Holiness effectively answered the false prophets who had
been so assiduously undermining the basic tenets of our faith; in thanksgiving
for the innumerable allocutions in which, week after week, your Holiness continues to
expose and refute the errors at present proliferating through the activities of irresponsible theologians and lay intellectuals who do not hesitate to scandalise the faithful by
"new catechisms" which by silence or ambiguity leave open to question even the
most certain of truths.'
[2] See p. 147 above.   [3] See the *Daily Telegraph*, 31 July 1968.
[4] See 7 August 1968.

strengthen his authority and bring solutions which can be worked out especially in view of the poor and uneducated.'[1] Dr André Hellegers, an obstetrician and a member of the papal Commission commented: 'I cannot believe that salvation is based on contraception by temperature and damnation is based on rubber.' Other lay critics were Mr and Mrs Crowley, founders of the Christian Family Movement, Professor Thomas Burch, the demographer at Georgetown University, and Mr Daniel Callaghan.

On the other hand the Encyclical was supported by Cardinal Krol of Philadelphia, who instructed his priests not to speak against the Encyclical, Bishop John Wright of Pittsburg who hailed it as 'a bold historic action', Archbishop Dwyer of Portland who expressed his gratitude to the Holy Father, and Monsignor Austin Vaughan, President of the American Catholic Theological Society, who declared that the Encyclical was binding on all Catholics.[2] Laymen, however, continued to criticise the Encyclical. The American Catholic Psychological Association, meeting in New York, issued a statement complaining that the Encyclical was based on 'inadequate knowledge' and demanding clarification.

[1] *The National Catholic Reporter*, 7 August 1968. Later in the month Fr Häring at a biblical-liturgical conference held at Holy Cross Abbey in Colorado, expanded his views, and declared it was necessary to 'rescue the Pope'. Fr Häring pointed out that he had been a member of the pre-Conciliar sub-commission and Commission on marriage. He stated: 'This pre-Conciliar sub-commission was thoroughly dominated by the Holy Office – people, in my eyes, cut off from the roots of life, an inbred group in which each had to prove to the other that he is more orthodox than the others, since their job was the hunting of witches. I told them: "you are professionally sick". I do not deny that they are good men, but I deny that they were living in a good structure. Pope John knew quite well how the situation was in that sub-commission and the result in the thrust on marriage, celibacy, and chastity. I heard that Pope John, receiving a friend, a simple father, a theologian, took the text which was sent to the bishops, took a ruler and said: "Look, five inches imperatives and then seven inches condemnation; here four inches condemnation, there three inches condemnation – how will this affect the Church's relationship to the world?"' ' Fr Häring was also a member of the papal Commission on birth control and commented on the fact that it had been constituted 'with all assurances for a conservative majority'. 'There were three people, Bishop Reuss, Canon Pierre de Locht, and to a modest extent myself, who dared to speak out for new solutions. It was amazing that, at the end, four-fifths of the Commission, four-fifths of the priests and almost one hundred per cent of the laity, came to the conclusion that there is no essential difference between the calculated use of temperature calendar tests in periodical continence and the more simple methods of birth regulation, such as the diaphragm or anti-fecundity pills.' See *Tablet*, 31 August 1968. Fr Häring elaborated his views in an article published in *Commonweal* on 22 September 1968.
[2] Bishop Wright was subsequently raised to the cardinalate and appointed to a curial post in Rome.

A New York group of ninety Catholic laymen declared 'loudly and clearly' their opposition to both the Encyclical and to Archbishop Cooke's pastoral letter supporting it. This group, the New York Association of Laymen, said that if Catholics considered such encyclicals as infallible 'we'd still be burning witches'.[1]

The American Press, both secular and religious, showed intense interest in the Encyclical. The *New York Times*, for example, devoted twenty-four columns to its coverage. The *New York Daily News* carried six separate stories on its first three pages the day after the Encyclical came out. The *New York Times* was gloomy about the Encyclical and its effect on the efforts being made to check a population explosion, but the *Daily News* refrained from any criticism of the Pope.[2] The Jesuit magazine, *America*, in an editorial published in August, said that the Pope's teaching should be most carefully and respectfully studied by all Catholics. It added, however: 'Theologians and married couples who are convinced after careful study, that other conclusions than those drawn by the Pope are possible for them, are not only free to follow their consciences, they must do so . . . the abdication of personal moral responsibility has never been a doctrine of the Church.'[3] The liberal Catholic weekly, *Commonweal*, was sharply critical of the Encyclical. It pointed out that 'for millions of lay people, the birth control question has been confronted, prayed over, and settled, and not in the direction of the Pope's Encyclical'.[4]

Faced with this conflict the United States bishops issued a preliminary statement through Archbishop John Dearden of Detroit, President of the National Conference of Catholic Bishops. The statement gave support to the Encyclical, but was moderate in tone. 'The Holy Father,' it said, 'speaking as the Supreme Teacher of the Church, has re-affirmed the principles to be followed in forming the Christian consciences of married persons in carrying out their responsibilities. Recognising his unique role in the Universal Church, we, the Bishops of the Church in the United States, unite with him in calling upon our priests and people to receive with sincerity what he has taught, to study it

[1] See *Catholic Herald*, 6 September 1968.   [2] See *Guardian*, 31 July 1968.
[3] See *Tablet*, 31 August 1968.   [4] See *Guardian*, 31 July 1968.

carefully, and to form their consciences in its light. We are aware of the difficulties that this teaching lays upon so many of our conscientious married people. But we must face the reality that struggling to live out the will of God will often entail sacrifice.'[1]

Dr Germain Grisez, Professor of Philosophy at Georgetown University, Washington, and author of the book *Contraception and the Natural Law*, was both more explicit and more uncompromising. 'The thing which is peculiar to Catholics,' he wrote, 'is that we are Papists. I think that the decision is undoubtedly a very hard one, and many people will have to decide whether they want to be Papists, that is Catholic, or not. If one is a Catholic, one is a Papist. And if one is a Papist, then one cannot say "Rome has spoken but the cause goes on". One has to say, "Rome has spoken the cause is finished." '[2]

These skirmishings were widely reported in the Press, but Washington was destined to be the centre of the struggle over the Encyclical in the Catholic Church in America and provided a forum for a confrontation between the liberal reformers of the Catholic University of America and of the Archdiocese of Washington on the one hand, and the ultra conservative Cardinal O'Boyle, Archbishop of Washington on the other. Two separate battles were fought, one between the Cardinal and the theologians of the University, the other between the Cardinal and his dissenting priests.

Fr Charles Curran, Professor of Moral Theology at the Catholic University of America, took the lead in organising a theological protest. A statement, criticising the Encyclical, was issued on Tuesday, 30 July, and signed in the first place by eighty-seven theologians. By the end of the week, two hundred Catholic theologians had signed it and eventually it was to attract more than six hundred signatures. The statement acknowledged the distinct role of the 'hierarchical *magisterium*' in the Church, but pointed out that theologians had a special responsibility in evaluating and interpreting pronouncements. 'The Encyclical,'

---

[1] *National Catholic Reporter*, 7 August 1968. After the issue of the letter, the Secretary of the National Conference of Bishops, Bishop Bernadin made it plain that the Bishops' statement was intended to endorse the Encyclical. They in no way intended to imply that there was any divergence between their statement and that of the Pope.
[2] *National Catholic Reporter*, 7 August 1968.

went on the statement, 'is not an infallible teaching. History shows that a number of statements of similar, or even greater authoritative weight, have subsequently been proven inadequate or even erroneous. Past authoritative statements on religious liberty, interest taking, the right to silence, and the ends of marriage, have all been corrected at a later date . . . furthermore, the Encyclical betrays a narrow and positivistic notion of papal authority, as illustrated by the rejection of the majority view presented by the Commission established to consider the question, as well as by the rejection of the conclusions of a large part of the international Catholic theological community. Likewise, we take exception to some of the specific ethical conclusions contained in the Encyclical. They are based on an inadequate concept of natural law: the multiple forms of natural law theory are ignored and the fact that competent philosophers come to different conclusions on this very question is disregarded.' The statement pointed out that it was common teaching in the Church that Catholics could dissent from authoritative, non-infallible teachings of the *magisterium* when there were sufficient reasons for doing so, and concluded: 'Therefore, as Roman Catholic theologians conscious of our duty and our limitations, we conclude that spouses may responsibly decide according to their conscience that artificial contraception in some circumstances is permissible and indeed necessary to preserve and foster the values and sacredness of marriage. It is our conviction also that true commitment to the mystery of Christ and the Church requires a candid statement of mind at this time by all Catholic theologians.'[1]

A few days later, five days after the issue of the Encyclical, fifty-one of the 300 priests of the Archdiocese of Washington took separate action and issued a statement of conscience expressing their opposition to the Encyclical.[2] Cardinal O'Boyle was out-

---

[1] *National Catholic Reporter*, 7 August 1968. Fr Bernard Häring signed the declaration and other scholars who signed included Christopher Mooney, head of the Theology Department at Fordham University, John O'Brien of the University of Notre Dame, David Burrell of Notre Dame, Aelred Tegels, editor of *Worship* magazine, Francis X. Murphy, Monsignor George Schlichte, and David Bowman, the Bishops' ecumenical aide assigned to the National Council of Churches.

[2] Cardinal O'Boyle sent a letter to all priests in his archdiocese forbidding them to question publicly the Pope's Encyclical or to preach doctrines contrary to those set forth in it. See *Tablet*, 17 August 1968.

raged by what he considered this act of defiance. He did not, however, take immediate action and waited until the beginning of September to show his hand. One priest, Fr Joseph O'Donoghue, was suspended for reading dissenting opinions on the Encyclical from the pulpit during the celebration of mass. Fr O'Donoghue was ordered to move out of his Washington parish at once.[1] On 4 September, the Cardinal held a Press conference, at which he was joined by five experts on canon law, on the moral and medical aspects of contraception. He declared that the real issue was not the Pope's Encyclical, but the authority of the Church hierarchy. 'The Catholic Church,' he said, 'is certainly not run in such a way that priests who will not follow the pastoral directives of their bishop can be allowed to go on as they like.' The Cardinal made public a letter he had sent to the dissenting priests the previous month saying: 'For a loyal Catholic the fact that his conscience tells him to do what the Church teaches is always forbidden is enough to warn him that his conscience is going wrong.' In an aside he added, if a priest could not follow the Pope's teaching, 'he ought to be his own Pope and get himself a church.'[2] By the middle of September the Cardinal had disciplined at least eight priests for persisting in their opposition to the Pope's Encyclical. This was announced at a news conference on 18 September, by Fr John Corrigan, Chairman of the Association of Washington Priests who, himself, had been disciplined. The sanctions included the suspension of one or more priestly functions, including that of hearing confessions. Other dissenting priests faced similar penalties unless they promised the Cardinal that they would not preach, teach, or counsel dissent from the Encyclical's teaching. The Cardinal was still interviewing priests at the time the Press conference was held. The most severe penalty imposed was that on Fr John Fenlon, of St Mary's Church, Rockville, Maryland. He

[1] *The Times*, 5 September 1968.
[2] The National Federation of Priests Councils (N.F.P.C.) wrote to the Cardinal on 9 September asking him to appoint an impartial panel to review Fr O'Donoghue's case. When no reply was received they asked the National Conference of Catholic Bishops to intervene. At the same time the Washington Priests Association asked Archbishop Dearden, President of the Conference, to submit the case to the Bishops' committee on arbitration and mediation. The Archbishop declined to do so. The N.F.P.C. was supported in its demand by the Baltimore archdiocesan senate of Priests. *Tablet*, 5 October 1968.

was forbidden to teach, preach, counsel, hear confessions, or to say Mass in public. Differing penalties were imposed upon the other priests. Fr Corrigan stated that all those who were disciplined were told that this action would later be confirmed in writing. The priests had appealed to Archbishop Dearden as President of the National Conference of Catholic Bishops to arbitrate in the dispute, but he had declined to do so.[1]

On 20 September, Cardinal O'Boyle issued a pastoral letter to be read at all Masses the following Sunday, 22 September, in which he denounced the attitude of the dissenting priests. He pointed out that a curse from the book of Deuteronomy would fall upon those who followed their own conscience rather than the divine law.[2] Having stated that he had made it clear to the priests that they could not be allowed to continue to act on his authorisation in a manner contrary to the teaching of the Church, the Cardinal went on: 'But they have assumed an inflexible position in defiance of my pastoral instruction. Every one of us, regardless of his station in life, is subject to a higher authority, and priests are no exception. I am sure you can clearly see why I have no choice but to act under the circumstances that face me.' The Cardinal then appealed to the laity to use their powers of persuasion to turn back to Catholic truth anyone whom they knew was following the divergent opinions.[3]

The Cardinal, himself, read out the pastoral at St Matthew's Cathedral in Washington, and it was also read in 129 other churches of his Archdiocese. Catholics walked out of the cathedral while he was reading the pastoral from the pulpit. When he had finished the congregation which remained burst into applause. It was estimated that 200 Catholics had walked out of the cathedral, and another 235 had walked out at four other churches when the pastoral was being read during morning services.[4]

The Cardinal's stand did not determine the issue. Eleven of the original fifty-one priests were reconciled with their pastor, but the remainder of the original group, together with an extra four sup-

---

[1] See *New York Times*, 19 September 1968.
[2] See Deut. 29:18–20.
[3] See *New York Times*, 21 September 1968.
[4] See *Charlotte Observer*, September.

porters, issued a joint statement reaffirming their stand on freedom of conscience. They pointed out that because the Cardinal had been interviewing priests individually, they felt it necessary to reaffirm their corporate position. The Washington Priests' Association announced that it had engaged a civil lawyer and two canon lawyers to investigate the position of the disciplined priests and to work for their reinstatement. The Cardinal's actions also provoked a protest from the executive board of the American National Association of Laymen, which represents 12,000 Catholic laymen. In a statement issued on 21 September, the board said: 'Cardinal O'Boyle says that by following his conscience in the matter of birth control, the layman is misled and could bring down on himself so horrible a curse as . . . the wrath and jealousy of the Lord. We find it hard to believe that Cardinal O'Boyle has such a punitive view of God. Moreover, we find such a view inconceivable. We appeal to the Cardinal and to all of this nation's bishops to realise that the laity is disheartened by the repeated lack of reality and charity toward dissenting bishops, priests, religious and laymen as exemplified so flagrantly in this particular instance.'[1]

Later, another group of laymen took a different view and issued a statement warning that the Church faced 'widespread apostasy and schism'. This statement came from an organisation called 'Catholics United for the Faith', and they made their views known in a letter published at a Press conference in Washington in October. The letter declared that the organisation intended to give its 'unswerving support to the teaching authority of the Church'.[2]

At the beginning of October Cardinal O'Boyle announced that he had ordered thirty-nine priests to stop exercising some or all of their priestly functions because they disagreed with him over the Encyclical. He warned the priests that if they continued to speak out publicly on birth control he would expel them from their rectories, a penalty which he had already imposed on five of the priests. Thirty-one of these priests came from the Washington Archdiocese, six were members of religious orders, and two were

[1] For this and the previous quotations, see *Tablet*, 28 September 1968.
[2] *Catholic Herald*, 11 October 1968.

N

from other dioceses doing special work in Washington. 'The real issue,' said the Cardinal in a statement, 'in this matter is simply this: Though some of these priests accept Pope Paul's Encyclical, *Humanae Vitae*, they insist on adding the qualifying sentence; "Spouses may responsibly decide according to their own conscience that artificial contraception in some circumstances is permissible and indeed necessary to preserve and foster the values and sacredness of marriage." Nowhere in the Encyclical does the Holy Father make any provision whatsoever for such an exception. I will loyally follow the teaching of the Church founded by Christ, entrusted to the care of Peter and the Apostles. Paul VI is the successor of Peter and the supreme teacher in the Church. I stand with the Pope.' The Cardinal said he was disciplining the priests 'reluctantly and sadly' but he had no other choice because of his obligation as a bishop. 'I delayed as long as I possibly could – in fact, nine weeks – in the hope that with reflection and prayer these priests would find themselves able to accept without reservation the teaching of the Church regarding contraception.' He had had more than a hundred meetings with priests individually and ten with them as a group and had written them long letters, but he added: 'It is now obvious that my efforts and those of others who have worked with me have achieved only a partial success. As I have said before, I am responsible to God for the soul of every Catholic in this Archdiocese. In good conscience I cannot stand idly by and see our good people confused and misled with respect to the teaching of the Church.'[1]

The Cardinal's statement provoked a reply from the Association of Washington Priests. Fr Corrigan, their chairman, speaking on their behalf, said they believed their position of respecting the responsible consciences of couples had been vindicated by a succession of statements from episcopal conferences in other countries: 'Thus for Cardinal O'Boyle to penalise 39 men and in 5 cases to fully suspend them and evict them from their homes with 3 days' notice is, in our judgement, an arbitrary, unjust and scandalous misuse of authority.' Fr Corrigan went on to say that the penalties imposed bore no evident relationship to the theological attitudes of individual priests or their pastoral practice.

[1] See *National Catholic Reporter*, 9 October 1968.

'Try as we may, we can find no discernible norm by which these penalties were inflicted.'[1]

Cardinal O'Boyle's stand caused intense controversy among American Catholics. Cardinal McIntyre of Los Angeles expressed his wholehearted support, and described Cardinal O'Boyle's pastoral letter as 'magnificent'. It should be read, he added, by all who wish to understand the controversy. Others were less enthusiastic, and regarded the whole dispute as totally unnecessary.[2] Certainly in the neighbouring diocese of Baltimore a group of priests had been as outspoken as those in Washington but, having held conversations with Cardinal Shehan, their Archbishop, no action was taken against them.

In March 1969 the National Federation of Priests' Conferences asked the American hierarchy to intervene in the dispute by setting up a fact-finding committee but the bishops declined to take action. By this time only nineteen of the original group of priests remained concerned since the others for the most part had left the active priesthood. Of the nineteen, nine remained active in the priesthood in the Archdiocese of Washington, three were working as priests elsewhere, and six were on leave of absence. The Board of the N.F.P.C. were then asked by the delegates to take 'appropriate action' and thereupon, took legal action within the

[1] The priests' association gave the following breakdown of penalties imposed by Cardinal O'Boyle.

Relieved of faculties to hear confessions, to teach, to preach, to say public Mass, and ordered to move out of rectory – Fathers John Corrigan, John L. Fenlon, Luke McArthur, a Salvatorian, T. Joseph O'Donoghue, and Joseph R. Schubert.

Relieved of faculties to teach, preach, and hear confessions – Fathers William Birdsall, S.J., Luke Caimi, Carl Dianda, John Dillon, Hugo Duhn, Ralph Dwan, James Kennelly, Shane MacCarthy, George Malzone, John McGarraghy, Paul Norton, George Pavloff, George Spellman, James Wintz, S.J.

Relieved of faculties to teach and hear confessions – Fathers Joseph Byron, pastor of St James, Raymond Machesney, Joseph O'Connell, William Porter, Frank Ruppert, and Gerald Sigler.

Relieved of faculties to hear confessions – Fathers William Berry, André Bouchard, John Cunico, Eamon Dignan, Charles Ebbecke, Joseph Haslinger, Paul Hill, Horace McKenna, S.J., John O'Laughlin, S.J., Francis Reardon, S.J., pastor of St Aloysius, Henry Slevin.

Granted leave of absence – Father William Meyer.

Uncertain – Fathers Robert Hovda and Hilary Benden.

See *National Catholic Reporter*, 9 October 1968.

[2] The Canon Law Society of America, without mentioning the Encyclical, went on record at Boston as being opposed to the use of ecclesiastical sanctions for suppressing 'the proper expression of dissent in an area where men of good conscience and theological competence are divided'. The *Tablet*, 5 October 1968.

system of Church courts to test whether priests who felt themselves wrongfully punished by their superiors could obtain a hearing from an impartial Church tribunal. In September 1969 the accused priests petitioned the tribunal of the Washington archdiocese for a hearing, aided by a panel of nine canon lawyers, who had volunteered for the task. The petition was refused on the grounds that under canon law only the Pope can judge the actions of a cardinal. The priests then took their case to the appeals court, the Cleveland diocesan tribunal. The appeal was made in October and in December 1969 the court rejected their plea that since their case consisted in a claim that they had been punished without being tried, they were not seeking to try the Cardinal but to turn themselves into defendants. The court held that if the case was accepted, Cardinal O'Boyle would be placed on trial, and they had no powers to try a cardinal. The court advised that their only means of redress lay in an appeal to the Pope. This would be an administrative review rather than a judicial process. Nevertheless the priests appealed to the Pope on 11 February 1970. They asked that administrative review and its weaknesses should be avoided by referring their case to the Rota, the Church's highest court, or to a special board of judges acceptable to Cardinal O'Boyle and themselves, which would hear the case in the United States.

The appeal was acknowledged by Rome on 18 April in a letter signed by the Apostolic Delegate in the United States, Archbishop Raimondi, and this was followed by a letter from Cardinal Villot, papal Secretary of State, urging the priests to seek a reconciliation with Cardinal O'Boyle. Negotiations with the Cardinal were opened but these broke down and in July Cardinal Villot referred the case 'for the examination and decision of the competent Sacred Congregation of the Clergy'. The prefect of this congregation was Cardinal Wright but he declined to begin the hearing of the case because of what he considered a threatening letter sent by the canon lawyers advising the priests, which was sent to him in August. The canon lawyers had stated that they no longer felt justified in advising their clients to avoid publicity: 'Unless the priests are guaranteed some sort of impartial hearing the N.F.P.C. is contemplating taking the case to every senate and association in its membership to solicit their support.' The Cardinal replied that he did not work under threat and temporarily shelved hearing the case or referring it to the Congregation.[1] Subsequently, on receiving an assurance from the canon lawyers concerned that there had been no intention of threatening publicity the Cardinal handed over the case to the Congregation of the Clergy.[2] At the time of writing, this tangled dispute continues.[3]

The dispute between Cardinal O'Boyle as Chancellor of the Catholic University of America, and the twenty professors who had spoken out against the Encyclical had a happier outcome. In April 1969 the academic senate, a forty-four member body which includes all of the University's deans, unanimously adopted the report of a five-man board of inquiry which had been appointed to investigate the whole situation. The trustees of the University ordered the investigation in September after the University became a centre of opposition to the papal declaration.[4] The report made a number of recommendations. First, that the University should recognise that the statement made by the professors on 30 July was adequately supported by theological scholarship and that in making it they did not violate their commitment to the academic or theological communities. Accordingly, no further

---

[1] See the *National Catholic Reporter*, 9 October 1970.   [2] Ibid., 30 October 1970.

[3] Clearly what American Catholic priests need is some means of obtaining 'due process'. A report as to how this could be achieved was made by the Canon Law Society of America to the National Conference of Catholic Bishops in October 1969. In November 1969 the Conference unanimously accepted the Report and recommended that bishops should experiment with procedures such as those outlined in the document 'adapted where necessary to local circumstances, and to the prompt implementation on the diocesan, provincial and regional levels of this and other well-conceived plans which may become advisable for that secure protection of human rights and freedoms which should always be among the goals of the Church'. In July 1970, the Archdiocese of Chicago established a 'due process' procedure. In October the Society meeting at New Orleans set up a legal aid agency for priests and others in trouble with their bishops. During a visit to Rome in April 1971 I ascertained that a compromise solution had been agreed by the Congregation of the Clergy and the dissident priests but details had not been made public. Whether this compromise will prove acceptable to Cardinal O'Boyle is another matter.

[4] The inquiry had to determine whether seventeen theologians in the faculty 'violated their commitments as teachers' in opposing in public the Pope's Encyclical on birth control. The investigation was carried out by the faculty, not by the bishops. The theologians were allowed to continue to teach pending the issue of the report if they agreed to abstain from making any public statements against the Encyclical. Those declining to make this agreement were to be suspended temporarily pending completion of the inquiry but were to receive their salaries. *Tablet*, 14 September 1968.

proceedings should be instituted which would question the fitness of the professors to teach at the University. The report went on to suggest that the University should proceed quickly to institute formally 'norms of academic freedom and academic due process'. Moreover, the University should reassure the academic community that 'in the future it will not resort even to a threat of suspension, much less actual suspension of faculty members, without first according the professor involved academic due process'. Finally, the report pointed out that 'while acknowledging the ultimate canonical jurisdiction and doctrinal competence of the hierarchy, the trustees remain sensitive to the devastating effect of any exercise of power in the resolution of academic difficulties.'[1] The report constituted a landmark in Catholic higher education because, for the first time, a controversial dispute over theology and dissent was submitted to academic rather than to ecclesiastical authority. An ironic point is that the Catholic University is the only institute of higher learning in the United States sponsored directly by the Pope.[2]

Meanwhile, the United States bishops had made a second statement at their biannual conference, which was held by chance in Washington in November. Some novel features were apparent. The dissident Washington priests and their supporters, with folk-singing cheer leaders, held a 'pray-in' outside the conference doors in the lobby of the Hilton Hotel where the bishops were meeting. They were praying for an independent tribunal of bishops to judge between them and the Cardinal. Senator Eugene McCarthy addressed a rally on the eve of the first meeting of the bishops and read poetry which he had specially composed for the occasion. Despite these efforts, the statement, which was issued in the form of an eleven-thousand-word pastoral, 'Human

[1] See *Tablet*, 19 April 1969. The 'devastating effect' of an exercise of arbitrary power might well have been seen in a reopening on a national scale of the dispute as to whether federal funds should be made available to institutes of Catholic higher learning. This consideration may well have influenced the trustees in accepting the report of the inquiry they had appointed.

[2] For an account of the report, see *The Times*, 16 April 1969, and the *Tablet*, 19 April 1969. The dissenting professors had been holding their teaching posts since September 1968 with the proviso that they should be silent during the seven-month inquiry. The board of trustees of the University included in its membership Cardinal Krol of Philadelphia, Cardinal McIntyre of Los Angeles, Cardinal Shehan of Baltimore, as well as Archbishop O'Boyle.

Life in Our Day', was notably conservative. The bishops had met from 11–15 November and adopted the document by a vote of 180 to 8. The letter had been originally drafted by a committee headed by Bishop Wright of Pittsburg. It stated that *Humanae Vitae* 'presents without ambiguity, doubt, or hesitation, the authentic teaching of the Church concerning the objective evil of that contraception which closes the marital act to the transmission of life, deliberately making it unfruitful'. Nevertheless, the bishops did recognise tenuously the rights of conscience. '*Humanae Vitae* does not discuss the question of the good faith of those who make practical decisions in conscience against what the Church considers a divine law and the Will of God. The Encyclical does not undertake to judge the consciences of individuals but to set forth the authentic teaching of the Church, which Catholics believe interprets the divine law to which consciences should be conformed.' But the bishops went on to remind Catholic couples that 'however circumstances may reduce moral guilt, no one following the teaching of the Church can deny the objective evil of artificial contraception itself'. Nevertheless couples were urged not to lose heart, but to continue 'to take full advantage of the strength which comes from the sacrament of penance and the grace, healing and peace in the Eucharist'.[1]

The United States bishops may have been more or less united behind the Encyclical, but the indications are that very many priests took a different point of view. In a national poll carried out in the autumn of 1968, it was indicated that almost exactly half of United States diocesan priests disagreed with Pope Paul's condemnation of artificial contraception, and that his Encyclical had little effect in changing their minds. In this first major survey of the opinions of United States priests since the issue of the Encyclical, it was found that 51 per cent of the priests who responded held, before the Encyclical, that artificial contraception was permissible in some circumstances, and 49 per cent held the same view after it. One per cent said they had become undecided. The split among the priests was heavily influenced by age with the older priests – about 95 per cent opposed to contraception – and the younger ones, about 95 per cent favouring it.

[1] See *Tablet*, 23 November 1968, and *The Times*, 16 November 1968.

The signs of trouble ahead are unmistakable.[1] Much will depend on the policy followed by the bishops and it is significant that outside of the Archdiocese of Washington there has been no sustained attempt to enforce the Encyclical. A sign of future attitudes may perhaps be traced in the statement of Cardinal Dearden, the Archbishop of Detroit, to the meeting of the National Conference of Catholic Bishops in Houston, Texas, in April 1969, where he told the bishops that they must bestir themselves to keep the obedience of their people. 'It is not authority that is questioned,' he said, 'but the way in which authority is exercised.' To remain credible, authority should function in a manner different from the past. There should be procedures to involve many people in making decisions – to a degree greater than the Church had known – that would permit 'a more intelligent exercise of authority through collaboration of those who are with us in the Church'.[2]

THE VIEWS OF THE HIERARCHIES

The views of the English and American hierarchies on the Encyclical have already been described.[3] In the months following the issue of the Encyclical, hierarchies in other countries also gave their views and they varied widely. The firmest and most unreserved backing for the Pope came from the hierarchies of Ireland, Scotland, Australia, New Zealand, and Italy. The Irish bishops declared that the Encyclical contained 'the authentic teaching of the Pope. We are confident that our people will accept it as such and give it that wholehearted assent which the Second Vatican Council requires'. With regard to the position of con-

[1] For a full account of the survey, see *National Catholic Reporter*, 9 October 1968. The survey was carried out by mail in late August to a random sample of about 3,750 diocesan priests or 10 per cent of all diocesan priests, and within 30 days 1,500 replies were received constituting a 40 per cent return. It was conducted under the auspices of the Center for the Study of Man, an institute on the campus of the University of Notre Dame and sponsored by the *National Catholic Reporter* and a number of other organisations. 45 per cent replied affirmatively to the question 'Did you advise married people prior to the Encyclical that in some circumstances artificial contraception was permissible?' and 41 per cent replied affirmatively to the question: 'Do you give this advice now?'
[2] See *The Times*, 17 April 1969.
[3] See pp. 151–61 and pp. 176–7 and 186–7.

science, the bishops contented themselves with quoting from the pastoral constitution on the Church in the modern world issued by the Council in which reference is made to the fact that husband and wife must not act arbitrarily in their sexual relations, but must always be governed by a conscience submissive to the divine law and the teaching authority of the Church. The bishops, however, did declare their conviction that priests in the confessional 'without compromise of principle' would show the 'understanding and sympathy which Christ himself displayed'.[1]

The Scottish bishops were forthright in their declaration that the Pope was teaching as supreme pastor of the Church, and calling for the assent of the faithful. 'In the Encyclical, he has not stated a new doctrine on birth control, but has reaffirmed the traditional teaching of the Church and this teaching is not in doubt.' Passing on to the issue of conscience, the bishops dismissed it in these words: 'In the Encyclical, the Holy Father has given us the principles according to which Catholics are to form their consciences in this matter. The obligation of a Catholic to accept the teaching of the Church on any grave moral problem can never justifiably be regarded as an offence against the freedom of his conscience. Rather, the free acceptance of that particular obligation is implicit in the free decision, already made and still continuing, to accept the claim of the Catholic Church to speak with the authority of Christ.'[2] In other words, the bishops confined the operation of conscience to the initial acceptance of the Church's teaching office after which it does not apply to those matters on which the *magisterium* has spoken.

The Australian bishops in a joint statement issued on 5 August, affirmed that the Encyclical was 'an official exercise' of the Pope's teaching authority. 'Although the Holy Father did not choose to use his teaching authority to its full extent by solemn definition,' they declared, 'the doctrine of the Encyclical is authentic and authoritative. Accordingly, every member of the Church must be considered bound to accept the decision given by the Pope. To refuse to do so would be a grave act of disobedience.' While conscience was indeed the ultimate guide of morality, the

---

[1] *Tablet*, 6 October 1968.
[2] *The Times*, 7 October 1968, and *Tablet*, 12 October 1968.

bishops stressed that Christians in the formation of their consciences 'must be guided by the doctrine of the Church'.[1] Further
support for the Encyclical came from Cardinal Gilroy, Archbishop
of Sydney, and Archbishop Cahill in Canberra, speaking on public
occasions. Archbishop Cahill rebuked four priests for making a
statement to a Canberra newspaper that there could be circumstances in which artificial contraception could be used by sincere
Catholics despite the Pope's stand. Archbishop Cahill said the
Pope's views were clear and called for obedience, while the
priests' opinions were 'not in conformity with the teaching
authority of the Church'.[2] Similar backing came from the New
Zealand bishops who stressed that throughout the history of the
Church there had been one essentially unvaried stream of teaching to the effect that artificial contraception was contrary to the
natural moral law and must be firmly and resolutely rejected,
together with abortion and sterilisation.[3] The Italian bishops also
gave strong backing to the Pope, but suggested that priests
should be patient with couples who failed to observe the rule out
of weakness.[4]

In South America a number of hierarchies came out in support
of the Pope. Thus in November 1968 the Colombian bishops
declared that the Encyclical 'binds Catholics in conscience even
if it is not an *ex cathedra* definition'. They went on to list the 'very
great evils' which could follow from the use of artificial means of
birth control, 'the wide, open, easy way to infidelity in marriage';
'the moral degradation of many sectors of society'; 'the loss of
esteem and respect for womanhood' and 'the placing of a dangerous weapon in the hands of public authorities who, uncon-
cerned with moral issues, could, as experience shows, drift into
racial genocide'. They dismissed the criticism of the Encyclical as

[1] *Tablet*, 17 August 1968.
[2] Ibid. In October, 70 professional men signed a statement saying that leaders of the
Church in Australia should not silence priests for expressing views disagreeing with
those of the bishops. They expressed their gratitude in particular to Fr Crotty for his
comment on the Encyclical. Ibid. 26 October 1968.
[3] Ibid., 17 August 1968
[4] *Daily Telegraph*, 16 September 1968. They advised confessors that those whose
'failings do not derive from an egoistic refusal of fecundity, but rather from the
difficulties . . . of reconciling the exigencies of responsible parenthood with those of
reciprocal love' must be judged less harshly than those whose violations 'were inspired
solely by egoism and hedonism'.

springing from confusion in people's minds and the lack of serious study of the document. 'No number or quality of theologians can gather valid opinion against the manifest teachings of the *magisterium*; therefore such opinions cannot be validly followed by Catholics.'[1] South American bishops seemed especially concerned lest contraception should be considered as a substitute for development in tackling population problems. Thus speaking at the Latin America Bishops' Conference in September, Bishop Villalba of Riobamba, Ecuador, stressed that population problems were complex and delicate. 'Any unilateral approach, any simple solution is obviously wrong. It seems particularly dangerous to follow an anti-birth policy that tries to replace, or avoid, the demands of a constructive, more difficult policy of development, which is the only acceptable solution. It is not a matter of limiting the mouths at the table, but of multiplying the bread.'[2] A year later the Chilean Bishops' Conference came out in strong opposition to the Government's birth control programme. 'We ratify,' they declared, 'our unconditional agreement with the Supreme Head of the Church, who recalled in the Encyclical *Humanae Vitae* the Christian meaning of matrimony and the need to obey the law of nature and who criticised the use of artificial anti-conceptive measures. We also affirm that although all must act according to their consciences, the Christian must form his in the light of the Gospel and the teachings of the Church.'[3]

Backing for the Pope also came from Asian bishops. The Indian bishops issued a statement pledging their loyal adherence to the teachings of *Humanae Vitae* and calling on priests, religious and laymen to give it full allegiance. The bishops added that they expected governmental and public bodies not to penalise or impose disabilities on those who had conscientious objections to

[1] *Tablet*, 16 November 1968.
[2] Ibid., 21 September 1968.
[3] Ibid., 16 August 1969. A division of opinion existed in South America in ecclesiastical circles as in other parts of the world. Thus Father José Neves, rector of the São Paulo Institute in Brazil, which trains priests for religious congregations, defended the position taken by the bishops of Germany, Belgium, and the Netherlands on the Encyclical. This led to a clash with the Archbishop of São Paulo, Cardinal Rossi. Ibid., 30 November 1968. In January 1969 the provincial superior of the Dominicans in Brazil resigned from the priesthood and married, giving as one of his reasons for his resignation that 'to accept the confused and thoroughly unsound teachings about birth control . . . would have made me live a lie'. Ibid., 18 January 1969.

the methods employed by the Government in promoting its family planning campaign.[1]

Very different was the position taken up by the Belgian, German, Austrian, Canadian, Scandinavian, and Dutch bishops. These hierarchies all recognised a right of objective dissent from papal teaching, while accepting the Encyclical as a fact of major importance. The Belgian bishops, for example, pointed out that the Encyclical made no claim to infallibility and that this being so 'we are not held to absolute and unconditional support of the sort which is required for a definition of dogma'. The Encyclical should be received with the respect and the spirit of docility which the teaching authority established by Christ can legitimately demand, but it went on: 'Someone, however, who is competent in the matter under consideration and capable of forming a personal and well founded judgement – which necessarily presupposes a sufficient amount of knowledge – may, after a serious examination before God, come to other conclusions on certain points. In such a case, he has the right to follow his conviction provided that he remains sincerely disposed to continue his enquiry.' Even in such a case he must maintain 'sincerely his adherence to Christ and to his Church and respectfully acknowledge the importance of the supreme teaching authority of the Church as the conciliar document *Lumen Gentium* enjoins'. Care must also be taken not to create an unhealthy unrest or to question the very principle of authority. The Belgian bishops then went on to deal with the position of those who felt practical difficulties were too great to enable them to follow the teaching of the Encyclical. In such cases they must try honestly to find a means of adapting their conduct to the rules, but if they could not achieve

[1] *Catholic Herald*, 18 October 1968. Cardinal Gracias, Archbishop of Bombay, had earlier denied British newspaper reports that he had sent a confidential letter to India's bishops deploring the Pope's ban on birth control. The Cardinal stated that he 'not only accepts' the Pope's teaching on birth control 'but also supports it'. See the *Tablet*, 31 August 1968. The Indian bishops' statement was made by the standing committee of the Catholic Bishops' Conference of India at a meeting held in Bangalore from 30 September to 4 October 1968. Clergy and laity, declared the bishops, 'should in keeping with the directives of the Holy Father, speak *without ambiguity*, and speak the *same language*; and in all dealings with the faithful, let them adhere to the norms clearly indicated by the Holy Father.' *Tablet*, 26 October 1968. The bishops of the Philippines also supported the Encyclical but left room for priests to entertain private opinions provided they taught those of the Pope. *Tablet*, 16 November 1968.

this straight away they should not believe themselves 'to be separated from the love of God'.[1]

The Scandinavian bishops took a similar attitude in a statement issued in Stockholm on 17 October 1968.[2] They stressed that the Encyclical should be honestly and conscientiously examined but went on: 'However, if someone from weighty and well-considered reasons cannot become convinced by the arguments of the Encyclical, it has always been conceded that he is allowed to have a different view from that presented in a non-infallible statement of the Church. No one should be considered a bad Catholic because he is of such a dissenting opinion.'[3]

The Canadian bishops took a similar standpoint. They declined to say anything until lay and clerical opinion had an opportunity to crystallise. Dissent poured in upon the bishops from across the country. The Catholic Physicians Guild of Manitoba, for example, declared that not only was the Encyclical unconvincing, but that they had come to the conclusion that conception control was 'not intrinsically evil'. It should be approved openly. The Western Canadian Conference of Priests submitted a statement bearing the signatures of 351 priests, which asked the bishops to issue 'an unequivocable explanation of the conditions for prudent dissent both internal and practical'. The Canadian Institute of Theology opposed the Encyclical. Messages supporting the Encyclical tended to come from individuals rather than groups and the weight of public opinion appeared to be with the objectors. The

[1] See *The Times*, 9 September 1968, and *Pope and Pill* (ed. Leo Pyle, 1968), pp. 158–63, where the full text of the statement is given. The bishops also added a gloss to the Encyclical's call to governments to prevent un-Christian practices being sanctioned by law. 'Without presuming to dictate the law to public authorities,' said the bishops, 'or wishing to judge her fellow Christians and non-believers, the Church believes that it is her duty to enlighten consciences in regard to family life and demographic problems. She claims, on the other hand, real freedom for all her sons to live according to their Christian conviction.' This asserted a right to freedom, but made no demand for compulsion.

[2] The statement was issued on behalf of the six bishops of Church jurisdictions in Denmark, Finland, Norway, and Sweden.

[3] *Tablet*, 26 October 1968. The bishops also dealt with the question of pastoral advice saying: 'The pastor will understand that there can be a development and a maturing process within the personal, intimate area of marriage. He should also take into consideration that one of the partners can be convinced that he or she – rightly or wrongly – is following the voice of conscience when deviating from the norm of the Encyclical, and that in this case, there may be no sin that must be confessed or that excludes the person from Holy Communion.'

Canadian bishops took full account of this situation when they issued their statement. They affirmed that they were in accord 'with the teaching of the Holy Father concerning the dignity of married life, and the necessity of a truly Christian relationship between conjugal love and responsible parenthood. We share the pastoral concern which has led him to offer counsel and direction in an area which, while controverted, could hardly be more important to human happiness.' The statement went on to express the solidarity of the bishops with the faithful, and to declare that 'the dignity of man consists precisely in his ability to achieve his fulfilment in God through the exercise of a knowing and free choice'. The Christian, however, has to form his conscience responsibly according to truly Christian values and principles, and this implies a spirit of openness to the teaching of the Church. The bishops went on to say that those who were commissioned by the Church to teach should refrain from publicly opposing the Encyclical, but they added an important modification: 'However, this must not be interpreted as a restriction on the legitimate and recognised freedom of theologians to pursue loyally and conscientiously their research, with a view to greater depth and clarity in the teaching of the Church.' The bishops then dealt with the difficulties of those who could not give an assent to the Encyclical. 'We must appreciate the difficulty experienced by contemporary man in understanding and appropriating some of the points of this Encyclical,' they said, 'and we must make every effort to learn from the insights of Catholic scientists and intellectuals, who are of undoubted loyalty to Christian truth, to the Church and to the authority of the Holy See. Since they are not denying any point of divine and Catholic faith, nor rejecting the teaching authority of the Church, these Catholics should not be considered, or consider themselves, shut off from the body of the faithful, but they should remember that their good faith will be dependent on a sincere self-examination to determine the true motives and grounds for such suspension of assent and on continued effort to understand and deepen their knowledge of the teaching of the Church.'[1]

[1] *Tablet*, 12 October 1968: *National Catholic Reporter*, 9 October 1968. The bishops also went on to deal with the pastoral question, and declared that: 'Confession

The German bishops adopted a similar standpoint. In a preliminary statement on 30 August, they upheld the rights of conscience and of continuing discussion.[1] The principles to be applied, declared the bishops were:

1. Everyone is required to consider seriously and sympathetically what the Encyclical has to say.
2. Everyone entrusted by the Church with the task of preaching the faith has the special responsibility of conscientiously explaining the teaching of the Pope's Encyclical.
3. In their work, particularly in the administering of the sacraments, pastors must respect the responsible decisions of conscience made by the faithful.

As for themselves they promised to 'continue the dialogue with the Holy Father and with the bishops of other countries in the spirit of collegiality'. A few days later on 4 September the biennial congress of German Catholics (the *Katholikentag*) opened at Essen. The congress held a full debate on the question of marriage and the family and the Pope's Encyclical was severely criticised. At the end of the debate a resolution was passed by 3,000 votes to 90 with 58 abstentions calling on the Pope to review and revise his decision on 'the methods of contraception' as expressed in *Humanae Vitae* which they could not 'in judgement and conscience' accept. The assembled Catholics also declared their right to free discussion: 'We share with Paul VI his concern for a right understanding of the nature of marriage, but in our faith we reject the governess-like attitude of *L'Osservatore Romano*, which tried to

---

should never be envisaged under the cloud of agonising fear or severity. It should be an exercise in confidence and respect of consciences.' The bishops also gave advice to priests on the counsel they should give: 'Counsellors may meet other persons who, accepting the teaching of the Holy Father, find that because of particular circumstances they are involved in what seems to them a clear conflict of duties: e.g., the reconciling of conjugal love and responsible parenthood with the education of children already born, or with the health of the mother. In accord with the accepted principles of moral theology, if these persons have tried sincerely but without success to pursue a line of conduct in keeping with the given directives, they may be safely assured that whoever honestly chooses that course that seems right to him does so in good conscience.' The bishops thus recognised the two problems of conscience, (*a*) that of those who could not accept the Encyclical intellectually, (*b*) those who found it impossible to put it into practice in their particular circumstances.

[1] *Tablet*, 7 September 1968.

relegate the well trained faithful and adult Christians into the role of mute receivers of orders.'[1] A message from the Pope was read to the assembly on 7 September, in which he criticised those who were 'demanding freedom to put their own purely personal ideas with an authority which is a clear challenge to he who alone has received this holy gift from God'. Some commentators interpreted this as a rebuke to the German bishops for their statement of 30 August, but since the papal statement bore that date, the final date of the German bishops' conference, this seems unlikely. In a further statement issued in September, the German bishops made it clear that in their opinion the opposition to the birth control Encyclical among Catholics was not based on a fundamental rejection of papal authority, and while maintaining that it was not permissible to question the competence of the teaching authority of the Church in regard to the moral order of conjugal life, made it clear that the consciences of those who reach different conclusions would be respected. Such a position could only justifiably be taken up after profound self-examination.[2]

The Dutch bishops first gave a cautious reaction to the Encyclical, saying that it needed 'lengthy and deep reflection' and that for the time being they could give only provisional guidance to priests on the matter. They emphasised, however, the importance of reverence for the word of the Pope: 'Personal conscience cannot ignore such an authoritative pronouncement.' The bishops clearly envisaged the discussion going on, and expressed the hope that this would contribute to a clearer appreciation and functioning of the authority in the Church.[3] This statement came at the beginning of August, and at the end of October a commission set up by the bishops expressed its view that birth control should be a matter to be decided by husband and wife. The attitude of the Dutch hierarchy was not, however, defined until January of the

[1] *Tablet*, 14 September 1968.
[2] See *National Register*, 22 September 1968. The German bishops raised a whole series of questions on the relation between the sacrament of marriage and revelation which they wished to have further investigated. The bishops were not happy about the *Katholikentag* meeting at Essen and criticised it at their autumn meeting at Fulda (23–25 September) for 'impatience', wrongly understood 'tendencies towards democratisation' and the application of 'the principle of majority rule to the truth of the faith'. *Tablet*, 5 October 1968.
[3] *The Times*, 3 August 1968.

following year. On 8 January 1969, a representative assembly of Dutch Catholics declared that the renewal of the ban on artificial contraception by the Pope was 'not convincing'. At the assembly a resolution to this effect was carried by 100 votes to 4 with 5 abstentions. All the nine Dutch bishops voted for the resolution. The motion passed by the assembly had been written by the bishops, and declared: '(1) The plenary assembly asks for further consultation with the world episcopate, the Pope, married people and experts about a present day Christian outlook on marriage. (2) It considers the absolute rejection by the encyclical, *Humanae Vitae*, of the artificial means of birth control not convincing on the basis of the argumentation given. The well-considered personal decision of consciences of married people should be respected. (3) Therefore, the assembly is of the opinion that the discussions about the way in which marriage is lived have not been closed, and that the activities in the field of pastoral and mental care can be continued, taking this into account.'[1]

Other hierarchies took up a middle position, and found a refuge from impossible choices in recognising conscience in the subjective sense. Ignoring the intellectual problem as such, they dealt with the matter pastorally. The statements of the English, American, French, Austrian, and Japanese hierarchies fall into this category. The French bishops made their first statement on 6 August, when they expressed their view that the Encyclical was binding. Cardinal Lefebvre, the chairman of the Episcopal Conference of France, said: 'The Holy Father has just recalled the teaching of the Church on the regulation of birth. The committee of family affairs of our Episcopal Conference is preparing a pastoral note which will present to priests and faithful the pontifical document and will help them to a better perception of its character as profoundly human as it is Christian.'[2] Individual

---

[1] See *The Times*, 9 January 1969, and *Catholic Herald*, 17 January 1969. The resolution strongly worded as it was, replaced one with even more forceful phraseology which declared that the papal ban was 'unacceptable' and said that it 'stems from a way of thinking that has become strange and unrecognisable for a majority of the faithful'. This draft resolution was never submitted and the resolution quoted in the text was devised by Cardinal Alfrink to replace it. Cardinal Alfrink who moved the subsequent resolution said that such a strong word as 'unacceptable' should not be used and that there should be room for dialogue. See *Daily Telegraph*, 9 January 1969.

[2] See *The Times*, 5 September 1969.

o

French bishops then issued statements, notable for their pastoral emphasis. Archbishop Guyot of Toulouse stated that the Encyclical called for 'an enlightened adherence on our part'. He emphasised that the first duty of spouses was to believe in the love that God has for them: and added 'having enlightened their consciences as far as they can, they will decide on the solution that they will judge most in conformity at present with that divine will'. The Archbishop also stressed that when the two spouses were not in agreement they should always, in the first place, act 'with concern to safeguard the fidelity of their love and the unity of their household'. Bishop Elchinger of Strasbourg warned against a legalistic interpretation of the Encyclical. 'The moral law,' declared the bishop, 'can never take the place of conscience. The law has the mission of enlightening and guiding conscience. It can never decide in the place of conscience. In particular cases, the ultimate decision is up to the conscience of the spouses, on condition that conscience is correct and enlightened, and if, in reverence to the doctrine of the Church, they have together, in complete loyalty, in complete generosity, weighed their common responsibility before God. It would be a bad interpretation of the Encyclical to harden requirements on this level.'[1]

The French bishops met in plenary session at Lourdes from 2–9 November 1968. They issued a statement which praised the spirit of the Pope's Encyclical for its integral vision of man, body, and soul. It pointed out that contraception can never be a good thing, 'it is always a disorder'. But having said that, they added: 'This disorder is not always sinful.' It was the lesser of two evils for the individual who found himself in a real conflict of duties, the conflict between his duty to obey the Church's teaching and his duty to preserve the harmony and stability of married life, the primary concern of a Catholic married couple.[2]

The Austrian bishops issued a compromise statement declaring that Catholics, who limited the number of their children for

[1] *Tablet*, 26 October 1968.
[2] 'On this subject,' explained the bishops, 'we simply recall the constant moral teaching; when one faces a choice of duties, when one cannot avoid an evil whatever the decision taken may be, traditional wisdom requires that one seek before God to find which is the greater duty. The married couple will decide for themselves after reflecting together with all the care that the grandeur of their conjugal vocation requires.' See *Tablet*, 16 November 1968, and see also the *Observer*, 10 November 1968.

ethical reasons dictated by conscience, could be admitted to Communion without having to confess their practice of birth control as a sin.[1] The Japanese bishops at a meeting in Tokyo in January drew up a pastoral note which asserted that the Encyclical 'defends the true values of family and society'. Catholics must receive it 'with the spirit of obedience'. The bishops added, however: 'We are well aware that the observance of this teaching will bring various difficulties to many married people. In such cases if, while exerting all good will to be obedient to the Encyclical one is unable to follow it in some point on account of unavoidable, actual and objective circumstances, the faithful should not think they have been separated from the love of God.'[2]

THE REACTIONS OF ROME

That Rome had expected some hostile reaction to the Encyclical is shown by the covering letter sent with it by Cardinal Cicognani, in which he made a special request for episcopal support, but the strength and violence of the reaction seems to have taken the

[1] *The Times*, 25 September 1968. This statement was believed to be a compromise between the liberal views of Cardinal Koenig and those of other more conservative members of the hierarchy. The bishops pointed out that the Church's *magisterium* is competent not only in teaching revealed truth, but in teaching natural truth. 'There is freedom of conscience,' they declared, 'but not freedom in the formation of conscience, which means that the formation of a conscientious judgement is dependent on God's law which must not be overlooked.' See *National Register*, 6 October 1968. The bishops, however, came very near to the German and Scandinavian hierarchies, etc. when they went on to declare: 'Whoever is an expert in this field and comes to a conviction different from that of the Encyclical after serious self-examination and not because of an emotional reaction is allowed to follow his conviction. Such a person does not sin if he is ready to continue examining the situation and otherwise shows respect and loyalty to the Church.' *Tablet*, 5 October 1968.
[2] Before this statement of the bishops there had been a controversy in the *Tablet* over the attitude to the Encyclical of Catholics and the hierarchy in Japan. The *Tablet* reported: 'The Catholic Press has carried little news about it and there has been as yet no translation. It was the apostolic delegate who called for a press conference after its release, not the bishops, and it was the apostolic delegate who tried to get the bishops to send a letter of joyful acceptance to the Pope. They did not do so.' (28 September.) The following month Cardinal Doi, Archbishop of Tokyo, requested the General Secretary of the National Catholic Committee of Japan to write to the *Tablet* and explain that the Vice-President of the Japanese Bishops' Conference sent a telegram to the Pope expressing allegiance to the principles of *Humanae Vitae*. 'Also, the bishops expressed in special letters the same allegiance.' The editor of the *Tablet* pointed out that there was nothing inconsistent with this and their own report which was not referring to the actions of individual bishops. See *Tablet*, 26 October 1968.

Roman authorities by surprise. Whatever had been expected in hostility from the non-Catholic world, Catholics themselves, it was believed, would show themselves more docile. As the varying reactions coming from Rome after publication showed, no coherent plan had been devised to meet with resistance on a large scale. It is customary for the Vatican to ignore any comment on its pronouncements, but faced with the turmoil throughout the Catholic world it proved impossible to maintain this traditional stoic and phlegmatic attitude.

The first Vatican comment came through *L'Osservatore Romano*, the Pope's official newspaper, which throughout the year that followed gave consistent support to the hard papal line. 'Obviously,' wrote its deputy editor on the evening of 30 July, with what Mr George Armstrong of the *Guardian* described as some flair for understatement, 'the reactions are not all favourable. Rather, there are reactions of complexity, uncertainty and doubts. One could not say that these reactions faithfully reflect the dominant state of mind of the Catholics, and those who have had some experience in contemporary social communications well know that "protest" is a literary style much in vogue.'[1] This fashion certainly never infected the pages of *L'Osservatore*, which for months gave space only to those supporting the Encyclical. By the beginning of November it had made no mention of the statements by the Dutch, Belgian, German, Austrian, Canadian, or Scandinavian hierarchies. The only material to be published from the *Tablet* was the article written by Dom David Knowles on 5 October, giving the Encyclical his full support. The massive resistance by the clergy was ignored save for the report of 'a few negative reactions' among the American clergy, in the issue of 7 August. This one-sided attitude was reported at some length in the *Tablet* in November[2] and was the subject of later criticism by Cardinal Suenens at the Synod in October 1969, when he complained that *L'Osservatore* evidently regarded only one type of theology as orthodox, that followed at Rome itself.

[1] See *Guardian*, 31 July 1968.
[2] See 'The Most Observed of All Observers' in the *Tablet*, 2 November 1968. The *Tablet* pointed out how many messages, letters, and telegrams of thanks, congratulations, and articles 'of positive exposition' *L'Osservatore* had published. On 18 October, *L'Osservatore* claimed that without it world opinion would lack a fundamental point of

The first comment from the Pope himself, given at his weekly audience at Castelgondolfo on Sunday, 4 August was mild. He thanked all those who had sent him messages of gratitude. In his experience there had never been so many messages of solidarity for a papal document: 'God bless you all.' The Pope went on: 'We know that there have been many who have not appreciated our teaching and not a few who are hostile to it. We can in a certain sense understand this incomprehension and even this opposition. Our word is not easy and is not in conformity with a practice which today, unfortunately, is becoming widespread as convenient and apparently favourable to love and to family equilibrium. We want to recall once more that the rule reaffirmed by us is not just ours, but properly of the structure of life, of love and human dignity – and thus derived from the law of God. It is not a rule which ignores the sociological and demographic conditions of our times: and it is not in itself contrary, as some seem to suppose, to a reasonable limitation of births, nor to scientific research and therapeutic cures, nor even less to genuinely responsible parenthood, nor to peace and harmony in the family. It is simply a moral rule, exacting and severe, and still valid today, which forbids the use of means which intentionally prevent procreation, and which thus degrade the purity of love and the mission of married life.'[1]

The following Sunday, 11 August, the Pope once again returned to this theme, claiming that the Encyclical was 'in defence of life, love and liberty'. He asked God to bless not only those who supported it but also those who opposed it 'so that their consciences may be illuminated and guided by doctrinal correctness and the superior morality'.[2] By the beginning of September the Pope was speaking with somewhat less serenity, referring to the suffering

---

reference for knowing the extent of the positive reception of the Encyclical. The fact that the Encyclical was controversial did not mean 'that it has not the almost universal obedience of the people of God behind it. And it is this obedience that we are documenting.'

[1] *Catholic Herald*, 9 August 1968.

[2] *Catholic Herald*, 16 August 1968. During his visit to Bogota, on 24 August 1968, the Pope strongly reaffirmed the teaching in his Encyclical. He welcomed the 'lively discussion' that it had evoked and expressed the hope that it might lead to a better knowledge of the will of God and 'a conduct that withholds nothing'. See *Tablet*, 31 August 1968.

which he was undergoing. 'The sharpest pain,' said His Holiness, 'was given by the unruliness and unfaithfulness of certain of her [the Church's] ministers and certain consecrated souls. The most disappointing surprises came from among the most helped, favoured and chosen.' He felt bitterness but had not lost confidence. Furthermore he recognised the fundamental goodness of heart and the considerations of justice, truth, authenticity and renewal which were at the root of certain challenges even if some of them were excessive and unjustified and thus to be reproached.[1]

L'Osservatore Romano maintained its intransigent position and as time passed the Pope seemed to move nearer to it and to become more and more depressed about the general state of the Church. The necessity for obedience became a favourite theme of the Vatican newspaper. A typical article was that published in mid-August, written by Monsignor Lambruschini, who had presented the Encyclical at the original Press conference on 29 July, and which stated that its teaching was binding on the consciences of all Roman Catholics, whether priests or laymen. A Catholic who could not see the reasons for the Pope's decision had no right to challenge it but must accept it humbly.[2] In early September *L'Osservatore* again called for obedience, even from those who had difficulties in following its arguments because 'this obligation is not based on reason, but on the authority of the Pope'. It went on to state that certain Catholics seemed to have lost sight of the character of the Church's *magisterium*. 'It is not a scientific *magisterium* but a *magisterium* of authority.' To oppose a papal decision with theological arguments the Pope has already rejected 'signifies putting the fallible light of human science on the same plane with the divine light of the pastors assisted by the Holy Ghost'.[3]

The Pope continued issuing rebukes to those who challenged

---

[1] *The Times*, 12 September 1968. *The Times* also reported that the Pope apologised for appearing weak and indecisive in dealing with the current Church crisis but he denied that he lacked confidence. Ibid., report from Rome, 10 September.

[2] *The Times*, 14 August 1968. Monsignor Lambruschini returned to this theme in September. He maintained that moral theologians were free to argue with each other but not to argue against the *magisterium*. On the rights of conscience he said: 'The Church is not a substitute for individual conscience. But it does indicate the moral principles from which conscience is formed.' See *Tablet*, 14 September 1968.

[3] *Tablet*, 7 September 1968.

his authority but there was also a counterpoint recognising that there was good to be found in the new spiritual movements within the Church.[1] On 18 September came a sharp condemnation of dissident Catholics. 'A spirit of corrosive criticism,' he declared, 'had become fashionable in some sections of Catholic life. For instance there are magazines and newspapers which do not appear to have anything else to do but print unpleasant reports about events and people in the ecclesiastical world – not infrequently one-sided and perhaps slightly altered and dramatised a bit to make them more interesting and spicy. Hence they accustom their readers not to making calm objective judgements, but to being in a mood of negative suspicion, systematic mistrust, and preconceived deprecation towards ecclesiastical persons, institutions and activities. Thus they incite their readers and supporters to abandon the respect towards and the solidarity with, the community and ecclesiastical authority that every good Catholic and every right-minded reader ought to have. They spread disquiet and indocility in the hearts of many Catholics, even some priests and many fervent young people.'[2] In November the Pope issued yet another warning about reformers who were trying to change the 'indispensable structures' of the Church to suit their own convenience. 'We are demanding of you,' he told an audience of 400 monks and friars, 'total and generous faithfulness to the Church – not, certainly, to an imaginary Church, which each could conceive and organise according to his own ideas, but to the Catholic Church as it is.'[3]

L'Osservatore Romano's denunciation of critics of the Encyclical continued unabated and space continued to be reserved for those supporting the Encyclical, some of whom used much more violent language than the Pope.[4] A new point was reached in late

---

[1] In his audience of 11 September, for example, the Pope praised 'the spontaneity of thought and action which has pervaded so many sons of the Church'. He looked upon this blossoming of spiritual energies with respect and sympathy. At the same time he warned against excesses. See *Tablet*, 21 September 1968.

[2] *Tablet*, 28 September 1968. Cf. speech at audience in October stressing the need to rehabilitate the virtue of obedience. See *Tablet*, 26 October 1968.

[3] *Tablet*, 16 November 1968.

[4] See statement of Cardinal Journet in *L'Osservatore* for 3 October, when he declared that those against the Encyclical 'are those who love sin', and the leading article of 19 October which stated: 'The polemic against the Encyclical is directed not against the Church, but against humanity.' Articles were also published in early October by Fr Ciappi, O.P., and Cardinal Felici.

November when Cardinal Pericle Felici, a noted curial conservative, published an article in the paper, calling for obedience to the Pope whether he was right or wrong. The Cardinal agreed that a superior could be wrong in giving orders and then added: 'But the possible mistake of the superior does not authorise the disobedience of subjects. The principle still remains supreme that authority is constituted for the good of society and of the subjects themselves, even though a superior made a mistake in prudence and wisdom. The subject can certainly explain to the superior in a frank exchange of views the reasons which lead him to believe that the order is wrong or not suitable. He can also invoke the intervention of a higher authority to re-examine the matter and correct the possible error. But the subject cannot arbitrarily refuse obedience or, as some theologians maintain today, have recourse to *epikeia*, whereby in such cases he could do as he pleases. If such a principle were to be established without any further specifications, arbitrariness would no doubt triumph, since many are inclined to see errors in an order which is legitimate but which implies some sacrifice. . . . It is therefore preferable that one should bear with a possible error that might occur rather than subvert the principle of authority, which could be fatal to all.'[1] In the light of the Bishop Defregger case, which was shortly to arouse world interest on the subject of obeying immoral orders, Cardinal Felici's statement was ironically ill-timed. The *Tablet* characterised it as 'insensitive and extreme' and I criticised it sharply in the *Catholic Herald*.[2]

Despite the calls from the Pope and the sabre rattling of *L'Osservatore* (which is hardly daily reading for Catholics even in

[1] See *Daily Telegraph*, 26 November 1968 and *Tablet*, 7 December 1968.

[2] *Tablet*, ibid. In the *Catholic Herald*, 6 December 1968, I ventured the opinion that the Cardinal had 'said a mouthful'. I pointed out that this was the first recognition by inference from a curial official that there might be error in *Humanae Vitae* and that the old doctrine of unconditional obedience to ecclesiastical superiors had been reasserted in the twentieth century. I pointed out further that nobody has a right to ask for obedience to any command that is morally wrong. I added that while the Pope is competent to make pronouncements that carry with them the full spiritual authority of the Church in the matter of revealed doctrine and morals, he is not competent of himself to act with the authority of the Church outside this sphere. In this area he should be listened to with respect but there cannot be binding obligation of obedience. An unthinking and unqualified obedience brings authority into disrepute everywhere. On 20 December, the *Catholic Herald* published an indignant reply from Fr John Flanagan of Polegate.

Rome) the controversy continued to rage. The dispute widened from birth control to that of the authority of the papacy. Bishops continued to add glosses to the papal statement. If the unity of the Catholic Church was to be preserved something further needed to be done. On 23 December 1968, the Pope announced that he would summon the international Synod of bishops to meet him in Rome in the autumn of 1969.[1] The meeting would be an extraordinary not an ordinary one. This news was given to the world in an address of thanks given by the Pope to the cardinals and members of the Curia in reply to their formal expression of good wishes for Christmas and the New Year presented to him in special audience. Having made a direct reference to the 'differing reactions' to his pronouncement on birth control, the Pope went on immediately to make known his decision about the Synod. There could be no doubt of the connection between the events. The issue of the Encyclical was evidently leading to most unexpected results.

During the first part of 1969 the Pope continued to issue a stream of warnings about the dangers facing the Church, normally utilising his weekly Wednesday general audience to do so. At times these seemed to have become a species of papal nagging. On 12 February, for example, the Pope defended his ban on artificial birth control and rejected the view that married couples should be left to decide the matter for themselves.[2] On 2 April at his pre-Easter audience the Pope used the strongest language to date in condemnation of dissident priests and laymen. They were, he said, 'crucifying' the Church. The Church was suffering from 'the restless, critical, unruly and destructive rebellion of so many of its followers, including the most dear, priests, teachers, the lay, dedicated to the service and witness of the living Christ in the living Church, against its intimate and indispensable communion, against its institutional existence, against its canon law, its tradition, its internal cohesion, against its authority, the irreplaceable principles of truth, of unity, of charity, against the very

[1] *The Times*, 24 December 1968. For a full discussion of the Synod see pp. 206–21.
[2] *The Times*, 13 February 1969. The Pope said: 'We must note that the conscience to be the valid norm of human action, must be right, sure of itself and true. . . . The voice of conscience is not always infallible, nor objectively supreme. And this is especially true in the field of supernatural action, where reason is not worthy by itself to interpret the way of goodness and must resort to the faith to indicate to man the norm of justice willed by God through revelation.'

requirements of sanctity and of sacrifice.'[1] The intensity with which the Pope spoke, reported *The Times* correspondent, Mr Peter Nichols, made a deep impression on his audience in St Peter's basilica. The following day, Maundy Thursday, the Pope went beyond even these words, declaring that the Church was now divided and fragmented almost to the point of 'schism'. 'How,' he asked, 'can it be a Church, that is a united people, when a ferment practically of schism divides and subdivides it, breaks it into groups attached more than anything else to arbitrary and basically selfish autonomy disguised as Christian pluralism or freedom of conscience?'[2] The speech seems to have marked the lowest point of gloom and depression reached by the Pope.

On the first anniversary of the publication of the Encyclical, 29 July 1969, the Vatican saluted it as 'a defence of man and of the highest human values'. Writing in *L'Osservatore Romano*, Fr Giuseppe de Rosa, S.J., claimed that the past year had served to enhance the validity of the Pope's teaching. All humanity should be grateful because he had defended man against himself and had taken the side of man against the alienating and dehumanising forces which found their strongest advocate in man himself. The view that the Encyclical was a step back from the teaching of the Council was 'facile and gratuitous'. In fact it proclaimed with vigour 'the inviolable value of human life; the value of conjugal love which has its source in God-love: the dignity of the human person, particularly the woman; the liberty and responsibility of married couples called to collaborate intimately in the creative work of God: the objectivity and the firmness of the moral order above the fluctuations of history and the caprices of man.'[3] So ended an eventful twelve months in the life of the Church.

THE SYNOD

In October 1969 an extraordinary Synod of the Roman Catholic Church was held in Rome to discuss the whole question of the

[1] *The Times*, 3 April 1969.
[2] Ibid., 5 April 1969. On 25 June the Pope, returning to the theme of the reactions to the Encyclical, suggested that opposition came from a secret wish to abolish a difficult law in order to have an easier life. He complained of the lack of a heroic element in modern Catholicism. See *The Times*, 26 June 1969.
[3] *L'Osservatore Romano*, 28 July 1969. See also *The Times*, 29 July 1969.

relationship between the bishops and the Holy See. The Synod did not discuss the encyclical *Humanae Vitae* as such, but the Encyclical had been the cause of the meeting since its issue had revealed wide differences in the approach to the problem of birth control laid down by the Encyclical.[1]

The synodical system had been set up by the Holy See as a result of the rediscovery of the concept of collegiality at the Second Vatican Council; namely that the bishops as a body in union with the Pope are the direct successors of the Apostles as teachers, and have a joint responsibility with the Pope for the government of the Church. To give practical effect to this idea, the Pope, on 15 September 1969, by the *motu proprio* 'Apostolica Sollicitudo', set up the machinery of the Synod by which certain bishops, elected by the national episcopal conferences, and others, appointed by the Pope were to meet together from time to time to advise him on the government of the Church. The Pope retained wide discretionary powers as to the calling of the Synod and the subjects which could be discussed. The first Synod met in 1967 under somewhat unfavourable circumstances since its freedom had been circumscribed from the start by the virtual exclusion by the Pope of discussion of the urgent problem of priestly celibacy. The Pope had pre-empted the issue by publishing a strongly worded papal statement upholding celibacy just before the Synod was due to meet.

After the crisis in the Church occasioned by *Humanae Vitae*, the Pope decided to call a second meeting of the Synod and the preliminary decision was announced by Bishop Rubin in October 1968. This was confirmed by the Pope in a statement on 23 December. The Synod was to be an 'extraordinary' one and was to deal with the general question of authority in the Church.[2] In

[1] Another result of the Encyclical had been the interview given by Cardinal Suenens to *Informations Catholiques Internationales* on 15 May 1969. In this famous interview the Cardinal outlined his view on the crisis in the Church and the way in which it could be solved.

[2] An extraordinary session of the Synod is defined as one in which 'the matter involves the good of the Universal Church and requires speedy consideration'. The main difference between an extraordinary and an ordinary Synod is that the latter does not include representatives elected by the national hierarchies. Membership is composed of the patriarchs, major archbishops, and metropolitans of the Catholic Churches of the Eastern Rite; the presidents of episcopal conferences in which the hierarchies of more than one country are represented, to cover cases in which national conferences

his announcement the Pope disclosed that the aim of the new Synod would be 'to examine the proper forms and to ensure a better co-operation and more fruitful contacts of the individual episcopal conferences with the Holy See'. He added that the Synod could result in 'mutual help based on a principle of collegial collaboration and common responsibility' and expressed confidence that it would have 'results of no little usefulness for the Church'.[1]

First reactions to the papal announcement were hopeful. It was felt that the Pope was seeking a reasonable way out of the impossible situation which had been created by the resistance of so many Catholics to his teaching on birth control. It was hoped that the Synod would provide a means of reconciliation, but this optimistic assessment gradually gave way to gloom. It became evident that the conservatives in the Curia saw the Synod not so much as a means of reconciliation but as one by which to reimpose full papal authority. When the names of the Pope's nominees were published they turned out to be nearly all of a conservative frame of mind. The agenda for the Synod was kept secret but its contents were leaked to the Press in August 1969. They caused further despondency. Professor Hans Küng revealed, in an article in *Le Monde*, the existence of what he called a secret draft resolution prepared by the Curia for the Synod. It demanded 'that episcopal conferences before making a statement on an important matter, seek the opinion of the Apostolic See in good time'. Dr Küng described this as an effort to 'muzzle the bishops' and so avoid a repetition of statements by national conferences of bishops – such as those on birth control – which might conflict with the position of the Pope and the Curia.[2] The principal points in the agenda were given in an article published in the *Tablet* on 23 August and

---

do not exist; three representatives of the religious orders; and cardinals in charge of the offices of the Roman Curia. An extraordinary Synod is likely because of the lack of an elected element to be more conservative than a meeting of the ordinary body. The extraordinary Synod of 1968 was made up of 93 heads of episcopal conferences, 36 bishops from the Curia, 17 nominees of the Pope, and 3 heads of religious orders, the Benedictines, the Friars Minor, and the Jesuits. Of the bishops 54 came from European countries, 43 from North or South America, 31 from Africa, and 29 from Asia.

[1] *Tablet*, 4 January 1969, and *The Times*, 24 December 1968.
[2] *The Times*, 14 August 1969.

again in greater detail with other documents on 13 September.
Further despondency was caused by these revelations.[1] Fr Karl
Rahner declared that judging by the agenda there was 'little
promise' of closer unity between the bishops' conferences and the
Holy See.[2]

In the event the outcome of the Synod was very different from
what had been expected – it created a new spirit of co-operation
between Pope and bishops, was marked not so much by confrontation as a spirit of toleration and mutual co-operation ('an
episcopal love-in' was the phrase used to describe it by Mr Robert
Nowell in *Herder Correspondence*), and decisions were taken which
brought collegial government of the Church appreciably nearer.[3]
It was ironical that this should have been brought about by the
issue of an Encyclical which was clearly a non-collegial act.

The Synod opened at the Vatican in the Hall of the Broken
Heads on 13 October, the seventh anniversary of the opening of
the Second Vatican Council. Its proceedings were adjourned on
Monday, 27 October.[4] The atmosphere was not auspicious
because of an address by the Pope to the International Commission of Theologians on 6 October. The papal teaching authority,
he proclaimed 'as you know derives from Christ himself, our one
and supreme Pastor, and is essential for the government, stability,
peace and unity of God's Church. He who refuses it or attacks it,
attacks the one true Church and therefore incurs a grave debt in
regard to the souls that have the faith or are seeking it, and

[1] The bishops had been asked to send in suggestions for the Synod in a letter from the
Vatican dated 8 December 1968. These had to arrive by 1 February 1969. Owing to
the requirement of secrecy there was no opportunity to discuss the proposed agenda
with the laity and other interested parties.
[2] See 'Primacy and Collegiality' in *Publik*, 3 October 1969. A less pessimistic article,
'The Significance of the Synod', by Bishop Butler was published in the *Tablet*, 20
September 1969. Nevertheless, the bishop declared 'the teaching of Vatican II on the
Episcopal College is not in issue today. What is in issue is, how in practice the principle
of collegiality should be made something more than a dead letter. Clearly there are
those in the Church today who, whether they are aware of it or not, are promoting or
advocating policies which would eviscerate this doctrine of its practical significance.'
[3] During the Synod the Pope pleaded for an avoidance of confrontation: 'It must not
excite in us the psychology, so to say, of sports fans, who dramatise things through
superficial and conventional expressions.' See *The Times*, 16 October 1969.
[4] Simultaneously, a meeting of the European Assembly of Priests numbering about
200 met in Rome. The Assembly called for a total reorganisation of the Church, local
election of bishops, the abolition of the college of Cardinals and the election of the
Pope by a synod of Bishops.

undergoes responsibility before God's judgement.' He urged the Commission to help defend Catholics from 'the numerous excessive and pressing errors that are assailing the divine deposit of truth in the Church'.[1] The Pope's address at the concelebrated mass which marked the official opening of the Synod on 11 October was noticeably milder. Its theme was that of charity and unity rather than the juridical aspect of collegiality and he stressed both the nature of the Church and of the episcopate as a communion: 'this communion is interpreted in a double way as communion with God in Christ and as communion in Christ with those who believe in him and potentially with the whole human race'.

On 13 October the principal doctrinal debate opened with the presentation of a schema on collegiality presented by Cardinal Seper, Prefect of the Doctrinal Congregation.[2] The schema was highly unsatisfactory in that it contained a restatement of the pyramidical and juridical view of the Church. It was, however, modified by an introductory paper, a *relatio*, of Cardinal Seper's, the head of the Holy Office, which preceded it. In the *relatio* the Cardinal stated that while the Pope was free to act alone he should normally do so in conjunction with his fellow bishops. 'Therefore,' said the Cardinal, 'a more suitable way of exercising the supreme power in the Church, whereby its unity and diversity would be more closely expressed and put into effect, will be the exercise of this power by the Supreme Pastor together with the college of bishops – in which, however, the Supreme Pastor retains intact his office of Vicar of Christ and Pastor of the Universal Church – since, in this case the sacramental communion of the bishops among themselves and with the Roman Pontiff in this hierarchically constituted episcopal college is shown more clearly in its visible aspect.' The Cardinal went on to add that

[1] *Tablet*, 11 October 1969. His address, however, contained a major assurance to the theologians who had been pleading for freedom of research: 'our intention is to recognise the laws and exigencies that belong to your studies; that is, to respect that freedom of expression of theological science and of research called for by its development. We do not wish that there should be wrongly fixed in your minds the suspicion of a rivalry between two primacies, that of science and that of authority.'

[2] The sources for my account of the Synod are as follows: *Herder Correspondence*, December 1969, vol. 6, pp. 355–84. *The Times*, 13, 15, 16, 27, 28 October. *Sunday Times*, 2 November. *Los Angeles Times*, 15, 16, 22, 23, 24, 25, 26, 28, 29 October. *New York Times*, 17, 18, 19 October. *National Catholic Reporter*, 15, 22, 29 October, 5 November. *Tablet*, 18, 25 October, 8 November. *Catholic Herald*, 17, 24 October.

though the Pope had freedom to exercise at will his supreme power over the Church, the exercise of his primacy was subject to the objective norms of faithfulness to the revealed word of God, the primary constitution of the Church, and the Church's tradition. The *relatio* was found so much more satisfactory by the bishops that it was suggested by Cardinal Alfrink, and agreed, that it should be accepted as a basis for discussion and for further investigation of the whole question.

A lively debate then followed in which some notable contributions were made. Outstanding among these was the contribution of Cardinal Suenens who stressed that while there was no disagreement either on the primacy of the Pope or on collegiality as such, there was disagreement over the manner in which they should be exercised: 'there are those who insist so strongly on the role of the primacy that they easily reach the point of presenting the Papacy as an absolute monarchy like the *ancien régime*, where everything depended on the sovereign discretion of the monarch. Such a one-sided insistence leads in practice to the negation of collegiality. The *sub Petro* eclipses the *cum Petro*.' Criticising the schema which had been originally submitted for the discussion, the Cardinal pointed out that the theology underlying the text exalted the primacy to such a point that the bishops seemed to be reduced almost to the roles of 'assistants before the throne'. This was a serious matter because this theology was *de facto* the only one underlying the articles which appeared daily in *L'Osservatore Romano*. This created the impression that only this theology was orthodox. The Cardinal expressed himself much more satisfied with the *relatio* although he had his reservations about this too. There was a need to give prominence to the nature and the importance of the local church in which the bishop was the proper pastor of the people entrusted to him and in intimate communion with him. Again the exact relationship between primacy and collegiality was not satisfactorily treated in the *relatio*; the exercise of the responsibility of the bishops for the Universal Church was unduly restricted. 'In actual fact the Sovereign Pontiff is shown as if he had the responsibility for the whole Church while the co-responsibility of the bishops appears limited to their helping the Sovereign Pontiff in this his own personal mission. This limitation is all the more serious since the faithful are often all too much inclined to share these views restricting the functions of the bishops to the government of their own individual church.' Cardinal Suenens also found that the discussion on the origins of episcopal power was lacking in precision and therefore misleading.

The Indonesian Cardinal, Archbishop Justinus Darmojuwono, was even more outspoken. He declared that while it was clear that the Pope had the right to act alone it was better, when important issues were involved, that he should do so in conjunction with the college of bishops. For those decisions which had greater repercussions on the life of the Universal Church it was both more convenient and seemed to be the only just way for the supreme authority in the Church to be exercised in a strictly collegial manner. He referred in particular to *Humanae Vitae* and its after-effects. Cardinal Willebrands, president of the Secretariat for promoting Christian Unity, also made a forthright speech. The Church, he said, had three principles of unity, the Holy Spirit, the Eucharist, and the Pope. The first two principles were primary and the third secondary. He added that unity could co-exist with pluriformity in theological thought, in worship and in spirituality. He criticised the language used in the schema since it could give rise to the idea that all the Church's activity proceeded from the Pope and that the bishops were mere executives. Representatives of the Eastern Churches also drew attention to the fact that for long in practice the Eastern Churches had combined practical independence with communion with the Holy See.

The more conservative speeches came at the end of the theological debate, and views in support of the papal primacy were voiced by Cardinal Wyszynski, Archbishop of Warsaw, Cardinal Gilroy, Archbishop of Sydney and Bishop Colombo, the Pope's personal theologian. The voices of the Asian and African bishops were on the whole raised in favour of a stronger conception of the primacy. Cardinal Wright of the Curia added a warning against the dangers of nationalism. Perhaps the most forthright statement of the conservative case came from Cardinal Danielou, also of the Curia, who declared that salvation for the Roman Catholic Church in a time of 'very grave crisis' lay in more 'firm and unique authority', more doctrinal rigour rather than less as the progressives advocated. 'To face up to this crisis, we need a firm and unique authority in the Church. Instead, there is insinuated doubt of the authority not only of the Pope but also of the bishops and priests.'

The Synod had certainly enjoyed a free and frank discussion, a course urged upon it by Cardinal Heenan early on in the proceedings. 'When we are at home,' said the Cardinal, 'and give interviews in the Press or on television judging and condemning the behaviour of the Pope and the Roman Curia, we do not help the Church. We may even harm it. We are all brothers here and, as the Holy Father said on Saturday, collegial charity has no limits. That is why we should speak openly. If we believe that the way in which supreme authority in the Church is exercised is deplorable, the Synod is the place to say so. Here in the Synod our brothers who work in the Roman Curia are present. We can prove our fraternal charity by telling them where they go wrong.' The Cardinal went on to say, 'after the publication of the Encyclical *Humanae Vitae* no small scandal was caused by dissension in certain parts of the Church. The Church of Rome which until that time had been regarded as the exemplar of unity, suddenly became a spectacle of discord. Our duty venerable brethren is clear. The unity and authority of the Church must once again be made transparently clear. This duty cannot be discharged in private meetings and conclaves. The only way to do our duty is to take part in free and open discussion in this synodal hall'.[1]

On 22 October a vote took place in the Synod and the *relatio* was officially accepted as the basis for further investigation and discussion. Of the 141 Fathers present, 72 voted *placet* (or approval), 63 *placet iuxta modum* (approval in principle with reser-

---

[1] At a Press conference on 18 October the Cardinal told the assembled journalists, 'the Curia is not made up of wild beasts, they are human beings'. The Cardinal also stressed that the growth of education had altered the attitude of both clergy and laity: 'they still want to belong to the one fold of the one Shepherd but they do not want to be treated like sheep.' The Cardinal also spoke on 24 October and criticised the secrecy which had surrounded the agenda: 'Needless secrecy provides grounds for suspicion and rumour.' He stressed that there was too long an interval between the first Synod's ending and any action on its proposals, for example, an entire year had passed before anything was done about the proposals about the International Commission of Theologians. Furthermore, there had been no report on the question of mixed marriages as the Synod had recommended.

P

vations or amendments), and one *non-placet* (disapproval). Two abstained and five votes were null because the ballots were unsigned. Many of those giving qualified approval wished the *relatio* to be referred to the International Commission of Theologians which would then report back. These suggestions in the qualified votes were not, however, subsequently put to the vote so it cannot be said definitely whether the proposal to refer the document to the Commission did have majority support.

A notable feature of the doctrinal debate was that the Pope himself was present throughout, except on the Wednesday when his weekly general audience prevented his presence. He was present as president among his fellow bishops but the actual chairing of the meetings was undertaken by three president-delegates. The Pope listened to the bishops as they debated with complete frankness the shortcomings of the Church and the difficulties which it faced. Later, when Cardinal Marty, Archbishop of Paris, brought up a suggestion that the Pope should be present at meetings of the Synod, the Pope intervened informally to remark '*Eccomi*' – Here I am.

The Synod then went on to discuss the practical problem of the development of closer links between the bishops' conferences and the Holy See. The *relatio* on this matter, which again was an improvement over the original schema was presented by Cardinal Marty. The *relatio* began by stating that the college of bishops with its Head was the subject of supreme and full power. It then went on to add: 'supreme and full power over the Church by virtue of his office as Vicar of Christ and Pastor of the Universal Church, is also possessed by the Supreme Pontiff, although he is always able freely to exercise this power of his, as the Head of the college of bishops always remains joined with this college'. The *relatio* emphasised that the one Church exists in and is formed out of particular Churches. It also enunciated the principle of subsidiarity, quoting the words of Pius XII: 'whatever individuals can do on their own and with their own resources should not be removed from them and handed over to the community – a principle which is equally valid for smaller and lower ranking communities with regard to larger and higher ones'. It declared that the responsibility of bishops for providing for the good of the

Church at the universal and particular levels could be better effected by the right application of this principle.

The document went on to discuss various practical suggestions for making collegiality more effective. Presidents of conferences should meet informally with the Pope from time to time: annual meetings of the presidents of episcopal conferences with the Pope might take place: the Pope should be present at meetings of the Synod: regular meetings of the Synod should be held.

The *relatio* then dealt with the difficult question of the Pope and bishops acting together especially on matters pertaining to the doctrine of the faith. It stressed that even the appearance of disagreement should be avoided on these fundamental and central issues, and it went on to draw the following conclusions: 'It is therefore the wish of many that, in dealing with matters of greater importance, there should be, in as far as circumstances permit, true co-operation between the Supreme Pastor and the bishops, so that before a declaration or decree is issued on such questions, the Supreme Pontiff should deign to ask their opinion, either by questioning bishops' conferences or by hearing their delegates in the Synod or by calling on them to co-operate in some other way. Of course, all recognise and admit the full freedom which the Supreme Pastor enjoys in settling these cases, but they are of the humble opinion that the collective responsibility of all the bishops, which Vatican II affirmed on many occasions, is in this way more fully stressed and at the same time delimited. By this co-operation more complete knowledge can be obtained of persons and matters involved, towards which end the bishops of the various regions can be of great help to the Supreme Pastor. Finally, by sharing in the preparation of such documents the bishops are better able to expound them to the faithful of their particular Churches.'

The *relatio* also dealt with the other aspect of the problem, the need to keep bishops' conferences in touch with the Pope and to see that their statements were not out of accord with papal teaching. It was this problem that had led to the fear that the Vatican intended to try and 'muzzle the bishops'. The *relatio* stated: 'On the other hand, moved by the same concern for pastoral communion, the bishops themselves and especially bishops' conferences, when intending in their exercise of their office of teaching to issue a declaration on some serious question which particularly refers to doctrine, and especially when this is of the kind to have an impact outside their own territory, should also be joined with the Apostolic See and should act so as to come to a common mind and a common purpose with it.' The qualifications expressed in this passage and the reference to coming to a common mind indicates that consultation with Rome need not be the one-sided affair which Professor Küng and others feared it would be.

Finally, the *relatio* discussed the relations between the bishops and the Curia. It stressed that the members of the Curia were servants of the bishops as well as of the Pope. It insisted that bishops should be able to co-operate directly with the Holy See and not be confined to the intermediary of nuncios. Further, it laid down that no decree having internal effect on a diocese should be passed without an opportunity of delegates from their diocese being heard and second that all declarations and instructions, etc., of the Curia should be sent to bishops' conferences before publication. Thus the situation would not be repeated, which occurred with *Humanae Vitae*, when the first news that many bishops received of the publication of the Encyclical came through the mass media of Press and television.

The bishops then split up into nine language groups to discuss the *relatio* in detail and various suggestions were put forward such as the setting up of a permanent secretariat, new arrangements for the election of the Pope, etc. From these discussions and the general debates, thirteen propositions were drawn up and presented to the Fathers on Saturday, 25 October, for voting on the following Monday, the day of the official closure of the Synod. Each one of these propositions achieved the necessary two-thirds majority, 96 out of 143 votes. The propositions stressed the need for closer collaboration between the Apostolic See on the one hand and the synods of the Eastern Churches and the bishops' conferences on the other. While acknowledging the full freedom which the Pope enjoyed by reason of his office the bishops offered to him their help and expressed their desire that 'according to his judgement'[1]

---

[1] 'According to his judgement' – 'pro sua prudentia' – this rather nebulous phrase could be so interpreted by the Pope as to emasculate collegiality.

the Supreme Pontiff will be willing to accept this collaboration. They themselves will seek the same collaboration in sharing a common mind with the Supreme Pastor, in their own declarations and decrees so that by joining forces with him they may foster the good of the Universal Church and of the particular Churches.'[1] Means should be established whereby closer co-operation could be fostered between the Curia and the bishops' conferences. A regular and expeditious exchange of information between the departments of the Roman Curia and the bishops' conferences should take place. In matters affecting the internal life of dioceses the local bishop should be heard. 'Statements, instructions and decrees issued by the Holy See should before any communication to the public press be communicated at least in substance to the bishops themselves, together with the reasons, if this should be useful, on which they are based and suitable explanations of them: these are to be made known to the bishops in a manner which the Holy See considers most suitable and expeditious after joint consultation with synods of the Eastern Churches and bishops' conferences.'

The propositions went on to declare that the structure of the Synod of bishops should be revised and its activity re-ordered so that the collegial concern of the bishops for the Universal Church could be better brought into effect. 'The secretariat of the Synod of bishops should be revised so that it forms a permanent institution, properly organised whereby suitable preparation can be made for the work to be done by meetings of the Synod and to which proposals decided on by the Synod of bishops and approved by the Supreme Pontiff can be entrusted for execution. The secretariat would do its work in consultation with a number of bishops, who, with the approval of the Supreme Pontiff, would be appointed by a meeting of the Synod itself, according to norms to be established, so that the secretariat would form a genuine link between different meetings of the Synod.' General meetings of the Synod of bishops should be held every other year as far as possible, furthermore, 'Synods of the Eastern churches and bishops' conferences should have the right before a meeting of the Synod to propose questions they think should be dealt with by the Synod.'

The response of Paul VI to these resolutions was swift. In his formal speech closing the Synod on Monday, he accepted many of them even before the Fathers themselves knew the full results of the voting. The Pope accepted that the Synod of bishops should be summoned at fixed times 'according to ways and forms established by law'. He went on to say that he approved of the resolution which called for a meeting of the Synod of bishops every other year. 'Equally we can here and now indicate to you that it is our purpose to make the Synod secretariat more effective. To this end the greatest account will be taken of the votes you have cast with regard to the assistance – which we think extremely useful – to be duly established in legitimate form and to be provided by pastors representing the episcopate scattered throughout the entire world. They will also be the means whereby the subjects can be indicated whose treatment in the Synod seems necessary.'

Finally, the Pope went on to accept the principle of subsidiarity[1] although the extent of its application was not entirely clear, 'While this principle without a doubt plainly demands a deeper understanding and clarification both in theory and practice,' said the Pope, 'we fully admit it in its main significance. However, it cannot come about that this principle should be confused with a certain demand for that kind of 'pluralism which would be injurious to the faith, the moral law, and the basic forms of the sacraments, liturgy, and canonical discipline that have as their chief aim the maintenance of the necessary unity in the Universal Church'.

The bishops themselves responded enthusiastically to this final statement of the Pope and themselves issued their own statement on Tuesday, 28 October, praising him and urging him to continue his work. 'Before concluding this extraordinary session of the Synod,' said the bishops, 'the Fathers of the Synod wish to express their devotion and love for the Supreme Pontiff, Vicar of Christ and Pastor of the Universal Church whose assiduous presence at the Synod as high testimony of his collegial love has been for them extremely agreeable. We thank the Supreme Pontiff for the doctrine constantly imparted by him in times in which the faith for many has been put in danger. We pray him not to desist

[1] See p. 214.

from the free exercise of this his office as universal pastor and we declare that we are ready with all our heart to help him in this duty. In our time in which rage storms in the Church and in the world, nothing is more important than the witnessing of union and the unrestrained expression of peace. This union in the Church so ardently desired by Christian people depends for the greatest part on the collaboration both between the Supreme Pontiff and the episcopal conferences, and between the same conferences.'

The Synod must be accounted a notable success.[1] While it did not provide solutions for the actual problems raised by *Humanae Vitae*, it created a framework within which they and other issues could be considered. In future Synods will be held regularly at two-year intervals, an enlarged secretariat is to become permanent, and the bishops are likely to be able to propose matters for inclusion in the agenda but they have not been given the *right* to draw up the agenda or to have specific items included. It seems that the final decision whether or not to include any particular topic for discussion remains that of the Pope. He could thus exclude discussion of a controversial topic such as priestly celibacy if he so wished. If collegiality is to be effective the Synod must clearly have an unfettered right to discuss anything it wishes.[2]

The Pope gave evidence of his good intentions when he reorganised the Synod secretariat a month later, providing for the permanent appointment of bishops from different parts of the world to the Synod's secretariat; of the fifteen bishops authorised three were to be appointed by the Pope, and twelve by members of the previous Synod voting by letter; these bishops were to hold office from one Synod until the next.[3]

Just as important as the consolidation of synodical structures was the creation of a better atmosphere of co-operation and communion between the Pope and the bishops. The Pope responded

[1] See Cardinal Heenan's pastoral letter of thanksgiving for the Synod. *Tablet*, 22 November 1969. For a welcoming Anglican view see E. L. Mascall, 'An Anglican view of the Synod', *Tablet*, 15 November 1969.
[2] The papal decision on this point is not wholly clear. In his closing address the Pope said: 'we shall also give the utmost considerations to your wishes concerning the possibility of bringing forward, by means of these bishops, themes which it is considered necessary to discuss in Synod'. See *The Times*, 28 October 1969.
[3] See *Tablet*, 6 December 1969.

fully in the synodical situation and appeared too, personally heartened by the encounter, although a certain note of pessimism has since come back into his public utterances. In future it will be important to reduce or abolish altogether the secrecy surrounding the preparation for the Synod. Clergy and laity need an opportunity to put forward their views to the bishops and they cannot do this if secrecy is observed about the agenda. It is important, too, that there should be direct reporting of the Synod proceedings.[1] Among pressing problems that need to be discussed are the whole status and purpose of the priesthood including the question of celibacy, a re-examination of the nature of the sacraments especially that of marriage, and further initiatives to be taken to allay world poverty and hunger.[2] It will clearly also be necessary in due course for the Synod to reconsider the doctrinal and moral position following on the widespread criticism of *Humanae Vitae*. The Church through the Pope and Synod needs to reassess the position and examine the scope and limitations of papal authority.

If the proposed Synod reforms are vigorously implemented and a new spirit of co-operation between Pope and bishops is created, then it will be impossible for a non-collegial event like the issuing of *Humanae Vitae* to occur again. Much will depend on the attitude of the Curia and the sincerity of its members in seeking to make a reality out of the synodical proposals. As Cardinal Suenens remarked on the eve of the closure of the Synod: 'We have tuned

[1] Another point of importance is that when the bishops put forward amendments at the Synod they should vote upon them. In fact the Synod adjourned with no vote having been taken on the 'modi'. This was sharply criticised at the time by various commentators; the primary responsibility for this omission rests on the bishops rather than on the Pope.

[2] On 24 October 1969, Cardinal Cooke of New York addressed the Synod and urged them to demonstrate their collegial concern for mankind by establishing a world fund for human development. The Cardinal recommended specifically that each national conference of bishops should arrange an educational programme to arouse people to a proper sense of their duty in helping the poor of the world, secondly that every nation should be ready to devote some of its resources to the effort of helping the poorer nations, thirdly, that a financial appeal should be made to conferences of bishops throughout the world and that every national conference should contribute to it, fourthly such a world fund would not replace existing aid programmes but would co-operate with them. Therefore, concluded the Cardinal, 'I propose that a committee of bishops be appointed to explore the possibility of establishing such a fund and that this proposal be brought to the attention of all the episcopal conferences throughout the world for their consideration and implementation.' See *National Catholic Reporter*, 29 October 1961.

up the engine, and with a well functioning motor one may go far.'[1]

The Synod has no executive power and remains an advisory body but if development continues it could acquire an executive role at some point in the future. Perhaps the outcome will be that described by Dr Ramsey, Archbishop of Canterbury, in a prophetic passage in his book, *The Gospel and the Catholic Church*, published in 1936. 'A primacy,' wrote Dr Ramsey, 'should depend upon and express the organic authority of the Body: and the discovery of its precise functions will come not by discussion of the Petrine claims in isolation but by the recovery everywhere of the Body's organic life, with its bishops, presbyters and people. In this Body Peter will find his due place, and ultimate reunion is hastened not by the pursuit of "the papal controversy" but by the quiet growth of the organic life of every part of Christendom.'[2]

THE POPE AND THE UNITED NATIONS

Despite the Synod, the Vatican has continued to forward the Pope's views on birth control with initiatives of its own. Paul VI has been especially concerned about international programmes of family planning and the part played in these by the United Nations and its associated organisations.[3] In November 1970, the Pope took the opportunity of a conference marking the twenty-fifth anniversary of the foundation of the United Nations Food and Agriculture Organisation (F.A.O.) to reject birth control carried out 'with methods and means which are unworthy of man'.

[1] *Tablet*, 8 November 1969. Karl Rahner, commenting earlier on the results of the Synod stated: 'I found out that I am not the only heretic in Rome', *Time*, 24 October 1969. Cardinal Suenens also compared the Synod to an elevator which had reached the third floor. Those on the ground in such a situation point out that it has *already* reached the third floor, while those on the tenth floor say it is *only* at the third floor.
[2] *The Gospel and the Catholic Church* (London, 1936), p. 228.
[3] For a full account of this and related matters see Chapter VII below 'World Population Growth and Christian Responsibility'. Pressure for programmes of international family planning have undoubtedly increased. Thus in July 1970 the Family Planning International Campaign revived its activities under the chairmanship of Lord Caradon, former British Minister of State at the United Nations. The Campaign's purpose is to ensure that all over the world 'every child is a wanted child' and to 'enlist financial support' for the International Planned Parenthood Federation, etc. In 1971 the I.P.P.F. programme of technical assistance and financial support to seventy-two countries envisaged an expenditure of $13·6 million for the year.

Certainly, declared the Pope, 'in the face of the difficulties to be overcome, there is a great temptation to use one's authority to diminish the number of guests rather than to multiply the bread that is to be shared. We are not at all unaware of the opinions held in international organisations which extol planned birth control which, it is believed, will bring a radical solution to the problems of developing countries. We must repeat this today: the Church, for her part in every domain of human action, encourages scientific and technical progress, but always claiming respect for the inviolable rights of the human person whose primary guarantors are the public authorities.' Being firmly opposed to a method of birth control which would be in accordance with 'methods and means which are unworthy of man', the Church called on all those responsible to work 'with fearlessness and generosity for the development of the whole man and every man'. The Pope went on to make what appears to have been a commendation of the rhythm method: 'This, among other effects, will undoubtedly favour a rational control of birth by couples who are capable of freely assuming their destiny.'[1]

In the opening months of 1971 came news of a diplomatic offensive by the Vatican against state and international contraceptive programmes. The diplomatic moves were aimed against all official programmes propagating artificial birth control methods.[2] The diplomatic initiative had been taken by the Vatican in the previous year with the issue of a confidential document, dated 14 November, to all papal nuncios and apostolic delegates and to the Vatican's permanent observers at the United Nations and its agencies, by Cardinal Villot, papal Secretary of State. The Cardinal noted that the United States was now 'at the head of the line among promoters of an international policy of birth control'. He went on to criticise the United Nations Organisation for promoting population-control programmes in the third world. His comment on UNICEF (the U.N. children's fund), for distributing contraceptives, was particularly sharp: 'It therefore puts itself in contradiction to the very objectives of the institution

---

[1] See *The Times*, 17 November 1970, and *Catholic Herald*, 20 November 1970.
[2] The existence of the Vatican moves was revealed in *Time* magazine on 1 February 1971. See also *Tablet*, 6 February 1971.

created for the well-being of children.' The Cardinal condemned high-pressure methods of salesmanship which in practice deny couples real freedom of choice and commented on the amount of money being devoted to contraceptive programmes: 'It is troubling to see funds channelled into family planning campaigns more easily than into other enterprises; for example, certain projects for fertilisation of desert zones.'

The Cardinal directed that governments should be persuaded to take positions 'in favour of Catholic morality'. Papal diplomats should press bishops in each country to build up relations with local representatives of international organisations. Good relations would facilitate the choice of delegates to international conferences 'who possess Christian convictions'. Predominantly Catholic countries should be persuaded to give their delegates 'unequivocal instructions, and if necessary suggest that those delegates make contact with representatives of the Holy See'. Papal representatives should take constructive action and offer 'positive and morally acceptable proposals'. These should include combating poverty and hunger, co-operating in 'prudent sexual education' and popularising the rhythm method of birth control. Cardinal Villot pointed to the success of rhythm in Mauritius and urged its study: 'This method has been tried not only in industrialised countries, but in the Third World where there is an elementary social structure and where the population is largely illiterate.'[1]

This letter has been interpreted by some as a sinister development but as far as can be gathered from that part of the text which has been published in the newspapers it has positive elements. A definitive judgement will have to wait publication of the entire text which so far has not been made available.

[1] *The Times*, 5 February 1971.

CHAPTER VI

Theological Perspectives

As far as Catholic theology is concerned the encyclical *Humanae Vitae* is if not of decisive at any rate of pre-eminent importance. While it would be an inadequate response to give it unthinking and unreflecting assent, it would be equally erroneous to attempt to brush it aside as an irrelevance, some kind of aberration which is best forgotten. The argument cannot be foreclosed by declaring that it bears the imprimatur of 'the Vicar of Christ'[1] but neither can it be avoided by treating it as if it were merely the private theological opinion of the Bishop of Rome. Its significance can only be assessed by a careful evaluation of its status, first of all, and then by analysis of the intrinsic worth of its arguments.

THE STATUS OF 'HUMANAE VITAE'

The standing of *Humanae Vitae* can only be classified after discussion of the nature of the *magisterium* in the Church. In what exactly does the *magisterium* consist? It can conveniently be defined as 'the Church's active competence to teach and bear witness to

[1] The exclusive reservation of the title 'Vicar of Christ' to the Bishop of Rome is a late development. In early centuries the Pope was styled 'Vicar of St Peter'. Down to the ninth century the title 'Vicar of Christ' was used of many bishops other than the occupant of the Roman See. The Orthodox today use it of every lawfully instituted diocesan bishop. In the dogmatic constitution on the Church, *Lumen Gentium*, issued by the Vatican Council II, a return is made to the ancient usage and bishops referred to as 'the vicars and ambassadors of Christ'. (para. 27. *The Documents of Vatican II* ed. by Walter M. Abbot, S.J., London, 1966.) Furthermore the title had in origin a sacromental and iconological significance rather than a jurisdictional one.

the nature and consequences of God's revelation in Christ'.[1] This competence to teach, which strictly speaking is the prerogative of the Pope and the bishops, should not be considered as something isolated from the life of the Church. It does not exist of itself or manufacture truth rather it delineates and defines what is already present in the consciousness of the people of God. Over the past hundred years the stress has been placed on the part played by the Pope as teacher but the Second Vatican Council has brought to the fore the role discharged by all the bishops in relation to the *magisterium*. The concept of collegiality adumbrated by that Council indicates that the bishops, as a body in union with the Pope, are the direct successors of the apostles as teachers and are not to be thought of merely as papal agents.[2] Are there then two supreme teaching bodies within the Church, the Pope acting on his own and the Pope and the bishops acting together? There is a prima facie logical contradiction in the idea of two bodies both with supreme power. A way out of the difficulty can be found by the realisation that even if the Pope acts on his own without the actual co-operation of the rest of the college, he is in fact acting for the college and as its head.[3] There is a distinction in the mode by which the supreme power is exercised but not in the base of legitimacy on which it rests.

The ecclesiastical teaching function can then be exercised either by the college of bishops together with its head, or by the Pope alone acting as head of the college. The function is normally discharged in what is described as an 'ordinary' manner through the constant teaching of Pope and bishops. This may take any of a wide variety of forms, liturgical acts, papal encyclicals, constitutions, admonitions, etc, episcopal pastoral letters, sermons, diocesan directives *et al*. Alternatively it can be exercised in an 'extraordinary manner' when the Pope defines in solemn form a doctrine on faith or morals to represent the view of the Church as such, or when the Pope and bishops do the same when gathered together formally in council. Exercises of the extraordinary

[1] Daniel McGuire's definition in *Absolutes in Moral Theology*, ed. Charles Curran (Washington, 1968), p. 57.
[2] See *Lumen Gentium*, Chapter III.
[3] See Christopher Butler, *The Theology of Vatican II* (London, 1967), pp. 106–9; also Karl Rahner, *The Episcopate and the Primacy*, pp. 76–100.

teaching power are rare. It was used at the first Vatican Council to define the doctrine of papal infallibility and has subsequently been used only once by the Pope acting 'without the college'; by Pius XII when he proclaimed the Assumption of the Virgin in 1950.[1]

When the ecclesiastical *magisterium* is exercised in the 'extraordinary' way described, Catholic doctrine holds that the teachers are 'infallible', prevented that is by the Holy Spirit from falling into error. Infallibility is therefore a preventative *assistentia* and not a positive form of inspiration. When the *magisterium* is exercised in the ordinary manner by the college with its head, it too *may* be infallible but is not necessarily so. There is the further point that whatever be the theory of the matter it is extremely difficult in practice to establish in particular cases that the ordinary *magisterium* is so universal and certain as to establish the necessary conditions for infallibility. Presumably this is why the extraordinary *magisterium* exists.

What the Pope or the episcopal college with the Pope teaches infallibly requires the assent of faith, a complete acceptance which is the response not only of the intellect but of the whole being. Even then there is still scope for discussion, clarification, and development. A theological definition can never be the final word since it deals with mysteries which cannot be confined within the strait-jacket of language. A lifetime could be spent in meditation and discussion of a single truth of the faith. What the Pope, or the episcopal college with the Pope, or the bishops alone teach noninfallibly commands respect and consideration but cannot ask for the assent of faith.

What in relation to these various categories is the position of *Humanae Vitae*? A virtually universal consensus exists that the Encyclical is not an example of the use of the extraordinary *magisterium* of the Pope.[2] In the first place it was not issued in the

---

[1] Before the definition of papal infallibility, in 1854, Pius IX had defined the doctrine of the Immaculate Conception of Mary. On this occasion and again in 1950 when the Assumption was defined, the Pope consulted the world-wide episcopate on their views and soundings were also taken among the laity. It is theoretically possible but practically inconceivable that the Pope would make a solemn definition of doctrine without overwhelming support from the bishops.

[2] Canon law puts the burden of proof of solemn definition on those wishing to establish it. 'Nothing is to be considered as dogmatically declared or defined unless there is unmistakable proof of the fact.' Canon 1323:3.

solemn form of a doctrinal definition but in the form of a letter.[1] Second there was the indication at the Press conference given in Rome by the papal spokesman Monsignor Lambruschini that the Pope did not intend to invoke his infallible prerogative.[2] The Pope of course could not make a definition infallible or non-infallible merely by a statement subsequent to the definition but the fact that acting through his spokesman he declared that it was not to be considered as an act of infallibility is a highly persuasive piece of evidence as to its status. Third, the subsequent judgement of the Church has been that the Encyclical is not a solemn defini-tion. Even its most ardent supporters have not suggested this.

Apart from these formal arguments the subject-matter of the Encyclical, birth control, would seem to exclude the invoking of the extraordinary *magisterium*. This form of the *magisterium*, as has been noted, is confined to one area of faith and morals, the revealed truths of salvation contained in the scriptures.[3] In the main these consist of what are strictly speaking doctrines of faith, but they also include certain revealed moral precepts such as the truths contained in the decalogue. These, however, are few, not least because of the number of variables in moral matters such as time, place, and situation as well as the intrinsic ambiguity of moral language. The whole of life is evolutionary and evo-lution and development play a special part in moral science. This is especially true of Christian morality which is inspired by a dynamic idea, that of love, which can never be reduced to a rigid legal code. Human reason which contributes so much to morality is likewise a dynamic force working on material which is constantly changing. While certain broad moral principles applicable to

[1] Daniel Callahan in an article in the *National Catholic Reporter* of 9 October 1968, says that the Encyclical is not infallible but goes on to ask why not since it is *ex cathedra*, addressed to the whole Church, and deals with morals. He concludes that the doctrine of papal infallibility is vacuous since there is no reliable means of ascertaining whether a statement is infallible or not. One sees his point but it is rhetorical rather than strictly logical.

[2] For Monsignor Lambruschini's statement see the *National Catholic Reporter*, 7 August 1968, and *Pope and Pill*, pp. 101–5. '*Humanae Vitae*', said Monsignor Lambruschini, 'does not suggest the theological note of infallibility; this is also shown by a simple comparison with the Profession of Faith proclaimed on 30 June, during the solemn rite in St Peter's Square.'

[3] The usual teaching is that the extraordinary *magisterium* extends beyond revealed truths to such presuppositions as are necessarily affirmed if the revelation itself is not to lose its certainty. This view of the extension of the scope of the *magisterium* is speculative.

the sexual life, such as the need for chastity both within and without marriage, can be said to be presupposed by revelation, or implied or laid down by it, a prohibition of contraception is not among them. Indeed *Humanae Vitae* does not seek to establish any scriptural foundation for its condemnation. Even the traditional references to Onan have been omitted. Nor can it be established with any certainty that contraception is forbidden by the natural law. 'It is certainly,' wrote Fr Bertke nearly thirty years ago, 'not among the immediate and evident deductions from first principles, and it has been seen that even acute minds are capable of erring concerning remote conclusions.'[1] Contraception as such, therefore, would seem to be a matter incapable of solemn dogmatic treatment.[2]

Just as *Humanae Vitae* is not an exercise of the Pope's extraordinary *magisterium*, neither does it pertain to the extraordinary *magisterium* of the episcopal college. In issuing the Encyclical the Pope acted alone and without any formal act of the college as such. It cannot even be considered an example of the college's ordinary *magisterium*, as is evident from the glosses and reservations on it in so many subsequent episcopal statements. Its status, one may conclude, is that of the ordinary teaching authority of the Pope. What are the limits and demands of this form of teaching?

The limits of the ordinary teaching authority of the Pope should in strict theory be the same as those operating in the solemn *magisterium*, namely the sphere of revealed doctrine and morals. The Pope cannot bind the consciences of the faithful by *teaching* on morals unless this is based on or presupposed by revelation. Neither Pope nor bishops have any title as religious teacher other than that conferred by revelation. If contraception is not a matter of revelation then Pope and bishops are simply acting *ultra vires* if they attempt to pronounce upon it.

This, I believe, is too narrow a view. It would confine the teach-

---

[1] S. Bertke, *The Possibility of Invincible Ignorance of the Natural Law* (Washington, D.C., 1941), p. 99. The members of the papal commission on birth control also appear to have concluded that it is impossible to show from reason that contraception is intrinsically evil.

[2] In fact there has been no solemn definition of any moral precept. Morality because of its complexity does not lend itself to this approach. To be universally applicable it would have to be so generalised as to border on vacuity.

ing power of the Pope to a very few matters which after centuries of development had crystallised into certainty. It is more reasonable to conclude that while the basis of the extraordinary and ordinary *magisterium* is the same, namely revelation, there is a difference in application. The ordinary *magisterium* includes a more remote application of the Pope's teaching authority derived from revelation to areas where variables and contingent factors are involved.[1] The Pope, for example, in the matter of birth control, is entitled to apply revealed moral principles concerning marriage, but he cannot do so with the certainty and definitiveness essential for the invocation of the infallible *magisterium*. He cannot in these matters, therefore, demand the assent of faith. What then can he ask for?

This is an extremely difficult question to answer since so little thought has been devoted to it by theologians. In the period between the two Vatican Councils the predominant tendency within the Church was to accept without challenge any official statement on doctrinal or moral matters which came from the Holy See.[2] The Church was in the grip of a process of 'creeping' infallibility.[3] Even so the manual moralists were clear that the ordinary *magisterium* of the Pope did not demand the assent of faith.[4]

The Constitution on the Church issued by Vatican II does throw some light on the matter while not disposing of it entirely satisfactorily. After stating that the bishops teaching in communion

[1] The Pope may of course be teaching 'infallibly' without using the solemn form when giving day-to-day guidance on matters of generally accepted doctrine in the Church, but the 'infallibility' here pertains to the episcopal college not to the Pope as such. It seems probable that the Pope has no ordinary infallible teaching authority independent of his participation in the *magisterium* of the episcopal college.

[2] In his encyclical *Humani Generis* (1950), Pius XII went so far as to say that when the Pope has pronounced on some hitherto controverted subject it can 'no longer be regarded as a matter of free debate among theologians'. (para. 29.) This statement of course does not end the matter since its own status is debatable.

[3] The Jesuit, George Tyrrell, commented on this after the condemnation by Pius X of Modernism in his encyclical *Pascendi Dominici Gregis* in 1907. '*L'église c'est moi*', seems to be his attitude, he wrote. 'The Pope is the steam engine; the episcopate is the carriages; the faithful are the passengers', and all that was left to the layman, or apparently the theologian was 'to pay his fare and take his seat as so much ballast in the bark of Peter, while the clergy pull him across the ferry'.

[4] For a discussion of such authorities as Palmieri, Salaverri, etc. see Joseph A. Komonchak, 'Ordinary Papal Magisterium and Religious Assent' in *Contraception* (London, 1969), ed. by Charles Curran.

with the Pope are to be respected as witnesses to divine and Catholic truth, it goes on to declare that their teaching on faith and morals must be accepted by the faithful and adhered to 'with a religious submission of soul'. No definition is given of this religious submission but the text goes on to apply the obligation to papal teaching. 'This religious submission of will and of mind must be shown in a special way to the authentic teaching authority of the Roman Pontiff, even when he is not speaking *ex cathedra*. That is, it must be shown in such a way that his supreme *magisterium* is acknowledged with reverence, the judgements made by him are sincerely adhered to according to his manifest mind and will. His mind and will in the matter may be known chiefly either from the character of the documents, from his frequent repetition of the same doctrine, or from his manner of speaking.'[1]

Before discussing the meaning of this passage a word of caution is necessary. Council declarations are not doctrinal definitions and exegetical interpretation while useful should not be carried to literal extremes. Furthermore the declarations must be seen as the end product of long debate and representing not always final words but compromise positions. One of the principal points of conflict at the Council was that between papal and episcopal prerogatives, and this must be borne in mind when assessing wording. Finally, the background of relevant parts of the declaration in so far as they are known have to be taken into account.[2]

---

[1] Para. 25 of *Lumen Gentium*. In *Humanae Vitae* (para. 28), when the Pope asks for 'loyal internal and external obedience' the footnote reference is to this paragraph of *Lumen Gentium*.

[2] Thus in the original schema presented to the Council in 1962 a direct adoption of the words of Pius XII in *Humani Generis*, stating that subjects pronounced on by the Pope were not to be considered as matter for free debate among theologians, was included but this was omitted from the draft finally accepted. An attempt to restore the words failed. See *Emendationes a Concilii Patribus scripto exhibitae super schema Constitutionis Dogmaticae De Ecclesia, Pars I* (Vatican Press, 1963), pp. 43–4. Another emendation proposed by Bishop Cleary that the text should include a statement upholding freedom of investigation was also rejected. Ibid., p. 43. Again three *modi* were presented to the doctrinal commission in relation to para. 25. The first (159) raised the question of the position of an educated person who could not for 'solid reasons' give internal assent to teaching proposed non-infallibly. The commission replied that on this point 'approved theological explanations should be consulted'. The next (160) wished to add after the words 'adhered to' in para. 25 'although not with an absolute and irreformable assent'. This was rejected by the commission on the grounds that it was incomplete owing to the fact that the ordinary teaching office 'often proposes doctrines which

Whatever 'religious submission of will and mind' may mean, it must be something other than the assent of faith since to identify them would obliterate the distinction between the ordinary and extraordinary *magisterium*. The Latin 'religiosum voluntatis et intellectus obsequium' does not resolve the issue because of the essential ambiguity of the word 'obsequium'. At least six renderings of its meaning are possible, ranging from assent through submission, obedience, compliance, and allegiance to deference.[1] The assent of faith is by nature unconditional, indeed it may be said that this is characteristic of all true assent. As Newman has put it: 'No one can hold conditionally what by the same act he holds to be true.'[2] 'Religiosum obsequium' cannot therefore be translated as 'religious assent' which is quite a different notion. The teaching of some of the manual moralists that the ordinary teaching of the Pope commands 'internal' assent must accordingly be rejected. The quality of assent is not determined by its external or internal manifestations but by its intrinsic unconditionality. If the ordinary teaching of the Pope is not infallible then it must be fallible: if it is not irreformable then it must be capable of being reformed.

The literal translation is 'religious obsequiousness' and this gives a clear pointer to its meaning. In modern usage 'obsequiousness' has acquired a pejorative meaning with undertones of cringing and fawning but that is not the meaning of its Latin root 'to follow'. 'Religiosum obsequium' indicates an obligation to follow for religious reasons. A statement by the Head of the Church on earth, even when not infallible, commands reverence and respect from members of the Church because of their religious relationship to him, but this is neither absolute nor unconditional.

---

already belong to the Catholic faith itself'. (This point would be covered by regarding this exercise of the papal ordinary *magisterium* as part of the *magisterium* of the college as a whole as I suggest at page 225.) The third modus (161), suggesting that an addition should be made indicating the freedom to be permitted for further investigation and doctrinal progress, was approved by the commission but its inclusion not thought necessary. See *Schema Constitutionis Dogmaticae De Ecclesia: Modi*, etc., III: III (Vatican Press, 1964), p. 42.

[1] See John McHugh, 'The Doctrinal Authority of the Encyclical *Humanae Vitae*', *The Clergy Review*, September 1969, LIV: 680. This is the second of three articles, the first published in August and the third in October.

[2] *A Grammar of Assent* (London, 1906), p. 172.

Coming from the Head of the Church there is a presumption that it is true but not an absolute presumption as in a solemn definition. The presumption accordingly is rebuttable.

The furthest one can go is to say that the Pope is in possession and that the *onus probandi* is not on him to establish the truth of what he is saying but on those who cannot agree with him to demonstrate otherwise. Yet even this statement needs modification. It represents a theoretical position abstracted from the real world. The ordinary teaching of the Pope is said to be 'authentic' and it is authenticity that the contemporary world demands, especially in religious matters.[1] Modern man needs to be convinced of the truth of a position by the presentation of good reasons. An exercise of authority alone generally does not convince. This is especially true in the sphere of morals where the moral response is so important. This presumably is why the Pope in *Humanae Vitae* did give reasons for his decision: in theory it would have been sufficient merely to have stated his decision. A Catholic then cannot, *a priori*, dismiss the ordinary teaching of the Pope as being of no more significance than the opinion of a private theologian, but he equally must recognise that the obligation to follow this teaching may be lifted by demonstration that it is defective or incomplete, by a change in the teaching by the issuing Pope or a successor, or by rejection by the Church as a whole.

The obligation to follow the Pope in his authoritative teaching is then a conditional one subject to a number of other factors, the principal of which are the dictates of an individual's own reason and conscience. Conscience is the response of the whole being in the context of matters of morality as to whether a certain proposition is true or false or whether a course of conduct is right or wrong. The intellect plays a part in this but conscience is not to be identified with purely intellectual processes. An act of conscience like an act of faith goes beyond these while not contradicting them. It would for example be possible to accept that a given course of

[1] Hans Küng writes of 'that basic attitude through which individuals or communities, in spite of difficulties, remain true to themselves without dissimulation and without losing their integrity: a genuine candour with oneself, one's fellows and with God, a genuine candour in thought, word and deed.' *Truthfulness: The Future of the Church* (London, 1968), p. 36.

conduct was wrong, while at the same time to be unconvinced by any reasoning put forward to condemn it.

The Church has always recognised, at least in theory, the peremptoriness and legitimacy of the rights of conscience, which she has rightly seen as part of the essential freedom of man's nature. For centuries theologians have taught the obligation to follow even an erroneous conscience.[1] The Second Vatican Council gave a high place to conscience, declaring: 'Conscience is the most secret core and sanctuary of a man. There he is alone with God, whose voice echoes in his depths. In a wonderful manner conscience reveals that law which is fulfilled by love of God and neighbour. In fidelity to conscience, Christians are joined with the rest of men in the search for truth, and for the genuine solution to the numerous problems which arise in the life of individuals and from social relationships.[2]

It is important to stress that the Church has not given an absolute value to conscience in the popular sense in which the word is sometimes used as meaning a right to think and act as one pleases. Conscience is a mode of apprehension of the divine law: a mode which man must be left completely free to exercise in accordance with his nature but which is directed to the discovery of God's law which is an objective fact. Cardinal Newman makes this distinction in his letter to the Duke of Norfolk in which he gives the highest human place to conscience, describing it in an arresting phrase as 'the aboriginal Vicar of Christ'. He goes on to hail conscience as 'a prophet in its informations, a monarch in its peremptoriness, a priest in its blessings and anathemas' and declares that even if the priesthood throughout the Church should cease 'in it the sacerdotal principle would remain and have its sway'.[3] Yet he makes it clear that conscience is not the source of

---

[1] For a twentieth-century pre-Vatican II formulation see Genicot: 'When conscience feels certain, whether it be correct or mistaken, one is always obliged to follow it when it enjoins or forbids; and one is always entitled to follow it, when it recommends or permits.' *Institutiones Theologiae Moralis* (Brussels, 1931), I:42.

[2] *Pastoral Constitution on the Church in the Modern World*. Para. 16. This passage appears to have been based on a radio broadcast of Pius XII of 23 March 1952.

[3] In *Newman and Gladstone*, a collection of documents, introduced by Alvan S. Ryan (Notre Dame Press, 1962), pp. 127, 129. Newman was answering Gladstone on the latter's strictures on the definition of papal infallibility which he maintained had deprived Catholics of all freedom. The letter to the Duke of Norfolk contains the famous words: 'I add one remark. Certainly, if I am obliged to bring religion into

right but a witness to it: 'the internal witness of both the existence and the law of God'. As a contemporary theologian has put it: 'Because his conscience judgement is the first stage in his response to God in any situation, the individual is obliged to listen to God as carefully as he can. He must use all the resources available to him to understand what God is saying as fully as possible.'[1] And since this is the first part of the response to God he must be left to make it on his own.

A true conscience cannot be in collision with the law of God and therefore, as far as a Catholic is concerned, cannot be in conflict with the infallible teaching of the Pope, since he accepts this as a manifestation of the divine law. The situation is different in relation to the Pope's non-infallible teaching where there is no divine guarantee and the conscience of the individual may be right or wrong. Is there then no way of mediating between the Pope and the individual in such circumstances? If the individual conscience is thought of as a purely private thing, there is not, but the conscience of the individual Catholic operates not only privately but publicly in the community of which the individual forms a part, namely in the Church. The conscience of the ecclesial community is a public thing made up of contributions coming from members of the community who are striving to apply their Christian insight to their lives. This public conscience can only be formed through rational public argument and discussion. Hence the need for freedom and openness in which conscience can be checked against conscience and eventually a consensus can emerge. So a mature community of men is created who have learned responsible attitudes in the formation of their consciences.

---

after-dinner toasts (which indeed does not seem quite the thing) I shall drink – to the Pope, if you please – still, to Conscience first, and to the Pope afterwards.' Newman demonstrated that Catholic acceptance of the Pope depended on a prior act of conscience and conscience continued to limit papal power. Yet he was cautious about resisting the supreme although not infallible power of the Pope: 'Unless a man is able to say to himself as in the presence of God, that he must not, and dare not, act upon the Papal injunction, he is bound to obey it, and would commit a great sin in disobeying it.' (See 'Letter to His Grace the Duke of Norfolk' in *Difficulties of Anglicans*, II: pp. 257–8). Protagonists in our present debates usually quote one or other of these passages but rarely both of them together.

[1] Enda McDonagh, 'Conscience: the Guidance of the Spirit' in *Truth and Life*, ed. Enda McDonagh (Dublin, 1968), p. 133.

In such a community law is both interiorised in consciences and consciences are externalised in law in a creative process of tension and dialogue. Such a community is essential for the growth and rule of responsible freedom, the only alternative to which is the dictate of fear-inspired laws.

Like conscience the *magisterium* of the Pope must be seen in the wider setting of the community of the Church if it is not to be distorted and absolutised. The subject of infallibility is the Church as a whole: the infallible *magisterium* is principally a defining power. The ordinary *magisterium* of the Pope is similarly operating within a *koinonia*, a true sacramental and mystical community, which is more than a mere aggregate of consciences or individuals and possesses a dynamic life of its own. In order to operate at all the papal *magisterium*, which has no private source of inspiration to which it can turn, must go back to the mind of the Church and find there the material for its definitions. Accordingly the papal *magisterium* always operates within the community of the Church not from outside it or above it, which has been a wide-spread misconception in recent times.[1]

The *magisterium* is a service to the Church not a subjugation of it. It is a lead in love, and should operate therefore by its own in-trinsic merits of truth, in persuasion rather than compulsion. St Paul shows this in his first epistle to the Corinthians where he con-ducts a dialogue with those who are expressing different opinions on the truths of faith.[2] 'He read,' writes John McKenzie, S.J., 'the incestuous man out of the Church, but he did not read his own critics out of the Church.'[3]

The ordinary *magisterium* of the Pope, being a more remote application of the truths of revelation to changing and contingent

[1] The definition of papal infallibility at Vatican I probably contributed to this with its declaration that the definitions of the Pope were infallible 'ex sese non autem ex consensu ecclesiae'. This definition was drawn up in an historical context in which it was thought necessary to repel Gallicanism and prevent the possibility of an appeal from the Pope to the episcopate. It does not exclude the 'sensus fidei' as an operative force.

[2] *First Letter*, Chapters 1–2. Cf. *Epistle to the Galatians*.

[3] *Authority in the Church* (London, 1966), p. 55. Father McKenzie's book is an extended treatment of authority in the Church. He points out that authority in this context has more in common with 'diakonia' or service than 'exousia' power. Use of the word 'magisterium' shows a shift from New Testament ideas to the Roman concept of the office or function of a schoolmaster (p. 123).

situations, is especially dependent on Christian experience and the mind of the whole Church.[1] This 'sensus fidei', the believing mind belonging to the faithful as a whole, was explicitly recognised by the Second Vatican Council. 'The Holy People of God,' declares *Lumen Gentium*, 'shares also in Christ's prophetic office. It spreads abroad a living witness to Him, especially by means of a life of faith and charity and by offering to God a sacrifice of praise, the tribute of lips which give honour to his name (cf. Heb. 13:15). The body of the faithful as a whole, anointed as they are by the Holy One (cf. Jn. 2:20, 27) cannot err in matters of belief. Thanks to a supernatural sense of the faith which characterises the People as a whole, it manifests this unerring quality when, "from the bishops down to the last member of the laity", it shows universal agreement in matters of faith and morals. For by this sense of faith which is aroused and sustained by the Spirit of truth, God's people accepts not the word of men but the very Word of God (cf. 1 Th. 2:13). It clings without fail to the faith once delivered to the saints (cf. Jude 3), penetrates it more deeply by accurate insights, and applies it more thoroughly to life. All this it does under the lead of a sacred teaching authority to which it loyally defers.'[2]

The 'sensus fidei' subsists in the whole Church, Pope, bishops, priests, and laity, joined in sacramental and diaological community: it is the common possession of Christians. The laity is only one component of the community but they are full members and their role in preserving and articulating the faith is not a merely passive one. In certain matters such as marriage, the views of the married laity are of particular importance since they are giving prophetic witness to things which are peculiarly within their own experience and competence. By virtue of the sacrament of matrimony, says *Lumen Gentium*, spouses have their own 'special

[1] The point is made in relation to infallibility in Bishop Butler's book, *The Theology of Vatican II* (London, 1967). 'At least for practical purposes,' he writes, 'the infallibility of the ordinary *magisterium* and of the *sensus fidelium* means that the Church conducts her doctrinal and theological reflections within a collective or collaborative climate of opinion which is, so far from being agnostic, controlled by the pervading presence of a total truth revealed by God, a truth which is always carried and in some measure expressed in "the mind of the Church" and in the teaching of her *magisterium*, and which is capable, when circumstances require it, of partial formulation in definitions of faith'. p. 25.
[2] Para. 12.

gift among the people of God', and goes so far as to describe the family as 'the domestic Church'.[1] Because of their incorporation into the life of the Church, the laity have not only a right but a duty to express their views. This, too, was recognised by the Council when it declared: 'An individual layman, by reason of the knowledge, competence or outstanding ability which he may enjoy is permitted and sometimes even obliged to express his opinion on things which concern the Church.'[2] A similar point is made in *Gaudium et Spes*.[3] So the Council laid the foundation for what Cardinal Suenens has judged its greatest pastoral achievement: 'the rediscovery of the people of God as a whole, as a single reality; and then by way of consequence, the coresponsibility thus implied for every member of the Church.'[4]

History, in fact, gives the laity an even higher place than the Council in preserving revealed truth. During the Arian disputes of the fourth century, the laity preserved the central Christian doctrine of the divinity of Christ against the teaching of many of the bishops. In 357 even Pope Liberius sided with heresy when he confirmed the condemnation of St Athanasius. Dealing with the Arian episode in his famous article in *The Rambler*, 'On Consulting the Faithful in Matters of Doctrine', Cardinal Newman commented: 'I am not denying that the great body of bishops were in their internal belief orthodox; nor that there were numbers of clergy who stood by the laity and acted as their centres and guides; nor that the laity actually received their faith, in the first instance from the bishops and clergy; nor that some portions of the laity

---

[1] Para. 11.

[2] *Lumen Gentium*: para. 37. The laity, states *Lumen Gentium*, share in the priestly, prophetic, and kingly role of Christ (para. 31). Christ as prophet speaks also through the laity (para. 35). The clergy are exhorted to 'respectfully acknowledge that just freedom which belongs to everyone in this earthly city' (para. 37) and it is stated that: 'Every person should walk unhesitatingly according to his own personal gifts and duties in the paths of a living faith which arouses hopes and works through charity.' (para. 41.)

[3] See para. 62. It is hoped that many laymen will receive training in 'the sacred sciences' and that some will develop these studies further. 'In order that such persons may fulfil their proper function, let it be recognised that all the faithful, clerical and lay, possess a lawful freedom of enquiry and of thought, and the freedom to express their minds humbly and courageously about those matters in which they enjoy competence.' It is interesting to note the Orthodox tradition where so many of the leading theologians are laymen.

[4] Leon Joseph Cardinal Suenens, *Coresponsibility in the Church* (London, 1968), p. 30.

were ignorant, and other portions were at length corrupted by the Arian teachers, who got possession of the sees, and ordained an heretical clergy: but I mean still, that in that time of immense confusion the divine dogma of Our Lord's divinity was proclaimed, enforced, maintained, and (humanly speaking) preserved, far more by the 'Ecclesia docta' than by the 'Ecclesia docens'; that the body of the episcopate was unfaithful to its commission, while the body of the laity was faithful to its baptism; that at one time the Pope, at other times a patriarchal, metropolitan or other great see, at other times the general councils, said what they should not have said, or did what obscured and compromised revealed truth; while on the other hand it was the Christian people, who, under Providence, were the ecclesiastical strength of Athanasius, Hilary, Eusebius of Vercellae, and other great solitary confessors who would have failed without them.'[1]

Newman was dealing not with the 'sensus fidei' but the 'sensus fidelium', a concept exclusively applicable to the laity. He listed five ways in which the consent of the faithful impinged on the manifestation of the tradition of the Church: 'Its *consensus* is to be regarded: 1. as a testimony to the fact of the apostolical dogma; 2. as a sort of instinct or $\phi\rho\acute{o}\nu\eta\mu\alpha$, deep in the bosom of the mystical body of Christ; 3. as a direction of the Holy Ghost; 4. as an answer to its prayer; 5. as a jealousy of error, which it at once feels as a scandal.'[2] He concluded from the Arian experience that this was sufficient to enable the *ecclesia docta* in certain circumstances to discharge the normal functions of the *ecclesias docens*. If Newman is right in this, and the actual historical unfolding of the Arian drama show reasonably conclusively that he is, then the distinction between the *ecclesia docta* and *ecclesia docens* is not as rigid and absolute as has sometimes been supposed. The *ecclesia docens* is not at every point of time the active instrument of the Church's

---

[1] *The Rambler*, July 1859, vol. I N.S. part II, pp. 98–230. He refers to Gregorius de Valentis who states that the consent of the faithful is such 'that the Supreme Pontiff *is able and ought* to *rest* upon it as being *the judgement or sentiment* of the *infallible* Church' (p. 208). Cf. St Cyprian: 'I have made it a rule, ever since the beginning of my episcopate, to make no decision merely on the strength of my own personal opinion without consulting you (the priests and the deacons) without the approbation of the people.' Epist. 14:4: 'nihil sine consilio vestro et sine consensu plebis mea privatim sententia gerere.' Cf. Epist. 34:4, 1, 32.

[2] 'On Consulting The Faithful', op. cit., p. 211.

infallibility.[1] If this can be the case with the infallible *magisterium* how much more easily can it be with the ordinary *magisterium*, where the subject-matter is so variable. How much more easily again can it be when that subject-matter comes within the special competence of the laity as is the case with marriage.[2]

From these general reflections and principles certain practical conclusions in relation to *Humanae Vitae* can be drawn. First a confirmation of the view that although the Encyclical is an important and significant document it cannot of its very nature decide the issue. It cannot be the final word and it would be rash and imprudent to try and make it so.[3] Second, it is essential that discussion should continue in the freest possible manner since without this the mind of the Church cannot emerge. Many of the bishops have given the lead in this sphere with hierarchies such as the Belgian, German, Scandinavian, and Canadian recognising an objective right of dissent. The laity, and especially the married laity have a positive duty to let their views and experience be known, whether these accord with the Encyclical or not. This duty is a manifestation of the 'sensus fidelium', a gift of the Spirit operating in both the individual conscience of laymen and women and the collective conscience of the laity as a whole, as part of the community of the Church.[4] The teaching Church learns from the living Church and *Humanae Vitae* will only be able to pass from the

[1] Bishop Butler suggests that 'the application of the notions of *ecclesia docens* and *ecclesia discens* might profitably be re-examined. It is commonly supposed that the former is materially identical with the bishops, and the latter with the rest of the Church's membership. It seems possible that, in fact, the whole Church is, under different and correlative aspects, both *docens* and *discens*. That the bishops have a peculiar magisterial role as representing the apostolic college cannot be denied. On the other hand, in modern ecumenical Councils, including Vatican II, some prelates who were not bishops had not only a consultative but a deliberative vote in doctrinal issues.' *The Theology of Vatican II* (London, 1967), p. 110, fn. 22. The point is only touched upon in a footnote and is not pursued.

[2] Or in other matters. What would St Thomas More have done if he had taken the guidance of the overwhelming majority of the English hierarchy?

[3] It would be an example of 'magisteriolatry'.

[4] The Church as a whole can only gain from the active participation of the laity in her teaching life. As Cardinal Newman puts it in the concluding words of his article 'On Consulting the Faithful in Matters of Doctrine': 'I think certainly that the *Ecclesia docens* is more happy when she has such enthusiastic partisans about her as are here represented, than when she cuts off the faithful from the study of her divine doctrines and the sympathy of her divine contemplations, and requires from them a *fides implicita* in her word, which in the educated classes will terminate in indifference, and in the poorer in superstition.' op. cit., p. 230.

status of authentic teaching of the Pope to that of authentic teaching of the Church if it commands the assent of the married laity.

In forming the opinion of the Church, theologians have a major part to play and need freedom of expression if they are to discharge this role in an effective and convincing manner. The position of the moral theologian has been described by Karl Rahner as 'analogous to a specialist who sees in his field of knowledge contradictory views which each have important (even if sometimes very different) reasons behind them'.[1] As to the practice of the laity, if they are not conscientiously convinced by the teaching of the Encyclical, they cannot be under an obligation to follow it. Even if they accept the general argument they may conclude that it is not applicable in their own particular circumstances. This is a different position from those who accept the conclusions of the Encyclical but who, through frailty, are unable to follow it consistently in their lives. In the confessional priests are under an obligation to take into account the complexity of the situation created by the existence of these different points of view. The dissent from the Encyclical has been on such a scale as to constitute a new theological factor which has to be recognised in giving pastoral guidance.

THE ARGUMENTS OF 'HUMANAE VITAE'

The authority of *Humanae Vitae* is assessable not only by its intrinsic status and the reception accorded it by clergy and laity, but by its own intellectual stature and inner consistency. The authority of Christ, a relevant consideration here, was not the authority of power, but of truth which evoked a response in his hearers' hearts and minds. The primacy of Rome in the early Church was established as much by the wisdom of her rulings in response to requests for guidance as by any Petrine claims. Speculation about the motives of those responsible for the issue of the Encyclical, whether for example they thought it necessary for the maintenance of the authority of the papacy or not, are not of

---

[1] See article published in the *National Catholic Reporter*, 18 September 1968. In the same article Father Rahner points out 'a non-defined declaration is really basically capable of reform, and a Catholic, especially a theologian, has the right, indeed, even the responsibility to take cognisance of this fact.'

primary importance: ideas should be judged on themselves and not on the supposed intentions of their originators.

The Encyclical opens by stating the gravity of the issue with which it deals and outlines the new factors which have to be taken into account in considering it, such as the problem of world population, the changed social conditions of modern life, the alteration in the position of women, the revaluing of the place of conjugal love in married life, and the progress made by man in the domination of nature. It goes on to make an express reference to the work of the papal birth control commission and the Pope expresses his gratitude for the work of its members.[1] From this point on, however, both the new factors listed and the report of the commission are simply ignored, no attempt being made to meet the arguments for the restatement of the traditional Catholic position on contraception which they raise.

The next section of the Encyclical, headed 'Doctrinal Principles', sets out a high view of marriage with a noble and moving description of the nature and value of conjugal love. It is hailed as human, total, faithful, exclusive, and fruitful. Responsible parenthood and family planning are commended as an exercise in co-operation between human beings and their creator. These paragraphs are a classic exposition, written in excellent Latin, of the new theology of marriage, hinted at in *Casti Connubii*, and developed in *Gaudium et Spes*.[2] With their general theme no Christian, let alone a Catholic, would be disposed to quarrel. Unfortunately these principles appear once more in isolation from the rest of the Encyclical and its principal decision.

There is no logical connection between them and the teaching on the nature and purpose of the marriage act contained in paragraphs 11 to 14, which constitute the heart of the Encyclical. The assertion that 'each and every marriage act must remain open

[1] The principal reason given by the Pope for not accepting the conclusions of the commission as definitive is because 'certain criteria of solutions had emerged which departed from the moral teaching on marriage proposed with constant firmness by the teaching authority of the Church' (para. 6). Such a statement, although admirably frank, indicates that the whole issue was prejudged.

[2] The paragraphs of *Humanae Vitae* are 7–10: those of *Gaudium et Spes*, 48–51. The latter states that 'authentic married love is caught up into divine love and is governed and enriched by Christ's redeeming power and the saving activity of the Church'. Conjugal love is said to be 'uniquely expressed and perfected through the marital act'.

to the transmission of life' made in paragraph 11 may or may not be true, but it is not entailed by the doctrinal principles earlier laid down.[1] The same may be said of the statement in the following paragraph, and which constitutes the second major declaration of the Encyclical, that there is an 'inseparable connection' which is 'willed by God and unable to be broken by man on his own initiative, between the two meanings of the conjugal act: the unitive meaning and the procreative meaning'. No demonstration is made of the truth of this, no authority cited in its support other than a further assertion that the conjugal act by its intimate structure 'while most closely uniting husband and wife, capacitates them for the generation of new lives, according to laws inscribed in the very being of man and of woman'.[2] Later it is stated that man does not have 'unlimited dominion' over his 'generative faculties' because of 'their intrinsic ordination towards raising up life, of which God is the principle'.[3] And that, as far as the central message of the Encyclical goes, is that, apart from the conclusion drawn in paragraph 14 that all forms of contraception are illicit.

The statement that 'each and every marriage act must remain open to the transmission of life' has been subjected to severe criticism because of the existence of acts of intercourse which in the natural order of things cannot lead to conception. Sexual intercourse during the sterile period, strictly defined, cannot result in procreation. It is a biological impossibility. What then is the point of talking about acts being 'open to life', when in fact by any ordinary meaning of words they are closed? The only reason seems to be an apologetic one. If one wishes to argue that the unitive and procreative aspects of intercourse may not be separated by man at will in any circumstances, one is not greatly helped in establishing the point by the fact that God himself through nature has already done so. The difficulty can be got round to some extent by maintaining that in some transcendental sense non-procreative

[1] The only connection is the half sentence contained in paragraph 10: 'human intellect discovers in the power of giving life biological laws which are part of the human person'. The precise meaning of this phrase is obscure. Is it a simple statement of biological fact or does use of the words 'part of the human person' imply some moral component?

[2] Para. 12.

[3] Para. 13. One can, of course, accept this statement without concluding that he has no control over them.

natural acts remain open to life in that they have not been shut to them by human intervention. One then ends up with a safe-open period which is something of a semantic and an intellectual monstrosity.

Some defenders of the Encyclical have blamed the translation for the difficulty and 'open to the transmission of life' may not be a happy choice of words. The original Latin reads 'quilibet matrimonii usus ad vitam procreandam per se destinatus permaneat' and can be literally translated 'any use of marriage should remain of itself destined to procreate human life'. But if sexual acts are incapable of leading to procreation it is difficult to see in what way they can be 'destined' to do so. Bishop Clark of Northampton has translated it as 'any use whatever of marriage must retain its natural potential to procreate human life'.[1] This is more a paraphrase than a translation but in any case is it any better? An act which has no 'natural potential to procreate life' can hardly be subject to a moral imperative to retain what it has not got. One cannot of course conclude from the existence of sterile acts that man does have the right to create them, but their existence aids those who wish to establish the proposition rather than those who wish to deny it.

The Encyclical recognises the existence of conjugal acts which cannot be followed by new life and adds: 'God has wisely disposed natural laws and rhythms of fecundity which of themselves cause a separation in the succession of births.' These words too are open to criticism on grounds of biological inaccuracy and failure to tell the whole truth. The point of alluding to them is that later in the Encyclical, at paragraph 16, permission is given to use the period during which infertile acts occur as a means of family planning. Once this is resorted to consciously by a married couple, it is not the rhythms which act 'of themselves' in preventing birth taking place but their manipulation by the couple. Accordingly an act can be said to remain 'open' to the transmission of life and therefore legitimate when a 'time' obstacle is placed in the way of procreation but not when a 'spatial' obstacle is used. There is no

---

[1] See *Tablet*, 25 January 1969. Bishop Clark explains that the couple must be as fully man and as fully woman as they have it in their power to be at the time of the act. His use of the word 'procreate' is better than 'transmission' which has echoes of the false biological view that life is transmitted from man to woman.

doubt a physical difference between these situations but that this constitutes a moral differentiation will not be meaningful to many rational persons.

The distinction between the two classes of act becomes even finer in the light of other passages in the Encyclical. In paragraph 24, for example, the Pope, echoing the words of Pius XII calls upon medical science to provide 'a sufficiently secure basis for a regulation of birth founded on the observance of natural rhythms'. This could refer exclusively to assessment of the present infertile period as found in different women, but many commentators, including Cardinal Heenan, have interpreted it as an invitation to scientists to replace the often unpredictable and variable natural rhythms by a cycle of fixed duration created by artificial means. What then has become of the wise dispositions of natural rhythms which are said to have been provided by God? Why can the anatomical pattern be varied in this way but not in others? A possible answer is that irregular ovulation is to be regarded as a disease and intervention is therefore a medical rather than a contraceptive action. The Encyclical itself states that the Church does not in any way consider 'illicit', the use of 'those therapeutic means, truly necessary to cure diseases of the organism, even if an impediment to procreation, which may be foreseen, should result therefrom, provided such impediment is not, for whatever motive, directly willed'.[1] It seems, however, somewhat fanciful to treat ovulation irregularity as pathological however convenient this may be in this particular context.

Sanctioning of the creation of an artificial cycle also undermines the distinction made in paragraph 16 between the legitimate use of a natural disposition, which justifies resort to the infertile period for purposes of family planning, and the impeding of 'the development of natural processes', which rules out contraception. The Encyclical commends the use of the infertile period since it enables restraint to be practised at other times, which it claims is not possible when contraception is used. But is this true? There is no logical nor practical reason why the use of contraceptives should be considered as incompatible with abstinence and restraint. The Pope's assertion here seems to rest on the view that once

[1] Para. 15.

contraceptives are admitted into married life it is turned into licensed debauchery, but there is no evidence that this is so. Indeed, the experience of couples, both Christian and non-Christian, who use contraception, positively contradicts it.[1] The infertile period and contraceptives alike, may be used selfishly or unselfishly. It is true that use of the infertile period necessarily involves abstinence but is abstinence always a spiritual good? Whether it is spiritually beneficial or not must depend on other factors such as the spirit in which it is approached.[2]

A further question of major importance arises from the statement in the Encyclical that the unitive and procreative purposes of intercourse should not be separated at will.[3] What is the basis for this assertion? It requires explanation, all the more since theologians have not held that this applies to the animals committed to man's care. Why should man have dominion over processes in beasts which in human beings are removed from his control? If the biological pattern is primary and determines the morality of actions should it not apply to all creation? The Encyclical states that the ban on separation rests on the teaching authority of the Church: 'a teaching founded on the natural law illuminated and enriched by divine Revelation'.[4] But the natural law and Revelation are two different and exclusive modes of apprehending the law of God. It could be, of course, that one could apprehend the law of God on one point by both these methods but not by one 'enriched' by the other, which merely confuses two different means of knowledge. The suspicion is aroused that the two sources are linked together because it is impossible to establish the needed proposition by either alone. This conclusion is strengthened by an examination of the text.

As far as Revelation is concerned the Encyclical does not attempt to adduce scriptural evidence in support of its central

[1] The approach of many moral theologians to marriage appears to be excessively abstract and lacking the dimension of the actual. Intercourse in marriage is subject to a great number of restraints other than the desire to avoid children. One obvious example is that husband and wife must simultaneously consent to sexual relations.

[2] One school of moral theologians extols the use of the infertile period as an art or way of life. See S. de Lestapis, *Family Planning and Modern Problems* (London, 1961). It will surely strike many people as a distortion that a technique of questionable effectiveness should be treated as 'a way of life'. It indicates a more fundamental flaw of too biological an approach to sexuality.

[3] Para. 12.   [4] Para. 4.

R

proposition. Scriptural references are found in footnotes at other places but many of these do not seem to be appropriate.[1] As to the natural law, it is certainly not self-evident to reason that the sexual processes alone are not subject to the control of man or that the law of God is immanent in biological processes. It was agreed by all members of the papal birth control commission that reason alone could not establish the evil of contraception. Reason, in this context, means not merely the subjective judgement of individuals but an objective consensus of the people of God, developed within the whole life of the Church. The Encyclical recognises this when it calls in aid in its condemnation of contraception 'the moral teaching on marriage proposed with constant firmness by the teaching authority of the Church'. Certain elements in this teaching come from Revelation but some from the natural law as crystallised by theologians and others in their writings and discussions. *Humanae Vitae* declares that the Church 'has always provided – and even more amply in recent times – a coherent teaching concerning both the nature of marriage and the correct use of conjugal rights and the duties of husband and wife'.[2] In fact this teaching has not been as coherent and constant as the Encyclical makes out.

The Church's teaching on marriage has been in a continual state of development over the centuries. Certain propositions which were once taught have been abandoned and others, which were not laid down, included. It is no doubt true that certain basic values which the Church has sought to protect in marriage have remained constant, but the perspective in which these values have been seen has certainly altered, as well as the means employed to advance and protect them. Among the marital values consistently maintained by the Church have been the good of procreation, the importance of permanence in marriage, the need to educate the children, the personal dignity of the spouses, and the holiness of conjugal love, but she has not committed herself to a changeless body of ethical rules to embody them. Furthermore at different

---

[1] Thus in para. 4, where it is stated that the apostles were constituted guardians of the moral law there is a reference to Matt. 7:21, but this is a passage in the sermon on the mount of no obvious relevance.

[2] Para. 4. The reference to 'recent times' recognises that the fullest official Roman condemnations of contraception have come within the last hundred years.

times she has drawn on different sources for her matrimonial insights: for example, only in recent times has the actual experience of the married laity been made available.

The corpus of the Church's teaching on marriage has been laboriously built up over the centuries with different emphases at different periods. St Augustine's teaching on marriage greatly influenced the official position of the Church but today the inadequacy of his approach to married love is universally recognised.[1] Again, St Thomas Aquinas's emphasis on the importance of male semen which at one time greatly affected Catholic moral theology has declined in importance at the present time. Attitudes to intercourse during the infertile period have also radically altered over the years. Condemned at one point as sinful by St Augustine, accepted only grudgingly by theologians at others, it has today been sanctioned by two Popes as a means of family planning, and has been commended to married couples in countless Catholic marriage manuals and family planning clinics. Family planning itself has passed from the status of near delinquency to that of a positive moral duty.[2]

The encyclical *Humanae Vitae* itself, even in its condemnation of contraception, illustrates this process. It bases its rejection of contraception not on Revelation as such, nor on the sanctity of semen, nor even on the perception by reason of a purpose of procreation in sexual intercourse, but on the existence of biological laws and rhythms which are held to reflect the law of God. The official Roman position may not have altered in its proscription of contraception but the theological reasoning behind it has undergone a revolution. This shift from the basis of procreative purpose to that of the maintenance of a particular anatomical

---

[1] St Augustine taught that intercourse without procreative purpose was sinful although not mortally so. No Catholic theologian teaches that today.

[2] Another sphere where development has taken place is sterilisation, where the absolute condemnation has been relaxed to allow nuns or others in danger of imminent rape to take sterilising pills. This has been explained on the grounds that the intrinsic malice of condemned forms of sterilisation is only realised when the act seeks to deprive the *voluntary* exercise of the sexual faculty in intercourse of its natural procreative potentiality. Use of steroids as a safeguard against the effects of an unjustly enforced act of intercourse would not be within this prohibition. Victims of forseeable rape do not have the alternative of abstention. Does not this determine the morality of an action by intent? What then has become of the categorisation of sterilisation as 'intrinsically evil'?

pattern of union can be seen most clearly in the condemnation of artificial human insemination by a husband, made by Pius XII in 1956.[1] The Pope insisted that matrimony gave no right to artificial fecundation but only to 'the natural conjugal act'. Nor, said the Pope, could the right be derived from any right to a child: 'The matrimonial contract does not give this right, because it has for its object not the "child" but the "natural acts" which are capable of engendering a new life and are destined to this end. It must likewise be said that artificial fecundation violates the natural law and is contrary to justice and morality.'

The sacrosanctity of the biological structure is the premise from which the conclusions of the Encyclical flow. Only if this is accepted can it be maintained that contraception is in itself intrinsically evil. It is not enough to attribute procreation as a general end to the institution of marriage since this does not entail that every sexual act should in some way be directed to the procreation of children, although it does require that procreation as such should not be excluded from the marriage. The general procreative end of marriage can be maintained even with the use of contraceptives. Their employment would be judged on the same principles of morality as apply to the use of the infertile period. Was it necessary to maintain the education of existing children? Had the wife's emotional resources been exhausted? Would another child place an intolerable strain on the husband's financial resources? The imperative to maintain the physical pattern rules such considerations out.

One is compelled to ask again: how is this imperative arrived at? As has been seen, there is no demonstration or argumentation in the Encyclical: it is simply asserted as a fact. It can, however, only be arrived at by isolating the physical acts of intercourse from the whole pattern of the marriage in which they occur. Is this sensible? Can such acts even be comprehensible if the structure which gives them spiritual, as opposed to physical meaning, is

[1] See 'Address to Second World Congress of Fertility and Sterility' (19 May 1956), *The Pope Speaks* (Washington, D.C., 1956–7), 3:191, and *Acta Apostolicae Sedis*, 48:468. See also two previous addresses: 'Address to Fourth Convention of Catholic Doctors in Rome' (September 1949), *A.A.S.*, 41:557 and 'Address to Second World Congress of Fertility and Sterility' (October 1951), *A.A.S.*, 43:835. I expressed surprise in my book *Life, Death and the Law* (London, 1961), that this attitude should be taken because of Catholic stress on the importance of procreation in marriage) see p. 122.

simply ignored?[1] The structure of the body does not by itself reveal the purpose of the body. A simple inspection of the sex organs will not tell one very much about man unless one also considers his relationship to other men and to the world around him. It is difficult to accept that the natural or obvious purpose of man's organs or of an act also constitutes an imperative of what a moral use of them or a licit act will demand. Human intercourse is certainly biological but it is more than that and can only be fully understood within a wider anthropological concept of man.[2] Man it is true is partly determined and limited by the necessities of his nature yet he also possesses a rational freedom which enables him to transcend it. There is a 'given' in man but the Encyclical confers upon it too dominant a role. Even on that biological basis the argument of the Encyclical is difficult to sustain. As Julian Pleasants has pointed out, a biological action is ordinarily multi-functional, and inhibition of a function which is not needed is the typical means of achieving the integrated control required by living things.[3] For its own purposes the Encyclical assumes that the biological act has only one specific purpose and that all other effects are subsidiary to it.

If one takes the biological argument as adumbrated by others such as Elizabeth Daugherty, one is led to a conclusion different from the Encyclical. Summing up her approach she writes: 'I have attempted to give a careful demonstration of the evidence, which can be voluminously documented, that human beings have a reproductive system unique in the entire animal kingdom where sub-primate reproduction is strictly physiologically controlled and regulated. This system permits the bearing of relatively small

[1] For a philosophical discussion of this point see G. Egner, *Birth Regulation and Catholic Belief*, pp. 53–8, where he seeks to demonstrate that the scholastic approach is merely a variation of the empiricist fallacy of significance, which selects certain phenomena for examination and ignores others. In *Gaudium et Spes* there is a statement to the effect that the moral evaluation of intercourse must depend on objective as well as subjective factors based on 'the nature of the human person and his acts' (51). The mixed commission explained this in the following language: 'By these words it is asserted that the acts are not to be judged according to the mere biological aspect, but as they relate to the human person integrally and adequately considered.'

[2] Accordingly one cannot say that an act of adultery is intrinsically evil: what makes it wrong is the situation in which it occurs. Can any purely physical procedure be described as *intrinsically* good or bad?

[3] See 'The Lessons of Biology' in *Contraception and Holiness* (1964). Intr. Archbishop Thomas Roberts, p. 93.

numbers of offspring who require prolonged care and training, combined with the continued and permanent use of sex in the marital relationship. My principal thesis is, therefore, that conception as a result of the sexual act is meant to be occasional, but the function of the formation and maintenance of monogamous marriage as a result of the act is meant to be permanent and continuous.'[1] The permanent use of sex in marriage represents a major evolutionary development. The Encyclical makes not only an identification of the moral with the physical but an identification with a particular and static view of what constitutes physicality.

The implicit rejection of the evolutionary in man's affairs is one of the most surprising features of the Encyclical. Man, nature, reason, all are treated as though they were static not dynamic concepts, yet, by definition, reason should conform to the level of knowledge reached in contemporary developed societies. Newman made the point succinctly, nearly a century and a half ago, when he wrote: 'Here below, to live is to change, and to be perfect is to have changed often.'[2] Writing in our own day, Bishop Butler makes the same point in relation to the Church and draws attention to the fact that modern man's total environment is changing so rapidly and fundamentally that man himself in response is undergoing something analogous to a biological mutation: 'Not that his physical structure is being radically altered, but that his psychological pattern is becoming almost fundamentally different from that of earlier generations.'[3] Evolutionary theory in part causes and in part expresses 'the new sense of the universality of orientated change'. Thus the outlook of modern man is evolutionary and historical while that of the Encyclical tends to be static and based on the old Aristotelian–Thomist model. The theology of the Encyclical is of this order, in contrast to the dynamics of salvific history which lie at the roots of contemporary theological interpretations. 'We no longer,' writes E. R. Baltazar, 'regard the Church as a static juridical

---

[1] See 'The Lessons of Zoology', op. cit., p. 126. Miss Daugherty adds that she questions the usage by which the ends of the sexual act, which are accorded only to man, are called 'secondary' and those which are shared with the lower animals 'primary', p. 129.

[2] J. H. Newman, 'An Essay on the Development of Christian Doctrine' (New York, 1960), p. 63.

[3] Christopher Butler, op. cit., p. 10.

structure as scholasticism would present it, but as a Mystical Body which is in process of growth toward the *pleroma Christi*.'[1]

It would be strange indeed if in this new world, evolving at unprecedented speed, morals alone were to remain static and not be subject to change. Morality must change and evolve since it represents man's response to other men in a state of bio-cultural evolution. Accordingly human nature, while it has certain fixed elements, contains others which are subject to continuous change. The pace of change today in the relationship of men and women appears to be especially rapid.[2] A natural law which is to be meaningful to modern man must take account of this changing situation and recognise variables which were ignored in previous times. It has been defined by Michael Crowe, who has carried out much pioneer work in this field as 'a *dynamic existing reality*, an ordering of man towards his self-perfection and his self-realisation through all the concrete situations of his life and in intersubjective dialogue with his fellow man and with God'.[3] In this situation the old arguments from the use of faculties to the adoption of moral positions are less attractive than ever, since the faculties themselves are no longer seen as directly created but as being in a state of ceaseless alteration and adaptation, which has characterised them from the beginning. Altering the function of a faculty can accordingly be seen not as a frustration of the will of the Creator but as a fulfilment.[4] Such a conceptual approach is not even considered by

[1] See 'Contraception and Process', in *Contraception and Holiness*, p. 157.
[2] For a discussion of 'biologie théologique' see Teilhard de Chardin, 'L'Evolution de la Chasteté', an article written in Peking in 1934.
[3] See Michael Bertram Crowe, 'Natural Law Theory Today: Some Materials for the Re-Assessment' in *The Irish Ecclesiastical Record* (1968), CIX: 353–83, p. 383.
[4] A favourite analogy which used to be employed by defenders of the Catholic ban on contraception was that of the Roman vomitorium. It was pointed out that the Romans separated the pleasure of eating from its purpose of nourishing the body in the same way as users of contraceptives separated the pleasure of the sexual act from its procreative purpose. But the vomitorium, repellent although it undoubtedly is, does not show that vomiting in itself is wrong. What of a self-induced vomit to get rid of a poison from the stomach? The wrongness of the vomitorium is established not by looking at the physical act of vomiting but at the purpose for which it was induced, i.e. to indulge gluttony. The analogy is not with contraception as such, but with contraception used for some wider immoral purpose, e.g. to indulge lust. One does therefore in both cases have to look at the context in which the devices are employed. This also applies to the argument used by Catholic apologists in the past about the use of machines and their misuse to establish the illicitness of contraception. To know the use of a machine one has to take into account the whole context in which it is to be operated. In any case human beings are rather more complex than even the most intricate machines.

the authors of the Encyclical, who distinguish between the morality of recourse to the infertile period as a means of family planning and the immorality of the use of contraceptives by stating: 'In reality, there are essential differences between the two cases: in the former, the married couple make legitimate use of a natural disposition; in the latter, they impede the development of natural processes.'[1] The shock of seeing this ancient argument put forward so baldly in a document of such importance as *Humanae Vitae* is considerable.

The Encyclical not only takes no account of the modern evolutionary world but is dominated by a cultural pessimism which presumes that the world is headed for a moral breakdown. The assumption behind the section headed 'Grave Consequences of Methods of Artificial Birth Control' is that man is not to be trusted with the powers that these methods place in his hands and that unless they are banned they will lead him down a Gadarene slope to disaster.[2] Thus the reader is asked to reflect on 'how wide and easy a road' would be opened up towards 'conjugal infidelity and the general lowering of morality'. This of course could be the consequence of contraception but there is no necessary connection between contraception and immorality. The Encyclical then stresses the need to protect the young without showing that a total ban on contraception is necessary to do so.

There follows one of the oddest passages in the whole document. 'It is also to be feared,' says the Encyclical, 'that the man, growing used to the employment of anti-contraceptive practices, may finally lose respect for the woman and, no longer caring for her physical and psychological equilibrium, may come to the point of considering her as a mere instrument of selfish enjoyment, and no longer as his respected and beloved companion.' The male-orientated approach of the Encyclical at this point creates a major distortion. Did none of the authors of the Encyclical reflect on the fact that women may possibly enjoy sexual relations as well as men? Did they not wonder what effect successive pregnancies can have on a woman's 'physical and psychological equilibrium'? Apparently they did not.

[1] Para. 16. The notion that the 'impeding' of natural forces is in itself immoral is hardly self-evident, as the Encyclical appears to suppose. 'Natural processes' is an ambiguous phrase.
[2] Para. 17.

The Encyclical goes on to offer some tentative prophecies of doom. Would not the acceptance of contraception place a dangerous weapon in the hands of 'those public authorities who take no heed of moral exigencies'. Who, it is asked rhetorically, 'could blame a government for applying to the solution of the problems of the community those means acknowledged to be licit for married couples in the solution of a family problem? Who will stop rulers from favouring, from even imposing upon their peoples, if they were to consider it necessary, the method of contraception which they judge to be most efficacious?' These results might, of course, follow from moral approval of contraception, but then they might equally well ensue from approval of the infertile period as a means of family planning. No logical connection exists between allowing contraceptives to be used by married couples on a voluntary basis and their compulsory imposition by the state. One cannot establish that the only way of avoiding state invasion of the marital rights of individuals is by a total ban on contraception. Any advance in knowledge or power carries the risk that there may be misuse but that is part of the human condition and obscurantism is not an answer as the Encyclical appears to suggest.[1]

In any case if contraception is wrong in itself the consequences argument cannot be of decisive importance. The Encyclical recognises this when, at the beginning of the section, it explains that men can 'even better convince themselves' of the truth of the teaching if they reflect upon the consequences of resort to contraception. If these consequences can be shown to be bad the general argument that contraception is against the will of God certainly becomes more persuasive: God's laws are not mere arbitrary whims but are designed for the benefit of man: if then they are broken one would expect some ill consequences to appear. If on the other hand necessary bad consequences cannot be demonstrated the argument is correspondingly weakened.

[1] 'Consequently', it declares, 'if the mission of generating life is not to be exposed to the arbitrary will of men, one must necessarily recognise insurmountable limits to the possibility of man's domination over his own body and its functions; limits which no man, whether a private individual or one invested with authority, may licitly surpass.' This statement, unhappily, begs a whole series of questions.

This section of the Encyclical betrays a deep mistrust of man: he needs to be protected against his own wickedness, especially in the sexual sphere. The Encyclical is here reflecting a more general distrust of the body which is rooted in early Christian tradition. The equation of the erotic with the sinful was one which was made by some of the Fathers of the early Church and which has influenced the Christian approach to sexuality over the centuries. In this respect the Encyclical is the latest manifestation of a long tradition.

Apart from these general points, a number of individual criticisms can be made of the Encyclical. It confuses, for example, abortion with contraception. In a key passage it links them together when they are in fact separated by a wide gulf: 'We must once again declare that the direct interruption of the generative process already begun, and, above all, directly willed and procured abortion, even if for therapeutic reasons, are to be absolutely excluded as licit means of regulating birth.'[1] Contraception deals with a pre-life situation: abortion with a situation in which life has actually begun. It goes on to treat sterilisation as if it was a matter of similar moment to abortion and contraception: 'Equally to be excluded, as the teaching authority of the Church has frequently declared, is direct sterilisation, whether perpetual or temporary, whether of the man or of the woman.' Sterilisation, like contraception, is concerned with a pre-life situation and is therefore of a different order from abortion. It is more reasonably classified with contraception but it is hardly helpful to dismiss it in so summary a fashion.

Mutilation of the body without just cause has certainly been strongly condemned by Christian writers. This view can be traced back to the teaching of the Church Fathers. In the early Church, certain zealots, misinterpreting the Gospel passage 'there be eunuchs which have made themselves eunuchs for the kingdom of heaven's sake' (Matt. 19:12) castrated themselves. These practices were condemned in both canon law and the writings of the Fathers.[2] The body, they taught, could only be mutilated if a portion were diseased and it was essential for the welfare of the

[1] Para. 14.
[2] See Conc. Nic., Can I: Apost. Can. 21–4: Chrys., Hom. lxii in Matt.

body as a whole that the diseased portion be severed. Self-castration in order to preserve chastity failed in its object and was also contrary to Christian doctrine, since it posited the body as intrinsically evil and denied the use of man's free will.

These arguments were developed by St Thomas Aquinas and other ecclesiastical writers in the Middle Ages. St Thomas maintained that a man who multilates his body without cause sins in three ways: he violates the natural law of self-preservation and proper self-love; he offends against the community of which he is a part; and he commits an offence against God. The motive of curbing unchastity may be laudable but the method is both ineffective and disproportionate. St Thomas allowed only one exception: 'If, however, the member be decayed and therefore a source of corruption to the whole body, then it is lawful with the consent of the owner of the member, to cut away the member for the welfare of the whole body, since each one is entrusted with the care of his own welfare. The same applies if it be done with the consent of the person whose business it is to care for the welfare of the person who has a decayed member; otherwise it is altogether unlawful to maim anyone.'[1]

The traditional teaching was reaffirmed by Pius XI in his Encyclical on 'Christian Marriage', when he declared: 'Christian teaching establishes, and the light of human reason makes it most clear, that private individuals have no other power over the members of their bodies than that which pertains to their natural ends; and they are not free to destroy or mutilate their members, or in any other way render themselves unfit for their natural functions, except when no other provision can be made for the good of the whole body.'[2] Pius XII confirmed his predecessor's teaching.[3] All direct sterilisation was forbidden by a decree of the Holy Office of 21 February 1940.[4]

---

[1] *Summa Theologica* (London, 1929), II. lxv.
[2] *Casti Connubii* (New York, 1931), p. 33.
[3] See Address to Italian Catholic Society of Midwives, 29 October 1951, *A.A.S.*, 43:843. The Pope stated: 'Direct sterilisation, that is, that which seeks as means or end to render procreation impossible, is a serious violation of the moral law, and therefore illicit.' Cf. Statement to Italian Urology Society, *L'Osservatore Romano*, 10 October 1953, and Address to the Seventh International Congress of Hematology, 12 September 1958, *A.A.S.*, 50:734.
[4] See *A.A.S.*, 32:73.

Since sterilisation is a serious operation, depriving a man or woman, permanently in most cases, of the ability to procreate, it clearly should only be undertaken for grave reasons. This point would be conceded by most reasonable people, whether Christian or not. Man is deprived by sterilisation of his freedom to choose in an important sphere and is left with only his previous choice against procreation. In so far as freedom of choice is an essential part of the human condition, man is to a certain extent dehumanised by sterilisation. The Christian, with his concept of the creatureliness of man and his consequent desire not to flout the 'given' which comes from God, is likely to view sterilisation with even greater doubt and suspicion.[1] Yet to say this is not to accept the Roman position in its entirety. The Roman position is not an absolute one despite its wording. It forbids all 'direct' sterilisation but allows sterilisation to be carried out for the good of the body as a whole. 'Direct' here does not have a physical connotation necessarily since sterilising operations may have the same physical act accompanying them but very different intentions, and it is these intentions which will determine their morality. Thus according to the Roman view, a sterilisation undertaken for a contraceptive purpose would be immoral but one undertaken to lessen the risk of disease spreading to other parts of the body would be legitimate, although the physical act of sterilisation would be the same in both cases.[2]

Again the Roman position does not interpret the good of the whole body in a narrow physical sense but in the wider one of the good of the whole person. Thus in 1952 Pius XII declared to a medical congress: 'by virtue of the principle of totality, by virtue of his right to use the services of his organism as a whole, the patient can allow individual parts to be destroyed or mutilated when and to the extent necessary for the good of

---

[1] See report of Church of England Moral Welfare Council on sterilisation in 1951: 'Man does not belong to himself. He was created by God and for God, and therefore belongs to God. Consequently he has not an unqualified right to dispose of himself as he wishes; his right is limited by the laws of his Creator (which are also the laws of his own nature), and by the nature of his destiny.' *Human Sterilisation: Some Principles of Christian Ethics* (London, 1951).

[2] An example of the latter type of operation could be the sterilising of the testicles after the removal of a cancerous prostate. The casuistry of these cases is discussed fully in Noonan, op. cit., pp. 451–60.

his being as a whole'.[1] Subsequently, in 1958, he approved of the practice of plastic surgery for the purpose of improving physical beauty.[2]

But if the good of the whole person justifies resort to mutilation why should not sterilisation be used for contraceptive purposes when the good of the individual or family requires the avoidance of further pregnancies? Or, applying the principle of love of neighbour, why should it not be used if it would materially contribute to the welfare of society? If a married couple, for example, are likely to transmit defective genes, have they not an adequate ground for having themselves sterilised? If a country is facing a population crisis is there not a social case for sterilisation? I am presuming that in all these examples the sterilisation would be voluntary and not compulsory.

The Roman authorities give a negative reply to these queries, but why? The line drawn between different cases seems extraordinarily arbitrary. Thus a uterus which is judged unlikely to be able to bear the strain of another pregnancy may apparently be removed, but oviducts may not be excised to prevent a pregnancy likely to be dangerous to other organs such as the heart. The latter was ruled out by no less an authority than Pius XII.[3] The basis of the Roman prohibition must be, as in the case of contraception, the sacrosanctity of the biological processes but with a significant difference. In contraception only the physical act is taken into account whereas in sterilisation one is allowed to look at the context of the act to decide its lawfulness, at any rate to the extent of looking at the intention which accompanies it. Yet once that exception has been admitted, the sacrosanctity of the physical act has been destroyed and the absolute prohibition is left without any basis at all. I conclude therefore that it is both more rational, and in no way in conflict with Christian doctrine,

[1] Allocution to the First International Congress on the Histopathology of the Nervous System, *A.A.S.*, 44:782. A number of theologians have taken the use of the expression 'being as a whole' as an extension of 'good of the whole body'.
[2] Address to the Tenth National Congress of the Italian Society of Plastic Surgery, *A.A.S.*, 50:958-9.
[3] Address to the Twenty-Sixth Congress of the Italian Society of Urologists, 1953, *A.A.S.*, 674-5. In the same address the Pope reaffirmed that a healthy organ can be sacrificed if it threatens the organism as a whole. For the uterus opinion see Gerald Kelly and John Ford, 'Notes on Moral Theology 1953', *Theological Studies*, 15 (1954), 68-70.

to hold that a sterilisation may lawfully be carried out provided there are sufficiently grave reasons for doing so.

Humanae Vitae makes a general appeal to educators and rulers to create 'an atmosphere favourable to education in chastity, that is, to the triumph of healthy liberty over license by means of respect for the moral order'.[1] Few would be disposed to quarrel with this exhortation although the distinction between 'healthy liberty' and 'license' is not quite so obvious as is evidently supposed. It goes on, however, to make a highly over-simplified analysis of the problems facing mass media in the sexual field and draws a tendentious conclusion about the limits of artistic freedom. 'Everything in the modern media of social communications,' it declares, 'which leads to sense excitation and unbridled customs, as well as every form of pornography and licentious performances, must arouse the frank and unanimous reaction of all those who are solicitous for the progress of civilisation and the defence of the supreme good of the human spirit.' It concludes: 'Vainly would one seek to justify such depravation with the pretext of artistic or scientific exigencies, or to deduce an argument from the freedom allowed in this sector by the public authorities.'[2] The relevance of this outburst to the question of birth control is by no means clear, but even if it can be tenuously established, this kind of rhetorical approach to one of the most complicated of social problems, namely the limits of freedom of media of communication in liberal societies, is hardly helpful.

Equally unrealistic is the appeal which follows immediately for a legislative ban on contraception: 'To rulers, who are those principally responsible for the common good, and who can do so much to safeguard moral customs, We say: Do not allow the morality of your peoples to be degraded; do not permit that by legal means practices contrary to the natural and divine law be introduced into that fundamental cell, the family.'[3] Such an appeal might have some relevance in certain exclusively Catholic

[1] Para. 22.
[2] There is a footnote reference at this point in the Encyclical text to the Vatican Council decree on the instruments of social communication. This decree is the most inadequate of all those issued by the Council and has been subject to widespread criticism.
[3] Para. 23, 'Appeal to Public Authorities'. This passage could be interpreted as an appeal not to impose contraception compulsorily, but this is not its obvious meaning.

THE ARGUMENTS OF 'HUMANAE VITAE' 259

countries, such as Spain or Ireland, but addressed to the rulers of pluralist societies it seems singularly ill-judged. Laws on moral matters are only enforceable in free societies if they are supported by a general moral consensus among the people. In most of the nations of the free world no such consensus exists on the subject of contraception. The appeal is disturbing because it shows that the authors of the Encyclical to be extraordinarily out of touch with political and social realities.

A final point of criticism is the very tenuous treatment in the Encyclical of the problems of world population growth. They are touched on in the opening passages of the Encyclical but are not alluded to again until near the end of the document. It confines itself to a denunciation of an insufficient sense of social justice, of selfish monopoly of resources and of apathy among the richer nations, and to an exhortation for more co-operation in the international field: 'may mutual aid between all the members of the great human family never cease to grow: this is an almost limitless field which thus opens up to the activity of the great international organisations'.[1]

From all these considerations one may legitimately conclude that the rational arguments contained in *Humanae Vitae* do not stand up to close examination. The good intentions of its authors need not be doubted, any more than the imperative need for a restatement at the highest level of the doctrine and implications of Christian marriage, but the need unfortunately has not been met. A major problem of the Western world is an obsession with sex but *Humanae Vitae* itself mirrors this obsession by its concentration on the physical and biological aspects of marriage, thus in turn exaggerating the importance of the sexual in the marriage relationship. Clearly Christianity must have something to say about the regulation of sexuality, yet there is no obvious connection between the commands of God and the demands of the physical structure of man. No doubt it is true, as the Encyclical stresses, that there has been a longtime Catholic condemnation of contraception, but this condemnation is part of a tradition on sexuality and

---

[1] Para. 23. It may be said in defence of the skimpy treatment of world population problems that the whole matter was fully discussed in Paul VI's earlier encyclical, *Populorum Progressio* (1967).

marriage which is generally recognised to be fragmentary and incomplete, and at times positively misleading. The *magisterium* of the Church has reflected both the good and the bad in this tradition. A vital element of the tradition has been to protect the procreative value of marriage and of sex but one cannot conclude from the tradition that a total ban on contraception is a necessary means for doing this.

The teaching of the Church on marriage is a social as well as a doctrinal teaching and thus even more than dogmatic teaching has been in a continual state of development. In modern times the theological emphasis in matters concerning marriage and the family has shifted from nature to person. Bishop Butler points out that the Second Vatican Council constitution on the Church in the Modern World 'moves towards a theology of marriage which lays stress rather on the human persons existentially involved in marriage and the family, than on the bodily nature called into play in the marriage act. It speaks of "the conjugal, family, fellowship" as "a fellowship of love", and of the "intimate union" of husband and wife, and the "mutual self-giving of two persons" which constitutes this union.'[1] The tragedy of *Humanae Vitae* is that it ignores this revolution and harks back to the theology of a previous age. In a theology based on nature its stress on the biological would make sense: in a theology based on person it does not. The absolutising of the biological pattern in intercourse which *Humanae Vitae* contains, lingers on like the ghost in a machine which has changed, a potent and gibbering spectre it is true, but a spectre none the less.

THE CASE FOR 'HUMANAE VITAE'

Humanae Vitae has been severely criticised both inside and outside the Church but it has also elicited widespread support from

[1] See Christopher Butler, op. cit., p. 158. The relevant paragraphs of *Gaudium et Spes* are, 48–51. Cf. a secular analysis of the new Copernican revolution of our time in *Science and Human Values*, by J. Bronowski (New York, 1956). Dr Bronowski writes: 'To a world population at least five times larger than in Kepler's day, there begins to be offered a life above the animal, a sense of personality, and a potential of human fulfilment, which make both the glory and the explosive problem of our age. These claims are not confined to food and bodily comfort. Their larger force is that the physical benefits of science have opened a door and will give all men the chance to use mind and spirit. The technical man here neatly takes his model from evolution, in which the enlargement of the human brain followed the development of the hand,' p. 86.

Catholics and others. Supporters of the Encyclical like to describe themselves as 'the silent majority' but whether they are in the minority or majority is impossible to establish.[1] Certainly they have been silent in the sense of being less vociferous than opponents of the Encyclical, and they have suffered from a less sympathetic treatment by the mass media of communication. A conservative and defensive position is in any case much more difficult to articulate than a progressive and critical one but it can of course be just as strongly held. The arguments put forward in *Humanae Vitae* itself have already been considered and need not be recapitulated here. The attitudes of those who have supported the Encyclical need however to be briefly examined.

Supporters of the Encyclical have employed various versions of the natural law argument, maintaining that contraception is contrary to man's nature, that it frustrates the purpose of the sexual act and separates the procreative and relational aspects of sexuality to the detriment of both.

Others have accepted the teaching of the Encyclical because it was issued with the authority of the Pope. They are not especially interested in what they consider niceties of distinction about the extent of papal powers: the Pope has spoken on a matter of major importance, and that is the end of the matter. They have been supported by the fact that a long tradition within the Church has condemned contraception, and feel that if the Church is taken to have been wrong on this point, she can hardly be relied on in any other. To resist the Pope in such a matter, would, they feel, ultimately destroy the Papacy.

A more sophisticated and spiritual argument has been put forward by some Encyclical supporters on the ground that contraception destroys the total giving implied in the marriage act. Christopher Derrick in his book *Honest Love and Human Life*, gives the most extended development of this view. 'Marriage,' he writes, 'begins with the declared gift of self, a mutual commitment that is formal, public, and unqualified; and the happier kind of liaison will begin with a private and implied kind of commitment, limited in scope and duration but analogous in

---

[1] It must also be remembered that many critics of the Encyclical, especially clerics, have remained silent for reasons of prudence.

kind. In either case, the initial commitment will then be made concrete in many acts of erotic surrender. But if that word "love" is to have any of its higher meanings, every such act must retain the character of a gift, a surrender in fact as well as in seeming: in so far as it involves a withholding of the central self, it will be a pretence, incompatible with the original commitment. And this pretence will not acquire the character of honesty simply because it is desired on both sides. Even then, contraceptive love-making will be an act of erotic hypocrisy, agreed and mutual, but a great sin against love and truth.'[1] Others have supported the Encyclical on the grounds that it lays down an ideal and an ideal is necessary for human beings, even if one knows that it will only be attained in a limited number of cases. Yet another group have welcomed the Encyclical as a declaration of asceticism in an increasingly hedonistic world: a reassertion of the principle of 'cost' in a world which has lost sight of it. Cardinal Wright uses the ascetic argument in his defence of the Encyclical, published in the United States.[2] He considers it an example of Christian personalism and a defence against both perversion and totalitarianism. Finally, some have supported the Encyclical on psychological grounds: it constituted a relief to have a definite answer.

SOME DIFFICULTIES

If as a Catholic one concludes from a consideration of the various arguments that the Encyclical is in part erroneous – that its teaching on birth control is not wholly correct – some real difficulties have to be faced. If the teaching is not correct how was it taught for so long, and taught not only by Popes but by bishops and clergy as well? How was it accepted by the majority of the

---

[1] Published by Hutchinson (London, 1969 and Coward-McCann, New York). The publishers present the book as a 'forthright' defence of *Humanae Vitae*, but Mr Derrick's argument (which I personally find attractive) does not seem to have all that in common with the physical and biological finalities of the Encyclical. Nor would Roman theologians approve of his absolution for prostitutes and their clients, who have recourse to contraceptives. They may do this, without guilt apparently, because there is 'no question of love and honesty'. Wives may also use contraceptives when threatened by too amorous husbands, which he regards as a form of rape. I wonder what Paul VI would make of that? (See p. 278, fn. 4 of this book for Father Mahoney's views on this point.)

[2] *Los Angeles Times*, 5 October 1969.

laity? And how can these facts be reconciled with the concept of a Church guided by the Holy Spirit? The point is put clearly in the 'minority report' of the papal birth control commission. 'The Church,' it declared, 'could not have erred through so many centuries, even through one century, by imposing under serious obligation very grave burdens in the name of Jesus Christ, if Jesus Christ did not actually impose these burdens. The Catholic Church could not have furnished in the name of Jesus Christ to so many of the faithful everywhere in the world, through so many centuries, the occasion for formal sin and spiritual ruin, because of a false doctrine promulgated in the name of Jesus Christ.'[1]

This point can only be answered if one accepts that morality is not a wholly static concept but contains a dynamic element as well. The idea of development in morality as in doctrine is based on a realisation of the essential historicity of human existence.[2] Man's existence unfolds itself through thought and with the passage of time in the material world. Thinking is a fundamental activity of man's becoming. Since morality is the product of human thought in relation to God's law, it too is historical and constantly involved in development. Newman's *Essay on the Development of Christian Doctrine* is an extended application of this idea to revealed dogma as such. As far as doctrine is concerned, he perceives an identity in change which preserves its substantial form throughout all the changes, and this identity assimilates new elements to itself. It draws forth from its own principles new conclusions rendered imperative by its own growth. And these later developments are already faintly foreshadowed at an earlier stage although they only become explicit when the original principles are thrust into new contexts. 'Principles,' writes Newman, 'require a very various application according as persons and circumstances vary and must be thrown into new shapes according to the form of society which

[1] See *Tablet*, 29 April 1967, p. 480. For a discussion of the difficulty see Michael Dummett, 'The Documents of the Papal Commission of Birth Control', *Blackfriars*, February 1969.
[2] Cf. earlier treatment of this theme in this chapter, pp. 249–52. See also the 'majority report' of the papal birth control commission: 'In creating the world God gave man the power and the duty to form the world in spirit and freedom, and through his creative capacity, to actuate his own personal nature. . . . And it should be seen that man's tremendous progress in control of matter by technical means, and the universal and total "intercommunication" that has been achieved, correspond perfectly to the divine decrees.' See *Tablet*, 22 April 1967, p. 449.

they are to influence.'[1] Yet the original identity is always preserved.

If these principles operate in the field of dogma, where the fixed element is high, how much more likely are they to be found in that of morals which is marked by the contingent and by a changing social context. Scholastic thought on moral matters was dominated by the Greek view of nature which saw man's history as an unfolding of eternal values, which themselves do not change. Modern thought on the other hand has moved from nature to person and stresses the creative freedom of man. Thus in marriage the emphasis has passed from the physical body as such to a consideration of the situation of two persons existentially joined together. This is only the latest development in a marriage teaching which has been in constant if slow development. Certain elements have been dropped while others have been added. The third report of the papal birth control commission points out that for many centuries in the Church 'it was all but unanimously taught that marital intercourse was illicit unless accompanied by the intention to procreate – or at least (because of the words of 1 Cor. 7) to offer an outlet for the other partner'.[2] No Catholic theologian holds this view today. On the other hand positive developments in the Catholic view of marriage have included the acceptance of family planning and responsible parenthood, the licitness of rhythm, and a new stress on the value of sexual intercourse as such.[3] The question that has to be asked today is whether the acceptance of contraception, in certain circumstances as legitimate in marriage, is a true or false development. If it runs counter to the fundamental values constantly set out in the Catholic view of marriage it cannot be a true development: if it does not it may well be.

What, then, have been the fundamental values protected in

---

[1] *An Essay on the Development of Christian Doctrine* (New York, 1960), p. 79. Later he quotes Bishop Joseph Butler who wrote: 'The whole natural world and government of it is a scheme or system; not a fixed, but a progressive one; a scheme in which the operation of various means takes up a great length of time before the ends they tend to can be attained.' See p. 93.

[2] *Tablet*, 6 May 1967, p. 511.

[3] This should not cause surprise since as the third document of the papal birth control commission points out: 'The sources of life, just as existent life itself, are not more of God than is the totality of created nature, of which he is the Creator . . . God has left man in the hands of his own counsel.' *Tablet*, 6 May 1967, p. 511.

the Catholic marriage tradition? They have been the good of procreation and the holiness of married love and it cannot be demonstrated that contraception intrinsically destroys either.[1] Acceptance of contraception can thus be seen as the latest development in a tradition which has been continually evolving and in which the static element has been greatly exaggerated.

If this latest development has come more quickly than its predecessors that is because of the greatly increased pace and number of changes in the modern world. The papal birth control commission listed some of them in its third report: 'the social change in marriage, in the family, in the position of woman: the diminution of infant mortality; advances in physiological, biological, psychological and sexological knowledge; a changed estimation of the meaning of sexuality and of conjugal relations; but especially a better perception of the responsibility of man for humanising the gifts of nature and using them to bring the life of man to greater perfection. Finally one must consider the consensus of the faithful, according to which a condemnation of the spouses to a prolonged and heroic abstinence from the helpful and appropriate expressions of conjugal life must be erroneous.'[2]

It must also be remembered that when the earlier tradition condemning contraception was formed two vital elements were lacking. There was no freedom of discussion on the issue within the Church so that the validity of the tradition could not be openly and scrupulously examined. Accordingly, inadequate argumentation could not be exposed. The second element lacking was the witness of the married laity who had no opportunity of effectively expressing their views. Even at the Second Vatican Council the laity went unrepresented.[3] The point of lack of freedom of speech was put graphically by Canon Drinkwater in his book *Birth Control and the Natural Law*, published in 1965. Canon Drinkwater

---

[1] Thus the 'majority report' of the papal birth control commission sums up the tradition in these words: it was 'intended to protect two fundamental values: the good of procreation and the rectitude of marital intercourse.' John Noonan adds three other constant elements, the completion of procreation in the education of children, the sacredness of innocent life, and the personal dignity of spouses, op. cit., p. 533.

[2] See *Tablet*, 6 May 1967, p. 511.

[3] In fact the first and second Vatican Councils were the only Councils at which the laity were totally unrepresented. Before this there had been for many centuries a lay representation in the person of the Holy Roman Emperor.

stressed that there should have been continual discussion of *Casti Connubii* over thirty-five years, instead of which there was 'a whole generation of frozen silence, the silence of intellectual death, or at least of paralysis'. How did this come about? The canon gives his own answer: 'Perhaps root-responsibility lay with the lower pastoral clergy, the parish priests on the spot. They knew the facts. But also they knew that nothing would come of individuals speaking out, except suspension or a convent-chaplaincy for themselves; whereas if they kept their misgivings to themselves, they knew half-a-dozen ways of protecting their own flock from the worst effects of the freezing east wind. Rightly or wrongly, and more or less consciously, most of them would put their own parishioners first. The point is that in such an atmosphere the true living voice of the ordinary and universal teaching of the Church is not to be easily heard. There is heard only, so to speak, a single gramophone record playing on and on.'[1] Freedom of speech and discussion was only gained when Pope John called the Second Vatican Council, and at the same point the voice of the married laity began to be heard.

PREVIOUS EXAMPLES OF CHANGED TEACHING

It becomes easier to accept the possibility of a modification of the Church's traditional condemnation of contraception when one reflects that this has happened before in moral and social matters in Church history without destroying ecclesiastical credibility or the Church's claim to teach. The most pertinent example is that of usury.[2] Midway through the fifteenth century the ecclesiastical condemnation of usury was at its height. It was considered a mortal sin against justice to take profit on a loan, although profit on an investment in a partnership where the partner took risks was not forbidden. Biblical authority was cited for the prohibition, with texts being produced from both the Old and the New Testaments.[3]

---

[1] *Birth Control and Natural Law* (London, 1965), p. 62.
[2] For two authoritative articles on this subject by John Noonan see: 'Authority, Usury and Contraception', *Dublin Review*, 240 (Autumn 1966), pp. 201–29, and 'Tokos and Atokion: An Examination of Natural Law Reasoning Against Usury and Contraception', *Natural Law Forum*, 10 (1965), pp. 215–35.
[3] See especially Ezek. 18:5–9, Ps. 14:5, and Luke 6:35.

The Church Fathers were also referred to as authorities for condemning the practice, including St Ambrose, St Jerome, and St Augustine all of whom were forthright in their rejection of usury. Church Councils could also be cited in support of the ban. Thus the Second Council of the Lateran (1139) over which Innocent II presided, enacted the following canon: 'We further condemn what has been rejected as detestable and repugnant to divine and human laws by Scripture in the Old and New Testaments, to wit, that insatiable rapacity of usurers, and we separate them from every consolation of the Church.'[1] The Third Council of the Lateran under Pope Alexander III denied Christian burial to notorious usurers. In 1314 at the Council of Vienne, Clement V decreed that rulers enforcing the payment of usury by debtors should be excommunicated. This condemnation of usury was much more severe than any rejection of contraception which has been dealt with only by local councils and has never been condemned by a general council.

Popes and bishops were also active in condemning usury. Gregory IX in the first part of the thirteenth century set out a comprehensive condemnation of usury in his 'Decretals'.[2] Usury was condemned as being contrary to Scripture and a sin which no power could make right, and a whole range of penalties was laid down to punish it. As John Noonan points out: 'There are few moral rules of the Church which have been so fully articulated by papal decree.'[3] As to the bishops, he has ascertained 'as far as can be determined from any written record' that in 1450 they and the theologians were unanimous in condemning the taking of profit on a loan as a violation of both natural and divine law.[4] The laity however resisted the rule and eventually it was abandoned.[5] No trace of it remains today save in the condemnation of the charging of excessive rates of interest. This development can only be explained by looking at the purpose for which usury was condemned; it was condemned in the interests of justice and charity to protect the poor from exploitation and to ensure a proper distribution of capital. When these ends could be achieved

---

[1] G. D. Mansi, ed., *Sacrorum Conciliorum Nova et Amplissima Collectio*, 21:529–30.
[2] See Title 19, Book V.   [3] *Dublin Review*, op. cit., p. 213.
[4] Ibid., p. 219.   [5] It was gradually modified between 1450 and 1600.

by other means the condemnation was modified. The parallel with contraception is clear.

The institution of slavery provides another example of modified moral attitudes on the part of the Church. In the fourth century it was largely taken for granted by bishops and theologians. Thus St Augustine in the City of God writes: 'The state of slavery is understood to be a just imposition on a sinner. Thus in Scripture the word "slave" is nowhere to be found until the time when the just man Noah punished the sin of his son (Gen. 9:25). So it was not nature which merited slavery but sin.'[1] St Augustine concedes that slavery is contrary to nature but is ready to accept it *de facto*. Pope Gregory I held it to be morally lawful for the Christian laity to hold slaves and to recapture them if they ran away. Gratian in his collection of ecclesiastical laws, compiled about the year 1140, included the following ordinance: 'If anyone, on the pretext of religion, teaches another man's slave to despise his master, and to withdraw from his service, and not to serve his master with goodwill and all respect, let him be anathema.'[2] In 1452 Pope Nicholas V is found writing to King Alfonso V of Portugal authorising him to reduce into 'perpetual slavery' the people of the newly discovered territories in West Africa and America.[3] During the seventeenth century a number of Popes made slave purchases to provide rowers for the papal galleys. Right up to the early nineteenth century there was unanimity among Catholic theologians about the moral lawfulness of slavery and slave-trading. As late as 1866 the Holy Office could issue the following decree: '. . . slavery itself, considered as such in its essential nature, is not at all contrary to the natural and divine law, and there can be several just titles of slavery and these are referred to by approved theologians and commentators of the sacred canons'.[4] In the nineteenth century Catholic theologians and others began to protest against slavery but their inspiration came not from Catholic theology but from the Enlightenment.[5]

[1] *De Civitate Dei*, XIX, 15.
[2] *Corpus Iuris Canonici, Decreti Gratiani*: II, Causa XVII, Q.4, cap. 37.
[3] Brief *Dum Diversas*, 16 June 1452.
[4] Instruction 20 June 1866. *Collectanea S.C. de Propaganda Fide*, I, n. 1293, 719 (Rome, 1907).
[5] Slavery was condemned in forthright terms by Montesquieu in his book *On the Spirit of the Laws*. This was placed on the Index in 1751.

It was not until the Second Vatican Council that the old Catholic doctrine on the legitimacy of slavery was finally repudiated.[1]

Equally radical has been the change in the ecclesiastical attitude to religious liberty, at one time denounced by the Popes, but subsequently at the Second Vatican Council declared to be the inalienable right of every human being. Thus in his encyclical *Mirari Vos* (1832), Gregory XVI declared: 'And from this most putrid source of indifferenterism flows that absurd and erroneous opinion or rather mad raving that freedom of conscience should be accorded and secured for everyone.' With this may be contrasted the Declaration on Religious Freedom of Vatican II: 'This Vatican Synod declares that the human person has a right to religious freedom. This freedom means that all men are to be immune from coercion on the part of individuals or of social groups and of any human power, in such wise that in matters religious no one is to be forced to act in a manner contrary to his own beliefs. Nor is anyone to be restrained from acting in accordance with his own beliefs, either privately or publicly, whether alone or in association with others within due limits.'[2] The doctrine has clearly 'developed'.[3]

Other doctrines which have been modified include those on

[1] See *Gaudium et Spes* (1965), paras 27, 29, and 67.
[2] *Declaration on Religious Freedom*: 1, 2.
[3] Much ingenuity can and has been expended on interpreting papal encyclicals on religious liberty in the nineteenth century so that they can be shown as not being in conflict with modern ideas on religious freedom. Thus it has been pointed out that the *Quanta Cura* and *Syllabus of Errors* of Pius IX were condemning 'liberty' in the sense of an absolute, and a liberty which would subjugate the Church to the State. There is much in this approach and certainly encyclicals should be seen and judged in their historical context, but there does not seem to be much point in trying to deny that the thought of the Church has changed on religious liberty and that today it takes a much more favourable attitude towards it than in the past. At Vatican II, and not without a struggle even then, the Church finally caught up with what for long had been the common consensus of free and civilised mankind. The Declaration of Religious Freedom then is not exactly an epoch-making document save in its own narrow ecclesiastical context. I myself was brought up on the 'thesis-antithesis' solution to the problem of religious liberty, by which the thesis or ideal was considered the establishment of the Catholic religion and the suppression of 'error', but practicalities – 'the antithesis', rendering this out of the question, the Church put up with the existing situation of *de facto* liberty. Monsignor Chigi, papal nuncio in Paris in the nineteenth century, said the last word on this preposterous theory when he commented: 'The thesis is burn the Jews: the antithesis, dinner with Monsieur de Rothschild.' For a discussion of religious liberty see Norman St. John-Stevas, 'Catholicism and Religious Toleration: Notes Towards a Restatement' in the *Dublin Review*, 488 (Summer 1961), pp. 99–108.

salvation outside the Church and the nature of the Church itself. 'Extra ecclesiam nulla salus' – outside the Church there is no salvation – was at one time literally interpreted; today it has been almost metaphorised out of existence. In his encyclical *Mystici Corporis* (1943), Pius XII declared that the mystical body of Christ and the Roman Catholic Church were one and the same reality. He reaffirmed this identity in his later encyclical *Humani Generis* (1950) but it was abandoned by the Second Vatican Council which declared only that the mystical body of Christ subsists in (*subsistit in*) the Roman Catholic Church.[1]

[1] *Lumen Gentium*, para. 8. Thus Bishop Butler writes: '. . . It is hard to resist the conclusion that the Conciliar Constitution of the Church *Lumen Gentium* contradicted the papal Encyclical *Mystici Corporis*.' See *Tablet* 17 April 1971, p. 374. On these points the following letter which appeared in the *Catholic Herald*, 20 November 1970 is illuminating:

'The trend of "Mystici Corporis" is to establish a simple division between those who belong visibly to the Catholic Church and those who do not. The relevant section (Denzinger, 2286) states: "It follows that those who are divided from one another in faith or government cannot be living in the one body so described (i.e., the Mystical Body) and by its one Divine Spirit."

'That is surely clear enough? Non-Catholic churches, being divided from the Catholic Church in faith and government, do not live by its Divine spirit.

'The Decree on Ecumenism (n. 3) states that: "The separated churches and communities, though we believe that they suffer from deficiencies, are by no means destitute of significance and importance in the mystery of salvation. The Spirit of Christ does not refuse to use them as means of salvation, means whose effectiveness is derived from that fulness of grace and truth which has been entrusted to the Catholic Church."

'It is not possible to argue that the Divine Spirit of "Mystici Corporis" is in any way distinct from the Spirit of Christ of the Decree. If the Spirit of Christ uses non-Catholic churches, precisely *as churches*, as means of salvation, how can they be said *not* to live by the same Divine Spirit as the Catholic Church, as "Mystici Corporis" states?

'To take the matter further, though it means treading well-trodden ground, if words have any meaning, then the meaning of the bull "Unam Sanctam" (Denzinger, 469) is that only Catholics can be saved.

'The Council of Florence makes it even clearer: 'We firmly believe, profess and proclaim that no one who is not within the Catholic Church, not only pagans, but neither Jews, heretics nor schismatics can possess eternal life, but will go into the eternal fires prepared for the devil and his angels, unless before the end of life they adhere to that same church. . . . No one, no matter how great his alms-giving, no matter if he sheds his blood for the Name of Christ, can be saved, unless he abides in the bosom and unity of the Catholic Church." (Denzinger, 714.)

'Now, however much we wriggle round the words, it is surely obvious what is *intended* by these statements – anyone who is not a Catholic, no matter how good his life, is damned.

'From such pronouncements was distilled the teaching "No salvation outside the Church." It is a logical deduction from their words. With the passage of time, this teaching became less and less credible, but it was never revoked. That would be to admit error. Instead, it was gradually emptied of all meaning, so that we said, in effect, "No one outside the Church can be saved, but in fact everyone is inside the

The attitude to the Bible has also undergone a revolution in recent years. In 1920, Pope Benedict XV in his encyclical *Spiritus Paraclitus* rejected the idea that there were two elements in the Bible one religious, not subject to error, and another human and historical which was. Yet it was this distinction which was to a considerable extent accepted by Vatican II when it declared that Scripture teaches without error 'the truth which God, for our salvation, willed to be recorded' there.[1]

Doctrine apart there are numerous examples of papal errors which history affords and which have subsequently been put right. One does not have to be a member of the Protestant Truth Society to see that something can be learned from these incidents. Thus Pope Honorius I became involved in the Monothelite controversy and forty years after his death was declared a heretic by a Church Council.[2] In the ninth century, Pope St Nicholas I had condemned the use of judicial torture as being contrary to both human and divine law and was supported in this by the twelfth-century canonist Gratian. Nevertheless in 1252 Innocent IV is found commending the use of torture by the Inquisition and it was also employed to maintain the government of the Papal States. Boniface VIII (1294–1303) in his bull *Unam Sanctam* (1302) maintained that temporal authority should be subject to the spiritual authority of the Church, advancing papal claims of jurisdiction to a new high point: 'We further declare, state, and define, and pronounce as entirely necessary for salvation that every human creature be subjected to the Roman Pontiff.'

Church in some way or other." Which is very charitable, but makes absolute nonsense of the original statements.

'From such statements as "Unam Sanctam" flowed the teaching that non-Catholic churches, far from being used by the Spirit of Christ, were false religions and to participate actively in their services was held to be contrary to Divine, ecclesiastical and Natural Law. Such participation is now permitted, so either the Church has changed its teaching or it has changed Divine, ecclesiastical and Natural Law.'

University of Sussex   (Fr) A. W. Beer

[1] *Dei Verbum*, para. 11. This and related points are discussed by John McHugh, 'The Doctrinal Authority of the Encyclical *Humanae Vitae*' in the *Clergy Review*, October 1969, pp. 791–802. This is the second of two articles on the subject, the first appearing in the *Clergy Review*, August 1969.

[2] Pope Honorius I (625–38) who had been drawn into the controversy about the teaching of Sergius, Patriarch of Constantinople, which maintained that there was only one source of action or energy in Christ. Honorius spoke of there being 'only one will in Christ'.

Both Innocent III and the Fourth Lateran Council forbade Jews to exercise any authority over Christians and they were excluded from public office. The Lateran Council required them to wear a distinctive costume. All these and other similar papal aberrations concerned matters of major moral and social importance.[1] A more recent example on a comparatively minor matter was the apostolic constitution *Veterum Sapientia* of John XXIII, issued to preserve the use of Latin in seminaries. 'We will and command,' wrote the Pope, 'that in seminaries and universities, "the major sacred sciences" should be taught in Latin and that textbooks used by professor should be Latin and that teachers should speak Latin!' No attempt has ever been made to enforce this directive and it has become a dead letter.

All these considerations point to the need for a cautious approach to papal statements, a willingness to see their limitations and to read them in the context of their time. They are a warning against 'creeping infallibility', the tendency to endow all papal utterances with a sacrosanctity which history has shown them not to possess. By rigorously defining the limits of papal infallibility, seeing it in the context of the infallibility of the Church as a whole, certain absurdities and exaggerations can be avoided.

Hans Küng has adopted a more radical approach to reconcile the traditional formulation of papal infallibility with past papal errors and what he sees as the present papal error of *Humanae Vitae*.[2] Professor Küng asks why *Humanae Vitae* was ever issued and finds the answer in the existence of the previous encyclical, *Casti Connubii*, and the traditional teaching of the Holy See and the Church on the subject of contraception. Paul VI could not bring himself to go against these previous commitments, since he could only have done so by admitting that the old attitudes were

[1] Other errors that might be cited include that of Urban VIII who acquiesced in the condemnation of Galileo by the Inquisition in the seventeenth century and that of Gregory II who wrote a notorious letter to St Boniface in November 736, in which he appears to have authorised bigamy in a case where a wife was ill and unable to allow the exercise of conjugal rights. This piece of advice was given with some solemnity: 'we will state with all the authority of apostolic tradition what you must hold'. See ed. C. H. Talbot, *The Anglo-Saxon Missionaries in Germany* (London, 1954), pp. 80–3.
[2] This account of his reasoning is reconstructed from notes I took while listening to a lecture he gave at the London School of Economics on 16 April 1970.

mistaken. Professor Küng does not see any room for 'development' in papal teaching since it cannot explain a contradiction: 'there cannot be a development between a "yes" and a "no".' He accepts that *Humanae Vitae* does not qualify as an 'infallible' document but that the teaching behind it can lay claim to the title. How then can a Catholic who accepts the infallibility of the Pope reconcile his position with a rejection of *Humanae Vitae*? Professor Küng finds an escape route in looking again at the meaning of infallibility.

He points out that the Second Vatican Council merely took over the notion of infallibility from its predecessor and neither Council answered the question of what constitutes infallibility either of Pope or Church. Professor Küng rejects the idea that infallibility can be defined in terms of infallible propositions, but holds that its true meaning is that the Holy Spirit remains with the Church, in spite of all aberrations and errors over the ages. The miracle is that despite defections the Holy Spirit never abandons the Church, is always with her, so that she is truly indestructible. In this notion of 'indestructibility' Professor Küng finds the real meaning of 'infallibility'.[1]

Professor Küng's answer is one response to the question of how *Humanae Vitae* came to be issued but it is not the only one. I agree with him that in some sense the issuing of an encyclical like *Humanae Vitae* was almost inevitable. Given Paul VI's past theological background, the view taken by the Vatican of papal prerogatives, his own cultural principles, his celibacy, his life passed in the service of the Vatican, in short his 'formation', something of a miracle would have been required for an encyclical of a different character to have been issued. But God does not (although of course he could) normally act on human history by way of miracles. He does not alter human attitudes by blinding displays of power, he rather allows the consequences of human actions to work themselves out, leaving to other human beings the duty to correct them. I believe, then, that the Holy Spirit allowed *Humanae Vitae* to be issued in its existing form since it was only

---

[1] He has not however as yet satisfactorily dealt with the question of the exact status of infallible propositions. This and other questions will be discussed in his book *Infallibility*, which is to be published in England by Collins in the autumn of 1971. See also p. 280.

through such an act that Catholics could be brought to see the need for reform in the existing structures of the Church. *Humanae Vitae* did not emerge from a vacuum but out of an existing state of Church order. Through *Humanae Vitae* many Catholics, while continuing to accept the need of the Church for the Papacy as a centre of unity, have also come to see that in its present form and mode of operation it is unable to provide it adequately in the conditions of the modern world. In this sense *Humanae Vitae* can be seen as a providential event and one in which the negative operation of the Holy Spirit is present.

The minority on the papal birth control commission raised a related difficulty. 'If contraception were declared not intrinsically evil, in honesty it would have to be acknowledged that the Holy Spirit in 1930, in 1951 and 1958, assisted Protestant Churches, and that for half a century Pius XI, Pius XII, and a great part of the Catholic hierarchy did not protest against a very serious error, one most pernicious to souls . . .'[1] Perish the thought! And yet, if one considers the point, why not? Ecumenical theology is still in its infancy but the Dogmatic Constitution on the Church, approved by Vatican II, nevertheless had this to say: 'The Church recognises that in many ways she is linked with those, who being baptised, are honoured with the name of Christian, though they do not profess the faith in its entirety or do not preserve unity of communion with the successor of Peter. . . . Likewise, we can say that in some real way they are joined with us in the Holy Spirit, for to them also He gives his gifts and graces, and is thereby operative among them with His sanctifying power.'[2] The Holy Spirit is then found in the Anglican and Protestant Churches although the theological implications of this remain to be worked out. They cannot then be wrong on everything! And it is at least possible that because of their more flexible structure, because in these communions the voice of the laity has been heard in a manner which in the past at any rate has not been possible within the Roman Catholic communion, that they may have developed a more reasonable attitude to contraception rather more quickly than members of the true Church.

[1] See *Tablet*, 29 April 1967, pp. 483–4.
[2] *Lumen Gentium*, para. 15.

THE EFFECT OF REVISION ON THE ATTITUDE TO
SEXUAL ABERRATIONS

Another fear expressed by the minority on the papal birth control commission was that if contraception were to be accepted as lawful the way would be opened up to accepting all kinds of sexual aberrations and irregular sexual conduct as lawful.[1] Extra-marital relationships could be justified in certain circumstances: oral and anal copulation in marriage could be justified: the door would be opened easily 'to the licitness of masturbation among youths', etc. It could be concluded that homosexuality is 'good for those who are affected with abnormal inclinations and seek only friendship with the same sex for their balance'. All these undesirable results might result from abandoning the position that contraception is 'intrinsically evil'.[2]

These prophecies of doom will strike most people as unlikely to be fulfilled and as placing too much responsibility on an isolated course of conduct, the employment of contraceptives. They do however point to a significant weakness in Catholic moral theology, the basis of which as far as it concerns sexual morality seems over a long period to have been the fact of procreation rather than the idea of love. Now that sexual intercouse need no longer result in children, procreation can no longer be the basis for condemning adultery and fornication, or for arguing for the stability of marriage. In a contraceptive age these issues must be judged from the point of view of a personalist rather than a physicalist theology.

Acceptance of contraception does not lead on inevitably to the acceptance of anal or oral copulation, provided one remembers that in both these situations human beings as well as orifices are involved. Oral and anal copulation respect neither the dignity of love nor that of the spouses. To most people they are aesthetically as well as morally repellent. As to extra-marital relations, these are ruled out since in such relationships there is in most cases no

---

[1] See *Tablet*, 29 April 1967, pp. 484–5.
[2] Ibid. The minority report reaches this conclusion by the following reasoning: 'However, many theologians, who maintain that contraception is not intrinsically evil, seem to come to this conclusion from a more general principle: that, namely, which denies *all absolute intrinsic morality* to external human acts, in such a way that there is no human act which is so intrinsically evil that it cannot be justified because of a higher good of man.'

intention of permanent commitment and self-giving nor any intention to have children.[1] As to masturbation, it is essentially an egotistical and selfish act and has no intra-personal significance, and can be distinguished from contraception on these grounds.[2]

Neither does it seem necessary to conclude that acceptance of contraception implies acceptance of homosexual conduct.[3] The rejection of homosexual relations does not rest on unproven theories of the purpose of individual acts of heterosexual intercourse but on the natural facts of creation, which present two sexes as part of the 'given' of the human condition and makes intercourse between them essential for the continuance of the race. This is not to say that the Christian attitude to homosexuality does not need revision in the light of contemporary knowledge. It does. Homosexuality can be seen today not as a wilful perversion, but as a condition which affects certain people who are exclusively attracted towards members of their own sex. For this condition they are in no way responsible, it is not known how it is caused, and in the vast majority of cases there is no means of altering it. One might describe it as a natural variation from the norm of human heterosexuality. It seems quite inappropriate to judge homosexual conduct from any moral point of view, Christian or otherwise, without taking this factual situation into account. Christian moral and pastoral guidance to homosexuals needs radical rethinking but this has nothing to do with contraception.[4]

[1] I am confining 'extra-marital' relationships here to casual sexual encounters and am not thinking of those situations where there is a permanent personal commitment, but for some reason or other there cannot be a secular or ecclesiastical sanctioning of the relationship.
[2] In Catholic moral theology in the past masturbation has been condemned with a vehemence which in the light of contemporary psychiatric knowledge seems to have been rather unbalanced. One has to distinguish between different phases of life as well as between different people to make any meaningful moral assessment.
[3] Thus G. Egner points out in *Birth Regulation and Catholic Belief*, that if one condemns any form of non-generative insemination then one must logically condemn both contraception and homosexual conduct, but it does not follow that if one allows one type of action which involves non-generative insemination, one must therefore allow any other. Apart from this shared quality of non-generative insemination, contraception and homosexual conduct are entirely different. See pp. 268–70.
[4] One of the few attempts at rethinking has been carried out by Dr Norman Pittenger. See his article in *New Christian*, 9 March 1967, 'Time for Consent', later published in pamphlet form and his later article, 'An Ethic for Homosexuals' in *New Christian*, 19 March 1970. In the later article he proposed four guide lines for 'the conscientious Christian homosexual'. In the same issue Sebastian Helmore, a Roman Catholic, puts forward a form of Christian vow for homosexuals living together. See 'A Time for Commitment'.

Neither does the morality of abortion which concerns a situation where a new life has been created, whereas contraception deals with a pre-life position.

In considering Christian moral attitudes to sexuality one should not place a burden on natural theology which it is not fitted to carry. Christianity is a religion of revelation: one does not have to go to the natural law to find a condemnation of adultery, it can be found in the decalogue: fornication is not primarily rejected by Christians because of abstruse arguments about the purpose of intercourse but because it is incompatible with following the law of love as revealed in the person of Jesus Christ. Far from leading to a total moral relativism, the law of love, mediated through the New Testament, and comprehended by one attempting to lead a Christian life, leads to a commitment much more complete than any that can be mediated through the alleged fixities of the law of nature.[1]

CONTRACEPTION – A SIN?

Is contraception categorised as a grave or mortal sin by the encyclical *Humanae Vitae*? In view of its total rejection of contraception this might be thought a superfluous question, but a substantial body of theological opinion holds that even if one accepts the argumentation and conclusions of *Humanae Vitae*, this does not entail a condemnation of contraception as sinful. This conclusion applies to the objective situation: clearly if a person does not in conscience accept that contraception is wrong there can be no sin, in the subjective sense, in its use.

Whereas *Casti Connubii* used strong and emotional language to condemn contraception, *Humanae Vitae* is notably more temperate in tone, a point noted by Dr Beck, Archbishop of Liverpool, early in the controversy. The later Encyclical states that the contraceptive act in marriage is 'intrinsece inhonestum' but it does not stigmatise it as gravely wrong. Indeed the only reference to 'sin' as such in the Encyclical is an oblique one during a passage encouraging those using contraception to frequent the sacrament

[1] See Reinhold Niebuhr, *Love and Law in Protestantism and Catholicism* (London, 1954), especially Chapter 10. Cf. Paul Ramsey, 'Love and Law' in *Reinhold Niebuhr. His Religious, Social and Political Thought*, ed. C. W. Kegley and R. W. Bretall (New York, 1956), Chapter IV.

T

of penance.[1] As to *Casti Connubii* (para 56), Fr John McHugh points out, that Pius XI was not asserting that the sinfulness of contraception was a truth revealed by God but that the Church, as a matter of historical fact, had always held that contraception was gravely sinful, because the contrary opinion was not compatible with revealed teaching concerning marriage and sexuality.[2] That, of course, is a different point.

Dr James Good characterises *Humanae Vitae* as a Platonic document, similar in this respect to the *Syllabus Errorum*, dealing with the ideal rather than the real world. While ideally contraception is always wrong: in reality it may have to be accepted.[3] He suggests therefore two interpretations of the Encyclical: (*a*) 'Contraceptive intercourse is generally evil but in married life it is lawful where there are serious reasons for it'; (*b*) 'Contraceptive intercourse in married life is good, but it may be abused, e.g. by selfishness.'[4]

[1] Married couples are exhorted to face up to their difficulties: '. . . let them implore divine assistance by persevering prayer; above all, let them draw from the source of grace and charity in the Eucharist. And if sin should still keep its hold over them, let them not be discouraged, but rather have recourse with humble perseverance to the mercy of God, which is poured forth in the sacrament of penance.' (para. 25)

[2] See 'The Doctrinal Authority of the Encyclical *Humanae Vitae*', *Clergy Review*, October 1969, p. 798.

[3] '*Humanae Vitae*, A Platonic Document', *Tablet*, 19 April 1969. Dr Good compares the position of contraception with that of religious liberty and the theory of thesis and antithesis.

[4] With this may be compared Father Martelet's views. He raises the question: Does the Encyclical in condemning contraception as an objective disorder also condemn by this very fact someone whose conscience causes him to have recourse to such deviation as being in his view the lesser evil? Father Martelet gives a negative reply. See G. Martelet, S.J., 'Pour Mieux Comprendre L'Encyclique *Humanae Vitae*', in *Revue Nouvelle Théologique*, Louvain, November 1968, pp. 897–917 and December 1968, pp. 1009–66. Father Martelet's views have particular significance as he is credited with having played an important part in compiling the Encyclical.

For another modification see John Mahoney, S.J., Dean of Moral Theology at Heythrop College in the *Clergy Review*, April 1969, p. 260. He asks the question: Can a woman who has had three children – all spastics – use contraceptives when her husband wants intercourse and refuses to abstain? He replies affirmatively. Father Mahoney starts from the decision of Vatican theologians in 1961 that nuns in imminent danger of rape in the Congo could use contraceptive pills. This was extended to cover assaults on a married woman by a drunken husband. Father Mahoney suggests that whenever a woman has sound reasons for refusing intercourse to her husband (because of the possible consequences of the pregnancy) she may, if his will prevails, take the same steps to protect herself as a woman faced with physical assault.

Father Mahoney is to be congratulated on his ingenuity, but whether this kind of super-subtle approach will be considered relevant by many people today is another matter.

Confessional practice is as important in this sphere as theological theory and it is plain that many Catholics have simply given up confessing contraception as a sin and are not being disturbed by their confessors. Many priests when consulted by anxious penitents put the onus of decision on the penitent as to whether the act is sinful in their case or not. It does not seem likely that many individuals are being barred from approach to the altar for Communion in England and the United States because they are practising contraception: it seems to have been down graded in status from mortal to venial sin.[1]

THE MAGISTERIUM

A final difficulty which must be considered is the possible effect on the authority of the *magisterium*, or teaching authority of the Church and the Pope, of a revision of the traditional condemnation of contraception. 'If,' said the minority on the papal birth control commission, 'the Church should now admit that the teaching passed on is no longer of value, teaching which has been preached and stated with ever more insistent solemnity until very recent years, it must be feared greatly that its authority in almost all moral and dogmatic matters will be seriously harmed.'[2] Given that the argument is being conducted on this level, rather than that of truth or falsity, one is entitled to ask whether the *magisterium* would not be even more seriously affected by persisting in clinging to a position which has been shown to be intellectually undemonstrable?

Furthermore the credibility of the Roman Catholic Church might well be enhanced by an act of humility, admitting that on non-infallible doctrine she could in fact make mistakes. By doing so, far from undermining her authority she would be likely to extend it. In the field of ecumenism the papacy will never become a centre of reconciliation until the mentality of the Roman Curia is got rid of: it is this attitude of always being right, of lack of

[1] In this situation it cannot be argued that acceptance of the Encyclical should be made a condition of a valid marriage or of reception into the Church.

[2] *Tablet*, 29 April 1967, p. 485. Still concerned about the position of the *Ecclesia Anglicana*, the minority asked once more: 'Is it nevertheless now to be admitted that the Church erred in this her work, and that the Holy Spirit rather assists the Anglican Church?'

honesty and free intellectual discussion and inquiry, that actively repels non-Roman Catholic Christians from the Papacy.[1] Were the idea of authority as omniscient power to be replaced by that of humble service, the position of the Holy See in Christendom could be transformed from that of stumbling-block to reconciling agency and papal influence immeasurably increased.

[1] It is in this context that the contribution of Dr Hans Küng to the issue of papal infallibility has to be evaluated. His thought on the subject has been set out and criticised by Bishop Butler in two articles in *Tablet* for 17 and 24 April 1971. Bishop Butler recognises the value of Dr Küng's contribution even though he dissents from some of his conclusions, especially on the question of propositional infallibility. As the Bishop points out, in the second of his articles, the crucial question that Dr Küng raises concerns the Church's power to fashion and publish infallible definitions of faith. 'Is it possible to say *anything* about the faith which is true in such a sense that the proposition expressing it is "irreformable" and will never have to be contradicted? And can we be certified of this irreformability *a priori*?' Dr Küng concedes that the faith has to have linguistic expression and that accordingly there must be propositions of faith. He holds however that the early definitions of the Church were not doctrinal laws so much as 'free expressions of the faith of the community.' Bishop Butler stresses that a convert could not be received into the early Church if he declined to profess the truth in terms of the baptismal creed with which he was presented.

Dr Küng claims that Vatican I failed to prove the existence of infallible propositions either from scripture or from tradition: 'it was simply taken for granted by the Council, just as the Fathers of the Council of Trent took for granted the Ptolemaic cosmology.' So Küng regards the issue of infallible propositions as still open for Catholics. Küng, criticises the language used to define the doctrine of papal infallibility and Bishop Butler comments: 'One can agree with much of this criticism of language, and yet hold that what it points to is not necessarily the impossibility of "infallible propositions", but the need to apply sensitive exegesis to such propositions.' One may conclude, says Bishop Butler, 'that when Vatican I stated that papal definitions are "irreformable" it meant that they were irreformable within the conventions of the language in which they were expressed. That language may of course become an obsolete thing; in which case the definition will cease to be immediately intelligible to the common man and may even be misleading to him. This however does not mean that the definition was not true when understood within the convention in which it was made.'

Bishop Butler asks whether there is not a danger that the Church may be saddled with unnecessary definitions and concludes that there is and that the supreme authority in the Church ought to be 'extremely sparing' in its use of defining authority. As to the grounds for believing that the Church has authority to utter infallible definitions the Bishop writes: 'I suggest that the Church is not only a believing Church but a proclaiming Church. It exists not only to believe its own faith (and this belief might be largely inarticulate) but to proclaim the truths of revelation.' Finally Bishop Butler concludes: 'And particularly in regard to papal infallibility, it is most necessary that the papacy should exercise its visible and real role, not outside the general mental life of the Church, but within it; and as a court of final and really necessary appeal, not as an initiator of new ideas or a promoter of speculative development, nor on the other hand to short-circuit the laborious but legitimate dialogue of differing theologies.'

CHAPTER VII

World Population Growth and Christian Responsibility

The fact of a world population problem cannot be denied. Emphases may vary, calculations may differ as to the actual size of the population of the world by the end of this century or of the next one, but it is known with moral certainty that if the present growth rate of world population continues intolerable strains are likely to be placed on world resources.

It is not necessary to go all the way with Lord Ritchie-Calder, who entitled his paper on the effects of world population growth, delivered to the Conservation Society in London on 23 November 1968, 'Hell on Earth', but one must go beyond the complacent optimism of writers such as Colin Clark, who hold that the economic growth stimulated by population expansion will in itself solve our major problems. The world population is growing at an unprecedented rate which is likely to double the number of inhabitants of the globe within thirty-five years. By the year 2000 the population of the world is likely to number about seven billion: the equivalent of an additional world will have come into existence. It took the world twenty-five centuries to reach a population of 750 million and another two to reach a total of 2,500 million. Today one must think not in terms of centuries but in single years, and what took the world hundreds of years to achieve will be surpassed in the lifetime of one generation. The average rate of world population increase is at the moment between 1·9 and 2 per cent and if maintained will double world population in 34·6 years.

The temptation is to think that somehow or other this increase will not come about, that it is an exaggeration of statisticians, that it is of the order of prediction which can show that if the egg of every housefly was hatched, the whole surface of the globe would be covered by a mass of flies to a height of three miles within ten years.[1] Such ridicule was resorted to in order to discredit the findings of the United Nations report on *The Future Growth of World Population* when it was published in 1958, but looking back to the report from a standpoint over a decade later, it can be seen that its warnings have been fully and indeed more than justified. In 1958 the population of the world was approximately 3,000 million and the annual rate of population increase was 1·6 per cent. Today there is a world population which in ten years has grown by 500 million and a rate of population growth which is between 1·9 and 2 per cent.

These global statistics, alarming as they are, do not reveal the urgency of the problem in particular parts of the world. Rates of population growth are taking place in the main in the poorest and least developed areas of the world. The growth of population is concentrated in Latin America, in Africa, in South-East Asia, and in Asia itself.

In Asia only four countries have a rate of population increase below 2 per cent and ten countries are over 3 per cent. India has a population of 536 millions which is increasing at the rate of 2·5 per cent per year – Pakistan's population of 131·6 millions is increasing even faster at an annual rate of 3·3 per cent.

In Latin America the average rate of population increase is 3 per cent per year. In Brazil, for example, the population is expected to increase by 30 million in ten years and this in a country where the average income per head is only £80. In Venezuela the rate of increase is 3·6 per cent per year. Even within individual

---

[1] Of course this type of criticism may be valid for individual countries and the term 'population explosion' should not be used indiscriminately as a slogan. For a valuable corrective approach re the United States see 'The Nonsense Explosion' by Ben Wattenberg in the *New Republic*, 4, 11 April 1970. Mr Wattenberg points out that 'America is not by any standard a crowded country and that the American birth rate has recently been at an all time low.' He goes on to suggest that what has been happening in the U.S.A. in recent years has not been a population explosion, but a population redistribution – 'And the place people have been redistributing themselves *to* is a place called "suburb" '.

countries the impact of population growth is increased for some areas by regional variations. Arthur McCormack, the distinguished Catholic demographer, has pointed out that in Caracas, the capital of Venezuela, the more affluent sectors have a population increase of 2 per cent while those living in the slums have a population growth rate of 5 per cent.[1]

What are the effects of this spiralling growth of world population likely to be? There is the obvious and ever-present danger of famine and the spread of malnutrition but the situation is not as desperate in this respect as at one time it was thought likely to be. In fact there has been a 'green revolution' which began in 1967. A new era in agriculture opened with the discovery of new varieties of wheat and rice with very high yields and many other advantages compared with the conventional varieties. The use of these new strains has spread very rapidly in the developing countries and has laid, for the moment, the spectre of mass starvation.[2] Precious time has been gained during which world population problems can be resolutely tackled.

In many countries, however, it is not only food supplies that are threatened but the whole rate of social advance. As Paul VI states in his encyclical *Populorum Progressio*: 'It is not just a matter of eliminating hunger, nor even of reducing poverty. The struggle against destitution, though urgent and necessary, is not enough. It is a question, rather, of building a world where every man, no matter what his race, religion or nationality, can live a fully human life, freed from servitude imposed on him by other men or by natural forces over which he has not sufficient control; a world where freedom is not an empty word and where the poor man Lazarus can sit down at the same table with the rich man.'[3]

In underdeveloped countries with a high rate of population

---

[1] See *The Population Explosion and the Encyclical* (unpublished paper).
[2] For an account of the 'green revolution', see M. Cépède, 'Victoire sur la crise alimentaire', *Jeunes et Développement*, No. 1, January 1969. See also the optimistic four year study completed by the Food and Agriculture Organisation in 1969. The study, known as *The Indicative World Plan for Agricultural Development*, concludes: 'In many respects the conclusions of this study are optimistic. They show that given the adoption of the technical, institutional, and economic measures proposed, the main problems of hunger and malnutrition could be overcome, trade flows could be improved and a substantial contribution made to providing additional employment.' See *The Times*, 20 October 1969.
[3] Para. 47.

increase, unemployment constitutes an endemic and demoralising problem. 'Unemployment,' writes Goran Ohlin, 'in the large cities of the developing world is staggering. Apart from the waste that this implies that a poor country can ill afford, and from the deep privations entailed, it is a serious threat to the minimum of political stability that development policy requires.'[1] One reason for the high unemployment figures is the movement of the population in many countries from rural to urban areas: another is the high rate of population growth: a third is the slowness of change in methods of farming and cultivation. Developing economies are also afflicted by underemployment: in Pakistan the figure is as high as 22 per cent of the working population.

Poverty also undermines family life. 'Many families in the developing world,' writes Arthur McCormack, '(it is impossible to secure accurate data in this field but the number may be as high as 150 million) live in sub-human conditions. This means that hundreds of millions of children are growing up in conditions which menace not only their physical development but also their spiritual welfare, exposed as they are to the dangers of vagabondage, prostitution, delinquency, promiscuity, etc.'[2] In this situation large families serve only to increase the sum of human misery. They exacerbate a housing problem which already condemns millions to live in the most appalling slums.[3]

High population growth creates even greater pressure on limited educational resources. The spread of education in underdeveloped countries is the prerequisite for any form of industrial take-off and already in every one of these countries is in desperately short supply.[4] There are not only too many schoolchildren per potential teacher but too many potential schoolchildren per

[1] *Population Control and Economic Development*, p. 58.
[2] *Population Growth and Economic and Social Development*, paper prepared for the fourth assembly of the Pontifical Commission on Justice and Peace at Rome, September 1969.
[3] Writing on Calcutta, Arthur Hopcraft notes: 'The squatters already nest with the rats on every square foot not built upon. If we imagine their number doubled we are moving towards the unspeakable.' *Born to Hunger*, London, 1968, p. 110.
[4] Cf. Paul VI, *Populorum Progressio*: 'It can even be affirmed that economic growth depends in the very first place upon social progress: thus basic education is the primary object of any plan of development. Indeed hunger for education is no less debasing than hunger for food: an illiterate is a person with an undernourished mind. To be able to read and write, to acquire a professional formation, means to recover confidence in oneself and to discover that one can progress along with the others.' para. 35.

adult. Excessive population growth cancels out any hope of higher educational and therefore of higher social or living standards. This threat although less dramatic than starvation is even more urgent.[1] In Kenya, for example, where population growth is going forward at a rate of 3 per cent per year and the Government is pushing on vigorously with plans for educational expansion, it is estimated that by 1990 the number of those unable to obtain a school place will have doubled. On the other hand, if fertility could be halved all children would be able to find a school place by 1985.[2]

Is all this any concern of Christian theology and has theology anything of specific usefulness to say on the problem, or should it be left to other disciplines? Theology is the science which tells us about, discusses, and attempts to define the great truths of existence, of the existence of God and man's relationship to him, of man's purpose on earth and his final end. In one sense, therefore, whatever concerns man concerns theology: as Cardinal Manning once put it, all conflicts are basically theological. This is not to deny other disciplines their reasonable autonomy but theology regulates them by pacing their findings in a wider perspective. Theology itself is of course not a disembodied set of *a priori* principles and is profoundly influenced by advances in the secular sciences and by man's increased knowledge of himself, but being based on revelation is not determined by them. The population problem concerns man's relation with man, but this relationship cannot be understood without considering man's relationship with God, and both relationships are the concern of theology. In regard to the population problem, theology can throw light on two questions. First, whether we are obliged to do anything about the problems raised by high population growth and, second, if that question is answered affirmatively what are the limits on the

[1] Cf. Ohlin: in *Population Control and Economic & Social Development*, where he writes: 'The stress and strain caused by rapid population increase in the developing world is so tangible that there are few, and least of all the planners and economists of these countries, who doubt that *per capita* incomes would be increased faster if fertility and growth rates were lower indeed in some cases they might otherwise not increase at all.' O.E.C.D. (Paris, 1967), p. 53.

In 1969 a UNESCO report revealed that in this decade the number of illiterates in the world had risen by almost 60 million to about 300 million. High birth rates caused this rise by outstripping educational programmes in underdeveloped countries. See *New York Times*, 19 October 1969.

[2] See *Population Report of Kenya* (Population Council of New York, 1965).

means to be employed to solve them. It cannot, however, tell us what are the best means to be employed which is the function of other sciences or disciplines, economics, sociology, politics, and demography.

The most basic teaching of theology is the fatherhood of God. Theology tells us that God created the world and with it the human race. The ultimate purpose of man is to be with God for all eternity, and having passed through the transformation of death to be with God in a special way, but already by the very act of creation he is in relationship with God here and now. The modality of the relationship will be changed by death but the relationship as such already exists and is shared by all.

Since every man has the same destiny of happiness with God, the whole human race is linked and joined by a shared final end although man is free to frustrate this end, to turn away from God and reject him if that is his will. In the ontological sense then, men are brothers, members of one family, placed in the world to work towards a common destiny where their relationship with God and one another will be more immediate than it is now.

It follows from this relationship, and indeed is declared specifically in the Old Testament, that the world which is the theatre of the linked human-divine drama belongs to no individual or nation but is the common property of mankind.

The point is summed up clearly in the Second Vatican Council document *The Church Today*: 'God intended the Earth and all that it contains for the use of every human being and people. Thus, as all men follow justice and unite in charity, created goods should abound for them on a reasonable basis. Whatever the forms of ownership may be, as adapted to the legitimate institutions of people according to diverse and changeable circumstances, attention must always be paid to the universal purpose for which created goods are meant. In using them, therefore, a man should regard his lawful possessions not merely as his own but also as common property in the sense that they should accrue to the benefit of not only himself but others.'[1] What applies to individuals is equally applicable to nations.

[1] See *Gaudium et Spes*, para. 69. Cf. paras. 83–6, 87, and 90 on the issue of the community of nations, etc.

Rich nations have a duty to help those which are poor.[1] The general duty to help those who are poor or in need, founded in Old Testament theology, is reinforced by the explicit New Testament message of charity and love for all mankind. The theme of feeding the hungry and succouring the needy is one that recurs throughout the gospels. At the supreme moment of the *Parousia*, the second coming of Christ, as described in St Matthew's gospel, the contrast is sharp between the grandeur of the setting and the simplicity of the dialogue. With the whole human race gathered before the throne of their judge, he is concerned with only one thing, whether they have fed the hungry, given drink to the thirsty, and clothed the naked.[2]

There could hardly be more dramatic evidence of the priority given to physical help of neighbour in Christian teaching. In recent years three Popes, Pius XII, John XXIII, and Paul VI in a series of addresses and encyclicals have thrown the weight of the papacy behind the effort to bridge the gap between the rich and poor nations.[3] Paul VI set up a pontifical commission in 1967 with the explicit purpose of rousing the faithful throughout the world to a sense of their duty in this respect and to urge their governments to action.[4] Through its own foundation *Caritas*, the Vatican has tried to set a good personal example.

This general obligation is reinforced by a particular moral duty that rests upon Western nations from the actual cause of the population explosion. The rise in world population has been caused not by a rise in the birth rate or an increase in human fertility but by a falling death rate. For this the Western nations are directly responsible. Western medicine has succeeded in reducing the infant mortality rate, while at the same time taming the killer diseases which at one time decimated nations and acted as crude means of population control. We have thus altered the equilibrium between birth and death rates in the underdeveloped countries

[1] Disraeli's 'two nations' finds its modern equivalent in 'two worlds'. Western Europe plus the white Commonwealth countries plus the U.S.A. constitute 16 per cent of the world's population and enjoy 70 per cent of its wealth. The other 84 per cent of the world has to subsist on 30 per cent.

[2] See Matt. 25:31, et seq.

[3] See Pius XII's first encyclical *Summi Pontificatus* (1939), John XXIII *Mater et Magistra* (1961), and *Pacem in Terris* (1963), and Paul VI *Populorum Progressio* (1967).

[4] Pontifical Commission on Justice and Peace. This was set up on 21 April 1967.

and the population explosion has been the result. This responsibility is the immediate ground of a specific moral duty to assist in ameliorating a situation which we ourselves have created.

All this has taken place in a world which thanks to the advance of technology has been psychologically transformed. For the first time in history man has been able to develop a true world consciousness and hence a world conscience: he cannot ignore, even if he wishes to, the fact that he lives in one world. Technology, while it has created the conditions for this psychological revolution, has at the same time placed in the hands of man the means by which he can effectively help his fellow beings. Today mankind really does have the opportunity to escape from the dreadful treadmill of famine and poverty and want, and the potentialities for full human development, hitherto confined to a few, could within a measurable time be brought within the reach of all. A major contribution of theology is to issue to mankind an ethical categorical imperative to create conditions and devise plans and programmes by means of which what is still a dream can be transformed into a reality. Charity in this sphere is not enough. A physical redistribution of goods would result in the consumption of the excess goods of the minority but would not lead to the poor being permanently helped. What is needed is the creation on a world-wide basis of a strong, prosperous and efficient society, capable of economic growth according to needs. This is the moral imperative. Such an imperative does not arise from enlightened self-interest, although it may well be supplemented by it, but from the very nature of man himself, as seen through the theological spectrum.

I have established the ethical and theological grounds for world-wide action in attempting to solve the problems raised by population growth but what forms should this take? Only three principal courses of action are available for helping the underdeveloped nations: programmes of trade and aid, liberalised immigration laws providing greater freedom of movement throughout the world; and programmes promoting population policies and family planning. All three approaches are necessary if world population problems are to be satisfactorily dealt with, and it is misleading to pretend that any single one can provide a panacea. Of the three, the least likely to be effective is emigration. The principle of freer movement for individuals and peoples is in itself desirable, and in the past emigration has been an effective and practical way of relieving population pressures. After the Civil War in the United States, the North American continent provided a haven for millions of European immigrants and enabled their homelands to cope with population increase in a much more satisfactory manner than would otherwise have been possible. Emigration saved at least one million Irish from starvation in the potato famine of the 1840s, an event incidentally which shows that a population catastrophe can be more than a delusion of the fevered imaginations of Malthusian pessimists. Conditions for mass emigration are unhappily much less favourable in the twentieth than in the nineteenth century, and the capacity of a host country to absorb immigrants, especially if they are of a different race, is limited. The recent experience of Great Britain is relevant where the effort to accommodate a coloured population of under 2 per cent has caused grave social strains. As a result of the pressure of public opinion, immigration into England from the Commonwealth has been drastically curtailed.[1]

These practical considerations have to be placed against such unexceptionable statements of general principle as that of Pius XII to the American bishops in 1948 when he declared that man had a natural right to emigrate since God had provided material goods for the use of all. 'If then,' concluded the Pope, 'in some locality, the land offers the possibility of supporting a large number of people, the sovereignty of the state, although it must be respected, cannot be exaggerated to the point that access to this land, is for inadequate or unjustified reasons, denied to decent and needy people from other nations, whenever this does not hinder the public welfare as measured on honest-weight scales.'[2]

[1] Until the Commonwealth Immigration Act of 1962 every citizen of the Commonwealth had a right to settle in Britain. This was done away with by the Act and a system of control by voucher introduced. Today these number a few thousand a year and are confined to skilled and professional workers. Dependent children under sixteen of Commonwealth immigrants settled in Britain have a prescriptive right of entry. The Conservative Government of 1970 proposed to abolish this right for the future and to equate the position of Commonwealth citizens with that of aliens.

[2] Letter dated 24 December 1948 (*A.A.S.*, 2nd series, XVI, pp. 69–71). For other statements of Pius XII on migration see *Exsul Familia*, *A.A.S.*, 2nd series, XIX, pp. 649–704.

One factor that has to be weighed in the 'honest-weight scales' is that the capacity of individuals to cross from one culture to another of a radically different nature is limited, and a wholesale immigration can be destructive not only to the migrants but also to the social structure of the receiving countries.

Although personally prejudiced in favour of free movement, I am pessimistic, after my experience of race relations problems in Britain, of the degree to which immigration can solve population problems. Liberal immigration policies have greater symbolic than practical value. The underdeveloped nations are suspicious at times of Western motives in spreading family planning policies on the grounds that these may be a new form of imperialism or colonialism to keep the lesser races within bounds.[1] The ending of the white Australia policy and the adoption of more liberal immigration policies in the United States could make a real contribution to the removal of such doubts, and so facilitate international family planning programmes. Temporary immigration also has a part to play in helping countries carry the burden of an excessive population.

AID

The underdeveloped countries cannot reach the threshold of industrial take-off by means of trade alone since this is insufficient to raise the capital they need. This necessary capital can only be supplied by joint governmental action on the part of the richer nations. Voluntary organisations can play a unique role in mobilising individual citizens to take a personal and responsible part in aiding poorer countries, but the problem is so vast and complex that it needs concerted intervention at government level. The point is put clearly in the 'Pastoral Constitution on the Church in the Modern World' (*Gaudium et Spes*), issued by the Second Vatican Council: 'The international community should see to the co-ordination and stimulation of economic growth. These objectives must be pursued in such a way, however, that the resources organised for this purpose can be shared as effectively

[1] See the section 'The Case of Latin America' in 'American Goals and Family Planning' by J. Mayone Stycos in *World Population and U.S. Government Policy and Programs*, ed. Franklin T. Brayer (Georgetown, 1968).

and justly as possible. This same community should regulate economic relations throughout the world so that they can unfold in a way which is fair.'[1]

The case for aid is simply that the free workings of the market are insufficient to achieve justice between the richer and poorer nations. Under this mechanism – the rich nations become richer – the poor remain poor or become poorer. 'Left to itself,' writes Paul VI in his encyclical *Populorum Progressio*, 'it works rather to widen the differences in the world's levels of life, not to diminish them: rich people enjoy rapid growth whereas the poor develop slowly'. Concerted action is necessary, local and individual efforts are not enough. 'Only world-wide collaboration,' writes Paul VI, 'of which a common fund would be both means and symbol, will succeed in overcoming vain rivalries and in establishing a fruitful and peaceful exchange between peoples.'[2] It is indeed tragic, as Mr Robert McNamara, has pointed out, that whereas the world is spending $175 billion a year on armaments, it is only spending one-twenty-fifth of this amount on all foreign assistance programmes.[3]

Various attempts have been made to mobilise world resources. In 1958 the World Council of Churches suggested that the more developed countries should devote 1 per cent of their national income for aid purposes. In 1960 the United Nations General Assembly recommended that this objective should be accepted by all its members. The United Nations inaugurated the first development decade which was to last from 1960 to 1969. Unfortunately, at the end of this decade the poorer countries did not find themselves substantially better off. In 1964 the first United Nations Conference on Trade and Development was held and the members present agreed that 1 per cent of gross national income should be devoted to helping the developing countries. Four years later at the second *UNCTAD* meeting at Delhi this target was reformulated as 1 per cent of the gross national product of

---

[1] *Gaudium et Spes*, para. 86.   [2] *Populorum Progressio*, para. 51.
[3] See 'Address to Columbia University at New York', 20 February 1970. Mr McNamara adds: 'What is even worse is that defence spending is increasing by some 6 per cent a year, a growth rate in destructive power that is greater than the growth rate of the world's total production of all goods and services. And the final irony in this litany of irrationalities is that arms spending in the less developed countries is rising at the rate of 7·5 per cent a year, as against the world average of 6 per cent.'

the nations concerned. The Conference also supported the principle of granting a generalised preference for imports of manufactured and semi-manufactured goods from developing countries. Unfortunately, the preparations for this conference were badly handled and the conference itself was not a total success.

Accordingly, the second development decade from 1969 to 1979 opened with only modest achievements and with a general disillusionment about the utility of aid. Ironically enough the 1 per cent target had been reached before its official adoption in 1964 but had not been met since. The total official development aid of the member governments of D.A.C. amounted in 1969 to only 0·36 per cent of their combined GNPs. The relative decline in the position can be seen by looking at the United States' figures. In 1949, when the Marshall Plan was inaugurated, American economic aid amounted to 2·79 per cent of GNP and 11·5 per cent of its federal budget. In 1970 the aid programme constituted less than 0·3 per cent of GNP and less than 1 per cent of the budget.

Against this generally gloomy picture the achievements of the World Bank stand out. It was the World Bank which on 27 October 1967, took the initiative in launching a major inquiry into world aid. The then President, Mr George Woods, suggested a 'grand assize' in which an international group of 'stature and experience' would 'meet together, study the consequences of twenty years of development assistance, assess the results, clarify the errors and propose the policies which will work better in the future.' In August 1968 Mr Lester Pearson, a former Prime Minister of Canada accepted the invitation of the World Bank's new President, Mr Robert McNamara, to form a commission to undertake this study. This commission presented its report in September 1969 and it has become known as the Pearson Report.[1]

Meanwhile, on 30 September 1968, in what will probably come to be regarded as an epoch-making speech, Mr McNamara launched the World Bank on a new and vigorous course. Mr McNamara first made it plain that he had always regarded the Bank as more than a mere financial institution, in fact as 'a

[1] The Commissioners, apart from Mr Pearson, were Sir Edward Boyle (United Kingdom), Mr de Oliveira Campos (Brazil), Mr Douglas Dillon (United States), Dr Wilfried Guth (Federal Republic of Germany), Professor Arthur Lewis (Jamaica), Dr Robert Marjolin (France), and Dr Saburo Okita (Japan).

development agency'. The Bank, he said, would produce a survey for the next five years for each developing nation, to see what the Bank would need to invest to meet each country's needs. The survey would proceed on the basis that there was no shortage of funds, the only limitations being 'the capacity of our member countries to use our assistance effectively and to repay our loans on the terms on which they were lent'. Mr McNamara stated that it was the intention of the Bank to double its rate of lending over the next five years. 'This means,' he said, 'that between now and 1973 the Bank group would lend in total nearly as much as it had lent since it began operations twenty-two years ago.' Bank lending should thus run at about $2 billion a year between 1969 and 1973 instead of $1 billion a year. Mr McNamara also announced that the Bank was seeking to tap new sources of funds throughout the world and not confining itself to the conventional money centres in Germany and the United States. It would expand its investment in Africa and Latin America. Greater emphasis would be placed on investment in education, in collaboration with UNESCO, and in agriculture.

The great advantage of the use of the World Bank as a development agency is that it can act swiftly and immediately. Its disadvantage is that it has to charge interest rates which at the present time are in the region of $6\frac{1}{2}$ per cent. Mr McNamara's speech contained no reference to funds for the soft loan agency, the International Development Association.[1] Although several governments, including the British, have authorised the planned 60 per cent increase in subscriptions, the United States Congress has hung back.[2] On the other hand, the very fact that the World

[1] The I.D.A. was established in Washington on 1 October 1959, with the aim of promoting economic development by providing finance on terms more flexible and bearing less heavily on the balance of payments of the recipient countries than those of conventional loans. It is closely affiliated to the World Bank.

[2] The planned increase would produce $400 million a year for three years. Up to March 1966 the I.D.A. had extended 86 credits amounting to the equivalent of $1,262 million to help finance development projects in 32 member countries. These credits are for the development of electrical power, transportation, telecommunications, educational projects, etc. All were made for terms of 50 years with no repayment for 10 years, then 1 per cent per annum for the next 10 years, then 3 per cent per annum for 30 years. No interest is charged but there is a service charge of $\frac{3}{4}$ of 1 per cent on amounts withdrawn and outstanding to meet the administrative costs of I.D.A. Repayments are due in foreign exchange. See *Text Book of International Organisations* (1966–7), p. 641.

U

Bank is a financial institution acting on commercial principles gives a reasonable guarantee that the money it raises will be well spent, and this could play an important part in counteracting the growing revulsion in the richer countries from the idea of aid because some funds have been squandered. The Bank is in a strong position to counter this kind of opinion by continuing to maintain its own high investment standards in its commercial operations, and ensuring that these are followed in its daughter organisation, the I.D.A. The I.D.A. could certainly be more fully utilised. The World Bank and the I.D.A. are the institutions which can make the most effective contributions to the world's most important need, the creation on a global basis of a strong, prosperous and efficient society, capable of economic growth according to need.

In September 1969 in his annual address to the board of governors of the Bank, Mr McNamara was able to make an encouraging progress report. He told the directors that the Bank, the I.D.A., and the International Finance Corporation had been able to increase their financing of development projects by 87 per cent over the previous year. New loans, credits, and investments had totalled $1,877 million as compared with the 1968 financial year total of $1,033 million. He revealed that plans for 1970 aimed at an expansion of loans, credits and investments to an approximate total of $2¼ billion. Mr McNamara also emphasised that there had been a shift in emphasis in granting of loans in favour of Latin America and Africa. 'We increased loans and credits to African member countries, for instance, by nearly 150 per cent this year. And lending operations in Latin America are rising sharply to meet our goal of more than doubling them by 1973.' The Bank was also placing new emphasis on population planning, educational advance, and agricultural expansion. In education greater attention was being given to functional literacy for adults with less emphasis on physical construction. A greater commitment had been made to educational innovation and experimentation. The number of agricultural loans had doubled over the past year. The aim of the World Bank was to contribute to an increase in the growth rate of underdeveloped countries of at least one-third to a level of at least 6 per cent per year. As a step towards that end the Bank had established an Industrial

Projects Department, to make practical recommendations to the developing countries as to how they could best accelerate their own industrial growth.

A further encouraging report came from Mr McNamara in September 1970. After completion of the first two years of the five-year programme to double the Bank Group's operations he was able to report that the Bank was on schedule and that he remained confident that the goal would be reached. The Bank was in a sound commercial position with profits amounting to $213 million, the highest in its history. Mr McNamara was also able to report that the developing nations had achieved in the previous year an historically unprecedented growth rate of 5 per cent a year.[1]

Mr McNamara's speech was also significant for the new emphasis it laid on policies of social transformation. 'We must,' he said, 'secure a 6 per cent growth rate. We must deploy the resources necessary for it. But we must do more. We must ensure that in such critical fields as population planning, rural renewal, fuller employment, and decent urbanism, positive policies support and hasten the social transformation without which economic growth itself becomes obstructed and its results impaired.' Certainly psychological, sociological, and anthropological factors need to be taken into account if the best is to be got out of aid. As Mr Colin Clark has bluntly put it: 'The trouble in Latin America is not shortage of food, nor unduly rapid rate of growth of population, it is politics.'

Miss Barbara Ward has also drawn attention to the need to look beyond the crude target of growth. She is particularly concerned about the attitude of young people, radicals and internationalists, dedicated Christians who have reservations about the

[1] Throughout the year the Bank was announcing a series of loans to underdeveloped countries, e.g. in March 1970 two loans totalling $8·5 million were announced for education projects in Chile. $7 million were for raising the quality of primary education and better teacher training, and expanding and improving agricultural secondary education. $1·5 million were to help finance expansion of programmes of vocational training already operating and so provide more skilled workers for agriculture, industry, and fisheries. The terms of the first loan were a loan for 25 years with 10 years' grace and 7 per cent interest. The terms of the second loan were for 25 years with 5 years' grace and 7 per cent interest. Other loans were made to the Ivory Coast, Egypt, Brazil, Costa Rica, Mexico, etc.

commercialism of the Western system. 'They,' she says, 'are beginning to question whether a straight forward extension of the same
economic drives and incentives to the developing world can
produce anything but a comparable perversion of goals and mal-
distribution of wealth and responsibility. In this reservation they
are met half way by many of the younger leaders in the developing
world, who have begun to denounce foreign aid as well as foreign
investment as simply a prolongation of Western imperialism under
a neo-colonialist disguise. Capital assistance from the West, they
assert, simply reinforces the position of the local powers that be.'[1]
This is an important warning that economic aid should promote
not only growth but better distribution as well. Ideas of development need to be supplemented by those of social justice. As
Barbara Ward points out young people in particular 'do not wish
to go *slumming* in developing lands, graciously offering patronage
and gifts. They are not bent on producing crumbs of aid from the
rich man's table. They search for a genuine transformation of
international order for a more truly just, co-operative, fraternal
world.'[2]

The exclusive concentration on increase in economic growth
came under attack at a conference on unemployment in developing countries held at Cambridge in the autumn of 1970. Mr David
Morse, a former Director-General of the International Labour
Organisation, maintained that a mistake had been made in
assuming that the unemployment problem would gradually solve
itself if the rate of economic growth was accelerated. 'Experience
has shown,' said Mr Morse, 'that in developing countries an automatic mechanism linking increases in production to increases in
employment, let alone anything approaching full employment,
simply does not exist.' He went on to recommend the 'dethrone-
ment of GNP' as the main development objective, and its replace-

[1] See 'The Politics of Aid', *Tablet*, 19 September 1970.
[2] Ibid., 'It follows,' she concludes, 'that the form and style of development policy in
the 70s may well determine the ability of Western nations to continue the work. If it
is co-operative; if it is divorced from the narrower and more egoistic forms of national
interest; if it takes full account of justice and social needs; if it abandons all taint of
Western control and expresses the world's open and fraternal attempt to redress its
profound imbalance – it will be supported and it may indeed become a means of
redemption for the inexorably growing wealth of the already semi-saturated Atlantic
World.'

ment by policies aimed more directly at increasing employment.[1]

One especially pressing problem is that of debt servicing of money borrowed by developing countries. Their debt service burden has in fact been growing much faster than their GNP. Over the past decade the rate of growth of the external debt of developing countries and its service has been about twice the rate of growth of their export earnings and nearly three times that of their combined gross domestic product. Mr McNamara showed himself aware of this problem in his report to the governors of the World Bank in September 1970, and he announced the initiation of a series of studies of the debt servicing difficulties facing a number of countries. 'The external public debt of developing countries,' said Mr McNamara, 'has increased five-fold since the mid-1950s, and debt service payments have grown at a rate of 17 per cent annually while foreign exchange receipts from exports have risen only 6 per cent per year. Obviously such trends cannot be allowed to continue indefinitely.' Perhaps the best solution to these difficulties would be a general moratorium on debt service payments for a period of years and the greater use of 'soft' loans made available through the I.D.A. whose resources have been replenished.

THE PEARSON REPORT

Undoubtedly one of the most significant achievements of the World Bank, in the long term, was the publication of the Pearson Report in September 1969.[2] This report surveyed the development of the poorer countries over two decades, analysed their problems, including those of population, unemployment, and urbanisation, set out the shortcomings of the aid programme and looked ahead to the needs of the future. The Pearson Report set out as the principal aim of aid the promotion of self-sustaining growth. It hoped that by the end of the century a situation would be created in the underdeveloped countries which would enable them to achieve a growth rate of 6 per cent without any further need for aid in concessional terms; it made recommendations

[1] See *Sunday Times*, 27 September 1970.
[2] *Partners in Development*, Report of the Commission on international development: New York, Washington, London, 1969.

covering the whole field of trade and aid. Among the more important of its recommendations in the trade field, the following
should be noted. Developed countries were exhorted to eliminate
as soon as possible excise and import duties on non-competing
products of special interest to the developing countries. It went on
to suggest that financing of reasonable buffer stocks in support of
well-conceived commodity agreements and policies should be
recognised as a legitimate object of foreign aid. No new quantitative restrictions should be imposed on products of special interest
to developing countries, and all existing quantitative restrictions
on these products should be abolished during the 1970s as rapidly
as possible. These recommendations are of particular significance
in view of the proposed enlargement of the European Economic
Community to include Great Britain. Clearly special arrangements
will have to be made if the developing countries are not to find
their primary and manufactured exports excluded from a protected market.

With regard to aid, the report recommends that each developed
country should increase its resource transfers to developing
countries to a minimum of 1 per cent of its GNP as rapidly as
possible and in no case later than 1975. Furthermore, each
developed country should increase its commitments of official
development assistance to the level necessary for disbursements
to reach 0·7 per cent of its GNP by 1975 or shortly thereafter, but
in no case later than 1980. The report suggests that all member
nations of the Development Assistance Committee should prepare
plans for reaching the 0·7 target and that these should be discussed at the 1971 meeting of the board of governors of the World
Bank. The national plans should be submitted for publication to
the Chairman of the D.A.C. by 1 January 1971. The Report was
also concerned to increase the flow of private foreign investment
to the poorer countries and recommended that developing
countries should structure their tax systems so as to encourage
profit reinvestment by foreign companies. It further suggested
that governments of developing countries should establish
positive incentives for all companies foreign and domestic to share
ownership with the public by the sale of equity in suitable forms.
The 1 per cent target if achieved would probably give to the

developing world a capital investment from the richer countries of from $17 to $18 billion a year. It has been calculated that this would meet their capital needs including the financing of policies for creative urbanisation and the building of an adequate urban infra-structure.[1]

The Pearson Report was also particularly concerned with development debts, recommending that aid giving countries should consider debt relief a legitimate form of aid and permit the use of new loans to re-finance debt payments, in order to reduce the need for full-scale negotiation. It further suggested that in future the terms of all official development assistance loans should provide interest of no more than 2 per cent, a maturity of between twenty-five and forty years and a grace period of seven to ten years. Finally, it set out a series of recommendations for creating an improved international framework for development. The Pearson Report aroused world-wide interest and while its full objectives have certainly not been accepted by all developed countries, and it has been subject to criticism for being in some sense 'dated and not sufficiently aware of the need to cure the defects of the present aid system', it has undoubtedly had the effect of reviving interest in the whole aid issue.[2] In Britain and the United States in particular it seems to have had a beneficial effect.

GREAT BRITAIN

Traditional British trade policy has been of great help to the underdeveloped countries. The policy of creating an open market for most primary products has helped them considerably, as has the policy of successive governments in favour of concluding international commodity agreements. Britain has also given considerable aid to developing countries over the last decade. In all 120 countries have been aided, 90 per cent of the aid being afforded through bilateral agreements and 80 per cent to Commonwealth countries; about half of the aid has been tied to purchases in Britain. In 1958/9 £90 million of aid was granted and in recent

[1] See Barbara Ward, 'The Politics of Aid', *Tablet*, 19 September 1970.
[2] For some sharp criticisms of intellectual and political inadequacy see 'Development in Partners?' by Paul Streeten, *New Society*, 27 November 1969.

years it has averaged about £200 million. While the aid programme has not been cut back directly in absolute terms nevertheless aid has declined in terms of the proportion of GNP devoted
to it and it has also been eroded by price inflation. On 27 November 1969, the Minister of Overseas Development, Mrs Judith
Hart, announced her forward programme for aid over the next
three years. She recalled that the white paper on public expenditure published in February 1969 had given estimates of £227
million for aid in 1969–70, and of £235 million for 1970–1.
Excluding defence elements this gave figures for total economic
aid of £219 million for 1969–70 and £227 million for 1970–1.
Mrs Hart announced that the Government had now decided that
in 1971–2 all economic aid would be consolidated into one official
aid programme and that this would be increased by £18 million
from £227 million to £245 million. In 1972/3 it would be further
increased to £265 million, an increase of £20 million and in
1973/4 it would accelerate by a further increase of £35 million to
£300 million. It was impossible, said the Minister, to go beyond
these years since 1973–4 was the last year of the existing public
expenditure survey. Mrs Hart said that Britain could expect to
reach the 1 per cent target recommended by the Pearson Commission not much after the appropriate date 1975. The snag,
however, of Mrs Hart's figures is that they depend for their
achievement on an increased flow of private investment and this,
of course, cannot be guaranteed by the Government. She went on
to say, however, that the Government intended, unless the balance
of payments position should preclude it, to reach the target of
1 per cent total flow by the end of the second development decade,
that is by 1980. Mrs Hart was criticised from both sides of the
House for failing to accept the Pearson recommendation that
official aid should reach a level of 0·7 per cent of the GNP by
1975.[1] The day after the government announcement on 28
November, the House of Commons debated the Pearson Commission Report and passed the following resolution without a
division: 'That this House welcomes the Report of the Pearson
Commission and supports the full participation of the British
Government and British private investment in international

[1] See *The Times*, 28 November 1969.

development effort but regrets the continued fall in the proportion of Gross National Product voted to overseas aid.'[1]

In December 1969 the white paper on public expenditure (Command 4234) stated that over the next four years the aid programme would rise by one-third. Priority would be given to help to multilateral institutions. Since 1965 Britain has followed a policy of providing interest-free loans to needier developing countries. Ninety per cent of the loans made have been interest free with a grace period for repayment of the principal.

In 1970 the new Conservative Government made it plain that although it had been returned to office, pledged to reduce government expenditure, the aid programme would not be affected. Speaking at the United Nations during its twenty-fifth anniversary session on 23 October 1970, the Prime Minister, Mr Edward Heath, pledged the help of Britain in promoting the growth of trade and aid to assist the underdeveloped countries. 'The British Government,' he said, 'has contributed generously to the development for many years. We are committed to a substantial reduction in public expenditure. This is essential both to our own economic growth and to the control of inflation. In spite of this, we are planning to increase our official Aid programme for the next few years and I reaffirm our acceptance of the 1 per cent target agreed at the second UNCTAD conference in 1968. In accordance with the strategy for the second decade we shall do our best to reach this target by 1975.'[2]

Britain has also been the first country to set up a separate Ministry of Overseas Development. This grew out of the Department of Technical Co-operation which was set up in 1961 and which was turned into a separate Ministry by the Labour Government. On the return of the Conservatives to power in 1970 the Ministry of Overseas Development was absorbed into the Foreign Office. The Minister remains an independent Minister but heads a Foreign Office department. This was intended as a rationalising of the structure of government rather than a down-grading of the

[1] See *Hansard*, 28 November 1969, columns 773–872.
[2] This pledge was redeemed when the white paper *New Policies for Public Spending*, was published in October 1970. The commitments for the aid programme made in Cmd. 4234 were reaffirmed with the addition of a promise that aid would increase further to £340 million in 1974–5. See *The Times*, 28 October 1970.

Ministry, the advantage of the new arrangement being that the Minister of Overseas Development now has direct access to the Cabinet through the Foreign and Commonwealth Secretary.[1]

Britain has also operated a voluntary assistance programme, 'The British Volunteers', since 1962. In 1968 20,000 British citizens, most of them in their early twenties were engaged in the programme. The majority of these were graduates or professionally trained. The cost of the support of these men and women is met by the countries in which they are resident. The cost of their travel is met 75 per cent by the British Government and 25 per cent by voluntary societies. Those taking part in the programme are required to serve for a minimum period of one year.

Despite these initiatives the aid programme seems to have lost support in Britain. In February 1969, the Gallup Poll put the question, 'Do you think it is right that the British Government should spend a part of the taxpayer's money in assisting poor countries raise their living standards or not?' – 42 per cent replied affirmatively, 47 per cent negatively, and 10 per cent said they did not know.[2]

THE UNITED STATES OF AMERICA

Since the end of the war the United States has born the major burden of the world aid programme, but in common with other countries the amount devoted to aid by the United States has declined.[3] While progress has been made in sponsoring international family planning programmes this has not been matched by advances in the aid programme as such. In October 1969, when President Nixon sent a $2·7 billion foreign aid request to Congress, it ran into considerable trouble and received a negative

[1] The white paper stated that the Government had come to the conclusion that 'in order to unify ministerial responsibility for overseas policy, overseas aid should become the ultimate responsibility of the Secretary of State for Foreign and Commonwealth Affairs. They recognise, however, that the management of overseas aid is a function distinct from the general conduct of foreign affairs and that it is important to maintain the valuable body of expertise and skill in aid administration which has been developed in the Ministry of Overseas Development and its predecessors.' It went on to say that the status of the Minister for Overseas Development would be 'equivalent to that of a minister in charge of a separate department not represented in the Cabinet'. See *The Times*, 16 October 1970.
[2] Source *Vox*, April 1969.
[3] See p. 292 for comparative figures.

reception. Yet as President Nixon pointed out in a special message to Congress, the $2·7 billion figure was the smallest request in the history of foreign aid programmes. He added that small though it was it was 'vitally needed to maintain our relationship with the developing world'.[1]

In March 1970 the presidential task force on international development, which had been appointed by the President under the chairmanship of Mr Peterson, presented its report. The report recommended that it should be a cardinal aim of American foreign policy to help developing countries but added that the United States should not try to build a world in its own image but should contribute to the development of 'self-reliant and healthy' societies and an expanding world economy from which all countries would benefit. While declining to give a specific annual figure for the aid programme the task force recommended as a first priority the substantial raising of the low level of American economic development assistance. It further recommended that international development programmes should be independent of those American military-economic programmes which provide assistance for security purposes. The United States should also support efforts to make international lending institutions the main channel for development assistance. In a statement accompanying the report, the President said that 'a new United States approach to foreign affairs based on the proposals of the task force, will be one of our major foreign policy initiatives in the coming year.' He promised that he would submit legislation to Congress in January 1971 to carry out the new policy.[2]

President Nixon gave a more detailed account of his intentions in a special message to Congress 'Foreign Assistance for the '70s' issued on 16 September 1970. In his message he declared that he was proposing a major transformation in American foreign assistance programmes. The answer to declining amounts spent on foreign aid was not to slash them further but 'to reform our foreign assistance programmes and do our share to meet the needs of the '70s'. The President's first proposal was to create separate organisational arrangements for each component of the assistance effort which he divided into security assistance,

[1] *New York Times*, 19 October 1969.   [2] See *The Times*, 9 March 1970.

humanitarian assistance, and development assistance. His second principle was to strengthen multilateral institutions and to channel an increasing share of development assistance through them as rapidly as possible. The President went on to suggest that in order to provide more effective bilateral development assistance in the changed conditions of the 1970s, two new and independent institutions should be set up. The first would be a United States international development corporation to handle bilateral lending and the second a United States international development institute to help bring American science, technology, and research to the lower income countries. The President also suggested that all the industrialised countries should move rapidly towards initiation of a system of tariff preferences for the exports of manufactured products from the poorer countries. Another change announced by the President was 'the elimination of those tying restrictions on procurement which hinder our investment guarantee programme in its support of United States private investment in the lower income countries'. He added a proposition that all donor countries should take steps to end the requirement that foreign aid be used to purchase goods and services produced in the nation providing the aid. Perhaps the most imaginative of his set of proposals was, that in order to provide a permanent source of funds for the poorer countries, all nations should enter into a treaty which would permit the utilising of the resources of the sea-bed in order to promote economic development. Any royalties obtainable from sea-bed operations should be utilised principally to provide economic assistance to developing countries participating by treaty. The President ended by stressing that while economic development in itself could not guarantee political stability, this latter would be unlikely to occur without a preceding sound economic development. President Nixon's proposals if followed through could provide a new point of departure in the history of American aid.[1]

[1] The President gave immediate directions that American aid should be 'untied for procurement in the lower income countries themselves'. A few days before the President's message Japan promised that it would consider extending aid to developing countries with no strings attached at any date agreed upon by the industrialised nations within an agreement worked out by the Development Assistance Committee of the 21-nation O.E.C.D. See the *Financial Times*, 15 September 1970.

THE ROLE OF THE CHURCHES

The particular role of the Churches is to create and sustain a world conscience on the problems of world poverty and aid to the underdeveloped countries. 'There is no inherent reason,' writes Barbara Ward, 'why the Christian Community, stretching as it does from one end to the other of our planetary society, should not be, in developed and developing societies alike a catalyst of energy, devotion and reform. Christian citizens could take a lead in supporting and publicising the proposals for reform, in demanding from the rich a sense of justice and equality, from the poor a readiness for forgiveness and constructive co-operation, from all men of goodwill a vision of a planetary community in which development and justice are sought together and man's vast resources set to work for the building of the common good.'[1] If the problem of world poverty is to be solved it will require an unprecedented degree of international commitment, not for one decade alone but until the end of the century. Towards sustaining this commitment the Christian Community can make a vital contribution.[2]

The Catholic Church has made a number of important contributions to this end. The Second Vatican Council showed its deep concern for the plight of the poorer countries of the world and suggested a number of principles on which to base practical action in its document *The Pastoral Constitution on the Church in the Modern World*.[3] Paul VI's encyclical *Populorum Progressio*, issued in the spring of 1967, is a profound, compassionate and in its way revolutionary document which has served to concentrate Catholic attention on world poverty and the duty of Christians to alleviate it. In the same year in order to give practical effect to the principles laid down by the Council, the Pope set up the Pontifical Commission for Justice and Peace. Its aims and objectives were defined as follows: to arouse the whole Church to a full awareness of its

[1] See 'The Christian Response', *Tablet*, 3 October 1970.
[2] Barbara Ward has compared the situation to that of the movement for the abolition of slavery in the last century. William Wilberforce and Thomas Clarkson began their campaign in the 1760s but did not achieve a break-through until 1807 and were not finally victorious until the 1830s. See 'Poverty and Politics', the *Tablet*, 18 May 1968.
[3] See especially section 2: Building Up the International Community.

mission at the present time, when the world is so glaringly divided between the 'haves' and the 'have-nots'; to promote the development of the poor countries of the world; to encourage social justice between nations; and in doing so, to help the less-developed countries to promote their own material progress. The foundation of this Vatican commission was followed by the setting up of national commissions in individual countries. In May 1969 the English Commission for International Justice and Peace issued a report with the approval of the bishops. It recommended that individuals should devote 1 per cent of their personal income to overseas aid, that dioceses and parishes and Church institutions should do the same and that the Government should be urged to raise its total aid contribution to 1 per cent by 1972.

The World Council of Churches has also given a series of leads to world opinion. In May 1968 the World Council and the Catholic Church organised a conference at Beirut to study in depth questions of economic co-operation for world development. For the first time the Churches publicly and jointly pledged themselves to intensify and give structural form to the work for international social justice.[1]

In January 1970 the World Council of Churches sponsored a further conference of Church leaders and economic experts at Montreux in Switzerland. The principal purpose of the conference was to give guidance to member Churches in the developed and developing countries on the proper use of the growing amount of Church funds being made available for development. In England in October 1969, a local initiative was taken by a number of Christian and other organisations when they published 'a manifesto on action for world development'. The sponsors pledged themselves to work for the cause of world development. One result of the manifesto was the organisation of a sign-in on world poverty, the text of which was agreed by the steering committee of the Church's action for world development. The signing of this text was the centre of a series of activities to arouse Church members and others to a sense of their responsi-

[1] For the common agreed statement see *Tablet*, 4 May 1968, and for a descriptive article see Arthur McCormack, 'Beirut Summed Up', *Tablet*, 18 May 1968.

bility. The text was presented to various members of Parliament.[1]

In May 1970 the Archbishop of Canterbury, the Cardinal Archbishop of Westminster, and the Moderator of the Free Church Federal Council called upon the Prime Minister, Mr Wilson to discuss the aid situation; they urged that government aid to underdeveloped countries should be augmented as rapidly as possible and that Britain should achieve the Pearson Report's target as quickly as possible. Other Church activities and efforts are being prepared.

FAMILY PLANNING AND CHRISTIAN RESPONSIBILITY

Trade and aid have been dealt with first because these are positive contributions towards increasing the wealth of the poorer countries and provide the context in which international family planning policies can best be considered. These policies have a vital role to play, but they cannot of themselves create new wealth although they can help to prevent it being used up by excessive population growth. What do the Christian conscience and Christian theology have to say on proposals for international family planning?

The first point to establish is that family planning is accepted as a good by all major religions. Religious opinion on this point is

[1] The text reads as follows: 'We, the undersigned, believe that mass hunger, disease and illiteracy are intolerable anywhere in the world; that the skills and resources to change these unjust conditions now exist; that to obtain justice among men the international financial and trading system can and must be changed; that as a first step the poorer countries must receive more aid and that the terms of international trade must no longer discriminate in favour of the rich. We ask you, as our representative in Parliament, to support as immediate practical aims: (1) the achievement by 1972 of the target of 1 per cent of the wealth (i.e. Gross National Product) of the United Kingdom for overseas aid, with at least $\frac{3}{4}$ allocated in the form of effective government aid; (2) an increase in the amount of U.K. aid channelled through international agencies, encouraging other rich nations to follow this lead; (3) the negotiation by our government of trade agreements favourable to the poorer countries. We hereby commit ourselves to continuing action for world development.' I received a petition signed by members of various churches in my own constituency of Chelmsford and attended a meeting where the petition was presented. I forwarded this to the Prime Minister, Mr Wilson, and received a reply from him in which he said: 'I welcome the increasing expression of concern in this country about the world's poorer people and also the general commitment to continued action for world development.' The then Prime Minister added, however, that he and the Government had important reservations on specific points in the declaration.

in accord with what appears to be the general conviction of man-kind. In 1968 the International Conference on Human Rights meeting in Teheran, at which eighty-four United Nations' states were represented, proclaimed the right of parents to free and responsible determination of the number and the spacing of their children.[1] All the Christian Churches today stress the need for responsible parenthood. Parents are under an obligation not to bring into the world more children than they can physically and emotionally support. The point is made explicitly in *Humanae Vitae*: 'The responsible exercise of parenthood implies, therefore, that husband and wife recognise fully their own duty towards God, towards themselves, towards the family and towards society, in a correct hierarchy of values.'[2] There has, in fact, been a profound shift of emphasis within and without the Christian Churches away from stressing the absolute good of a large family towards encouraging a family size which is within the parents' capability to cope. A large family is no longer an automatic signal for clerical praise.

If family planning is a good it follows that its promotion in the international sphere is of the same order of moral obligation as the provision of aid to the poorer countries. The United States' President's scientific advisory committee on the food problem was unanimous in its report of 1967 in expressing the need for 'continuing and increasing emphasis upon research, technical assistance and capital funding in family planning'. The com-mittee went on to state that 'only by such continuing emphasis and effort can the outpacing of food production by population growth be avoided as a problem that might continue well into the next century. The long lag period that necessarily precedes the main effect of family planning programmes adds to the urgency of the need for action now'.[3]

---

[1] This resolution was agreed by 56 votes to 0 with 7 abstentions (Brazil, Beo-Russia, Malawi, Poland, The Ukraine, U.S.S.R., and Zambia). The General Assembly of the United Nations Resolution 2211 (xxi) of 17 December 1966 recognised *inter alia* the sovereignty of nations in formulating and promoting their own population policies with due regard to the principle that the size of the family should be the free choice of individual families.

[2] See para. 10.

[3] *Report*, Washington, May 1967, p. 14. The United States' President's report on population family planning, which was published on 9 January 1969, and compiled by a panel of experts in various disciplines, stated the attitude of the United States to

The World Bank under the leadership of Mr McNamara has recently undertaken a new role as a promoter of population policies. In his address to the governors on 30 September 1968, Mr McNamara made it plain that the World Bank intended to support family planning programmes. He justified this by referring to the crippling effect of a high rate of population increase on economic growth in developing countries. He estimated that in a typical situation involving two countries with similar birth rates, halving the rate and reducing it to one above that in most developed countries, would raise the standard of living in the reducing country by '40 per cent above the other country in a single generation'.[1] He proposed the following three courses: 'First: to let the developing nations know the extent to which rapid population growth slows down their potential development, and that, in consequence, the optimum employment of the world's scarce development funds requires attention to this problem. Second: to see opportunities to finance facilities required by our member countries to carry out family planning programmes. Third: to join with others in programmes of research to determine the most effective methods of family planning and of national administration of population control programmes'.[2]

Mr McNamara incurred a sharp rebuke from the Vatican for his address but it was welcomed by many. He returned to the

---

international assistance in family planning. 'The policy of the United States for international assistance in this field is based on the fact that excessive rates of population growth impede economic and social progress and on the principle that effective access to family planning information and services should be universally available', p. 15.
[1] Mr McNamara took India and Mexico as examples of countries with the same birth rate of 40 per thousand and suggested halving this by 20 per thousand. Cf. the position with regard to the Aswan Dam in Egypt, which on completion will raise the wealth of the country by 18 per cent, but by that time the population will have increased by 32 per cent. See also the situation in tropical South America (Bolivia–Brazil–Columbia –Ecuador–Peru–Venezuela–Guyana), where the population growth is at an annual rate of 3·2 per cent whereas the economic growth has been in a region of 1·5 per cent to 2·2 per cent. See 'Facts from Latin America', George Hills, *Tablet*, 31 August 1968.
[2] In fact Mr McNamara was building in his statement on a declaration of a former President, Mr G. Woods, which was made in the spring of 1958 when he said: 'We in the World Bank favour all responsible policies and programmes to reduce birth rate in countries where excessive population inhibits economic development . . . in particular as possibilities for action in this field expand we are giving increasing heed to our borrowers' policy on population as one indication of their commitment to economic growth.'

theme in subsequent addresses at Buenos Aires on 18 October 1968, and at Notre Dame University in Indiana on 1 May 1969.[1] At Notre Dame Mr McNamara made it clear that he fully accepted the principle that in a free society the parents themselves must ultimately decide the size of their own family. 'We would regard as an intolerable invasion of the family's rights,' he said, 'for the state to use coercive measures to implement population policy.' At the same time he stressed that developed nations had a duty to give every measure of support they could to countries which have already established family planning programmes and to assist others to come to a decision by helping with the demographic and social studies which would reveal the facts and point out the urgency of the issue. 'It is essential, of course, to recognise the right of a given country to handle its population problems in its own way. But handle it it must.'

In his address to the board of governors in September 1969, Mr McNamara told them he had established a population projects department within the Bank. Although this department was not fully operative he had already found that the immediate need of underdeveloped countries was not so much for financial assistance in family planning programmes as for technical advice and counsel. Once again in September 1970 in his presidential address Mr McNamara returned to the theme of population planning, stating that the Bank had received requests for help in this field from countries such as India, Indonesia, Jamaica, and Tunisia. At the same time he was constrained to admit that with the exception of Singapore and Hong Kong, special cases, there was only evidence in two developing countries Taiwan and Korea that the rate of population growth had been significantly reduced by family planning programmes. Mr McNamara explained this lack of success partly because of the overwhelming size of the

[1] In a Press conference after his speech to the Inter-American Press Association at Buenos Aires on 18 October, Mr McNamara answered the following question in these words: 'Question: Is it true that we are making loans conditional on the recipients using artificial means of birth control? Mr McNamara: No, this is not so. Population policies, as I will emphasise again in a moment, must be decided by national governments in relation to their people. Parents have a right of freedom of choice in the means they use to limit family size. But as advisers on development policies and partners in development programmes it is our duty to point out the severe limitation on economic progress imposed by too rapid increases in population.'

problem and the difficulty of adapting programmes to countries with different social and cultural traditions. Nevertheless, some progress had been made. In 1960 only three countries had population planning policies and only one government was actually offering concrete assistance. No international development agency was working in the field of family planning. In 1970, on the other hand, twenty-two countries in Asia, Africa, and Latin America, representing 70 per cent of the population of those continents, had official population programmes. More than a dozen other countries representing 10 per cent of the world population provided some assistance to family planning, although without an officially formulated policy. A number of international agencies were working in the population field.[1] Mr McNamara also stressed that many citizens lacked access to the information and assistance required for family planning. He recommended that there should be a greatly expanded research effort in basic reproductive biology and that a strong administrative organisation and a comprehensive data analysis and evaluation service should be set up in connection with international family planning.[2]

The attitude of the United Nations and its associated organisations towards birth control has radically altered. Attempts to

[1] The United Nations Population Division, U.N.D.P., UNESCO, W.H.O., F.A.O., I.L.O., UNISEF, O.E.C.D., and the World Bank had all stated a willingness to participate in population planning activities.

[2] Support has been given to Mr McNamara's views from a computer model of an underdeveloped country's economy devised by Steven Enke and Richard G. Zind and the General Electric Company of the United States. The model showed that the cumulative rate of return on money invested in birth control programmes in underdeveloped countries is about 65 times over 25 years, compared with a usual rate of about 4 times on money invested in factories, irrigation canals, and other capital projects. This conclusion is based on a computer model of an underdeveloped country's economy which relates the growth of GNP to the labour force, capital stock, and other factors. After 30 years the GNP of the country with the birth control programme is slightly smaller than that without it because of the increased labour force in the latter case. But the GNP a head starting at $150 a year has risen to $255 with the birth control programme compared with $206 without it. The extra income a head represents the value of the programme to the existing population. Dividing the extra income by the cost of the programme the researchers calculate that the undiscounted cumulative rate of return on the programme is 13 times after 5 years and 80 times after 30 years. The model also predicts that a birth control programme costing an annual 30 cents a head of the population or about 3 per cent of the total budget for economic development would raise average income over 15 years by almost twice the percentage that it would rise without the programme. See *Journal of Bio-Social Science*, 1:41 (1969); and *Science*, 7 February 1969, 163:533.

use the United Nations to exert influence in order to encourage world-wide family planning were made in the 1950s but all attempts to secure the adoption of such policies were blocked by Roman Catholic and Communist countries.[1] Thus, in 1952, the World Health Organisation dropped the Norwegian proposal to study contraception as part of its official programme after opposition from Catholic delegates.[2] The United Nations accordingly at first adopted a policy of neutrality on the subject, one of the agreed principles of co-operative action established at the 1954 world population conference being to respect different ethical and religious values and to promote mutual understanding.[3]

The change in the attitude of the United Nations was shown in July 1968 when by 12 votes to 7, with 4 abstentions, the United Nations Economic and Social Council adopted a recommendation to the effect that the United Nations Development Programme should be ready to finance projects 'designed to assist developing countries in dealing with population problems'.[4]

In September 1969 President Nixon made it clear that he was in favour of international family planning when speaking at the United Nations. He said, 'International co-operation is . . . indispensable for the reduction of the population growth.' On the other hand, the Brazilian representative criticised this position and the one adopted by the World Bank under the presidency of Mr Robert McNamara. This Brazilian hostility to birth control appears to be based partly on a nationalism which has visions of populating Brazil's vast and empty interior but it was also

[1] Communism maintains there is no true population problem; the shortage has been created by the capitalist system. This doctrine has not always been rigidly applied in Communist countries; Lenin, for example, allowed contraceptives to be made available, a policy reversed by Stalin in 1936. The Soviet position was stated at the population conference in 1954 when contraception was condemned. China adopted a birth control programme in 1956–7, but at the end of the year it was rumoured that it had been abandoned.

[2] *New York Times*, 20 May 1952, 13:5.

[3] Opposition to contraception is not confined to Christians. Thus, in Mauritius, Hindu members of the Legislature have joined with Christians in declaring their opposition to the propagation of contraception. See *The Times*, 29 April 1960.

[4] *The Times*, 1 August 1968. France and Panama were among the countries voting against this recommendation, but another Catholic country, Venezuela, supported it. This resolution was significant since it came after the issue of the Papal Encyclical, *Humanae Vitae*.

influenced by the encyclical *Humanae Vitae* to which the Brazilian hierarchy rallied. The Government then went on record in support of the Pope's ban on artificial contraception and refused to implement the national population control programme.[1]

If family planning is to be made effective in underdeveloped countries, such policies must be promoted from the top: they will not arise spontaneously as is the case in advanced countries. This increases the need for inter-governmental action. Paul VI in his encyclical *Populorum Progressio* comes out in favour of publicly sponsored family planning programmes, putting the point frigidly but clearly: 'It is true,' says the Pope, 'that too frequently an accelerated demographic increase adds its own difficulties to the problem of development: the size of the population increases more rapidly than available resources and things are found to have reached apparently an impasse. From that moment the temptation is great to check the demographic increase by radical measures. It is certain that public authorities can intervene within the limit of their competence, by favouring the availability of appropriate information and by adopting suitable measures, provided that these be in conformity with the moral law and that they respect the rightful freedom of married couples.'[2] On the other hand, in his later encyclical *Humanae Vitae* the Pope appealed to public authorities in the following terms: 'Do not allow the morality of your people to be degraded; do not permit that by legal means practices contrary to the natural and divine law be introduced into that fundamental cell, the family. Quite other is the way in which public authorities can and must contribute to the solution of the demographic problem: namely, the way of a provident policy for the family, of a wide education of people in respect of the moral law and the liberty of citizens.'[3]

What then are the moral principles which should inform international policies of family planning? First and most important, they should be so designed as not to violate fundamental human values and basic human rights. Freedom is the essential characteristic of human nature. The human person is autonomous, free, and inviolable. The human person is not explicable in terms of

[1] See *The Times*, 23 September 1969.   [2] Para. 37.
[3] Para. 23.

social forms, nor should he be subordinated to their purposes. He transcends them. Theology confirms this fact about man's nature. 'Freedom,' writes Cardinal Feltin, 'lies at the very heart of Christianity, which seen from without might look like a system, but thought and lived from within is a living bond between persons, a religion of the spirit. Faith is the encounter of a free gift and a free acceptance: a call on the part of God and a conscious and submissive response to God's voice.' By faith man is able to participate in the redemption, and redemption itself is both given and received by love. Love, like faith, is a free act. 'When one has known the love of free men,' says Péguy, 'the prostrations of slaves are worthless.' Through grace, man is liberated from the servitude of sin and becomes a free man in the theological order. He enters, says Danielou, freedom in a new sense. 'It means that man's relationship to God is no longer merely that of a servant of his Lord but also that of a son to his Father.' Such a relationship is inconceivable unless it is free.

One of the greatest perils of our age is that the technology which promises an earthly paradise could also be used to deliver a hell. *Humanae Vitae* gives a warning of the danger that governments could impose population policies without regard to the moral status and values of human beings. Where the Encyclical exaggerates is that it appears to state that this will be an inevitable result of acceptance of contraception.[1] One does not have to accept this exaggeration to see that governmental promotion of contraception could have this effect. In this connection it is relevant to study the unintentionally horrific paper by Richard and Gitta Meier delivered at the Georgetown symposium on world population and U.S. Government policies in July 1967.[2] Reference is made in that paper to the brave new world where each couple upon marriage will be granted the right to bear twenty-two deci-children. This is a scheme of Kenneth E. Boulding's in a society where infertility will be the norm for adults, and the rights to raise children will have to be bought up on the open

[1] See para. 17 and the reference to 'the consequences of methods of artificial birth control'.

[2] 'New Directions: A Population Policy for the Future' in *World Population and U.S. Government Policy and Programmes*, ed. Franklin T. Brayer (Georgetown University Press, Washington, 1958).

market.[1] I think also of the statement in Britain made in 1968 by Mr Douglas Houghton, Chairman of the Parliamentary Labour Party, that large families would come to be considered 'a form of social delinquency'.[2] Provided that the voluntary principle is adhered to these horrific results need not arise. This means first of all that individual citizens must always retain the ultimate responsibility for the size of their families.[3] Governments may legitimately attempt to persuade them of the necessity of having fewer or more children by exhortation or by tax measures, but the final decision must remain a parental one.

What if the national interest runs counter to the collective personal preference of married couples? This may possibly be happening in the United States where the population is increasing because the birth rate remains obstinately higher than that required to replace the population. This is not because of lack of knowledge of birth control so much as the desire to have large families.[4] While the state has the right to formulate a population policy and publicise it: while it is entitled to use persuasion to arouse couples to a sense of their moral responsibility to the community: it has no right to resort to compulsion. As to incentives and deterrents, it is hardly human to impose positive tax disabilities on those who have more than a given number of children

[1] Kenneth E. Boulding, *The Meaning of the Twentieth Century* (New York, 1964), p. 128. For a satirical appraisal of such attitudes see 'A State License to have children' by Alan Barth, the *Washington Post*, 26 December 1969.

[2] The speech was made by Mr Houghton to the Sociological Research Foundation on 2 July 1968. 'Already,' he said, 'large families are a form of social irresponsibility. Shortly they will be regarded as a form of social delinquency.'

[3] Cf. *Populorum Progressio*: 'Finally, it is for the parents to decide with full knowledge of the matter, on the number of their children, taking into account their responsibilities towards God, themselves, the children they have already brought into the world, and the community to which they belong. In all this they must follow the demands of their own conscience enlightened by God's law authentically interpreted, and sustained by confidence in Him.' (Para. 37.)

[4] See 'Nixon's Population' by Peter J. Smith, *New Society*, 24 July 1969, where he writes: 'The main reason for the growth of population in the U.S. is thus not any real or imagined inadequacy in birth control and family planning services but is, quite simply, that on average American parents *want* more children than the average maximum number required to stabilise the population. . . . Generally speaking, the mean number of children considered ideal goes down with increasing education level and economic status of parents. Thus highly educated upper income parents desire on average about three children; and poorly educated lower income parents desire closer to four.' It should be noted that in recent years the birth rate has declined sharply in the United States from its previous postwar high.

since if they are incurred it is the children who will be likely to suffer. On the other hand it is less objectionable to hold out positive inducements for parents not to have children or not to have more than a certain number, through a system of tax rebates or graded family allowances, e.g. no allowance for any child after the fourth.[1]

Again, nations must remain free to accept or reject family planning programmes and pressure should not be brought to bear upon them making, for example, the acceptance of a particular form of family planning a condition precedent for the conferring of some other benefit, such as a loan or capital grant. The policy of the United States Government in promoting population programmes for foreign countries is fully in accord with this principle.[2] United States policy has evolved from the position of refusal to do anything to promote international family planning enunciated by President Eisenhower in 1959 to its acceptance as a duty by President Johnson in his State of the Union message of 4 January 1965, when he declared: 'I will seek new ways to use our knowledge to help deal with the explosion in world population and the growing scarcity in world resources.' Again in his State of the Union Message for 1968, President Johnson stated: 'Unless the rapid growth of population in developing countries is

[1] Dr John Marshall draws an analogy between education and population policy. 'It is the right and duty of the parents to educate their children, but we accept interventions by the state which limit considerably the exercise of this right. A similar situation must exist with regard to population. Indeed it exists already; the moment a government imposes taxes, it adopts a stance on this issue by the generosity of the scale of its allowances for children; still more is this so with family allowances and other measures which, though primarily social in objective, have indirect demographic effects.' See 'State Planning and the Family', *Tablet*, 3 October 1970.
[2] See the address of Robert Barnett, Deputy Assistant Secretary of State for Far Eastern Affairs, given at Columbia University on 25 March 1966. Mr Barnett stated: 'Participation in the family planning components of programmes must be entirely voluntary.' He went on to say that 'the use of family planning services must not be a prerequisite to receipt of benefits or participation in any other programme or activity funded by government agencies.' Mr Barnett's third requirement was that 'such programmes must provide, and make known to participants, the availability of advice and assistance on a variety of family planning methods and techniques sufficient to ensure that persons may make choices consistent with their personal beliefs.' Cf. Declaration of policy made by the Secretary of Health, Education and Welfare of 24 January 1966, when he said: 'Programmes conducted or supported by the Department shall guarantee freedom from coercion or pressure of mind or conscience. There shall be freedom of choice of method so that individuals can choose in accordance with the dictates of their consciences. The Department will make known to state and local agencies that funds are available for programmes of the sort described above, but it will bring no pressure to bear upon them to participate in such programmes.'

slowed, the gap between rich and poor will widen steadily. Governments in the developing countries must take facts into consideration. And we in the United States are prepared to help them in those efforts.'[1] On 29 July 1968, just before the publication of *Humanae Vitae*, President Johnson reiterated this policy in signing a law putting new emphasis on U.S. aid to developing countries which voluntarily adopt birth control programmes.[2] This policy has been followed and developed by President Nixon. In July 1969 he became the first American President to send a formal message on the problems of United States population growth to Congress. He went further than this, setting as a national goal the provision of birth control advice to all American women who want it, adding in an aside that no advice would be forced upon women and their religious convictions would be respected. The President proposed to raise federal expenditure on birth control to $150 million, asked for a commission to consider population growth, shifts of population and the American governmental agencies, federal, state, and local, involved in birth control projects.[3]

Population policies sponsored by richer nations must, then, be based on voluntarism, and must respect the freedom and the ethical values of the countries they are proposed to benefit, but what of the promotion of international family planning from the point of view of the promoting country? Here again, ethical limitations apply. The United States, for example, could hardly help to promote foreign programmes of euthanasia as a means of population control even if it could be shown that such a programme was entirely voluntary. What, then, are the criteria to be employed? I state them as follows: first, that population programmes promoted by one country for the use of another should

[1] See *World Population and U.S. Government Policy and Programmes*, ed. Franklin T. Brayer (Washington, 1968), p. 5.
[2] See *Guardian*, 30 July 1968. For an account of the development of U.S. policy in this field see my article, 'An Ethical Appraisal' in Brayer, op. cit., p. 89. Asked at a Press conference for his reaction to the papal Encyclical, President Johnson replied: 'I have done what I could to encourage all nations to materially increase their food production. In connection with population control, the government has been willing to provide counselling and monetary assistance to countries and people who desired that assistance. As long as I am President, we will continue to do so.' Congress, which in 1967 had earmarked $35 million of aid funds exclusively for population and family planning, increased the earmarked funds to $50 million.
[3] *Economist*, 26 July 1969.

not violate the general moral consensus held by citizens in the promoting country. Second, that for prudential reasons and for the sake of preserving civil peace, a country in its foreign population programmes should not advocate or co-operate in methods of family planning which outrage a considerable proportion of its citizens. The question then becomes a factual one, namely whether for a given country a particular means of family planning does or does not do this. I intend to confine my consideration of the problem to pluralist societies, such as Great Britain or the United States, where a wide variety of ethical and religious viewpoints are represented among the citizens.

Abstinence apart, which does not present problems, save perhaps in practice there are only four methods of family planning that are reasonably effective: use of the sterile or safe period, abortion, sterilisation, and the various forms of contraception. Use of the rhythm method in international family planning programmes would present no problem to either Britain or the United States since the vast majority of citizens regard it as morally acceptable. The issue tends, however, to be academic since whatever may be said for the use of the safe period by reasonably advanced and educated people, it is not a practical proposition where these conditions are lacking. Experiments in India have been very discouraging and difficulties of correct usage, combined with fluctuating periodicity in many women, combine to make it an unsuitable means of international family planning. If scientists respond to the exhortation in *Humanae Vitae* and succeed in developing a pill which will pinpoint the day of ovulation in women it will be a different matter, but no such pill is yet in existence.

Abortion has been used by a number of countries notably Japan and certain countries of eastern Europe as a substitute for birth control. Would co-operation by the Western states in the promotion of such schemes, or the supply of abortifacients be morally acceptable? The answer must be negative: it would both be out of accord with what I take to be the general moral consensus on this controverted matter, and it would outrage a considerable number of citizens, many, but by no means all, Roman Catholics. The law in Western countries has traditionally, and to some extent still does, protect the life of the unborn child. Killing a foetus remains a statutory crime in all American legal jurisdictions and in the English legal system. There are, it is true, important glosses on the law. An abortion is not considered criminal in many jurisdictions in the United States if carried out to preserve the life of the mother or to protect her health: in Britain a statute has recently been passed which allows abortion on a wide variety of grounds, but even in that statute there is no suggestion that abortion should be accepted as a means of population control.[1] The consensus appears to be that while the community stops short of equating the foetus with a human person, it is nevertheless agreed that as a living organism, potentially at any rate, a full human being, it has rights which should be respected. These rights should only be taken away when they cause a conflict with other rights, such as those of the mother, or for some overriding reason such as the likelihood of the child being born deformed. Popular morality draws a reasonably clear distinction between contraception which concerns potential life and abortion which concerns life already in existence. In this respect it is particularly unfortunate that *Humanae Vitae* should link the two and in a single sentence enunciate its condemnation of contraception and abortion.[2] This error, made by some of the early Fathers of the Church, was understandable in the limited medical knowledge of those days.

Unlike abortion, sterilisation is much more of a border line case. Its moral status has been fully discussed in Chapter VI, 'Theological Perspectives', where I concluded that provided sufficiently grave reasons exist its employment is not in itself contrary to Christian morality.[3] Yet because of the seriousness of

[1] The Abortion Act 1967 (Ch. 87) provides that an abortion by a doctor is justified if 'two medical practitioners are of the opinion, formed in good faith, (a) that the continuance of the pregnancy would involve risk to the life of the pregnant woman, or of injury to the physical or mental health of the pregnant woman or of any existing children of her family, greater than if the pregnancy were terminated; or (b) that there is a substantial risk that if the child were born it would suffer from such physical or mental abnormalities as to be seriously handicapped.' (s. 1). Owing to concern about the Act a government inquiry into its workings was ordered in February 1971. *Hansard*, February 23, 812: 313–14.
[2] See *Humanae Vitae*, para. 14. 'In conformity with these landmarks in the human and Christian vision of marriage, we must once again declare that the direct interruption of the generative process already begun, and, above all, directly willed and procured abortion, even if for therapeutic reasons, are to be absolutely excluded as licit means of regulating birth.'
[3] See pp. 254–8, 257–8.

the operation in reducing human choice, if other means are available they should be used first. Ethical objections to sterilisation are reinforced by undefined but strong feelings that there is something degrading in sterilising operations, feelings reinforced by its compulsory use in Nazi Germany.[1] In these circumstances I would think it imprudent for developed countries to include measures for sterilisation in their aid programmes. The gravity of sterilisation rests on its irreversibility, but if techniques are developed which make it easily reversible it would in effect become merely another form of contraception, and would be governed by the principles applicable to contraception in general.

I turn now to contraception as such, by which I mean birth control practised by methods other than the use of natural rhythm. In England and the United States contraception is generally accepted as a normal part of married life. The Catholic Church and Orthodoxy officially condemn contraception, but many Catholics undoubtedly approve of contraception and use contraceptives, and a strong body of Catholic theological opinion supports the use of contraceptives subject to certain conditions.[2] Does the Roman Catholic position which condemns contraception entail the conclusion that contraception should be banned by law? Even if one holds contraception is contrary to the natural law one cannot conclude with some rigorists that the question is immediately answered in the affirmative, since all contraventions of natural law are not subjects for legislation. Fornication, adultery, lying, for example, are contrary to natural law, but civil sanctions are not advocated for such offences. Non-philosophic criteria must be applied before the question can be disposed of. A breach of natural law must be a fit subject for legislation, and injure the common good substantially, before it is forbidden by law. The law must be capable of enforcement and equitable in its incidence. Finally, if it would cause greater evils than those it is intended to avoid, recourse to legislation is undesirable.

The banning of the use of contraceptives by law as was the case

[1] In Nazi Germany a comprehensive sterilisation statute was passed in 1933, and in its first year of operation 56,244 sterilisations were ordered. *Eugenics Review*, 29:9 (1937–8). For a full discussion of the ethical, social, and legal aspects of sterilisation see Norman St. John-Stevas, *Life, Death and the Law* (London and Bloomington, 1961).
[2] See Chapter 4 *The Catholic Revolution*, and Chapter 6 *Theological Perspectives*.

in Connecticut until the relevant statute was declared unconstitutional, fulfils none of these criteria. Using a contraceptive is essentially a private act, and though it may have harmful social consequences, it is impossible to isolate any particular act and demonstrate the harmful consequences that flow from it. In practice such a law is obviously unenforceable, and the attempt to enforce it would involve an intolerable interference with the private life of individuals. Private individuals and married couples would have to be subjected to constant supervision, the home would be invaded by investigators, and the police state advanced to a new point.

Banning the sale of contraceptives and the dissemination of birth control information, on the other hand, is a possible subject for legislation, since these are public acts, capable of regulation by law. Certainly such laws are difficult to enforce, but their effect would be far from nugatory, given a climate of moral opinion which approved their content. Thus in a country where the population predominantly rejected contraception, such laws would not be unreasonable, and in fact they are found in certain Catholic countries such as Spain, Italy, and Ireland.[1] It might, of

---

[1] In Spain the 1928 Penal Code made it a criminal offence to propagate contraceptive theory or practice. Existing law in Spain, enacted under General Franco, forbids the sale or 'public divulging in any way of means or procedures to avoid procreation as well as any kind of contraceptive propaganda (*Codigo Penal* 416). Nevertheless, contraceptive pills appear to have been manufactured in Spain since 1966. See *The Times*, 31 July 1968. Exhibition or offering for sale of contraceptives are forbidden by the Act of 24 January 1941. Customs regulations forbid the importation of contraceptives. Doctors are not forbidden to prescribe contraception but birth control advice may not be given as part of any public health service and there are no birth control clinics in Spain.

In Ireland Section 16 of the Censorship of Publications Act (Ireland No. 21 of 1929) forbids the sale or publication of material 'which advocates or might reasonably be supposed to advocate unnatural prevention of conception. Section 17 of the Criminal Law (Amendment) Act 1935, forbids the sale or importing of contraceptives. Penalties under both statutes are a fine of not more than £50 or imprisonment for not more than 6 months, or both.

In Italy birth control propaganda was forbidden until 1971. The sale of contraceptives was limited to pharmacies and birth control clinics could not operate. In March 1971 however the law providing these restrictions was abolished by Italy's constitutional court as being in conflict with article 21 of the Constitution upholding freedom of thought and word. The ban on pro-abortion propaganda was upheld.

Contraception is also restricted in Belgium. See the law of 20 June 1923, which makes it a criminal offence to distribute 'objects specifically designed to prevent conception'. Writings describing means of preventing conception are also restricted by this law.

course, be maintained that moral condemnation renders a law superfluous, but this view is unrealistic since law is closely connected with the moral opinion of the community, and is a powerful, although subsidiary means of maintaining moral standards.

Does the Catholic theological position condemning contraception oblige those Catholics in non-Catholic countries who subscribe to it, and specifically those in England and the United States, to work for prohibitory laws or to defend them where they exist? Such a question can certainly not be answered by means of a logical deduction from an alleged natural law premise, but the particular social situation in the country under consideration must instead be carefully examined. By the constitution and philosophy of both England and the United States, Catholics certainly have a right to work for the passage of such laws, using all the normal political means, such as public campaigns and lobbying of legislators, to attain their end. By such means in the past, laws restricting gambling, betting, and drinking, have been added to the statute book, but not by Catholics. Indeed Catholics reject the doctrinal suppositions which these laws embody, and might argue that their personal freedom was unfairly diminished. The right then exists, but whether Catholics would be wise to follow Protestant precedent and exercise it is very dubious.

Laws embodying moral precepts are only enforceable if they are supported by a corresponding moral consensus in the community. The Volstead Act should have made this plain enough. A law forbidding the sale of contraceptives would be effective only if the vast majority of citizens believed their use to be wrongful and possibly not even then. Catholics then in campaigning for the maintenance of such laws gain little for public morality. They do, however, increase the fear of Catholicism in the minds of non-Catholics, and increase the likelihood that when Protestants visualise the Church the image will not be that of a religious body, but of a political power structure. This is a high price to pay for the maintenance of ineffectual statutes.

Aside from metaphysics, Catholics could justify a prohibitive law if they could show that demonstrable evils flow from the practice of contraception. If a declining population and a falling standard of life could be traced directly to birth control, then a strong case would have been made out for banning it.

On these grounds birth control in the past has been banned in France, the law being inspired by imperial and sociological rather than theological reasons.[1] Again if contraceptive methods could be shown to be harmful to health, a prohibitory law might be justified, but the evidence on the point is conflicting and allows no such conclusion. Finally the argument that recourse to contraceptives increases lust and promiscuity, would, if established, give grounds for a ban, but increase in such vice is not measurable and if it were, it could not be conclusively demonstrated to result from contraception. In these circumstances a strong case exists for the abandonment of Catholic effort to secure a legislative ban on contraceptives. Efforts to preserve public morality would be more constructive if confined to measures commanding general support, such as the maintenance of individual freedom of choice and the avoidance of any employment of compulsion by the state. Statutes regulating contraception belong more appropriately to the field of public nuisance than to the criminal law proper. There may well be a case for restricting advertising of contraceptives or their sale in areas where they might be obtained by minors.[2]

[1] The restrictive law was that of 31 July 1920. Use of the mails was restricted by Article 91 of the Decree Act, 20 July 1939. Importation of contraceptive propaganda, etc., was restricted by a Decree of 5 February 1946. While this legal situation existed no birth control clinics were allowed to operate nor could advice be given under public health services. Exemptions on the other hand existed for doctors to prescribe contraceptives, such as danger to a mother's health from further pregnancies. These restrictions were largely repealed in February 1969 when a new law governing contraception was brought into effect. In fact, even before this law, male contraceptives had been freely available allegedly as a protection against venereal disease, and the pill was available on prescription for 'therapeutic purposes' including, ironically, treatment of infertility. It was estimated in 1969 that 1 million 'infertile' French women were using the pill. The new law allows instruction to be given in family planning and authorises the sale of contraceptives but a number of restrictions remain, including restrictions on advertising, and the sale of the pill. Users of the pill or intra-uterine devices can only obtain these through a doctor. The doctor issues the woman concerned with a voucher from a book kept by him which she takes to the chemist with her prescription. Doctors and chemists must keep stubs and vouchers for three years for official inspection and the prescription is valid for one year only. Minors are required to have written consent of one parent and their age as well as their identity is entered on the prescription. See The Times, 26 February 1969. In 1971 restrictions on the sale of contraceptives at chemists were further relaxed.
[2] In October 1966 a statement was issued by the Canadian Catholic Conference of Bishops on the proposal, made to the Canadian legislature that Article 150 of the Criminal Code, making it a criminal offence to sell or advertise any contraceptive

What of family planning programmes sponsored by the State both on a national and international level? So long as the desirability of such State intervention was in doubt and Catholics constituted a body united in their opposition to contraception it was not unreasonable to suggest (and I did) that the State should be neutral on this issue and leave family planning to private organisations. Government neutrality in this sphere is not an ideal position but one which may be necessary because of an irreconcilable conflict of moral and social values within the community. In countries with such a strong Catholic minority the majority might well be wise to recognise the susceptibilities of the minority. In 1961 I wrote: 'To dub such a policy, allowing the minority to dictate to the majority, is to mis-state the issue. It would be better described as a judicious recognition of the existence of a considerable minority opinion, the flouting of which would inevitably lead to a serious diminution of civil peace. Reasonable concessions to such opinion offers a better as well as a more effective basis for the working of a democracy than the mechanical application of the principle that the will of the majority must always prevail.'[1]

Since 1961, however, the situation has been radically transformed. Contraception has become much more widely accepted as a normal part of married life. The law in countries such as the United States, France, and even Italy has been relaxed. Family

information or materials, should be repealed. In their statement the bishops approved the principles which are laid down in the text above and indeed quoted them virtually verbatim from my pamphlet 'Birth Control and Public Policy', published in 1960. The Canadian bishops' statement ended: 'Provided then that safeguards against irresponsible sale and advertising are built into the law and that protection of personal freedom is ensured, we do not conceive it as our duty to oppose appropriate changes in Article 150 of the Criminal Code. Indeed, we could easily envisage an active co-operation and even leadership on the part of lay Catholics to change a law which under present conditions they might well judge to be harmful to public order and the common good.' Conditions which must be fulfilled before a law should be passed turning a wrongful act into a statutory crime were listed by the bishops as follows: '(i) It should first of all be clear as indicated already, that the wrongful act notably injures the common good; (ii) The law forbidding the wrongful act should be capable of enforcement, because it is not in the interest of the common good to pass a law which cannot be enforced; (iii) The law should be equitable in its incidence – i.e. its burden should not fall on one group in society alone; (iv) It should not give rise to evils greater than those it was designed to suppress.' See *Western Catholic Reporter*, 13 October 1966.

[1] See *Life, Death and the Law*, pp. 99–100.

planning has come to be accepted as a proper concern of the state. In 1968 for example, in the United States, federal spending on birth control projects amounted to $70 million. At the same time, as has been described earlier in this book, a revolution in thinking has taken place within the Roman Catholic Church. Many Catholics now accept contraception as legitimate, and they are supported in this view by priests, bishops, and theologians.[1] Others, including Pope Paul VI, continue to condemn it. The encyclical *Humanae Vitae* was issued to restore the old position but it manifestly failed to do this. Faced with this internal disagreement the Catholic Church has had in practice to allow the issue to be decided by the consciences of individuals. It would surely be absurd in this situation for Catholics to attempt to deny to the non-Catholic conscience what has been conceded *de facto* to the Catholic one. The new situation has made it morally unnecessary as well as practically impossible for Catholics in pluralist societies to oppose state-sponsored programmes involving dissemination of contraceptive information and distribution of contraceptive devices, provided, that is, that certain principles are respected. Catholic social action today should be directed to ensuring that in the national and international field the moral principles of voluntariness, the maintenance of public decency, the observance of the distinction between abortion and contraception, etc. are observed.[2] In the international field adoption of programmes of family planning should not be made a condition precedent to the granting of aid.

Catholics who are uneasy about contraceptive programmes at

[1] In July 1970 the Catholic Renewal Movement in Britain decided to distribute 100,000 leaflets suggesting that Catholic families, whose consciences allowed it, should consult the F.P.A. *Catholic Herald*, 10 July 1970.

[2] In September 1970 an example of such action took place in the United States when the Committee on Inter-State and Foreign Commerce reported to the House a rewrite of a measure providing contraceptive services to indigent families. The following section 1008 was added: 'None of the funds appropriated under this title shall be used in programmes where abortion is a method of family planning'. The voluntary principle was contained in section 1007 'the acceptance by any individual of family planning services or family planning or population growth information (including educational materials) provided through financial assistance under this title (whether by grant or by contract) shall be voluntary and shall not be a prerequisite to eligibility for or receipt of any other service or assistance from, or to participation in, any other programme of the entity or individual that provided such a service or information.' The Bill with these sections included became law on 24 December 1970 – 'The Family Planning Services and Population Research Act', Public Law 91–572, 91st Congress S. 2018.

home and abroad might also reflect on the alternative means of population control which is likely to be resorted to in the absence of contraception, namely abortion. They might then find contraceptive programmes acceptable as the lesser of two evils.[1]

'The tragic truth,' said Mr Robert McNamara in his address to the University of Notre Dame, 'is that illegal abortion is endemic in many parts of the world. And it is particularly prevalent in those areas where there is no adequate, organised family planning assistance. The conclusion is clear: where the public authorities will not assist parents to avoid unwanted birth, the parents will often take matters into their own hands – at whatever cost to conscience or health.'[2] This is certainly true in many countries of Latin America, where women are prepared to use the most primitive methods of abortion rather than bring more children into the world. In Uruguay, for example, where rates of population increase are comparatively low a survey carried out by the Christian Family Movement some years ago showed that 75 per cent of conceptions ended in abortion. The abortion rate for Latin America as a whole is estimated to amount to between 25 and 30 per cent of all live births. In Chile, according to a statement by the Minister of Public Health, there is one illegal abortion for every two live births.[3] In Santiago, Chile, the principal hospital, University College Hospital, has not been able to keep pace with the number of cases coming to the hospital on account of complications after illegal abortions.[4] In 1966 it has

[1] Thus the President of Columbia, Mr Carlos Restrepo, in the course of an address to the inter-American conference on population studies in September 1967 stated: 'I have visited the poorest slums of the Republic and I recommend the same visit to the people who examine the population question above all from the moral point of view . . . what can we say of the frequent incest, of the primitive sexual experience, of the miserable treatment of children, of the terrible proliferation of prostitution of children of both sexes, of frequent abortion, of almost animal union because of alcoholic excesses? It is, in consequence, impossible for me to sit back and examine the morality or immorality of contraceptive practices without thinking at the same time of the immoral and frequently criminal conditions that the simple act of conception can produce in the course of time.' See *Pope and Pill* (London, 1968), pp. 86–7.
[2] 1 May 1969.   [3] See *Nature*, 3 August 1968.
[4] It has been calculated that in Santiago hospitals 40 per cent of the admissions, 25 per cent of blood for blood transfusions and 30 per cent of days hospitalised were results of illegal abortions. In greater Santiago 2·5–3 deaths out of 5 from obstetric causes are caused by abortion. See Statement of Professor Herman Remero, Professor of Preventive and Social Medicine, University of Chile, in 'Victor Fund Report', September 1966, p. 18.

been estimated that the number of induced abortions in Brazil was in the region of 700,000.[1]

These horrific abortion statistics must be taken into account by anyone attempting to assess objectively the need for family planning programmes. A society in which contraception is widely accepted undoubtedly faces grave new moral and social problems, and to the solution of those problems religion should make a real contribution, but that contribution can no longer take the form of a negative opposition but rather of a constructive shaping of social and moral attitudes.

[1] See Appendix 7, 'Abortion Statistics in some developing countries', in an unpublished paper by Arthur McCormack.

Index of Names

Subject Index